Reviews from Amazon.com Readers of Previous Editions

"...My productivity has increased tenfold."

There are over 100 five-star reviews for the previous editions of this book on Amazon. Here are some highlights.

★★★★★ **Excellent book,** May 4, 2013. Dale Sloan

"Well laid out with easy to follow directions for set up and use. Simple explanations and listing style made it a breeze to follow. Good examples throughout."

★★★★★ **Lifechanging,** April 14, 2013. CLTuptown

"I have been using the method now for a couple of weeks. I already feel more in control of my workday. It has allowed me to stop working at home every night and every weekend. It is life changing. I highly record this book to anyone whose work-day controls him/her!!"

★★★★★ **The best business book I've ever read,** Feb 28, 2013. CB

"Without a doubt, I benefited more from this book than any book I've ever read. From the very first chapter, Linenberger teaches you simple yet highly effective ways to get control of your Inbox. You're able to put these tools in place immediately while reading the rest of the book to build on the techniques..."

★★★★★ **A productivity book that actually delivers,** Jan 18, 2013. Greg Laxton

"I am a third of the way through the book (section one of three) and already I have seen a marked improvement in my lot in life with how I manage my workday and my e-mail. This book - and the techniques it espouses - actually work! Brilliant."

★★★★★ **This really works,** September 30, 2007. Beancounter

"I have been using Michael Linenberger's system for about 3 months now and my productivity has increased tenfold. With this system, I have a way to track important tasks and I feel that I am on top of my job."

★★★★★ **A well thought out and practical approach to email and task management,** December 31, 2012. PDX Paul

"Michael Linenberger has laid out a practical and effective approach to managing the on-slaught of email and tasks that many (maybe most) of us receive every day. One of the many things I like about the book is that the author not only discusses his philosophy or theory regarding how to manage emails and tasks, he provides specific instructions and examples on how to do it..."

★★★★★ **Finally, a time management book that is working for me,** December 15, 2012 John

"read this book ~ 8 months ago, and have applied principles ever since. I've been trying to be organized for 20 years... tried paper Daytimer, Franklin Covey. Tried Omnifocus. tried Outlook tasks a couple of times. read Covey (x3), David Allen, attended seminars, etc. read at least 5 other time management books by less advertised authors. always felt overwhelmed. This book is great for synthesizing and summarizing prior author's thoughts about getting organized. It is really EXCELLENT for putting step by step instructions at how to manage the "to do" list..."

★★★★★ **Changed my way of working,** November 18, 2012. Julio

"These have been the best 10 euro spent in many months. This book has changed the way I work, has given me more control over the hundreds of open tasks everyone manages these days. It offers a simple workflow to keep things under control using MS Outlook's standard features..."

★★★★★ **Brilliant process,** October 22, 2012. iparas

"Brilliant process. Quite complementary to GTD process of David Allen. Microsoft should include it to their preferred guides for Outlook training. Thanks for your contribution into my personal improvement!"

★★★★★ **Completely changed my life,** August 24, 2012. S. Gabriele (NJ)

"...this book has CHANGED MY LIFE. Using Mike Linenberger's system I now am more organized and focused and on top of things...and as a result, relaxed without the normal anxiety. I have been applying many of the principles he speaks of to my personal life and find that they work for that as well..."

★★★★★ **workday control totally manages the email files,** January 20, 2012. Linda

"I cannot believe that the secret is so well kept. This book has changed how I manage the in-box. The email programs are so complicated that I never would have been able to develop this process without serious help. Fortunately I found this book. It has changed my email life..."

★★★★★ **Best of both worlds - time management and MS Outlook,** December 6, 2011. cotrader

"The best book I have ever read on time management. The best book I have ever read on getting the most out of Microsoft Outlook. Incredible synergies here. Minimum of preachy philosophical thoughts on leading a productive life while providing a concise, hands-on approach for building tools that can and should be integrated into daily routines with email and task management. Practical sequencing that does not require reading from start to finish before being able to derive benefits from the effort. Great book!"

★★★★★ **Love this book,** November 19, 2011. KRF

"...I have purchased this book 4 times over the past 5 years. One for a friend and the rest because I am dependent on the task management system the author advocates and the movers keep losing the darn thing. I finally bought it for my Kindle!"

★★★★★ **Well Done!!!!!!!!!,** October 12, 2011. Alan D. Parker

"This is one of the most well thought-out books/concepts/systems I have ever come across. From the first 15 minute "Get you going" section at the beginning to the advanced Outlook concepts in the end the book shows a realistic understanding of how we do things and why we fail to get things done. The solutions actually work. And the Outlook utilization techniques are elegant and logical..."

★★★★★ **great time management,** March 29, 2011. Jules

"If you follow the steps in this book your inbox will be cleaner and your tasks will be managed. It truly reduced stress as long as you stick with it. I have shared this book with several co-workers."

★★★★★ **Gets into the organizing functionality of Outlook,** March 14, 2012. Citizen John

"I think Linenberger filled a crucial gap in organizational literature. His point is that if you're already using Outlook, you might as well use much of its functionality to organize your work life. There isn't an absolute need to use other software in addition to Outlook for work organization because Outlook does so much..."

★★★★★ **This book changed my life!,** December 19, 2010. Julie Davis (Darwin, NT Australia)

"I cannot tell you how grateful I am to Michael Linenberger for writing this fantastic book. I was constantly on the look out for how to become more efficient, pack more into each day, stop missing deadlines and reduce stress in my everyday work life - and this book has dealt with all of those issues. For the very first time in 18 years, I left work to go on holiday leave at a reasonable time (5.10pm) instead of working until 2am to get everything under control before I left. I cannot tell you how this had changed my life. Not only did I leave work at a reasonable time but I left feeling confident that I had completed all my important and urgent tasks and that all other tasks were in my task list dated appropriately and would be done in an orderly and timely manner when I returned. Working hard and working long hours is simply not enough in our current working environments. Michael Linenberger has changed my life for the better and I cannot recommend this book highly enough to anyone needing to get control of the myriad of tasks that come your way on a daily, if not hourly basis. I have bought 2 more copies to give to my friends who I know will benefit greatly from the systems that Michael recommends."

⭐⭐⭐⭐⭐ **Delighted with this book!,** March 17, 2010. LeaRae Keyes "cabin stuff creator and nurse e... (Minneapolis, MN USA)

"...When I began reading this book I had over 1000 emails sitting in my inbox. Now I am down to less than 200 and expect that in less than a week I will be down to zero emails in my inbox. I feel as though a heavy weight has been lifted…"

⭐⭐⭐⭐⭐ **Everything I hoped it would be...and more,** March 19, 2010. Antone M. Goyak (Wisconsin, USA)

"...I have learned how to competently organize my day, all while staying current with emails and tasks. Michael's thought process and approach to tasks and emails is getting the job done for me. Along with the crucial basics, I am now learning some of the finer aspects of workday management in later chapters so that my thinking is getting transformed along with my actions. I feel like my day is not disjointed anymore and that I am able to tackle what is most important and not let the menial tasks fill my day. What I received for the price of the book has been remarkable. Kudos to Michael for a text that is well-written, fully illustrated, and easy to read."

⭐⭐⭐⭐⭐ **I Love This Book,** July 2, 2009. R.D. (New York)

"I have a demanding job and get more mail than I can process every day, and I've often wished that I had some better strategy to deal with all of my incoming mail. One day I declared I would have a clean inbox, and then I just moved all of my mail out of my inbox... just to see some space in it. But after a day or two, I had an out of control inbox again... after a few weeks... I was basically back where I started and I was frustrated. When I first saw this book, I was intrigued. But what dragged me in was the clarity with which Linenberger seemed to understand modern workday problems. I found myself nodding my head over and over again and saying "this guy speaks the truth!" His language is direct, clear and concise, and he seemed to really understand what I had to go through every day. So I kept reading until I just had to buy the book…"

⭐⭐⭐⭐⭐ **Best and most practical book on managing your workflow,** August 18, 2009. Amy M. Leschke-Kahle

"I've read many many books and attended way too many classes on "time management" only to wonder what I was doing wrong when I couldn't sustain writer's magic method. That was until I found Total Workday Control. Michael Linenberger has finally developed a practical, real-world approach to managing the workday. It's clear that he gets how today's world in the office works. "

★★★★★ **Kudos to you, Michael!,** August 3, 2009. Mark B. Logan "marklogan"

"I don't say this often, but it is well deserved... reading this book and implementing its recommendations has been nothing short of life changing. I've been using the techniques and framework as outlined in the book and immediately recognized the benefits and realized significant time-saving and stress-reducing results. What a great feeling it is to zero out my inbox on a daily basis!"

★★★★★ **OUTSTANDING!!!,** April 28, 2009. Adam S. Farrah (Middletown, CT)

"Hands down the best Outlook book ever. What makes it so good is that Michael teaches a system of thinking and using Outlook within that system. If you just "learn Outlook" you'll be better with Outlook but not much better at managing your day and to-dos. Michael and his system (Manage Your Now) gives you a WAY to manage your days that uses Outlook as the platform. Michael shows you how to completely reconfigure Outlook AND use it's inherent power. Outlook is a great program - once you unleash its true potential using Michael's book!"

★★★★★ **Second most lifechanging book ever**, January 12, 2007. Cynthia Choi (Albany, NY)

"This book is the second most lifechanging book I've ever read. Completely awesome. His system is not overly cumbersome and lightweight enough to be realistic to use every day. Project managers can read the book and learn the system in one afternoon and have your inbox cleared from 800 down to zero by the next day."

★★★★★ **Total Workday Control Works**, August 3, 2007. W. Parks (Wilmington, DE)

"A colleague of mine recommended I get the book TOTAL WORKDAY CONTROL USING MICROSOFT OUTLOOK. I help operate 5 companies and found that the recommendations in this book are terrific in terms of integrating tasks along with the calendar function. The techniques eliminate paper post-it notes, organize tasks so that they prompt at the proper time, and yet keep the Microsoft Outlook Calendar clear of non-appointment type items. These techniques really do help personal productivity. I strongly recommend reading this book and trying its suggestions."

★★★★★ **Well worth its weight in gold!**, August 14, 2007. Dr. Eric G. Kassel "ekpharmd" (Shorewood, Illinois United States)

"I read David Allen's GTD and struggled to incorporate into my e-World. I then read TWC and eagerly jumped on board. It was exactly what I needed and in 1/2 a day I was reconfigured and recategorized with an inbox that read zero. I am a convert and preacher. I recently had Michael come in to address my group of 60 field scientists who often are challenged with email, follow up and loosing their drive. I am still getting compliment and people are excited to get back to work. EXCITED! To get back to email! Well worth the book, the live session…"

★★★★★ **Outstanding Book!**, October 2, 2007. David R. Drake (Iowa City, IA USA)

"I am a professor at a major research university in the US. I have struggled with dealing with multiple tasks and emails for years... until I have embraced the fantastic system described in this great book. If you use Outlook as your major portal for email and tasks, you MUST read this book. The approach here is logical and work for you. It is that good."

★★★★★ **Project manager**, January 15, 2007

Mark Marker (Chicago Illinois Area)

"Superb guideline. Even if you don't follow it line for line... it distills a task mentality in your daily work habits. It causes one to stop and take a moment to plan out the day. If you feel like you have 10 pounds of work in a 5 pound bag then this book will be of great help."

★★★★★ **A book I return to over and over again**, August 27, 2007

Barry J. Kurtz "Business Process Master" (New Jersey USA)

"As a person who practically lives in Outlook, this book has provided me with many tips and ideas on how to use the product better. Outlook has many capabilities hidden from the person who does not have the time or desire to study every technical nuance of the software. This book distills a lot of useful information into easily digestible chunks that you can make use of directly or build upon to suit your personal needs. If you use Outlook to help manage your computer-based life, this book should be on your desk."

★★★★★ **By far the best system I've ever used... you should get this book**, July 14, 2007

K. Vickers (Washington DC)

"I've tried them all and the thing about Michael's approach is that it not only works with a product I'm already familiar with and use extensively every day (Outlook) but it's also a system I can use without major disruptions to my work life—it just works. By implementing this approach I've gone from well over 1,000 emails in my in box to the point where I can now leave at the end of the day with less than 10. I'm also much more relaxed knowing that I have a handle on all the items I need to work on... In short, this approach has transformed my work life..."

★★★★★ **Great book - Easy system you will actually use**, November 4, 2006. Garafano (Massachusetts USA)

"Terrific book. I spent a few hours with Michael's system and the results were amazing. I have cleaned out my inbox and have a working, viable task management system that is showing some big results. It doesn't take weeks of studying or a massive effort to use. It is casual, simple, and really allows you to focus on the information rather than the system. I use it in combination with Clear Context and I couldn't be any happier."

Total Workday Control Using Microsoft® Outlook

Fourth Edition

By Michael Linenberger

 New Academy Publishers
San Ramon, California

First printing 2013

ISBN-13: 978-0983364726
ISBN-10: 0983364729
Library of Congress Control Number: 2013915258

Visit the publisher's website at www.MichaelLinenberger.com for additional information.

The following trademarks appear throughout this book: Microsoft, Windows, Windows XP, Microsoft Windows Vista, Microsoft Windows 7, Microsoft Windows 8, Windows Mobile, Microsoft Office, Microsoft Outlook 2013, Microsoft Office 365, Microsoft Outlook for Mac 2011, Microsoft Office Outlook 2010, Microsoft Office Outlook 2007, Microsoft Office Outlook 2003, Microsoft Outlook 2002, ClearContext, Toodledo, Master Your Now!, Now Horizon, Over-the-Horizon tasks, Now Tasks, Critical Now, Opportunity Now, Target Now, Defer-to-Do, Defer-to-Review, FRESH Prioritization, Day-Timer, FranklinCovey, Day Runner, Circa, Getting Things Done, GTD, Retrospect, Google, Google Voice.

Cover photograph of Michael Linenberger by Joe Burull

Preface to the Fourth Edition

What Has Changed in This Edition

If you are reading this after studying the third edition, since then approximately 30 percent of the existing material has changed. Nearly every page has updates of some kind.

If you are coming from the first or second edition, quite a bit more has changed, probably 70 to 80 percent, and I encourage you to study the earlier prefaces, before reading this preface, to help understand system changes. Following are links to the online PDF versions of those earlier prefaces.

Preface to second edition: www.myn.bz/preface-second-edition.pdf

Preface to third edition: www.myn.bz/preface-third-edition.pdf

Note: All links in this book are case-sensitive, so match capitalization exactly when typing these links in your browser. Also, the domain name myn.bz (used throughout this book) is a redirected domain for michaellinenberger.com. This shorter domain makes typing easier. However, some firewalls block such redirects, so if you get an error, replace myn.bz *with* michaellinenberger.com *when typing the links you see throughout this book.*

Book and System Changes in the Fourth Edition

Most changes in this book are related to the different versions of Outlook covered in this edition, but you will see many other changes listed below.

▶ Outlook 2013 support has been added. Compared to Outlook 2010, the changes in Outlook 2013 are mostly cosmetic, but some interesting changes have been made to some features. The effects on MYN are minimal, but the new To-Do Bar does take some study. All major impacts are listed briefly in the following list and are described in more detail in this edition in the lessons (chapters) that are affected. To read my online article about the general changes in Outlook 2013, including some changes not listed in this book, go to: www.myn.bz/blog/new-version-of-windows-outlook-coming-outlook-2013/.

▶ Outlook 2003 has been removed from the book, primarily to make room for the new Outlook 2013 material. If you need support for earlier versions of Outlook, previous editions of this book can still be found on Amazon and in other book sellers.

▶ In Outlook 2013, Microsoft changed the controls that display the To-Do Bar, which greatly affects the MYN system. The new controls and how they affect MYN are described in detail in Lesson 2.

▶ Good news for Outlook 2013 MYN users: Except for the To-Do Bar changes previously listed, Outlook 2013 task functionality is almost identical to that in Outlook 2010, so you do not have volumes of new material to learn. For example, the MYN configurations in Lesson 3 are identical in both versions.

▶ Many sections of the book have been simplified by removing redundant material and reorganizing the order of materials, leading to greater clarity and focus. Many areas have been expanded to cover new materials.

▶ All images have been updated for better quality and to reflect newer Outlook versions. The e-book now has color images.

▶ The e-book version of this book has been greatly improved. Changes include higher quality e-book formatting, color images, hyperlinked internal references (including to images), and a hyperlinked index.

▶ Since the previous edition, I've released a set of videos that you can purchase — they provide a summary of much of this book. They also, in some cases, better illustrate step-by step operations in Outlook. A number of the videos in that set are free. I've indicated in the book when it makes sense to watch these videos (and how to get at them). See the Quick Start for more information.

▶ The Quick Start has been rewritten to teach the One Minute To-Do List as the best way to get started quickly with MYN Outlook. The One Minute To-Do List is a simpler version of MYN, which you can learn in minutes. It's based on my 2011 book of the same name.

▶ The free video that corresponds to the Quick Start has been improved and includes instruction about Outlook 2013.

► You'll now see comparisons to the One Minute To-Do List throughout the book. That will be useful if you are moving to the complete MYN system from the simpler system.

► Many users are confused by flagged-mail tasks. The section of Lesson 2 that explains flagged-mail tasks has been expanded and clarified.

► The Mobile Systems section in Lesson 6 has been rewritten and expanded to include mobile-technology changes since the last edition.

► At the end of Part II (at the very end of Lesson 9), I've added an extensive new section titled "MYN-Outlook Flow Charts." There you will see work-flow diagrams that summarize most of the core MYN Outlook principles. Included is an extensive explanation of those workflows. I encourage even experienced MYN users to study this new section.

► I've provided instructions in Lesson 3 on what to do if it looks like you lose MYN custom configurations immediately after you set them.

► To ease converting e-mails to tasks, I added a section to Lesson 7 on how to create Quick Steps in Outlook 2010 and 2013.

► Near the end of Lesson 8, I have added a section on the Read Later category, and how using it can help you empty your Outlook Inbox daily.

► The step-by-step Outlook Rules section in Lesson 11 has been converted to a free online video, which is much easier to follow.

► The Intrinsic Importance custom task view shown in Lesson 12 has been simplified (fewer II levels are now used).

This captures the major changes, but nearly every page has been improved. And again, this list captures only the changes between the third and fourth editions. If you are moving to this fourth edition directly from the first or second edition, consider studying the prefaces from the previous editions, too. The links to free copies of those are shown at the start of this preface.

A Powerful New Edition

The book has been improved considerably to make understanding and using the MYN Outlook system easier. Enjoy the new edition, and do not hesitate to send me feedback. To contact me go to my website: www.myn.bz (or www.michaellinenberger.com) and click the Contact link.

Michael Linenberger
August 2013

Acknowledgments

Deep thanks go to the following individuals for their assistance in preparation of this latest edition: John Faulkner and Mark Rhynsburger.

Contents at a Glance

Contents

PART II: Advancing the MYN System 135

Total Workday Control Using Microsoft® Outlook

Fourth Edition

MYN Quick Start: The One Minute To-Do List

Introduction

Before starting the main lessons in this book, Windows Outlook users should consider using this optional Quick Start section to get going right away with a simple version of this system. Here, in about 15 minutes, you will learn enough to give you an immediate solution for many of your current workday-control issues. Even better: instead of *reading* this chapter, you might want to *watch* the video version of the chapter instead, as described next.

Video Course Version of this Book and Quick Start

Much of this book is summarized in the online video course *MYN-Outlook Complete Video Training,* which you can purchase at www.myn.bz/mvc.htm. A small number of the segments of the video course are free, and the videos of this Quick Start are among them. The video set roughly matches the daylong live MYN training I give for my corporate clients. It teaches you the complete MYN system, and it's good for those who prefer a video study approach. However, this book is more comprehensive, delivering many more details and additional MYN materials. For example, there is no Mac coverage in the video set, and much of the book's in-depth analysis is not in the videos.

Free Quick Start Videos

To access the free Quick Start videos:

▶ For Outlook 2007 or 2010, go to: www.myn.bz/mvc.htm and scroll down to the top of the video list. Select the video titled: Quick Start 2007-10.

▶ For Outlook 2013, go to: www.myn.bz/mvc.htm and scroll down to the top of the video list. Select the video titled: Quick Start 2013.

For the remainder of the videos, at the beginning of each lesson in this book, I'll indicate which video(s) in the series correspond to the lesson (nearly all are part of the paid set).

Note: *All links in this book are case-sensitive, so match capitalization exactly if typing these links in your browser. Also, the domain myn.bz (used throughout the book) is a redirected domain for michaellinenberger.com. This shorter domain name makes typing easier. However, some networks block such redirects, so if you get an error when using myn.bz with the following links, replace it with michaellinenberger.com.*

Versions of Outlook in Quick Start

Like these videos, this chapter is for Windows Outlook versions 2007, 2010, and 2013. (Outlook 2013 is sometimes called Outlook for Office 365.) Macintosh users, my apologies. Due to the design of the Outlook 2011 for Mac, there are no easy quick steps for you. Go directly to the Introduction or to Lesson 1.

The steps in this chapter vary depending on your Windows Outlook version. If you do not know which version you are using, jump to Lesson 2 to the section titled "How to Identify Your Windows Outlook Version." There you will find more help. Then return to this Quick Start.

Getting Started Quickly with MYN: The One Minute To-Do List in Outlook

To help you get started quickly, I am going to teach you a highly simplified variant of the MYN system called The One Minute To-Do List (abbreviated as 1MTD). It will take you about 15 minutes to learn it.

Let me set some context for this. As I travel the world teaching people how to dig out of stacks of e-mails and tasks, I actually teach *two* systems in Outlook. First is the system covered in the bulk of this book. It's called MYN, or Master Your Now! It's the one I recommend for serious business people because it can handle an unlimited number of tasks. But it does take some time to learn.

I also teach a simpler version called The One Minute To-Do List. It is the main topic of my short 2011 book of the same name. It is designed for people who have less-intense task management needs or just want to get started quickly. If you're juggling fewer than 100 tasks in your to-do list at any given time, you can get by with 1MTD for quite some time. You don't need to learn the complete MYN system, or you can upgrade later.

The reason I mention this now is that learning 1MTD is also useful as a way to get a *taste* of MYN in a short amount of time. It shares the same underlying principles as MYN, but leaves you free of the more complicated MYN features. You might say it's "MYN Lite."

I'm going to get you started on 1MTD in just a few minutes. You can experience the basic features of MYN, and you'll have a good set of tools you can use *right now*. After using this Quick Start, if you want to learn more about the 1MTD system, you can download a free PDF copy of the 1MTD book at: www.myn.bz/free1MTD.htm (this link is case sensitive).

The To-Do Bar

As a first step to using tasks in Outlook, let me show you the task area that you're going to work with in 1MTD and MYN. Note, you're *not* going to use the Outlook main tasks folder. Rather, you're going to use a smaller task list in a section called the To-Do Bar—it's what we use for tasks in 1MTD and in MYN. The To-Do Bar is an Outlook pane that usually (but not always) occupies the right side of your Outlook window. You can often recognize it by the mini-calendars at its top (see Figure Q.1). If you don't see it on the right side of your screen, or are not sure, go to your View menu or tab, choose To-Do Bar, and then choose Normal from the submenu (in Outlook 2013, select Tasks from that submenu). This will open the To-Do Bar.

Figure Q.1
The To-Do Bar occupies the right side of the Outlook window.

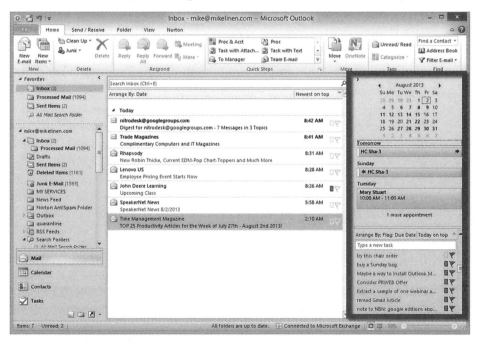

Note that the To-Do Bar has a task list area, usually at its bottom. That's the task list we're going to modify for use in 1MTD.

Modifying the To-Do Bar for 1MTD

The first modification is this: If the task list in your To-Do Bar is too short, as shown in Figure Q.1, we're going to make it taller.

To do that in Outlook 2007/10, right-click the very top of the To-Do Bar, just above the mini-calendars, and in the shortcut menu, clear the check mark next to Date Navigator. That will make the task list bigger.

In Outlook 2013, from the View tab choose To-Do Bar, and then clear any check marks next to Calendar or People. Make sure the check mark next to Tasks is selected.

Next, for all versions, if your To-Do Bar seems too narrow, drag the left edge a small amount to make it wider. But don't make it any wider than about 2 to 3 inches.

I also recommend that you clear any view settings you might have applied (knowingly or otherwise) to this To-Do Bar task list so we can start with a clean slate and so the settings that follow will work. Here's how. At the top of that task list, right-click the header label Arranged By (or Arrange By, or Task Subject). Near the bottom of the resulting shortcut menu, choose Custom or Customize Current View or View Settings. (You will see one of those three.) In the dialog box that opens, click the Reset Current View button in the lower-left corner. If that button is grayed out, your settings are already in default mode and you need to do nothing. In either case, click OK to close that window.

Now, the next step—the only real 1MTD setting you need to make in this Quick Start—is simple. Just click the Arranged By (or Arrange By) label at the top of the task list, and from the drop-down menu, select Importance. That's it!

At this point, if you already have tasks entered in your task system at various priority levels, you'll likely see a layout similar to Figure Q.2. In Figure Q.2, notice the High, Normal, and Low priority groups. If you do not see all these groups yet, no worries, read on.

Clean Out Old Flagged Mail

Look at your task list. It may be currently empty, or it may have a few tasks, or it may have tens or hundreds of tasks listed in there. If it has lots of tasks—tasks that you may not remember entering—they are probably virtual copies of old mail that you flagged. Outlook displays flagged mail in the To-Do Bar task list to remind you that they might need action. If there are lots of them, you should clean this list up by removing flags from that old mail. You can do that now by clicking the flags at the right of those tasks, one at a time, which removes them from the task list and removes the flag from the corresponding e-mail (but still retains the e-mail, wherever it is). If you have several hundred or more, you may want to wait till Lesson 2, where I'll show you how to clean those out in bulk. Also, ignore the red color you might see on the text of many tasks. We'll fix that in Lesson 3.

Figure Q.2
The 1MTD version of the MYN Tasks List (Outlook 2010 shown; other versions similar).

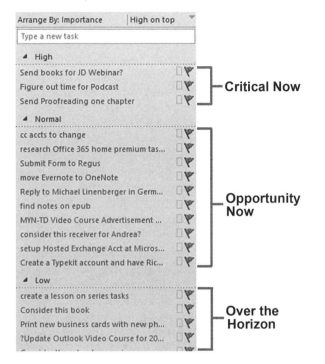

Adding Tasks to Your Task List

If you don't have many tasks, let's add some now. At minimum, I want to be sure you have at least a few tasks in each of the three priority groups. For all versions, to enter a task, just type a task name in the text box near the top of the list—it's usually labeled Type a New Task or it might be labeled Click Here to Add a New Task. After you type a task name, press ENTER. The task will drop into your task list at the top of the group labeled Normal. If you have just entered your first task ever, congratulations!

If you don't have at least one task in each of the three priority groups (High, Normal, and Low), let's enter some more. A group will not show unless you have at least one task in it. New tasks always default to Normal priority, so enter a few more tasks and change the priority level of some to High and some to Low. Here's how to change the priority: After you create a task, double-click it in the list, and in the middle of the dialog box that opens, you'll see the Priority drop-down menu. Select the priority from that menu. Ignore the date fields and other controls. We'll talk about start dates, due dates, and much more in later lessons. Click Save & Close in the upper-left corner of the Task dialog box.

You can mark a task complete by clicking the flag at its right edge. Doing that moves the task to the main Tasks folder, where it is marked with a line through it. You can delete a task by selecting the task and pressing DELETE.

Using the 1MTD Urgency Zones

Now you're ready to apply a few 1MTD principles—ones that also apply to MYN. After you have entered a few tasks at each of the three levels, you'll clearly see the three priority-labeled groups in your task list, as shown in Figure Q.2. These three groups correspond to three *urgency zones* in the 1MTD and MYN task systems. The key take-away of both systems is that tasks in each urgency zone require a different level of attention. If you place tasks in the correct zones and then apply your work intensity appropriately, you'll greatly reduce your stress level—and you'll get your tasks well under control. Let's see how to do that.

Critical Now Urgency Zone (High)

The first urgency zone is called Critical Now, and we'll use the High priority group in your task list for these (see top of Figure Q.2). These are tasks that are absolutely due today. You should list tasks here only if they are so critical for today that you would work late into the evening if they were not complete. You should have no more than five tasks here each day, preferably fewer. Having none is fine. You'll want to check this list often, perhaps even once an hour, to see what might get you in trouble (or keep you late at work) if not completed by end of day. It is very refreshing to have this list clearly delineated and well tracked.

Make sure the High priority group is *always* at the top of your task list. If the entire group is at the bottom, you can fix that by clicking the small downward-pointing arrow at the right end of the task list header.

Opportunity Now Urgency Zone (Normal)

The next urgency zone is called Opportunity Now, and this corresponds to the Normal priority group in your task list (see middle of Figure Q.2). Place tasks here that you would work on today *if you had the opportunity*, but that you could let slide till tomorrow or later, some even up to ten days or so. Plan to review this complete list at least once a day to see if anything there has been elevated in importance and needs to be done today. Here's the main rule: You should have no more than about 20 items in this list. If you have more than 20, drag the lowest-priority items to the third, or Low, zone.

Over-the-Horizon Urgency Zone (Low)

The third and final urgency zone in 1MTD is called Over-the-Horizon, and it corresponds to the Low priority group in your task list (see bottom of Figure Q.2). Place tasks here that you can ignore for longer than ten days; perhaps much longer. Then plan to review this list *once a week*. I recommend every Monday morning; however, the actual review day is up to you. If on review anything looks like it has become more important, drag that item to one of the higher-priority zones.

Converting E-mail to Tasks

To avoid losing tasks in your Outlook Inbox, and to keep your Inbox under control, do this: When you get an e-mail that has an action for you to do, drag that e-mail from your Inbox list to the Tasks label or icon at the bottom left of the Outlook window. In Outlook 2007/10, that icon looks like a clipboard with a check mark on it. In Outlook 2013, it is the large Tasks label (on a Windows tablet it might be an icon) in the bottom left of the Outlook window, just to the right of the large People label.

For all versions, when you drag the e-mail as described, a task window will pop open (like the one you saw earlier when you double-clicked a task). Immediately change the subject line to the task action and set the priority level as appropriate. Ignore the dates and other controls for now. Click the Save & Close button in the upper-left corner of the task window. The new task appears in the To-Do Bar task list.

After an e-mail is converted to a task, you should then work these tasks in priority order off your task list, along with all your other tasks.

Converting e-mails to tasks is very important and has a lot of benefits. It prevents you from trying to use your Inbox as a task management system. You'll have more success with tasks if you manage them in the task list. Why? The task list enables you to work incoming requests in the order of their priority. Converting e-mails to tasks prevents you from losing important action requests, ones that would get lost in your overflowing Inbox. With the 1MTD system, you can move mail out of your Inbox and file it more easily.

Converting e-mails to tasks also helps ensure that existing to-do's already on your task list are given equal or greater treatment to ones coming in by e-mail that day. Otherwise, new e-mail action requests might be the *only* actions you take all day, leaving higher-importance ongoing projects unattended to. This is a common problem in today's workplace when e-mail takes over. Converting e-mails to tasks is a great solution.

Next Steps

That's it—this 1MTD task list presents the most critical portions of the full MYN system in a nutshell. If you like, use this 1MTD task list for a while before proceeding with the rest of the book. I know it looks simple, perhaps overly so. But that's deceptive—it's actually a very powerful system even at this beginner 1MTD stage.

Here are my recommended next steps. First, reread the short section "Using the 1MTD Urgency Zones." This will help you embrace the simple 1MTD rules. Then start copying tasks from other lists and consolidate them into your 1MTD list. From now on, use the 1MTD list as your main to-do list. Next, glance at your Outlook Inbox and see if any of your e-mails should be converted to tasks. Finally, start reviewing your new 1MTD according to the cycles described earlier. You are now under way!

You can learn more about 1MTD by downloading and reading the free PDF version of *The One Minute To-Do List* book at www.myn.bz/free1MTD.htm. It's a very quick read and can help you extend 1MTD as an intermediate solution for a while, before advancing to the complete MYN system described in this book. It also shows you how to implement the 1MTD system on paper.

But obviously, 1MTD represents only a small portion of what you'll learn in the MYN system. MYN adds much more power—power you might even need right now. So when you are ready for more, take the next steps and proceed with the rest of this book. To that end, read the Introduction next, and then move to Lessons 1 through 12.

Introduction

The First Task, Time, and E-mail Management System That Will Work for You

This book is not a user manual on how to use Microsoft Outlook. Rather, this book presents a set of easy-to-use principles on time, task, and e-mail management. These principles, when used with Outlook as shown in this book, help you get your workday completely under control. With this system you can get ahead of your to-do's and e-mails, helping you feel much less stressed about your busy day. Its main focus is your to-do, or task, list: how to create and manage your list in Outlook with powerful, newly developed approaches. And it shows you how to keep it small, well managed, and well executed.

Equally important are the techniques for regaining control of your e-mail, primarily by identifying the action components of e-mail and managing them systematically as tasks in Outlook. I then show you how to file your important e-mails in an extremely fast and simple way. I will show you principles so you can empty your Outlook Inbox — easily — every day.

Learning these techniques and principles, you will learn the true potential and power of Microsoft Outlook. It will finally become the tool that you always hoped it would be, a tool to truly help you manage your very busy workday.

Note: *This lesson is summarized in video 1 of the MYN-Outlook Complete Video Training (see beginning of the Quick Start chapter for more information).*

A New, Low-Guilt To-Do List System

Many to-do list systems are available today — Day-Timer, FranklinCovey, Getting Things Done, Day Runner, Circa — more than we can keep track of. A few of them offer ways to use Outlook, supposedly to get ahead of your to-do's. So, does the world really need *another* to-do or day organizer system applied to Outlook? I say emphatically, yes, we do! And when the first version of this system came out several years ago with the first edition of this book (then called the Total Workday Control system, or TWC for short), it quickly became the best-selling Outlook volume on the market because readers found it really worked. With the publication of this fourth edition, the book remains the best-selling Outlook volume, and I am grateful that so many people have found the system helpful.

Why a New To-Do System?

The reason I developed and am teaching this to-do (and e-mail) management system is that I am convinced most popular to-do systems available today are not very good. I have tried and worked with all the major ones. And while some have useful features, they all fail in the long run.

The main problem with most of them is that they are overly based on *guilt*, and over time, positive-minded people like you and me give up on systems that overuse guilt. We become jaded when all our to-do's are colored red and appear overdue. Systems also fail due to lack of appropriate automation. Some are just dated. Most have no integrated solution for e-mail, which is a major source of workday inefficiency these days.

Instead I developed and teach my Master Your Now! (MYN) system, which I like to say is a low-guilt system and uses the best and latest features of Outlook. The system is fully automated and based on solid theory described in detail in Lessons 1 and 9. In fact the name itself, Master Your Now!, was carefully selected and describes the theory well. MYN is a system to successfully *master* the overload of work that you have on *your* plate right *now*. It truly does help you master that period of time you tend to be most anxious about: your *now*. It helps you choose what to-do's to do now, what e-mail to focus on now, what not to worry about now. You gain confidence that the important tasks are attended to, which greatly lowers any anxiety you might have about your workday. Based on feedback from tens of thousands of users, MYN can be the first to-do—and e-mail—management system that actually and consistently works for you.

But before describing that system, let's look at some of the current approaches out there and see why they do not work very well, starting with typical guilt-based systems.

Outlook's Default To-Do List System

The to-do list module built in to Outlook is called *Tasks*. Unfortunately, that module, if left unmodified, works poorly. That's because it is founded on 75-year-old principles of task management that don't work anymore. Therefore, as is, I do not recommend it. On the positive side, at least it is automated, which is good. But the problem with the unmodified Outlook task system is it places the oldest, most overdue tasks at the top of your To-Do Bar task list and marks them in bright red, which is bad. Why? Because it ends up emphasizing only *very old, very dead* tasks. All the recent, energized tasks are scrolled down to the bottom of the task list, way out of sight. The message seems to be this: "If you have not completed your oldest, least interesting tasks, you are a bad person, so these are what I am going to show you first. Don't do anything else until you complete these." That's a very discouraging message.

Outlook also does something even more discouraging. It takes every e-mail you have ever set a follow-up flag on (perhaps years' worth, perhaps thousands) and copies them as tasks into the To-Do Bar task list, also marked in a bright "you are a bad person" red. No wonder so few people use the standard Outlook task system for very long.

The good news is that the Windows Outlook task system is highly configurable, and with the Master Your Now! system, we change those configurations for the better, making Outlook a very useful and powerful tool. You'll see how to do those changes in Lesson 3.

Note: *While the Windows version of the Outlook task system is completely configurable, the Mac version is less so and has fewer features. Because of that, the Mac version might not be your best MYN task solution. While this book shows you how to use Outlook for Mac 2011 with MYN, alternative software is described in the mobile section of Lesson 6. (For more alternatives, go to www.myn.bz/Software.html. Notice that all links in this book are case-sensitive, so be sure to match capitalization exactly when typing this link in your browser.)*

Paper-Based Task Systems

I actually think the old paper-based task systems many of us use, both formal and informal, work better than an out-of-the-box Outlook task system. At least with paper-based systems, as you turn the pages and copy important tasks forward to the new days, you can leave the older, less energetic tasks behind, keeping your list fresh. And with paper systems you can make sure your highest-priority tasks, even new ones, are at the top and circled, underlined, starred, or otherwise dramatized.

However, there are two problems with most paper systems. First, you need to apply effort and discipline to copy older important tasks forward. Consequently, tasks often get inadvertently dropped or missed. The lack of automation hurts here. Second, and more critical, there is no easy way to move deferred e-mail actions into a paper list.

Action-List Systems

The buildup of too many tasks is also a problem with popular action list systems, whether automated or paper. These emphasize a generalized to-do list, action folder, or sometimes a next-action list, but they do not offer a well-designed prioritization system or a clean way to shorten the action list other than deleting. As a result these lists grow too large and they become unusable. More on that later.

Any System That Claims
Everything Must Have a Due Date Will Ultimately Fail

You've probably heard the expression: "Put a due date on every task or it won't get done." This approach works for large project tasks, but for small ad hoc tasks it ultimately fails. Why? Again, it is guilt-based and our psyche ultimately rejects this over time, especially when the system does not deliver. The reason it doesn't deliver is that artificial due dates on small ad hoc tasks just don't work—we adjust to them. We can smell a fake due date a mile away, and in the heat of the busy workday, we just skip over a task with such a date. Worse, this actually leads to *missed deadlines*. On those rare occasions when we *do* have a true hard deadline, we may ignore it, because we have become so accustomed to ignoring most of our other due dates. More on this in the next section.

A number of systems out there claim to have the task-management processes optimized. Over my many years in professional life, I have studied nearly every system on time and task management there is and used them in my own work, first as an engineer, then as project manager, manager, senior executive, and consultant. Most helped a little but not enough. The two systems that I have used the most are the FranklinCovey system and David Allen's Getting Things Done system, and these two are the best. All systems borrow from one another or from past time management books, and in that spirit I have also borrowed a few elements from these and other systems (and give credit in the book where I have). But 90 percent of the MYN solution is distinctly different from other systems.

MYN—the Unique Solution That Works

The MYN system is distinct in at least five ways:

▶ **It uses a new kind of to-do list called the MYN task list.** As you will see in Lesson 1, it's based on managing urgency and releasing the grip that out-of-control urgency has on so many of us. That way you can focus on your most important work with much less stress.

▶ **It integrates e-mail in a way no other system does**. MYN recognizes that many of our new tasks arrive by e-mail. And according to MYN, good task management is the solution to out-of-control e-mail, primarily by converting e-mails to tasks. No other system puts so much emphasis on an integrated e-mail solution.

▶ **It is a low-guilt to-do list management system.** MYN is probably the first system that recognizes that you, as a busy professional, will nearly always think of more things to do than you can possibly do—and that's a *good* thing. It's good because as professionals we should be constantly reaching for more. So this system does not punish or nag you when lower-priority aged items are not completed. Rather, MYN gives you a unique, trademarked approach for creating a short, usable, daily action list, and it adds scheduled solutions for the overflow items that have dropped in relative priority. This approach uses two key techniques called *Defer-to-Do*™ and *Defer-to-Review*™ to keep uncompleted lower-priority tasks out of sight but attended to responsibly. It does this successfully in a scheduled, no-regrets way. With MYN—finally—there is a positive approach to a busy professional's natural overload, one you can feel good about that doesn't drive you into frustration. Coverage of these two approaches is in Lesson 9.

▶ **It's the only system that emphasizes a start date, not a due date, as the primary management date.** As previously described, the idea that *every task should have a due date or it won't get done* is just plain wrong. In fact it's actually risky, because it leads to missed deadlines. MYN is the first and only system to identify the *start date* field as the key task management field for tasks. With start dates you control when you see tasks and when you want to think about tasks. It does not *ignore* deadlines, but rather emphasizes deadlines only when they are actually present. This is a much more positive, realistic, and *natural* approach to task management. It is introduced in Lesson 4.

▶ **It's optimized for the strengths of Microsoft Outlook.** While many systems have been "bolted" to Outlook, MYN, from top to bottom, has been designed specifically for Outlook. It started and grew entirely in Outlook, over seven generations of software versions. And you can apply the system without adding new software to Outlook. You just make some simple configuration changes (Lesson 3). That said, helpful software add-in options are available that support the MYN system, and these are discussed in the book. But again, because the system was designed from the ground up in Outlook, you will find that the methods and Outlook features work hand in hand.

Note: *While this system has been designed for Outlook, many of the MYN principles can be applied to other software or formats. I recommend one non-Outlook software solution—Toodledo—and it is discussed in Lesson 6 of this book.*

The result is that the MYN system really works for nearly everyone who tries it, so it might be the first to-do (and e-mail) management system that really works for you. Over 60,000 people are using elements of this system successfully. You can, too.

Getting Started

Let's begin this story by describing the problem and then some elements of the solution. I think this will help convince you that taking the time to learn the MYN system is worthwhile. However, if you are ready to start now, feel free to skip to Lesson 1.

The Problem Is Rampant

I have seen this in many places where I have consulted: Staff routinely complain of being overloaded with tasks, of putting in long hours to try to finish their work.

Managers complain that assigned tasks are not getting done. It's as if individual work assignments are deposited in a black hole, and the only way they get done is through repeated nagging by the task assigner.

And staff seem too busy to reply to or act on most of the e-mails they get. Important e-mails with requests for a reply are ignored. E-mails with clear requests for action get buried in the recipient's inbox, an inbox that contains hundreds or even thousands of unattended responsibilities in it.

In some cases the root cause of these problems is that staff really are assigned too many tasks, or get too much business e-mail. But in most cases the problem is lack of an effective task and e-mail management system. Tasks are never really incorporated into an effective system for getting them done and focusing on the highest priorities first. How to manage e-mail effectively is left to each individual to figure out.

Finding a Solution Is Important

Solving this problem so that you can get the most important work done at a reasonable pace is important. If struggling staff try to *do it all* by rushing through the day at 200 mph, they become even more inefficient. Dr. Edward M. Hallowell, in a January 2005 *Harvard Business Review* article, describes a near-clinical mental condition staff and managers can reach when they try to push through their out-of-control workday at a near-panic pace. When under this type of stress, the human brain functions differently, less effectively, displaying Attention Deficit Disorder (ADD)–like symptoms. The degraded functionality can grow worse, month after month. Or staff can mentally "give up" and divest from work goals, showing up physically but without spirit.

Either way, the results can be devastating to productivity. As task and e-mail volumes become unmanageable, individual productivity plummets. Perhaps worse is that team productivity suffers. Team collaboration suffers because teammates cannot trust one another to complete tasks they have agreed to, or to reply to simple requests for assistance. When team members cease collaborating and team collaboration becomes ineffective, the goals of the organization suffer.

You Know the Symptoms

▶   You work late and feel you have far too much to do.

▶ You have a sense that there is no time in the day to get things done.

▶ You leave important tasks uncompleted.

▶ You focus only on the work that is right in front of you and rarely plan tasks in advance.

▶ You might have a number of loose task lists, but you have them spread around and they are generally out of control.

▶ Rather than controlling your e-mail, you find yourself just barely reacting to e-mail.

▶ You know that buried in your e-mail are many requests for action and you regret not getting to them quicker.

▶ You find yourself practicing *reactive,* or crisis, management, acting only on the emergencies as they arise around you.

▶ You rarely gain a sense of completion of important tasks.

▶ You have a sense of forgotten or misplaced tasks.

▶ People are often reminding you of things you promised that are not yet completed.

▶ You almost always leave work knowing something important is not finished.

Unmanaged Tasks and E-mail Derail Work Effectiveness

While you may have too many required tasks, *it is more likely that your problems stem from unmanaged tasks.* The fact is, all of us will always have too many tasks. The secret is in managing them. Unmanaged tasks can derail your work effectiveness because:

▶ You spend too much time on low-priority tasks.

▶ You drop important tasks and actions in e-mails, and they then become emergencies that require inefficient activity to fix.

▶ You do no planning of synergies, which leads to inefficient task completion.

▶ You are forced into too much wheel spinning, rehashing of tasks, and rereading of e-mails.

▶ You have a sense of being out of control, leading to a poor attitude. You really don't expect to get to assigned tasks, or to get to all your e-mail.

Ambiguity Is a Problem

One problem with casual task and e-mail management approaches is ambiguity:

▶ We are not sure where task lists are and which are up to date.

▶ We are unsure how to plan and prioritize action on tasks.

▶ We do not know how to handle an overflowing task list.

▶ We are vague about what to do with items, such as e-mails, that have tasks implied in them.

The Single Biggest Problem: Inbox as Task Manager

This problem is the most important one. The single biggest mistake knowledge workers make these days is this: using their inboxes as a task management system. When we leave action-laden e-mails in our inbox with the intention to get to them later, we've unconsciously attempted to convert our inbox to a task management system, and that just won't work. The Outlook Inbox does not have the tools we need to manage tasks. They just aren't there. There are no easy tools to indicate various levels of priority and to sort by them, no easy tools to schedule action timing and sort by action date, and no tools to schedule revisits to postponed actions to see if their urgency has increased. Again, attempting to use the inbox as a task management system is the number one issue with workday management these days, and something we all do. And it's one that is easily solved by the MYN system.

Benefits of the Master Your Now! System

Increased Efficiency and Productivity

Getting tasks and e-mail organized with a system that finally works (and this one does) goes a long way. Having a way to capture tasks embedded either explicitly or implicitly in e-mails will bring your e-mail under control. Having your tasks clearly organized and prioritized in a usable system helps you work on the most important tasks first. When properly organized, tasks at the bottom of the list that you postpone or drop due to lack of time are usually the least important ones. So it's your low-priority tasks that fall off the end of the day, not the important ones.

Having your tasks and e-mail organized and under control makes you more efficient at accomplishing them or responding to them. You actually spend less time finishing more activities. Why? Because when all your important tasks are clearly in front of you, you can multitask in meetings. You can take advantage of chance encounters with people and places. You can, during unexpected free slots of time, see and pounce on your most important tasks and get many of them done. You can organize your day to attack tasks in optimum order while ensuring that only the lowest-priority tasks are dropped if you run out of time at the end of the day.

With a smooth system of processing e-mail, you will spend much less time in your inbox. You will greatly reduce inbox churn, where you reread many messages looking for items you left in the inbox. You'll spend less time processing new mail because you will learn how to immediately convert action mail to tasks and move on.

As a result, in my surveys of seminar participants who stick with the system (same content as this book), most users say they gain back at least 25 percent of their week. Many say much more, some up to 45 percent.

Reduced Stress and an Improved Attitude

Just as important is having your tasks and e-mail under control in a usable system to reduce your workday stress and improve your attitude. If you are like me, you probably tend to carry uncompleted tasks with you in your unconscious mind throughout the day (and sometimes night!). This stress is exaggerated when tasks are not well organized.

Our Mental Limit for To-Do's

Malcolm Gladwell in his book *The Tipping Point* describes long-standing research that shows the human mind cannot clearly remember more than six or seven items at once. This is called the channel capacity of the brain. This commonly known limit, among other things, led to early phone numbers being limited to seven digits. It also applies to tasks. After your mental task list exceeds that count, you forget what's on the list. Uncontrolled and forgotten tasks tend to nag us. We carry a sense of being behind the game, of being on the wrong side of the curve. A sense of something that we should do, something we have been remiss about. Not only is this very stressful, but it's also often what drives us to work late nights with the thought: "If I work more hours, I'll get it all done and this feeling will go away." However, *exhaustion* is what usually finally calms the feeling instead, along with the thought, "I have worked far more hours than is reasonably expected; surely I can go home now." Unfortunately, without a good task and e-mail management system, fate curses us to stay late night after night. Eventually, many workers do not expect to complete their tasks, even important ones, and they carry that expectation as an attitude that sabotages their success.

Burden Lifted

After you are controlling your tasks and e-mail correctly, as shown in this system, your burden is lifted. It is such a relief to know you have identified and organized everything on your plate. It is a relief to clearly identify what is most important (and what to work on first) and to know what can wait and how to defer it with appropriate follow-up. It is such a relief to be able to say to yourself, "That's all of it. I've got it all in sight, and there is nothing hanging out there that will bite me later." Achieving this organized state usually reveals that the critical portion of your list is much shorter than you think, and it enables you to finish the critical items first. Therefore, it enables you to know that you can leave the office guilt-free at the end of the workday without neglecting key responsibilities. Your mind is free and clear to enjoy the evening or the weekend.

When your mind is free from the subconscious message "I am out of control," you can more effectively execute activities. You can plan to get at tasks before they become emergencies. When you accomplish tasks in nonemergency mode, they fall into place more cleanly and easily and with less expenditure of energy.

You Might Even Find This System Enjoyable

This is not a guilt-based system. This is not a list of "shoulds" that you hope to find time to do but know you probably will not. Rather, I think you will find that you may even *enjoy* doing most of the steps in this book.

Really? you say. Actually *enjoy* the steps? Let me demonstrate this by asking you whether you feel bad about the following:

▶ Stepping into a nice warm shower every morning

▶ Setting the table in a pleasing way before a good meal

▶ Frosting a cake for your child's birthday

▶ Closing the garage door when you drive away from your house in the morning

These are all small efforts that we feel good about because they are mostly effortless, they keep our life tidy, and they lead to a richer experience in life. Many are fun in the process. In the same way, after you get past a few setup activities, the steps in this system are all simple, effortless, and actually enjoyable in most cases, primarily because, as you do them, you feel satisfaction. The results are a richer, more satisfying work experience.

So give this system a try.

▪   ▪   ▪

Designed for a Quick Start

After Part I You Are Ready to Go

This book is presented as lessons. I have designed this to be a smooth and compact learning experience for you. I have tried to keep theory at a minimum and practical application at a maximum. I have also carefully organized the book so you can quickly get started and then learn increasingly advanced material lesson by lesson.

To that end, I've provided the Quick Start chapter (just prior to this one), which within minutes gets you started with the simple One Minute-To-Do List version of the MYN system.

To make the next level of commitment easy, the rest of the book is divided into three parts. By the end of Part I, which is approximately the first 175 pages of the book, you will be using almost the complete MYN system and benefiting from it greatly. You can even stop at the end of Part I if you want to. Part II takes you to the next level by teaching more about tasks and filing e-mail—it's optional, but I highly recommend you study it. Part III and the Appendix are fully optional—they cover much more advanced system practice.

In general, you should plan to do the lessons in order because they build on one another. In some places I invite you to skip ahead to particular lessons if interested. After you get to Part III, however, feel free to skip around as much as you like, because all lessons there stand on their own.

Video Version of This Book

There is a video summary of this book on my website. This video course summarizes the most important contents of the book in an enjoyable and low-effort way. Many of these videos are complimentary, though most require that you purchase the series. (For more information, go to www.myn.bz/mvc.htm.)

Part I: The Basic MYN System

Part I teaches the basic MYN system. Lesson 1 is the underlying theory and an overview of the system. You can skip this lesson if you'd like to start using the system, but I think you'll find it very helpful and interesting.

In Lesson 2 you learn how to navigate across various Outlook task tools and the basics of entering tasks. I also introduce you to an important skill: how to convert e-mails to tasks. In Lesson 3 you learn how to quickly configure Outlook for the MYN task system. In Lesson 4 you'll learn the core principles of the MYN system, those for low-guilt, effective task management. In Lesson 5 you'll learn how to clear your Inbox and enjoy the bliss that experience brings. By the end of the five short lessons, you'll be using the system and gaining great benefits in your workday. You can even put the book down after these lessons and feel satisfied that you learned all you need to learn.

Part II: Advancing the MYN System

Part II is about advancing your usage of the MYN system. In Lesson 6 you will drill down on which tasks are best to put in Outlook and how you can use them in the MYN system. Mobile systems and alternate software are covered as well. Lesson 7 gives complete coverage of converting e-mails to tasks, an essential portion of the system and the cure to Inbox stress. In Lesson 8 you learn e-mail topic-filing techniques that really help you get ahead of too much e-mail. And in Lesson 9, I revisit the underlying theory of the system and use that as a basis for explaining the very important topic of Strategic Deferrals. If, after a few weeks or months of using the system, you find your task list has grown unbearably large, Strategic Deferrals will solve that for you. By the end of Part II, you will be totally proficient at converting e-mails to tasks, you will have a sophisticated e-mail filing technique under your belt, and you'll be managing your growing list of tasks effectively. I end Lesson 9, and Part II, with a set of flow charts that summarize the entire MYN system.

Part III: Mastering the MYN System

Part III is all about mastering the system completely. In Lesson 10 you will focus on techniques for assigning and managing delegated tasks. In Lesson 11 you will find a discussion of time management and time-saving approaches that add efficiency to your day. In the final lesson, Lesson 12, you'll find advanced ways to use the system to track high-importance tasks as well as ways to track projects, goals, deadlines, and other extensions of the system. You also learn how to create several optional Windows Outlook task views that will help you get the most out of the system.

Appendixes

Appendix A is about Outlook folders and how to use them. I also explain some difficult-to-understand features of Outlook.

In Appendix B, I teach you strategies for archiving the Outlook e-mail you store using the MYN system. I show strategies both for manual archive and for using Outlook AutoArchive. This appendix is a highly valuable explanation of this difficult topic.

Appendix C is a list of resources you may find useful when further exploring the topics of this book. I also provide a few quick guides you can tear out to use on your desktop.

Getting Started

Most important: getting started immediately using the MYN system and gaining relief from your out-of-control workday. If you've exhausted the Quick Start, study Lessons 1 through 5 and enjoy the benefits of the complete MYN system for a while. Then come back to complete the other seven lessons.

Book Website and Newsletter

I encourage you to go to my website: www.myn.bz or www.michaellinenberger.com now to see if there are any updates to this book, which are available free of charge. I also recommend that you sign up for my free monthly e-mail newsletter at my website. In that newsletter I announce system enhancements and changes, and give the latest tips on using the MYN system.

PART I

The Basic MYN System

Lesson 1:
Master Your Now! in Outlook:
Theory and Overview

Introduction

If you used the Quick Start and tried out the One Minute To-Do List (1MTD) version of the Master Your Now! (MYN) system, you should have a sense of what this system can do for you. Now it's time to move on to the complete MYN system.

Before you create the complete MYN task list in Outlook, let me show you some of the underlying MYN theories that guide this system and then a brief overview of the system's key components. This will help you understand *why* you are making the Outlook MYN configurations and why you are learning the new workday processes.

However, reviewing this theory is not a prerequisite to success with the MYN system. So if you're eager to start implementing MYN and want to skip this theory chapter, feel free to jump to Lesson 2 now. For readers of the first edition of this book who are upgrading directly to this edition, I encourage you to read the following theory, so you can understand how and why the new system is different. For readers of my 2010 book, *Master Your Workday Now!*, you've seen much of this, so you can skip ahead in this lesson, if you like, to the section "The MYN task list in Microsoft Outlook."

Note: *This lesson is summarized in video 7 of the MYN-Outlook Complete Video Training (see beginning of the Quick Start chapter for more information).*

Master Your Now—The Theory

Solving Two Harsh Realities of Today's Workday

The MYN system of task management is largely based on solving two harsh realities of today's typical workday. A blunt recognition of these realities is

3

what makes the system work so well. You see, this is not an idealized system that works only for those who do everything just right and commit to a new organized life. Rather, it recognizes your workday is currently overwhelmed and probably a bit out of control, and starts from there. The system is based on modeling such an overwhelmed work life and then attending to it. Most people when they learn the theory behind this system say, "Yes, that's my workday!" I think you will, too.

Here are those two harsh but absolutely true conditions of today's workday experience that are dealt with up front in the MYN system.

▶ You, as a busy professional, cannot possibly get it all done. You will think of, and be handed, way more tasks (and e-mail) than you can possibly act on completely. The MYN system acknowledges that and teaches you how to deal with these tasks and all that e-mail in a positive and productive way.

▶ While you know that your *goals and values* should rule your activities, usually it is *urgency* that rules what you do at work every day. So the MYN system starts with an urgency-based model. MYN teaches you how to manage the urgency in your current work life. Later you will learn to insert goal- and value-driven tasks as your processes mature with the system.

These two simple realities guide the theory behind the system. After using it awhile, as your workday becomes more manageable, you will find these realities are no longer so harsh.

The Now Horizon Model of Work

A Time- and Urgency-Based Mental Model

Let's talk more about how prominent urgency is in guiding most people's work activities. As busy professionals we all collect a very large number of near-term responsibilities and tasks. In a busy office we tend to focus first on immediate emergencies if any exist. Next, we focus on urgent things due soon and then on slightly less urgent things that are due a little farther out, and so on. In the midst of that are meetings, interruptions, and diversions, and hopefully some importance-based tasks. In general, though, our focus is based on time and urgency. One can describe this time and urgency focus in terms of a *mental model* of our workload, which I believe most of us unconsciously structure our work around. This model diagrams how we tend to interpret, mentally and emotionally, various levels of urgency. It helps explain our feeling of overload as well as define a solution to the overloaded workday.

An Exercise to Identify Your Now Horizon

To define that model, consider this. If someone (not your boss) tried to insert a half-day project into your currently very busy schedule—giving you no permission to drop other items — and then asked you to complete it *tomorrow*, I am pretty sure you would say, "No, I am too busy right now." However, even with the same workload, if that request were due, say, two months from now (and you had some interest in it), you would probably say "fine." Somewhere in the range between tomorrow and two months is what I call your Workday Now Horizon, or Now Horizon for short. It is the date after which you stop feeling too busy, as you mentally gaze into the future.

The Workday Now Horizon helps define the mental model of your current workload. It delineates which commitments you consider when you think about what is on your plate *now*. Most very busy people, when they think about work *inside* that horizon, feel anxious or stressed about their workload. When they consider work beyond that horizon, however, they usually mentally relax, even if there is no change in their job or commitments.

Typical Now Horizon Periods

Interestingly, across all the busy knowledge workers I have interviewed, the Now Horizon period is usually around 1.5 weeks. There are exceptions of course and it varies by industry and job type; for example, it is longer for senior managers, shorter for administrative staff. But 1.5 weeks (let's say ten days) is a typical average.

Using this average number, consider how many days your Now Horizon is. Keep that in mind as you continue reading.

A Model of Near-Term Work

Horizon as a Sight Limit

Think of what *horizon* means. If you imagine yourself standing on a flat beach and gazing out over a flat ocean, the horizon is that line on the ocean where you can see no further. (Sailors tell me it is 12 miles out.) No matter how far it is, your sight of the ocean is limited to that horizon. If you traveled toward it on a boat, it would remain 12 miles out.

Similarly, your Now Horizon is that time edge of work beyond which you do not mentally see your future work clearly. Day by day it stays the same distance out (about ten days) because it is a *rolling* time frame — and that brings us to the next point.

Combined Model: Conveyor Belt or Treadmill

Let's combine the horizon concept with another mental model that many people think of when they think of work. Factory workers often work next to a rolling conveyor belt in which physical objects are brought to them, perhaps machine parts they need to assemble or pack. Their speed of work is often controlled by the speed of the conveyor belt. Knowledge workers who work in offices do not have a physical conveyor belt, but their work life is often described in a similar way, like being on a *treadmill*.

Combining all the above, here is a useful model. Imagine a person walking in place on the left end of a moving treadmill-like conveyor belt that stretches to the right a far distance. For simplicity of discussion, let's assume it is a man for now. He is facing and walking toward the right end at a speed that just keeps him in place above the left end of the moving belt (see Figure 1.1).

Figure 1.1
Now Horizon conveyor belt workload model in ideal state.

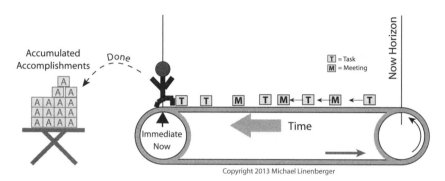

Copyright 2013 Michael Linenberger

The Flow of Work

Coming toward him on the belt are workday tasks and meetings that he needs to do and keep up with to do his job. Those things immediately in front of him are what he is working on now, or that are due now. As he accomplishes these tasks he tosses them into his mental accumulated accomplishments pile, shown in Figure 1.1, and takes the next work item in front of him.

A little beyond his immediate tasks are things that are going to impact him soon and that he may need to prepare for. Beyond that on the conveyor are less urgent things—but they are still in his awareness. Typically, the man works on tasks as they arrive to him on the belt. But occasionally he reaches out and picks items farther ahead, to get them done ahead of time, either because he wants to be proactive and get ahead of his work or, more likely, because the timing of related circumstances might be right to get them done *now*.

Now Horizon = End of Conveyor

At the far right end of the conveyor belt is the limit of what he can easily see coming. It is the Now Horizon we described earlier—about ten days out. It is not that no work exists beyond that horizon; it is just that work beyond that point is out of sight and therefore out of mind. So the man is not anxious about it and probably does not think much about it.

This is a good model for your workload. You tend to put all your attention on your work inside (to the left of) the Now Horizon. And you tend to get most anxious about work due soon (work that is next to you, at the left end of the conveyor belt). It's only logical.

Rate of Work

If the rate of work entering and the completed work leaving your Now Horizon is the same (as in Figure 1.1) you feel good. If, however, you complain about being overloaded with work, you are most likely complaining that the rate is too high and work is piling up inside the Now Horizon (see pile of tasks at the left end of the conveyor belt in Figure 1.2).

Figure 1.2

The Now Horizon model showing various "urgency zones" and an overloaded state.

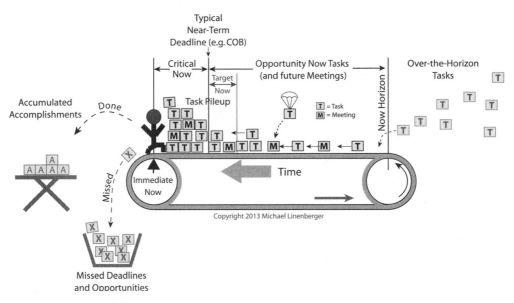

If the pileup is too great, you start to miss opportunities and deadlines, as depicted by the bucket added to the lower-left corner of the conveyor belt diagram in Figure 1.2. That leads to your sense of regret or anxiety about work. Again, whether overwhelmed or not, you still don't think much about work outside, or "over," the Now Horizon; that is, beyond about ten days.

Your Urgency Zones

You'll soon see that you can define what I call *urgency zones* in this model. Identifying these zones is extremely useful because doing so provides a way to manage within them. It gives you a way to apply work intensity appropriately. To identify the zones, let's add a bit of detail to this model.

Critical Now Tasks

Draw a line just to the right of where the man is standing on the conveyor belt, as shown in Figure 1.2. This line represents the typical deadline for things the man is currently working on or worried about. For most knowledge workers in most industries, this typical deadline is at the close of business (COB) each day, but it varies across industries. I call that time period, from the immediate now to the end of the typical deadline, the Critical Now. Naturally, tasks *due* inside that time frame have most of the man's attention and urgency. They probably have most of his anxiety as well. It is here where tasks typically pile up, which leads to missed deadlines and opportunities. Tasks due inside the Critical Now period I call Critical Now tasks.

You may wonder why I place the word Now in the title of this and the next two urgency zones, and in the term Now Horizon. It's because the time period of each zone is always with reference to now, to *today*. As the moving conveyor belt shows, our task lists are based on a rolling time period, so we will likely be updating these lists each day. The word *Now* emphasizes the immediate and dynamic nature of these lists.

Opportunity Now Tasks

Tasks to the right of the Critical Now deadline, but to the left of the Now Horizon, are tasks that the man is aware of and knows he needs to do soon or as soon as is practical, but he'll do them *now* only if the right opportunity is presented to him. For example, say the right person came by, or he had an inspired moment, or he completed all his urgent work. In those cases he might do these tasks, and therefore he wants them in his awareness just in case such an opportunity does arise. I call tasks in this zone of the conveyor belt Opportunity Now tasks.

Target Now Tasks

The man might also have tasks inside the Opportunity Now period he would *like* to do now but that are not urgently due. These are his most important Opportunity Now tasks. Getting them done now might make a client happy or ease the timing on downstream tasks, but he would not work late to get them done. I call these tasks Target Now tasks. You can see that in Figure 1.2, as well.

Over-the-Horizon Tasks

Finally, any tasks to the right of the Now Horizon, beyond the man's current consideration (again, beyond about ten days), are called Over-the-Horizon tasks. By definition, he's not very concerned about them. There are exceptions, of course. A big event might be a month out on his calendar and it might capture part of his attention. But regarding day-to-day responsibilities, these are tasks he does not think much about.

Again, all these task types are shown in Figure 1.2.

In my book *Master Your Workday Now!* I showed how to combine these zones into one paper list I called the Workday Mastery To-Do List (essentially the same as the MYN task list), and how to use it to manage your day. Here, I show you how to create that to-do list in Outlook—providing a much more powerful way to use this system.

The MYN Task List in Microsoft Outlook

Most people who see this model find it matches their work experience. That fact is encouraging because it appears we have the situation well defined. Defining a problem, however, is only half the solution. The rest comes when steps are provided to manage within the model. I do that by mapping components of the Outlook task system to this model, and by providing processes to manage within the model with Outlook. By following those steps and processes, you create the MYN task list in your copy of Outlook.

Grouping Outlook Priorities

The first part of the solution comes in Lesson 3. There, I will show you how to configure Outlook to group your tasks by the Outlook Priority field (and how to make many more changes, well beyond the ones you might have done in the Quick Start chapter).

Let me explain. If you have used the Outlook task system at all, you might know that built in to Outlook are three levels of priority: High, Normal, and Low. Any task must be set to one of these, with Normal being the default setting. At the end of Lesson 3, tasks in your Outlook task list will be visibly grouped by each priority and subsorted by start date (with future-dated tasks hidden). In Windows Outlook, all groups will be in the same list, with High being the top group, as shown in Figure 1.3. On the Macintosh, each group will be in its own folder as shown in Figure 1.4.

In terms of applying the Now Horizon work model, each of the Now Horizon urgency zones is going to map to these Outlook priority groups. Here is how.

Note: If you studied the Quick Start chapter, some of this is review; however, I suggest you read it because more details are added here.

Critical Now Tasks Use the "High" Priority of Outlook

The Critical Now tasks in this new model are going to be mapped to the High priority in Outlook tasks, so Critical Now tasks represent the top section of the list in Figure 1.3 (Windows), and the top folder at the left of Figure 1.4 (Mac). In the MYN system, the deadline for these tasks is today. Later in the book you will see a process that helps you identify those tasks early, track them all day, and get them done on or ahead of time. This greatly eases the tension of the day and enables you to leave work on time more often.

Figure 1.3

The MYN Task List in Windows Outlook, after being configured in Lesson 3.

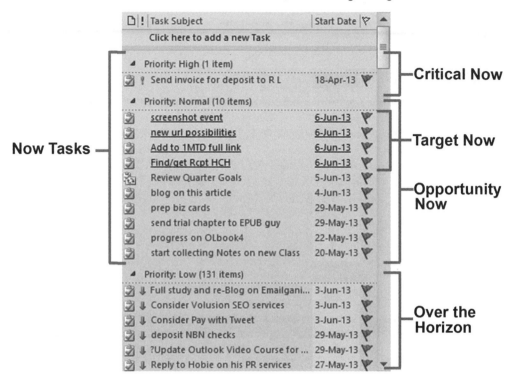

Figure 1.4

The MYN Task List in Outlook for Mac 2011, after being configured in Lesson 3.

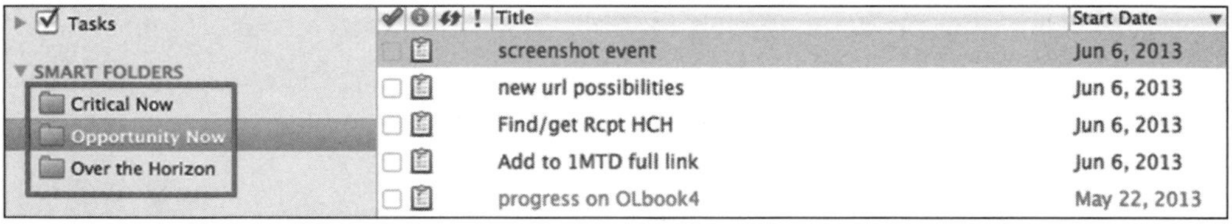

Opportunity Now Tasks Use the "Normal" Priority of Outlook

Tasks in the Normal (medium) priority section of Outlook tasks will correspond with the Opportunity Now tasks on the Now Horizon conveyor belt model as shown in the middle of the list in Figure 1.3 and the middle folder at the left of Figure 1.4. From now on, Normal priority Outlook tasks will be used for items not due today but that can impact you soon (within about ten days), and that you want to keep in daily sight to work on when possible. You do them when and if you have the opportunity, but you allow them to defer to the next day if you do not. Having this list well defined gives you a practical short list, which you can scan as you plan your workday and during any gaps in the day when you can get more work done. I provide a number of principles to help you manage that portion of the list in the lessons ahead.

Target Now Tasks Are at the Top of the "Normal" Priority Section of Outlook

The Target Now tasks list represents the upper portion of the Normal (medium) priority section of Outlook. In other words, they are your most important Opportunity Now tasks. (I'll discuss later how to indicate these and how to manage them. Delineating them represents an *optional* part of the MYN system for now.) See the underlined tasks at the top of the Opportunity Now section in Figure 1.3. These are not shown in Figure 1.4, but Mac users will see these tasks sorted to the top of the Opportunity Now Smart Folder after it is open. (However, no underlining is displayed.)

Over-the-Horizon Tasks Are in the "Low" Priority Section of Outlook

Tasks beyond about ten days are considered to be over the Now Horizon, and they are stored primarily in the Low priority section of Outlook. You will learn how and when to toss low-priority tasks over the Now Horizon to manage down the size of your Now Tasks list. This is an effective and legitimate way to improve your focus and decrease your workload anxiety. As you progress through the book and develop your use of the system, you will see a few variants of that, including a way to schedule reviewing and reentering of these tasks back inside the Now Horizon. More on that follows in the section "MYN Strategic Deferral," and then again in later lessons in the book. See the bottom tasks in Figure 1.3 and the bottom folder in Figure 1.4.

Critical Now Tasks + Opportunity Now Tasks = Now Tasks List

Combining the two main Now Horizon groups (Critical Now and Opportunity Now) together conceptually is useful. Together they make up what I call your Now Tasks list. On the conveyor belt model, they represent everything inside (to the left of) the Now Horizon line. By their definitions, you can see that Now Tasks are tasks you either must do now or would *consider* doing now if you could. These tasks are listed, visibly, in the upper two priority sections of your Outlook task list after it is reconfigured in Lesson 3 (see the upper portion of Figure 1.3 and the top two Smart Folders in Figure 1.4). I explain these further at the start of Lesson 4.

The Now Tasks list is an incredibly powerful list. It becomes your active daily to-do list. If you manage it as taught in this book, it places everything you need to prioritize in a relatively short collection of items. After you make a habit of adding *all* your tasks to the Outlook task list, including all tasks from e-mail, you can take comfort that you do not need to be concerned about anything *not* on the Now Tasks list. Having that clearly delineated and managed down to a reasonable size quickly leads to a reduction of stress in your workday. This Now Tasks list, along with your daily calendar and Inbox, places everything you need to know about your workday in one place. It becomes your control panel for what to do next, shown conveniently in Outlook.

The ultimate goal of applying your Now Tasks list is that your workday will start to look like Figure 1.1, at the start of this lesson. This is a smooth workday flow where tasks and e-mail processing are paced appropriately for your workday. Now you can experience mainly the satisfaction of accumulating *new accomplishments* every day, instead of the frustration of accumulating incomplete urgent tasks. The overloaded and chaotic picture in Figure 1.2 becomes a thing of the past.

All Tasks in One Place

In Lesson 6, I recommend you place *all* ad hoc tasks in your new Outlook MYN task list. Otherwise, if you need to look in multiple places, you won't have the confidence that you know everything on your plate. You won't be able to easily prioritize—and you won't be able to leave work at the end of the day with confidence that all important tasks are complete, that nothing is hanging out there at risk. Strategies for placing all tasks in Outlook are delivered in Lesson 6.

Converting E-mails to Tasks

As you progress through this book, you will soon find that successful e-mail management is largely accomplished through intelligent *task* management. At the very end of Lesson 2, I will show you how to convert e-mails to tasks. All of Lesson 7 drills down more on that critical skill. I hope you take the time to study and practice that, because you are going to find this skill is *the* fundamental step to getting e-mail under control.

Here's why this is so important. By converting e-mails to tasks, you can remove the tension from you Outlook Inbox by moving unreconciled actions into the task system. There they can be prioritized, scheduled, delegated, worked, or deferred—all with appropriate tools to do so effectively. With this skill you can speed through your Inbox because it gives you a way to process action e-mails without dwelling on them.

■   ■   ■

MYN Overview: Beyond the One Minute To-Do List

As I mentioned earlier, I teach *two* task management systems. The first is a simple one called the One Minute To-Do List (1MTD), which you saw in the Quick Start chapter and might have learned about elsewhere. The second, MYN (the topic of this book), is the more advanced one.

But what makes the MYN system so much more powerful? How is it different from 1MTD? Here is an overview of those additional features of MYN that cause it to rise above the 1MTD system (and above most other systems as well). You'll learn more details of these in the chapters ahead.

MYN Has a More Powerful Task Management Approach

Deadlines, Start Dates, and Follow-Up Tasks

Part of managing your priority of tasks is managing deadlines and when to do tasks. This is where many other task systems abuse our common sense. The old notion that you must place a due date on a task or it won't get done is appropriate for large project tasks, but no longer appropriate for the large number of small ad hoc tasks we get in today's business world. We get just too many tasks and too many new priorities every day to constantly be recalculating artificial due dates on tasks. We quickly reach the point that we ignore all due dates.

Instead, in MYN I teach you to put a *start date* on every task to guide task timing, and to use a deadline only on tasks with true hard deadlines. Using a start date in this system is a mechanical way to keep your Now Tasks list relatively short by hiding tasks until their start date arrives. Using a start date also gives you more fluidity when managing a constantly changing set of priorities, because starting a task past its original start date does not imply a missed deadline. Deadlines are managed separately and only when needed. Using start dates is covered completely in Lesson 4.

One place I do often recommend hard deadlines is on follow-up tasks, another MYN exclusive. These are tasks you set to track promises and progress on activities. Such tasks are quick to achieve and using them regularly helps keep your work streams on track. You'll see how to create and use these in Lesson 6 and again in Lesson 8.

FRESH Prioritization System

Inherent in any task management system should be a way to prioritize all tasks. Previously, you've seen the primary, urgency-based priority system applied in both 1MTD and the MYN task list. One layer below this is how to prioritize *within* the Opportunity Now tasks list. This is where MYN does a better job.

The Opportunity Now list (the Normal priority section in the Outlook task list) tends to get big, so an approach is needed to keep that list well managed. For this approach I teach you a new prioritization method called FRESH Prioritization, which is made possible by the use of start dates in MYN. This low-guilt method recognizes that task importance wanes over time. In today's fast-paced work environment, newer tasks tend to hold a higher priority, because they reflect the latest company priorities and urgencies, while older tasks tend to lose importance.

With the MYN FRESH Prioritization system, older tasks scroll lower in the list and eventually scroll off the page and out of sight if you let them. With

FRESH Prioritization, you can choose to move select older tasks back to near the top of the Opportunity Now list, if they are still important. But only if you decide they warrant it. In other words, older tasks need to *earn* their position near the top of your list. That is what FRESH Prioritization is all about, and it leads to a *self-cleaning* capability, something sorely needed in an automated task system that never forgets, such as Outlook. It is also what distinguishes this system from most other task systems that are guilt based and that promote *all* older tasks to the top of the list. I explain the FRESH Prioritization system thoroughly in the latter half of Lesson 4. The configurations in Lesson 3 are designed to support the FRESH Prioritization system.

MYN Strategic Deferral

After you start using the task system to manage your e-mail and tasks for a while, you will be recording in Outlook more tasks than ever before. Most of those will not be critical. They will be Opportunity Now tasks, as described earlier. Because Opportunity Now tasks are discretionary, they tend to build up over time. As your Opportunity Now tasks list grows in size, you'll be faced with a quandary: You'll have way more tasks recorded than you have time to do. Keeping the Now Tasks list to a reasonable number is important.

The typical way to manage excess tasks in any system is by using the "three Ds" — *delete, delegate,* or *defer*. In my experience, it is very hard for the average knowledge worker to delete or delegate many tasks. Rather, they need to *defer* activities in a strategic way, keeping their business well focused on a few important priorities while keeping track of the deferred ones, and over time deleting those whose usefulness has finally expired. That's what the MYN Strategic Deferral process does. Referring to the model above, I teach you how to toss lower-priority tasks over the Now Horizon, so they sit just out of sight and do not contribute to workload anxiety. I then show how to schedule these deferred tasks for review so they are not lost. Each task can get its most appropriate review date assigned. The review process is nearly automatic and does not distract from the primary task system.

This MYN Strategic Deferral process is a very powerful component of the system, and one that maps well to what you may already be doing when you ignore tasks you have no time to do. However, I suspect you're having trouble doing that in a very organized or satisfying way. MYN Strategic Deferral adds structure and a scheduled process to postponing lower-priority tasks, and it lets you relax knowing they are being managed in a timely fashion.

Note: *For those of you who used the master tasks concept in the first edition of this book, Strategic Deferral replaces most of its function of hiding low-priority tasks.*

I discuss a simplified manner of doing Strategic Deferrals in Lesson 4 and reserve complete coverage to Lesson 9. The Outlook configurations in Lesson 3 support all the Strategic Deferral processes and review steps.

More Powerful E-mail Management

Emptying Your Inbox

By converting e-mails to tasks, you can also achieve something that I find is very important and blissfully satisfying—an empty Inbox. You really want to get the Outlook Inbox back to a receiving-only function where it is emptied every day; otherwise, your Inbox becomes hopelessly cluttered. A cluttered Inbox represents a congestion of unattended responsibilities. Emptying the Outlook Inbox every day relieves that congestion in a very noticeable way. It also makes you more efficient, because without clearing your Inbox you'll be constantly glancing through old mail in search of passed over to-do's and unfiled information. Emptying your Inbox helps prevent responsibilities buried in e-mail items from getting away from you. It saves you time because it allows you to clearly delineate between mail that needs further processing and mail that you no longer need to read.

In both the 1MTD and MYN systems, I teach you a simple, no-brainer way of emptying your Inbox, with a single storage folder called the Processed Mail folder. With this straightforward technique, you can create a workflow in which you first extract tasks, and then drag all mail from your Inbox, every day, to that one folder. Students of mine who use this approach find the empty Inbox experience incredibly useful—and satisfying.

When you keep all mail in a single date-sorted folder, you'll find that it is a good way to find recent mail. You can also sort by sender in such a folder, grouping all mail from the same person together, and find mail that way.

In this book, with MYN, I go beyond that. In Lesson 5, I show you how to use a variety of search tools to find mail in that folder. In Lesson 8, I show you how to use Outlook Categories in that single folder to help find mail, as discussed in this next section.

Filing E-mail by Categories

While you can stop with Lesson 5 and just use a search tool to find mail and perhaps accomplish all of your e-mail filing needs, many people need more. Many people need a true topic-based filing system. So in Lesson 8, I discuss topic filing with various methods, including with multiple folders. I am not a big fan of using multiple folders, however, so I emphasize a more complete e-mail filing system based on tagging mail by topic with Outlook Categories. This is unique to MYN. Outlook Categories are an extremely useful way to file mail because they allow you to view your mail in folder-like *category* groups. You can even assign more than one category to an e-mail, and the item shows up in both places. If you need true topic-based filing, I strongly encourage you to give this method a try.

Optional Components of the MYN System

A number of other components of the system come into play in the latter part of the book. You might call these optional, depending on the role you play at your workplace. For example, if you have staff you delegate to, you'll definitely want to read Lesson 10 on delegation. Otherwise it is optional. If you manage projects, read Lesson 12. Here are some highlights from this more discretionary portion of the system.

Delegation

If you have a number of staff to delegate to, you might be frustrated by the lack of a clean way to manage delegated tasks. Failures with delegating often stem from lack of good systems to assign, track, and follow up on delegated tasks. They are not usually because of irresponsible subordinates.

What is often missing is a logical assignment and tracking system, so you can see what tasks are assigned and know when to check in on given tasks and when not to. Key to accomplishing this is setting follow-up tasks to yourself to track delegated assignments and to time contact with subordinates to check on assignments. I teach a simple task nomenclature and timing system to help you do this. The complete process steps are to identify a need, gain buy-in from your staff, and then enter an automated follow-up cycle until the task is done. Lesson 10 is devoted to this important process.

Time Management

When people say they need to learn time management, I find they usually need to learn *task* management. You can meet most of your time management needs by following the task management principles in the MYN system. You will use your time much more efficiently and effectively. As I mentioned in the Introduction, most users of this system say they gain back at least 25 percent of their workweek. Many say much more.

Beyond the task management principles taught in this book, however, a few simple time management techniques *are* part of this system. First, if your day is mostly full of appointments, you'll need to set some time aside to work your tasks. I encourage those using the MYN system to schedule general task time right on their calendar, which is discussed in Lesson 11.

Second, you might need to make sure that your time spent working your task list is well focused. In Lesson 11, I provide a number of techniques to ensure that. I also provide a simple process for identifying clearly whether you really are overloaded with high-importance tasks or just working inefficiently, which helps lead to a solution.

You can do many other things to make your use of Outlook and this system quicker and more efficient, which are all listed in Lesson 11, as well.

Intrinsic Importance

I've promised you that after you bring order to your workday chaos, and your work life is generally under control, you can use the system to track and manage intrinsically important tasks. What do I mean by *intrinsically important*? Tasks that are linked strongly to your values or goals are tasks that I say have high intrinsic importance.

I show in Lesson 12 a way to delineate and track such tasks. This optional lesson provides a very useful way of identifying these tasks and integrating them into your daily workflow.

Goal and Project Linkage

One useful way of prioritizing ad hoc tasks is to identify where they come from, why you are doing them, and what larger outcome they support. After you have tasks well under control, doing this exercise can help to add structure and can identify tasks that should be reprioritized. The main way to accomplish this exercise is to map ad hoc tasks to your *goals and projects*.

You can link tasks to goals and projects in a variety of ways. The simplest way is to create a goal and project list, and keep that list in mind as you create daily tasks. In other words, as you plan your day, look at your list of goals and projects and make sure you add tasks to your Now Tasks list, or appointments to your calendar, that support these higher-level priorities. To this end, I show a new way in Lesson 12 to build the master tasks list (a tool from the first edition of this book) that serves as a good place to list and review projects and goals.

A more elaborate solution is to actually link specific Outlook tasks to goals and projects, so you can see what tasks already on your list are contributing to a specific outcome. In Lesson 12, I show one way to do that in a new Outlook custom view with Outlook Categories. The Outlook add-in software ClearContext, which I highlight throughout this book, also provides a strong linkage between projects and tasks.

Beyond that, for more sophisticated goal and project management, I emphasize using other tools. Specifically for project management, after you reach a need to show clear linkages between dependent tasks, it really is time to move up to a tool such as Microsoft Project. For planning hierarchical relationships between goals, projects, and tasks, a tool such as MindManager is highly recommended. That said, I do show some ways to build Goal→Project→Task hierarchies. Lesson 12 puts all of this into perspective.

· ■ ·

Summary of System Theory and Key Components

So that's the Master Your Now! system in a nutshell. As a final overview, the following is a summary of the theory and major components of the system that you have just learned. All components are detailed in the following lessons.

▶ The system is based on an urgency model of a typical workday called the Now Horizon, which shows how nearly all our attention is placed on near-term tasks. This model provides a structure to manage those tasks.

▶ You will configure Outlook to map to the *urgency zones* in that model into a unified approach called the MYN task list. You will then learn ways to manage within each zone of that list.

▶ The Critical Now and Opportunity Now zones together make up what I call your Now Tasks list. These are tasks inside the Now Horizon — tasks you consider each day.

▶ After using the system for a while, you will want to take advantage of MYN Strategic Deferral — tossing low-priority tasks over the Now Horizon and scheduling reviews on them. This will keep your Now Tasks list at a reasonable size.

▶ You will learn two methods of prioritizing tasks, including the FRESH Prioritization system, which by default gives higher priority to newer tasks and uses start dates rather than due dates to guide task completion. Deadlines are used only when needed.

▶ Converting e-mails to tasks, and then managing those actions in your new MYN task system, is the number one way to get ahead of out-of-control e-mail.

▶ Emptying your Inbox every day will provide relief from the tension of unreconciled responsibilities buried in your Inbox. You will learn a simple way to do that.

▶ For people who need topic-based filing of e-mail, I recommend and teach a system of category-based tagging of Outlook mail, all within one folder, and then show how to display them in folder-like groups. Other options are discussed.

▶ The latter part of the book covers optional but important topics such as delegation, time management, intrinsic importance, and goal and project management. Consider exploring those topics after you have mastered the core skills of the system.

Next Steps

The ultimate goal of applying this model and corresponding management principles is that your workday will begin to look like Figure 1.1. This is a smooth workday flow where tasks on your list are paced appropriately for your workday, and you experience only the satisfaction of accumulating new accomplishments every day.

Using the task management system in Outlook is a key first step to doing that. In the next lesson, Lesson 2, I show you the basics of the out-of-the-box Outlook task management system. I then teach a simple version of the important skill of converting e-mails to tasks.

Then, in Lesson 3, I show you how to reconfigure the Outlook task system to match MYN principles. Detailed MYN principles to manage the task list and e-mail start in Lesson 4 and continue to the end of the book.

So get started now on Lesson 2, and you will soon have your tasks, e-mail, and workday well under control.

Lesson 2:
Learning the Outlook Task System

Introduction

Tasks and task management are at the core of the MYN system. Even though MYN also focuses on *e-mail* management, you'll see that my prescription for good e-mail management is built largely around having good *task* management in place. Everything in MYN centers around tasks.

Built in to the desktop version of Microsoft Outlook is an excellent task system, one that is highly configurable. In Lesson 3 you will use that configuration capability to modify your Outlook task system extensively — reconfiguring it to match MYN principles. But before you do that, you should learn how to use the basic, unmodified task system in Outlook. You'll need a thorough understanding of the Outlook task system before configuring it for your own use.

Note: *This lesson is summarized in videos 2 and 3 of the MYN-Outlook Complete Video Training (see beginning of the Quick Start chapter for more information).*

In This Lesson

In this second lesson, I will show you all aspects of the out-of-the-box task system in Outlook that are important to MYN. The Outlook task system is a rich and complex tool, so there is a lot to learn here. Specifically I'll show you:

► Outlook versions whose task modules are covered by this book.

► How to navigate inside the task system and how that varies depending on which version you have.

► The most important places to find tasks in Outlook, and the various ways to enter tasks.

► How flagging e-mail affects your task list—it can be a bit perilous!

► A quick way to convert e-mails to tasks, which is a core element of the MYN system.

Essentially, this is a lesson on the *mechanics* of using Outlook tasks. And while there are not many MYN principles covered in this lesson, I will teach you Outlook features that MYN depends on. I will also show you ways to change task layouts to make them easier to use with MYN. So, if you are a more advanced Outlook user and tempted to skip this lesson, stay with me. You'll learn quite a few new things that make the system easier to use. If you are not very experienced with Outlook tasks, this lesson is a core building block for you mastering the MYN system.

If You've Given Up on Outlook Tasks, Try Again

Most people I know who have tried the Outlook task system have given up quickly. I did too the first couple of times I tried it. However, do not let past failures with the task system stop you from trying it again. Let me tell a story that explains why.

Some time ago a company I worked for adopted Microsoft Outlook as its e-mail system, so it was natural at that time for me to try the Outlook task-management system. This was not the first time I had tried to manage tasks with an automated to-do list like the one in Outlook. I'd attempted this with many other automated packages, including Palm handheld software synchronized with the desktop version of the Palm software. I had also tried task software on a BlackBerry synchronized with Outlook.

However, in the past, and again this time, I found that within a few weeks the automated to-do list quickly got out of hand, and invariably I stopped using it. What happened was that a large list of tasks built up. These were tasks that I intended to get to but that I was unsure when I needed to complete them. Not wanting to lose sight of these tasks, I did not delete them from the task list, and the task list grew to a size that I found either psychologically overwhelming to look at or just impossible to scan through. I had trouble deleting tasks because even the lower-priority ones seemed significant after they were on the list.

Of course, I tried assigning priorities to tasks, but then I ended up with a large number of high-priority tasks, most of which were important but not important for any given day. Consequently, while they remained sorted high on the task list, I constantly skipped them as I used the list. So due to the overwhelmingly large size of the list, even the high-priority portion of it, the list became weak and useless. Outlook did not seem to solve the problem for me.

Having a Methodology Is Key

The solution that changed this was developing my own task and e-mail management methodologies that worked in Outlook. They involved reconfiguring Outlook in various ways to show only pertinent tasks, to provide ways to defer tasks, and to provide new approaches to task prioritization that work in today's business environment. After the methodologies were applied, and the configurations of Outlook changed, Outlook worked splendidly for managing tasks and e-mails.

The moral of this story is that while the tool was in place, a usable process or *methodology* was not. So even if you have tried and given up on Outlook tasks, give the task system another try with MYN. You now have a powerful new system to work with that will make it shine, especially if you use Windows Outlook. The Mac version has a much weaker task system, but you can still use it.

Next, let's discuss which versions of Outlook work with this system.

Outlook Versions Whose Task Modules Are Covered by This Book

Since 1997, nine major versions of the Outlook PC and Mac application have been released. Beyond that are mobile versions that many people think are Outlook (but aren't really). As Microsoft has evolved Outlook over those years, it has changed the task module in Outlook, often in significant ways.

Because of those variations, MYN is applied differently to each version. That's one reason this book is updated so often—to cover the newer Outlook versions. So it's important to know which version you have, both to confirm that it is covered by this edition, and to know which sections of this book to study.

Note: *When referring to Outlook labels, the instructions in this book cover only the English version of Outlook. Other language versions are not documented. If working in another language, do your best to translate the Outlook labels.*

Multiple Outlook Versions Are Covered

Updating this book every few years, I modify its scope to cover the most recent three to four Outlook versions. So with each new edition, I add a new version (or two) and remove one or more older versions.

Why not cover all versions of Outlook?

The book would be too long and many sections would be out of date.

Why not cover just one version per edition like many other computer books?

Because many users and companies are using multiple versions simultaneously. This way, readers are not forced to buy a separate book for each version they might use. Also, much of the material in the book is *not* version specific.

For those sections of the book that *are* version specific, I have labeled their titles to indicate which versions are covered. So it's important to watch for version information in the section headings as you study this book.

With that in mind, note that in this new edition, Outlook version 2003 and earlier are not included. The following describes what *is* supported in this latest edition.

Supported in This Edition: Outlook Desktop Versions 2007, 2010, 2011, and 2013 (Office 365)

Windows Outlook

Let's start with Windows Outlook. This latest book edition supports Windows Outlook desktop versions 2007, 2010, and 2013 (Office 365). If you are using an earlier version of Windows Outlook, earlier editions of this book may cover it. Most earlier editions of this book can still be found online. Specifically, if you have Outlook 2000 or 2002, get the 2nd Edition. If you have Outlook 2003, get the 3rd Edition.

Outlook 2013 is sometimes called *Outlook for Office 365*. However, that's misleading because Office 365 has both an online version of Outlook and a PC-installable desktop version. This book only supports the latter — the desktop version of Outlook in Office 365. The online version is Outlook Web App (OWA) and not robust enough for use with this book. More on that follows.

Outlook for Mac 2011 Is Supported in This Edition, But Not as Much as Windows

Over the years, because far more users of Outlook use it on a PC, the Windows versions of Outlook have been the main focus of this book series. But the latest Mac version, Outlook for Mac 2011, is catching on, so it is covered here, too. The earlier Microsoft product, Entourage, is not supported in this book.

Note that Outlook for Mac 2011 treats tasks quite differently than any of the Windows versions. For that reason I describe it separately in many of the instructions. Also, I cover it much less than the Windows versions. That's because, unfortunately, Microsoft chose not to implement as many task features in the Mac version as they have in the Windows version. The lack of those features makes it less powerful for tasks, and makes using MYN more difficult. That's the main reason you will see less coverage of it throughout the book.

Because of these weaknesses, some Mac users may be better off with a different software product for managing tasks according to the principles in this book. I discuss an alternative in Lesson 6 called Toodledo. You can read about it there or go to my website (www.myn.bz/ToodleDo.html) for more information. But before doing that, try out the Mac task features according to the instructions in this book and see if they work for you.

What About Web-Based Versions and Mobile Versions of Outlook?

Desktop Outlook Versions Are the Primary Topic of This Book

This book covers primarily the desktop PC or Mac versions of Outlook. Microsoft also has a large number of other PC, web-based, and mobile e-mail productivity products. Some of them even have the Outlook name (for example, Outlook.com or the old Outlook Express). But because these are not complete copies of Outlook, they lack the task features needed for MYN task management and are not the primary target of this book.

That's not to say that you can't use mobile versions if you are using the MYN system—you can. After all, many of us spend much of our day using e-mail on our mobile devices, and that's fine. However, I recommend you periodically (at least every day or two) touch base on your desktop copy of Outlook on your PC or Mac (or laptop or Windows 8 tablet), to do your complete MYN task and e-mail management and cleanup. I cover extending MYN skills to your mobile devices in Lesson 6. I also give tips on integrating mobile devices throughout the book.

Variants of Outlook Not Covered

Because only the desktop variants of Outlook are the target of this book, that means online implementations are not. So, for example, OWA and Office 365 web variants of Outlook are not suitable to implement the core MYN task principles in this book. That's because their task features are not sufficiently powerful. But note, if you have an Office 365 license, you might be eligible to download a free copy of the desktop Outlook 2013 application on your PC or Mac.

The myriad of other Microsoft-supplied mobile e-mail programs and mobile apps are not eligible to use as your primary e-mail and task management tool in MYN. So Outlook.com is not suitable, nor the Mail client on Windows 8 tablets. Many mobile e-mail and task products provided by mobile hardware manufacturers are also not covered, such as those by Apple for their mobile products, those by Google for their Android products, or those by BlackBerry—none are suitable for complete MYN task management. Feel free to use them for e-mail; however, be sure to find a good MYN-suitable mobile task application to use *with* them. There are lots of third-party mobile apps that work very well, as I discuss next.

The Mobile Solution: Third-Party Apps

With all major smartphones and tablets, you can install third-party mobile task apps, and there is at least one app that *does* support MYN available for each major mobile platform. I don't cover them *in detail* in this book because their features change so rapidly. Instead, I cover them on my website and keep those descriptions up to date. Lesson 6 lists those apps that support

MYN and provides links to my web-based instructions on how to use them. Using these mobile solutions throughout the day, along with periodic stops at your PC or Mac desktop version of Outlook, is definitely a viable plan.

So, even if you mostly use your mobile device for e-mail and tasks, my instructions for mobile usage in Lesson 6 assume you have first learned the MYN system using your desktop copy of Outlook. Consequently, I highly recommend completing Lessons 2 though 5 before moving to Lesson 6.

How to Identify Your Windows Outlook Version

Among the Windows Outlook versions supported in this book—2007, 2010, and 2013—there are many differences, so it is important that you know which of these you have. I'll show you how to determine that next. You are only looking for the version *year*. Service packs, dot releases, and so on are not important in making this determination.

Note: If you already know your Outlook version, you can skip to the next section.

Here is how to determine which version of Windows Outlook you are using.

All Versions Try This First

Before Outlook is started, try examining the Outlook icon on your PC—its label often displays its version year. If not, then hover your mouse over the icon, which might display the version year in the popup screen tip. If that does not work, then, when you start Outlook, examine the startup screen as Outlook starts. The version year might be prominently displayed. If you still do not know, read the following.

Identifying Outlook 2010 or 2013

After you launch Outlook, examine the top portion of the Outlook window. If you have a large set of tabbed icons at the top of your Outlook window with these exact tab names in this order, File, Home, Send/Receive, Folder, View (maybe more), then you are using either Outlook 2010 or 2013. To tell which, go to the File tab and if you see a Help entry in the left margin, click it and you will likely see a copyright statement on the right of the screen indicating it is part of Office 2010, which means you are using Outlook 2010.

To confirm that you have Outlook 2013, go to the File tab and you will likely see an entry on the left called Office Account. Select that and on the right you will see a button labeled About Outlook. Open that and you'll see a window with a copyright statement at the top indicating it is Outlook 2013 (or part of Office 365, which means it is the same thing).

Identifying Outlook 2007

If you do not see a large set of tabbed icons at the top as described above, but rather you see a set of menu names at the top labeled in this order, File, Edit, View, and more, then there's one more step to determine the version. Click on the Help menu at the far right of the main menu, and choose the About

Microsoft Office Outlook menu item. Then look at the copyright date at the very top of the small window that opens. That date is your version year and you are looking for 2007 (anything older is not covered in this book).

Note. The formal name for Outlook 2007 is Microsoft Office Outlook 2007. However, Microsoft dropped the word "Office" from that formal nomenclature starting with version 2010. For brevity in this book, I will refer to all the different Windows versions merely as Outlook 2007, Outlook 2010, and Outlook 2013, and sometimes I just use the version year.

Is there a "Best" Version of Windows Outlook for MYN?

I've mentioned that, when using MYN, the Windows versions of Outlook work much better than the Mac version. But I am often asked this: Among the supported Windows Outlook versions, is one better than the others for MYN?

Many task features were added starting with version 2007, so I recommend all versions 2007 and later. Outlook 2010 (and 2013) added the Quick Steps feature, and that can be very useful for the MYN system (described in Lesson 7).

I prefer the older Outlook 2010 over Outlook 2013 for the MYN system because in 2013, Microsoft changed the way the To-Do Bar works (which I'll discuss), and I do not like the new changes. However, Outlook 2010 has issues as well that were fixed in 2013, so overall I'd say either 2010 or 2013 are the best versions to use for MYN.

Navigating Through Outlook to Find Tasks (Windows and Mac)

Okay, let's get started with some Outlook basics. I want to show specifically how to navigate among various Outlook folders, because you will be doing that as you use the task module. Most of what follows applies to both the Windows and Mac versions, but I will call out some differences. If you are an experienced Outlook user, you might want to skip this section on Outlook folders and navigation, and go to the following section "Learning Basics of Outlook Tasks." However, if you have time, read this, too.

Data Types and Data Type Modes

Both Windows and Mac Outlook have five different data types, some of which you are probably familiar with. They are Mail, Calendar, Contacts, Tasks, and Notes. Windows Outlook 2007 and 2010 have one more—Journal.

Notice that Outlook can be in only one data-type mode at a time. You choose which mode is active by clicking the major navigation buttons in the lower-left portion of the Outlook window, as shown in Figures 2.1 and 2.2.

After a mode is selected, the entire Outlook window changes to reflect that data type. So if you click Mail, you'll see nothing but Mail items and Mail tools. Same with Calendar, Contacts, and so on. As you can see, these major navigation buttons are very important.

Figure 2.1
Navigation buttons in Outlook 2010 (2007 and 2011 are similar).

Figure 2.2
Navigation menu in lower-left corner of Outlook 2013 window.

The appearance of those buttons can be different depending on Outlook adjustments and on the Outlook version. In Outlook 2007, 2010, and 2011, the major navigation buttons in the lower-left corner can either be shown as vertically stacked, wide, labeled bars, as shown in Figure 2.1 (I call these *banner buttons*), or as smaller unlabeled icons that are arranged horizontally along the very bottom, as shown in Figure 2.3.

Figure 2.3
Alternate navigation buttons in Outlook 2010 (2007 and 2011 are similar).

They also can be displayed as a mixture of both. You can adjust which way they are shown by dragging the boundary at the top of that pane up or down.

Note: There are other ways to adjust the order and visibility of those buttons and icons. See Appendix A, section "Configuring Buttons and Icons at Bottom of Navigation Pane."

In Outlook 2013, four of those navigation buttons are usually shown as large, horizontally-spread *labels* named Mail, Calendar, People, and Tasks, as shown in Figure 2.2. If you click the ellipsis (…) at the right of that sequence, you'll get a menu that shows the remainder of the data types, as shown in Figure 2.4.

Figure 2.4
Additional navigation choices in Outlook 2013.

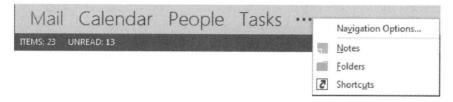

On that menu, choose Navigation Options to change whether to display large labels, shown in Figure 2.2, or smaller icons. (Select the Compact Navigation check box to display smaller icons. It's the default on Windows tablets.) With Navigation Options you can also choose which modes are shown or hidden in the ellipsis menu.

Outlook Folders

You might be using multiple Outlook folders to organize your mail. For example, you might be dragging mail you are done with out of the Outlook Inbox and into other mail folders. Actually, *all* data types in Outlook use folders. So, not only can you organize your *e-mail* in folders, but you can also use folders for organizing calendar items, tasks, and more.

New Outlook accounts normally start with one folder for each data type, and it's that folder that opens when a given data-type mode is activated. The Mail data type, however, starts with more than one folder (normally Inbox, Sent Items, Drafts, and Junk). You can create (or connect to) additional folders for all data types. You can have multiple tasks folders or contacts folders, for example, and move items among them.

When you have multiple folders for a data type, one of them is considered the default, and this default folder is usually favored in all navigation until you change the default (more on that follows).

Folders are data type specific, so a mail folder can hold only e-mail items and a calendar folder can hold only calendar events. However, there are two exceptions to this: The Deleted Items folder can hold all types (there is only one Deleted Items folder in an Outlook account), and some tasks folders can display flagged items from other data types, usually e-mail (more on that at the end of this lesson).

Choosing Folders in the Navigation or Folders Pane (All Versions)

After you have more than one folder for a given data type, you need to use a *folder list* to see them and open them. The usual way to see that folder list is to activate a given data type with the lower-left buttons. Then look on the middle-left side of the Outlook window. A list of folders that correspond to the currently open data type is displayed. Let's talk more about that left pane and how to use it to navigate around Outlook.

The left side of all Outlook windows is usually dominated by a large navigation form. In Outlook 2007, 2010, and 2011, it's called the Navigation Pane, and in Outlook 2013 it is called the Folders Pane (but it looks and acts the same in all versions). Figure 2.5 shows the Outlook 2010 Navigation Pane. All other versions including 2013 look similar.

Figure 2.5
Navigation Pane in Outlook 2010 (all other versions are similar).

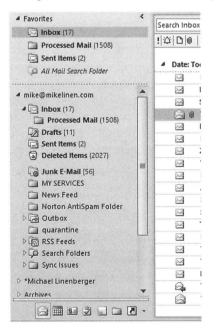

Note: *If something similar to the Navigation Pane shown in Figure 2.5 is not displayed on your screen, it might be closed or minimized. To open it, choose the View menu or tab, and click Navigation Pane (or Folders Pane in 2013), which in Windows versions opens a submenu from which you should choose Normal. In Outlook 2011 just click Navigation Pane to open it.*

The Navigation or Folders Pane is a powerful tool, but in many ways it is confusing. (I provide a complete explanation of the Navigation and Folders Pane near the end of Appendix A.) However, for now, follow this simplified two-step approach: Start by using the major navigation buttons in the lower-left corner of the Outlook window to select the data-type mode. This opens the current default folder and displays the complete folder list for that data type. Then, if needed, click in the middle or upper portion of the left pane to open other folders of that type.

Folder List Button (Windows Only)

I showed how, when a given data-type mode is active, the Navigation or Folders Pane displays only folders of that type. However, Windows Outlook has a unique and powerful version of a folder list that includes *all* data types (Mail, Contacts, Tasks, and so on), sorted by where they are stored. This can be useful if you have many local Outlook files or access to external data stores (network file storage, for example) and want to organize or search your data by location. To see that universal folder list, click the Folder List banner button or icon at the bottom of the pane (see Figure 2.6). In Outlook 2013, you can reach that same icon by clicking the ellipsis (…) at the right end of the major navigation labels (as shown in Figure 2.4). In 2013, it's called Folders.

Figure 2.6
Folder List icon in Outlook 2010 (other versions are similar).

After you click the Folder List, or Folders icon, a larger folder tree opens in the Navigation or Folders Pane that shows folders across all data types, grouped by location. I call this the Folder List mode. In this mode, you will see mail folders mixed with calendar folders, mixed with tasks folders, and so on. This Folder List choice is not available in Outlook for Mac 2011.

For more information about the Folder List mode, see Appendix A, section "The Three MODES of the Navigation or Folders Pane."

Learning Basics of Outlook Tasks (Windows and Mac)

Now that you know how to navigate among the various Outlook data types, let's focus on the most important one for this book: Tasks.

Accessing the Outlook Task System

A new Outlook account usually starts out with one task storage location. All tasks you create go in it. That task storage location can be accessed in multiple ways, but two are primary: the *Tasks folder* (all versions) and the *To-Do Bar* (Windows only). Tasks in each of these two views can appear sorted or filtered differently, but they are really the same single list of tasks. If you enter a task in one view, it is also displayed in the other view. Each view has advantages and disadvantages.

Using Tasks Folders

As described earlier, you select a Tasks folder by clicking the Tasks icon or label in the lower-left portion of the Outlook window. This puts Outlook in the Tasks data-type mode, so your entire Outlook window is dominated by your list of tasks.

Note: *After entering the Tasks data-type mode, I recommend you make the view easier to use by hiding the Reading Pane. In Windows Outlook, you do that by going to the View tab, clicking Reading Pane, and then selecting Off. On the Mac go to the Organize tab, click Reading Pane, and then select Hidden.*

While this appears to be the main way to view tasks in Outlook, in Windows versions we'll rarely use the Tasks folder. Instead, we'll be using the To-Do Bar on most occasions to use the MYN system. I'll explain why in a moment.

On the Macintosh the opposite is true. We'll use the Tasks folders exclusively for all our task work on the Mac because there is no Mac equivalent for the Windows To-Do Bar (one disadvantage of the Mac version).

Let's focus exclusively on the Windows To-Do Bar for a while, because that's where most of your task work will be done. Mac users jump to the section "Entering Tasks in Outlook for Mac 2011."

Why MYN Focuses on the To-Do Bar in Windows

In MYN, the most important place to access tasks in Windows Outlook is on the To-Do Bar. The To-Do Bar is a large pane that usually occupies the right side of the Outlook window. In Outlook 2007, it is labeled at the top, but in other versions it is not (Figure 2.7 shows Outlook 2010). If you can't see it on your copy of Outlook, I'll show you how to open it in the next section.

The To-Do Bar is where 99 percent of your MYN Outlook task management will be done. Why?

It's *simpler* than most other task lists in Outlook. You'll notice that it shows an abbreviated depiction of Outlook tasks. Out of the box, it shows a simpler set of columns of task information rather than the complex views in the Tasks folders just mentioned, making it a good quick-review location for tasks.

Figure 2.7

The To-Do Bar occupies the far right side of the Windows Outlook screen. (Outlook 2010 shown here; other Windows versions are similar.)

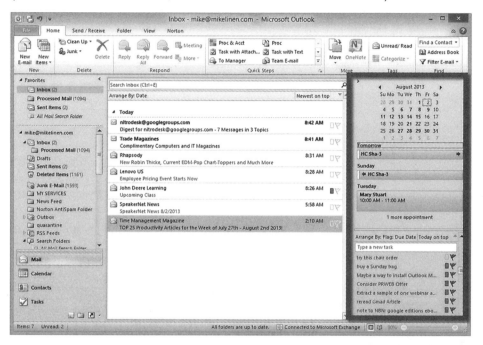

The most important behavior of the To-Do Bar is that it can be displayed no matter what mode Outlook is in. That's very important because it elevates the stature of tasks in Outlook. After you open the To-Do Bar in all the various Outlook modes, it is open all the time. You can quickly arrange it so you never lose sight of your important daily tasks, and thereby increase the probability of working them more consistently.

If you cannot see the To-Do Bar in your copy of Outlook, the next section shows you how to open it.

Note: *Do not confuse the To-Do Bar with the To-Do List, which is one of the Tasks folder views.*

Outlook 2007/10: Viewing the To-Do Bar Task List

The To-Do Bar is opened and resized differently in Outlook 2007/10 versus Outlook 2013. Let's start with 2007/10. (Outlook 2013 users can jump to the section "Outlook 2013: Viewing and Arranging the To-Do Bar.")

Opening the To-Do Bar in Outlook 2007/10

To open the To-Do Bar, use the Outlook View menu (2007) or the Ribbon's View tab (2010). Choose To-Do Bar and select Normal (see Figure 2.8 for Outlook 2010). The To-Do Bar opens on the right side of your Outlook window.

Figure 2.8
Opening the To-Do Bar from the View tab in Outlook 2010 (use the View *menu* for Outlook 2007).

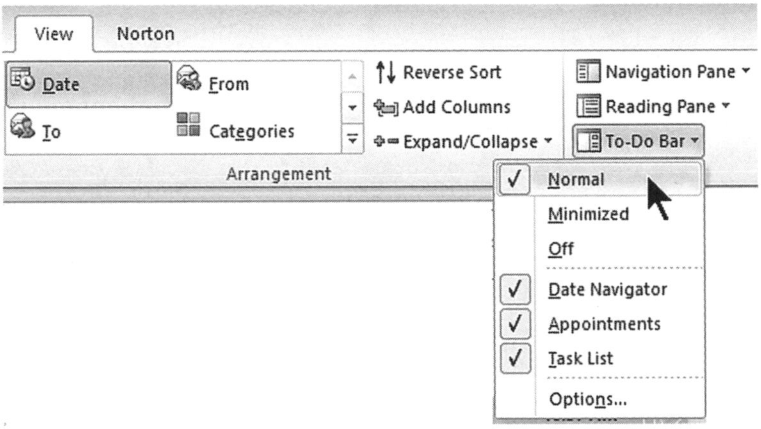

Examine the top of that menu as shown in Figure 2.8. The To-Do Bar has three display states: Normal (fully opened), Minimized (a narrow vertical bar at the right side of the Outlook screen), and Off (closed entirely). More on those in a moment.

Closing the To-Do Bar in Outlook 2007/10

To remove the open To-Do Bar completely, you can use the Off command just described. But in 2007, you can also use the Close button (x) in the upper-right corner of the To-Do Bar.

I recommend that you avoid the Close button or Off command because after you click the Close button, or close it from the menu, there are no buttons you can click to open the To-Do Bar again. To open the To-Do Bar you must redo the menu steps. That's a lot of steps, so, instead, I advise you to only *minimize* the To-Do Bar (more on that in the next section).

These To-Do Bar activation decisions are specific for each of the data types (Mail, Calendar, Contacts, Tasks, and so on). If you close the To-Do Bar while the Calendar data type is active, it closes only for that data type. When you navigate to Mail, the To-Do Bar is still open. If the To-Do Bar is closed for all major data types, and you want it open for all, you must open it one at a time while in each data type. After you open the To-Do Bar in any given data type, it stays open in that data type until you close it, again. Consequently, I advise all new MYN users to open the To-Do Bar in all views at the outset, and then *never close them again*. Always use minimize instead (described next).

Minimizing the To-Do Bar in Outlook 2007/10

I keep my To-Do Bar open much of the day. But sometimes when scanning my Inbox thoroughly, I like to close the To-Do Bar so it's out of the way. As previously mentioned, I can use the Off command to do that (or the Close button in 2007); however, that completely closes the To-Do Bar, and I'd have to go through all the menu steps to reopen it.

A better strategy is to *minimize* the To-Do Bar because this gives you quick ways to open and close the To-Do Bar. In Outlook 2010 it's easy, just click the small right-pointing arrow (>) in the upper-left corner of the To-Do Bar, as shown in Figure 2.9.

Figure 2.9
Minimize button in Outlook 2010.

In 2007, I use the double arrow (>>) in the upper right. When minimized, the To-Do Bar collapses to about one-half inch wide. To open a minimized To-Do Bar, click the same arrow, again, which opens it back to the Normal or completely opened state. This same minimize behavior can be applied to the Navigation Pane (the folder list that occupies the left side of the Outlook application window).

Temporarily Opening the To-Do Bar in Outlook 2007/10

There is actually a fourth view state for the To-Do Bar in Outlook 2007 and 2010 that I call popped open. Let me explain. Normally, when the To-Do Bar is completely open, it resizes whatever window is to the left of it smaller to make room, collapsing the width of columns as needed to keep them all in view. An example of this where the Inbox columns have all been squeezed smaller to make room for the To-Do Bar is shown in Figure 2.7.

In contrast, the popped open state causes the To-Do Bar to pop open *on top of* the Inbox without collapsing column widths, *actually covering* the right columns (as shown on the right side of Figure 2.10). To achieve this state, click in the lower portion of the minimized To-Do Bar. The resulting To-Do Bar display truly is a temporary popup. If you click anywhere else in Outlook, this temporary To-Do Bar is minimized again.

Figure 2.10
To-Do Bar temporarily popped open in Outlook 2010; 2007 is similar.

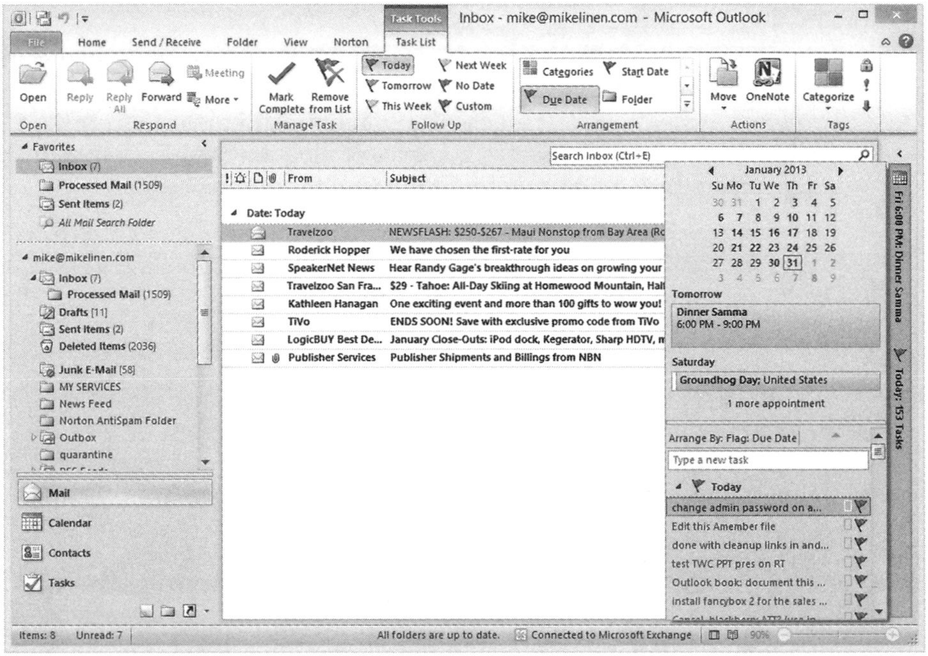

Why do this? If your screen is a bit small and you periodically want to take a quick peek at your to-do list, you can use this method. This also explains why the To-Do Bar disappears sometimes when you are using it. You probably opened it in the popped-open mode without realizing it.

Outlook 2007/10: The To-Do Bar task list

By now you probably have noticed that the To-Do Bar incorporates multiple sections. At the very top, it has a mini-calendar (called the Date Navigator, which you might have hidden in the Quick Start). Below that is an area that lists upcoming appointments, and the task list occupies the lower portion (see bottom right of Figure 2.7). Some organizations might also have a fourth section that lists frequently used contacts and even more.

Because in the MYN system the task list in the To-Do Bar is where you do 99 percent of your Outlook task management, the task list is by far the most important section on the To-Do Bar. So you want to be sure it is large enough for you to use.

To make it larger, make sure the To-Do Bar is wide enough—about 2.5 to 3 inches wide is perfect. You just drag the left edge of the To-Do Bar to change the width. Then you want to make sure the task portion of the To-Do Bar is tall enough, as described in the following.

How to See More Tasks in the 2007/10 To-Do Bar Task List

If you have a small screen, the task list portion of the To-Do Bar can be too short. If you have a very small screen, the task list portion can be almost unusable. In those cases, you need to decide if you really want to show all the other sections such as the Date Navigator and the Appointments preview. They are "robbing" vertical space from the task list. You won't miss much if you remove one or both.

For example, the Date Navigator is redundant. Clicking it merely takes you to your calendar, yet you can also do that by clicking the Calendar button in the Navigation Pane. More importantly, clicking the Date Navigator does *not* change what tasks are displayed in your task list. So you can remove that section without losing functionality. After you remove the Date Navigator, if the task list still seems too short, consider removing or decreasing the size of the Appointments preview, as well.

To remove these sections, right-click the very top of the To-Do Bar. A shortcut menu is displayed as shown in Figure 2.11. Clear the check mark next to Date Navigator, and possibly Appointments.

Figure 2.11

Right-click the top of the 2007/10 To-Do Bar to hide and show its components (Outlook 2010 shown; similar in Outlook 2007).

These same controls are available on the View tab or menu by clicking To-Do Bar, as shown in Figure 2.8. These changes are reversible, so I suggest you try them for yourself.

You don't have to remove the entire Appointments section. Instead, make a little more room by showing fewer appointments. To do that, keep the Appointments item checked. Then in 2007, use the Options item at the bottom of that same shortcut menu and specify a smaller number of appointments. In 2010, just drag the top edge of the task list up, which removes visibility of more distant appointments and makes the task list larger.

Outlook 2013: Viewing and Arranging the To-Do Bar

In Outlook 2013, Microsoft changed considerably how you open and close the To-Do Bar and how you arrange its sections (compared to Outlook 2007/10). Let's look at that.

Opening and Closing the 2013 To-Do Bar

You open the 2013 To-Do Bar one section at a time with the To-Do Bar button on the View tab. As shown in Figure 2.12, you have three commands that open corresponding sections: Calendar, People, and Tasks.

Figure 2.12
Use the To-Do Bar menu on the View tab in Outlook 2013 to open one or more of its three sections.

Opening each section is additive from top down. For example, if you click Tasks and then Calendar, the mini-calendar is added below the tasks section. The stacking order of those sections depends on what order you open them— their relative position is *not* fixed like in Outlook 2007/10. Figure 2.13 shows the 2013 To-Do Bar after opening all three sections one at a time.

When you open a section, by default it takes up an equal share of the To-Do Bar's height. You can change that share somewhat by dragging the boundary between the sections to optimize the size of each section (more on that follows).

Each section has its own Close button (the X in the upper-right corner of each section), which removes its section from the To-Do Bar. You can completely close the To-Do Bar one section at a time, or you can use a fourth command under the To-Do Bar button on the Ribbon's View tab called Off, as shown in Figure 2.12. That command closes all sections simultaneously and removes the entire To-Do Bar.

Figure 2.13
The 2013 To-Do Bar with Calendar, People, and Tasks sections open

Appointments Preview in the Outlook 2013 To-Do Bar

If you use Outlook 2007 or 2010, you might be wondering why there is no Appointments on the To-Do Bar menu (shown in Figure 2.12). In earlier Outlook versions, users could select an Appointments command that inserted a list of upcoming appointments on the To-Do Bar (usually turned on by default). In Outlook 2013, that section is now automatically combined with the bottom of the mini-calendar; that is, they open as a pair when you open the Calendar section. Figure 2.14 shows how this is displayed with one upcoming appointment highlighted.

Notice how an Appointments preview list is *not* visible in Figure 2.13. Why is that? The list is hidden due to the small height of the Outlook window. Notice the scroll bar at the right edge of the mini-calendar. If you scroll with it, the Appointments preview section rolls into view. If you resize the Calendar section larger (by dragging its bottom edge down), the Appointments preview is displayed. This is one example of why it is often important to adjust all sections and optimize their functionality after you add them in 2013.

Here's something new in Outlook 2013 that's worth mentioning: When you click on a specific date in the To-Do Bar mini-calendar, you are no longer moved to the Outlook Calendar mode. Instead, it leaves you in the current mode and changes the Appointments preview below the mini-calendar to match the selected date.

Figure 2.14
Outlook 2013's Appointments preview is part of the To-Do Bar Calendar.

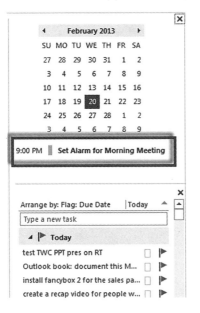

This is a useful new functionality with obvious advantages. However, because of this you can see only one day's worth of previewed appointments at a time. In Outlook 2007/10, the preview can display appointments for today, tomorrow, and more, all at once—as many as you have room for.

People Section in the Outlook 2013 To-Do Bar

The People section in the Outlook 2013 To-Do Bar is similar to the Quick Contacts section that some organizations optionally activated in previous Outlook versions, but it's now available to any user. As shown in Figure 2.13, it is empty unless you mark some of your contacts as *favorites*.

Marking a contact as a favorite is a little tricky in Outlook 2013. You must activate the new People view when in the People data-type mode. Right-click a person's entry, and select Add to Favorites. Unfortunately, if you use any of the other contacts views, there is no Add to Favorites command. Also, the People view might not be active by default when installing Outlook 2013 in an existing account. To activate the People view, on the View tab click the Change View button.

No Minimize Button in the 2013 To-Do Bar

If you are familiar with Outlook 2007/10, or have read the previous sections in this lesson, then you know that 2007/10 comes with a very useful Minimize button at the top of the To-Do Bar. That button is omitted from Outlook 2013. I'm not happy with the omission because it makes the 2013 To-Do Bar harder to use.

How is it harder? You must open the To-Do Bar one section at a time, and while you do that, you often need to make several adjustments to each section so that they're sized and organized just right. If you include opening and resizing multiple sections, it can take as many as eight mouse clicks or movements to display the To-Do Bar just the way you want. If you then close the entire To-Do Bar momentarily for some reason (say, to more easily view e-mail for a few minutes), you have to start all over again to reopen all sections. The Minimize button of earlier versions did that for you with one click.

For example, with Outlook 2010, I often opened and then hid the complete To-Do Bar many times per hour. The Minimize button made that easy. Moving to Outlook 2013 feels like a step backward, requiring much more work for this routine action. Let's hope Microsoft adds the Minimize button back to the To-Do Bar in future releases of Outlook. That said, there is a way to work around the lack of a Minimize button: install a Tasks button.

Outlook 2013: Installing a Tasks Button on the Quick Access Toolbar

I have long felt that if I could choose only one thing to use the To-Do Bar for, it would be for managing tasks — period. I feel the other uses for the To-Do Bar are much less important. If you agree, then one way to fix the lack of the Minimize button in Outlook 2013 is to display only tasks in the To-Do Bar and nothing else. When you decide to do that, the lack of a Minimize button is much less of an issue because showing or hiding *only tasks* requires few mouse clicks. It also provides an opportunity to build the equivalent of a Minimize button that works with one click with the Quick Access Toolbar in Outlook. Let's look at how to do that next.

Editing the Quick Access Toolbar

The Quick Access Toolbar (Figure 2.15) is an often-ignored feature that's present in all Microsoft Office applications.

Figure 2.15
Default Quick Access Toolbar in Outlook 2013.

It's a small row of two or three icons in the upper-left corner of the application window that provides one-click access to a few key commands. The application commands placed there by default in Outlook are Send/Receive and Undo.

What most people don't know is that it's easy to customize and add more commands to it. And as a replacement for a Minimize button, you can add a Tasks button there that opens and closes a tasks-only To-Do Bar. Here's how:

1. Close the To-Do Bar completely, including the Tasks, Calendar, and People sections.

2. On the View tab, click the To-Do Bar button.

3. On the To-Do Bar button submenu, right-click the Tasks choice and select Add to Quick Access Toolbar, as shown in Figure 2.16.

Figure 2.16
Adding Tasks to the Quick Access Toolbar in Outlook 2013.

This adds a small Tasks button to the Quick Access Toolbar, as shown in Figure 2.17. That's it. The button is installed and ready to use. Now click the new Tasks button and notice that it opens the To-Do Bar displaying only tasks. Click it again and the To-Do Bar closes. From now on, you can use it to instantly open and close the To-Do Bar. The Minimize button of previous versions is back, albeit with reduced functionality.

Figure 2.17
The newly added Tasks button on the Quick Access Toolbar, Outlook 2013.

However, this works well only if you do *not* activate any of the other sections on the To-Do Bar (for example, Calendar or People). Otherwise, odd behaviors can result. I don't miss the Calendar or People sections of the To-Do Bar, and I suspect you won't either. One reason for that is the Peek function, which is new to Outlook 2013.

Outlook 2013: Using Peek and Dock the Peek

A New Outlook 2013 Feature—Peek

Outlook 2013 comes with a new feature that you can use to take a quick look at Tasks, Calendar, or People data without switching to those modes. It's called Peek, and you use it by hovering your mouse over the corresponding label in the lower-left corner of the Outlook window, as shown in Figure 2.18.

Figure 2.18
Outlook 2013 Peek feature.

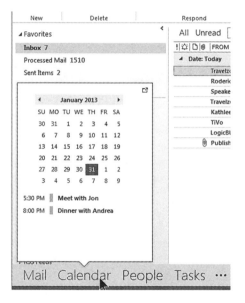

The Peek window can be useful for taking a quick look at your upcoming appointments, for example. This means that not having the Calendar section added to your To-Do Bar can be more acceptable.

Dock the Peek

Even more useful to me is the dock command that comes with Peek. If you right-click any of the main navigation labels, such as Tasks, the shortcut menu displays (along with other commands) Dock the Peek, as shown in Figure 2.19.

Figure 2.19
Outlook 2013 Dock the Peek command.

Choosing the Dock the Peek command does the same thing as choosing Tasks from the To-Do Bar menu on the Ribbon's View tab — it inserts (or removes) the Tasks section from the To-Do Bar. Another way to do this is to click the small icon in the upper-right corner of the Peek window.

Using Dock the Peek for tasks is essentially the same as using the Tasks button customized on the Quick Access Toolbar. So which of the two should you use? It's really a toss-up, but I prefer the Quick Access Tasks button because, after it's installed, it requires fewer mouse movements.

To-Do Bar Task List Appearance and Layout (All Windows Versions)

You probably realize by now that you can change the width of the To-Do Bar by dragging its left edge. But what you might not realize is that doing that can completely rearrange the structure of the task list portion of the To-Do Bar. Let me explain.

By default, the task list in an open To-Do Bar has two viewing modes — *compact* and *noncompact*. Which you see depends on how wide you make the To-Do Bar. By default, the compact mode is displayed.

Compact Layout

If the To-Do Bar has default settings and is less than about 7 inches wide, your task list looks something like the one shown in Figure 2.20. This default view is actually a special simplified presentation of tasks called the *compact layout*. It hides many columns and combines some columns together to make the list easy to read. However, for MYN, it does not show the right things.

Note: *If no tasks appear in your task list, skip ahead to the next section, which shows you how to enter tasks. Enter a few and then return.*

When the compact mode is active, each task in the list displays three things. Most prominently displayed is the *subject* of the task, which is normally a description of the action that you want to take. To the right of that, a small square that represents a category color is displayed (more on that later). And to the right of that you'll see a red flag (also described in this lesson).

Figure 2.20
Compact layout in To-Do Bar task list.

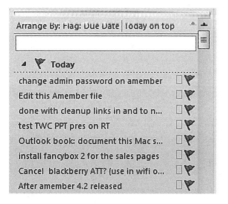

Noncompact Layout in the To-Do Bar Task List

Now try this: Drag the left edge of the To-Do Bar to the left, so it's about 7 inches or wider (you may need to enlarge your Outlook window to do that), and notice what happens to the task list layout. Figure 2.21 shows how it might look after being widened extensively.

Figure 2.21
Noncompact layout in the To-Do Bar task list.

Task Subject	Start Date	Remind...	Due Date	In Fo...	Categories	⌚	Outloo...	▽
	Thu 1/31/2...	None	Thu 1/31/...	To-D...				▽
▲ ▽ Flag: Due Date: Today								
change admin password o...	Tue 10/30/...	None	Tue 10/30...	Tasks			mike@...	▽
Edit this Amember file	Sun 11/4/2...	None	Sun 11/4/...	Tasks			mike@...	▽
done with cleanup links in ...	Tue 11/13/...	None	Tue 11/13...	Tasks			mike@...	▽
test TWC PPT pres on RT	Fri 11/30/2...	None	Fri 11/30/...	Tasks			mike@...	▽
Outlook book: document t...	Sat 12/8/2...	None	Sat 12/8/2...	Tasks			mike@...	▽
install fancybox 2 for the s...	Sun 12/9/2...	None	Sun 12/9/...	Tasks			mike@...	▽
Cancel blackberry ATT? (us...	Mon 12/10...	None	Mon 12/1...	Tasks			mike@...	▽
After amember 4.2 released	Mon 12/10...	None	Mon 12/1...	Tasks			mike@...	▽
create a recap video for pe...	Mon 12/10...	None	Mon 12/1...	Tasks			mike@...	▽
activate persoanl archives a...	Mon 12/10...	None	Mon 12/1...	Tasks			mike@...	▽
Review Book Orders and m...	Mon 12/10...	None	Mon 12/1...	Tasks			mike@...	▽
update InDesign file for 1...	Mon 12/10...	None	Mon 12/1...	Tasks			mike@...	▽
Consider this book: The In...	Mon 12/10...	None	Mon 12/1...	Tasks			mike@...	▽
3 study/write macro that ch...	Mon 12/10...	None	Mon 12/1...	Tasks			mike@...	▽
these books recommeded ...	Mon 12/10...	None	Mon 12/1...	Tasks			mike@...	▽
read this website: publlishi...	Mon 12/10...	None	Mon 12/1...	Tasks			mike@...	▽
close UBS accounts	Mon 12/10...	None	Mon 12/1...	Tasks			mike@...	▽
HCH training?	Mon 12/10...	None	Mon 12/1...	Tasks			mike@...	▽

Notice all the new columns. What's happened here? With the default Outlook settings, when you drag the To-Do Bar task list wider, the *noncompact layout* is displayed. This layout is not right for MYN either because there are too many columns displayed, many more than you need. In Lesson 3 you find the right balance, because I'll show you how to configure the noncompact layout to display in a narrower To-Do Bar. You adjust the displayed columns to a smaller, more appropriate set.

Note: In Lesson 12, after you become more adept at the system, I'll show you an optional way to use the compact view as part of the MYN system.

Best Width

For now, the best width for the To-Do Bar is about 2.5 to 3 inches, so adjust it and leave it at that width. If that seems too wide because it hides some of your mail information, then when reviewing mail just move the To-Do Bar out of the way with the Minimize button (2007/10) or the Quick Access Tasks button (that you added in 2013).

Note: To make more room to view your Inbox mail list, after you open the To-Do Bar, you might want to move the Reading Pane to the bottom of your Inbox. Go to the View menu or tab, choose Reading Pane, and select Bottom. Or you can choose Off to completely remove the Reading Pane. I remove mine because I find it distracting.

Red Flags on Tasks

The red flag that you see at the right edge of a Windows Outlook task appears in what is called the Flag Status field. This flag has a number of functions in Outlook, most of which you will not use in MYN. For now, you'll use it only for one thing — to mark a task complete (more on that to follow).

Notice that the flag looks similar to the flag at the right edge of e-mails in the Outlook Inbox (if an e-mail is flagged). The two share similar functions. For example, you might see flagged mail listed in your task list. I'll cover that extensively near the end of this lesson in the section "All About Using Flags in Outlook (Windows and Mac)." For now, just remember this: All items in the To-Do Bar task list have red flags whether they correspond to a flagged mail or a regular task. The only purpose for the task flag in the MYN system is to mark the task complete. That's all you need to know about flags for now. I'll cover much more about flags later in this lesson, and then again in Lesson 7.

Entering Tasks (All Versions)

Entering tasks is easy, but there are a few different ways to do it. Let's start with Windows Outlook. Mac users jump ahead a few pages to the section "Entering Tasks in Outlook for Mac 2011."

Windows Outlook: Two Methods of Task Entry

There are two primary methods of entering tasks in Windows Outlook. You can use either method according to your preferences and current needs. Both work whether you are working from the To-Do Bar or from one of the Tasks folder views. However, as mentioned, I recommend using the To-Do Bar for virtually all your task management activities. The two entry methods are the *quick entry* method and the *full entry* method.

Normally you access both methods by clicking in the New Item row, which is located at the very top of the To-Do Bar and Tasks folder. Notice the blank line at the top of the task list in Figures 2.7 and 2.13 that is labeled Type a New Task: that's it. In a noncompact To-Do Bar layout, it is displayed as Click Here to Add a New Task.

Clicking once there starts the quick-entry method and double-clicking there starts the full-entry method.

Note: If the New Item row is missing from your copy of Outlook, go to: www.myn.bz/new-item-row.htm to see how to add it.

Quick Entry Method of Creating Tasks

To use the quick-entry method in Windows, single-click anywhere in the New Item row and that line will become editable. Enter the name of your task. Press ENTER *or* just click off the task line. The new task is saved.

Note: If you have more than one cell in that row to click in, I prefer to click in the wide cell in the middle (Subject or Task Subject), because that selects it for editing, and this is normally the first piece of information I enter in a new task.

Full Entry Method of Creating Tasks

To use the full-entry method, instead of clicking the New Item row once, double-click the row. This opens the standard Outlook Task dialog box as shown in Figure 2.22. Enter a subject and start date, and set Priority. Then click Save and Close.

Note: This double-click method of opening the Task dialog box also works on existing tasks, if you want to edit them. More on that follows.

When to Use Each Method

So which method of creating new tasks do I use? I nearly always use the quick method from the To-Do Bar. To me, it is quicker and easier. I use the full-entry method when I know I need to change fields not displayed in the task list view.

Using New Button and Keyboard Shortcuts

In Outlook 2007, you can use the New button to open a new task window. Click the drop-down arrow next to it and select Task. If you are in Tasks mode, rather than click the drop-down arrow next to the New button, click the button itself. If that operation is available, the button has a task icon embedded on it.

Figure 2.22
New Task dialog box (Outlook 2010).

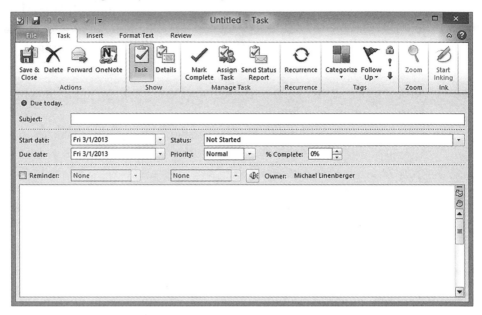

In Outlook 2010 and 2013, the button is labeled New Items. Click it and choose Task. If a Tasks folder is open, a New Task button is also displayed.

In all Windows versions, you can also use a keyboard shortcut. If you are in Tasks mode, use CTRL+N. No matter what mode you are in, you can use CTRL+SHIFT+K.

Three Ways to Set Outlook Priorities on Tasks (Windows)

You'll soon see that the Priority field (see middle of Figure 2.22) in Outlook tasks is the most important field for implementing the MYN system, so you'll be setting and changing it frequently. There are three ways to set priorities on tasks. However, at this point in studying the book, because the Lesson 3 settings are probably not in place, the first method might be all you can do on the To-Do Bar.

The first method works with a Task dialog box open where you'll find the Priority box right in the middle. Click it and select one of three priority levels.

With the next method, you to set the priority in the task list view. If you are editing an existing task, this is faster than opening the task window, but it works in the To-Do Bar only after you've added the Priority column, as we will do in Lesson 3. When it's added, you just click the task's Priority box (the column space with the ! label above it) and the three Outlook priority choices pop up, as shown in Figure 2.23.

Figure 2.23
Priority selector in the To-Do Bar task list (Outlook 2010 shown).

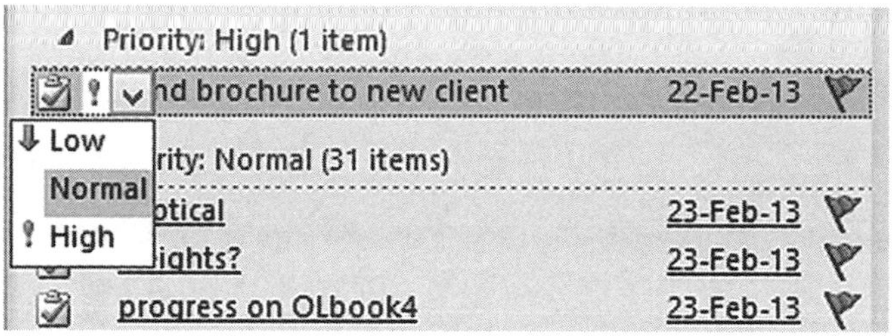

The third method also works in the task list view of the To-Do Bar, but works
only if your tasks are grouped by priority. (How to group tasks by priority is shown in the Quick Start, and in Lesson 3.) Then, all you need to do to
change the priority of a task is drag a task to a new priority group. The task's
priority setting adjusts to match the new group.

Entering Tasks in Outlook for Mac 2011

Outlook for Mac has fewer ways to create new tasks. There is no quick
method like the Windows versions. All new tasks are created by opening a
new, blank Task dialog box, which can be done in three different ways:

▶ With a Tasks folder active, click the Task button at the left end of the
Home tab.

▶ With a Tasks folder active, press CMD+N.

▶ If you are in a non-task folder, click the New button at the left of the
Home tab and select Task.

When the Task dialog box opens, enter a subject for the task in the wide text
box near the top of the dialog box. To enter a due date or start date, click No
Date next to each of the Due or Start labels. Figure 2.24 shows how the task
screen looks after values are entered.

How to Set Outlook Priorities on Tasks (Mac 2011)

Inside an open task, at the right end of the Ribbon's Task tab, High Priority and Low Priority buttons are displayed (see top of Figure 2.24). Clicking
either one highlights the button and sets the task to that level. New tasks are
set to Normal (medium) priority by default (neither button is highlighted).
After you set a priority to High or Low, click that same button again to set the
task back to Normal.

You can also set the priority level from the task list view. At the top of the
list view in the middle of the Home tab of the Ribbon, the same two High
and Low Priority buttons are displayed. Select a task in the list and use those
buttons the same way you did in an open task. You can also set the priority

another way: Press CTRL and click the item in the list. Choose a priority from the Priority submenu.

Figure 2.24
Mac 2011 Task dialog box.

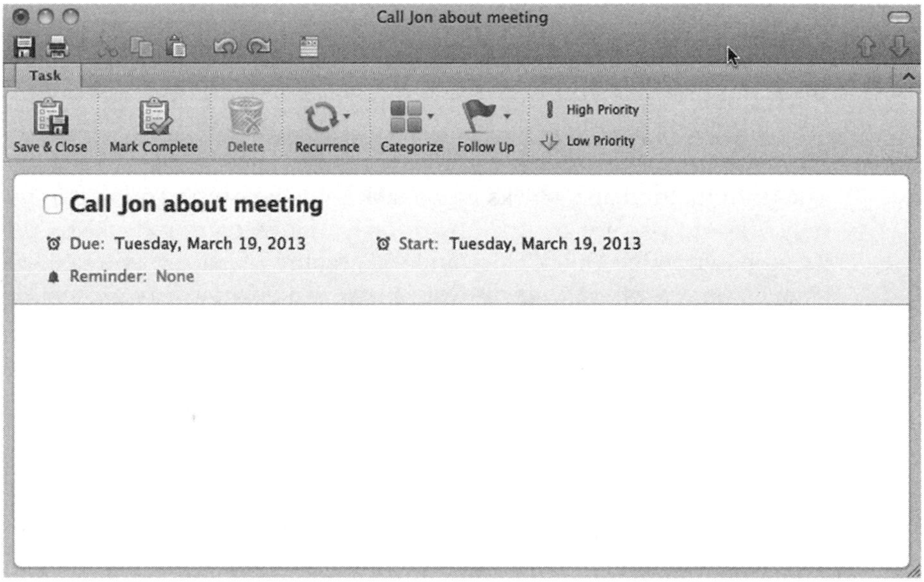

Practice Entering and Editing Tasks Now (Windows and Mac)

Entering Tasks

If this is your first time using Outlook for task management, you might want to practice entering a few tasks now. Both Mac and Windows users, try using the New or New Items button and keyboard shortcuts previously described to enter a number of tasks. For this practice, enter today as a start date and due date.

Windows users, try the quick-entry method—find the New Item row, click once, and enter the subject or action there. Do the same with the full-entry method (double-click), and practice setting the priority there.

This is all just for practice. I will go over proper use of these boxes and fields later.

Editing Tasks

Windows and Mac users, you can edit in the open Task dialog box by double-clicking the task in the list view.

Windows users note that you can also edit existing task information right in the task list. For example, you can change the text in the subject line by clicking once on the subject text and retyping. If date fields are shown, you can edit them by clicking them.

While as a Mac user, you can't edit in a task list like that, you can press CTRL and click an item, and reset the priority from the submenu. You can use the Follow Up command on that menu to reset the dates.

Marking Tasks Complete (Windows and Mac)

Later, after you complete working on the task and no more effort on that task is required, you should either delete the task or mark the task complete. The advantage of marking it complete is that it removes or changes the appearance of the task in the active task list, but Outlook still saves the task for later reference. That can be useful if, for example, you intend to write a status report later, describing completed tasks for the week or month.

The easiest way to mark a task complete is to do it from one of the list views of Tasks, but how to do that varies with version and view.

Marking Windows Tasks Complete

In Windows Outlook, with out-of-the-box configurations, to mark a task complete, click the flag at the right edge of the task. You can also mark tasks complete in the open Task dialog box. To do that, click the Mark Complete item in the Tasks tab. Or you can change the Status box to Completed, but notice there are many other status values available in the Status box—which can be confusing—because most of them you won't use in the MYN system.

Marking Mac Tasks Complete

In the Mac version, to mark a task complete, select the check box in the Complete column at the left edge of the task in the list, as shown in Figure 2.25.

Figure 2.25
Mac 2011 Complete column.

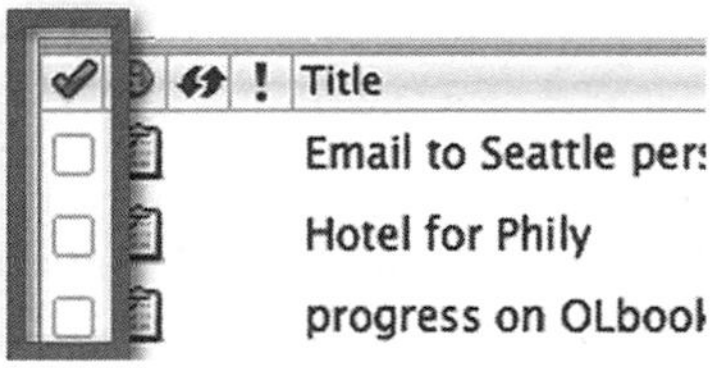

Also in the Mac version, there is a Completed check box inside the task window itself, just to the left to the task title as shown in Figure 2.24, which you can select. Or you can click the Mark Complete button on the Task tab, which is also shown in Figure 2.24.

What Happens When You Mark Tasks Complete

Depending on your configurations, after you mark a task complete, it either disappears from the list view, or it remains visible—but with a check mark next to it (in Windows it also turns gray and has a line through it).

The first time you mark a task complete with the flag in Windows, if it disappears, it can feel a bit disturbing. That's because you are probably used to flags on e-mail. Clicking an e-mail's flag just removes the flag—it doesn't remove the e-mail! But you'll get used to this task behavior shortly. I discuss task flags in great detail near the end of this lesson.

Changing Task Views to See Completed Tasks

You may want to view completed tasks to find old information or to create a status report. How you view completed tasks depends on your version of Outlook. Showing completed tasks in Mac 2011 is easy. From the Tasks folder, just click the Home tab on the Ribbon and select the Completed check box at its right end. This adds completed tasks to the task list view.

In Windows, you find completed tasks in the Tasks folder, but it can be a little difficult because a number of specialized views are available, and many of them hide completed tasks. Consequently, you need to activate a view that displays them. Make sure you are in the Tasks mode (click the Tasks button in the lower-left corner of the Outlook window). Then find the My Tasks pane in the upper part of the Navigation or Folders Pane, and then select the second item (Tasks). The next step depends on your version of Windows Outlook.

In Outlook 2007, look in the middle of the Navigation Pane on the left and in the Current View section, click the view named Simple List, which displays all tasks including completed ones. You can also choose the Completed view, to see only completed tasks.

If you're using Outlook 2010 or 2013, when you're in the Tasks mode with Tasks selected (*not* To-Do List) in the My Tasks pane, go to the View tab. At the tab's left end, click the Change View button. Then click either the Simple List or Detailed view, which displays all tasks including completed ones. You can also choose the Completed view, to see only completed tasks.

Note: *For Windows users, the My Tasks pane can be confusing. I discuss it in more detail in Appendix A, and I discuss task views in Lesson 12 in the section "Understanding Outlook Task Views."*

Reversing Completed Status (Windows and Mac)

If you mark a task complete by accident, and (depending on settings) it disappears from your list view, you can always use the Undo command to restore it quickly (CTRL+Z in Windows; CMD+Z in Mac). Or later, you can find the completed task and reverse its completed status. For all versions (Windows and Mac), when you find a completed task in the Tasks folder, if you wish to reverse its status to incomplete, you can remove the check mark in the left column by clicking it. This restores the task in your Tasks folder (and in the Windows Outlook To-Do Bar).

Deleting Tasks (Windows and Mac)

Marking a task complete might remove it from your main task view, but the task still takes up storage space. If you know you are completely done with the task and no longer need to view it, you can select it and press DELETE. The task is moved to the Outlook Deleted Items folder. To recover its storage space, empty the Deleted Items folder. Or, if you change your mind, you can restore a recently deleted task by dragging it from the Deleted Items folder to the Tasks folder.

■ ■ ■

Using Other Fields in the Task Dialog Box (Windows and Mac)

In the Task dialog box, other fields are available that you might want to use. Some appear in both the Windows and Mac versions, and others in Windows only. I'll go over the most important ones one at a time; however, feel free to skip this section because most of these are not used in the MYN system.

Reminder Check Box

About halfway down on the left of Figure 2.22 and 2.24 is a small item labeled Reminder. If this is new to you, reminders are small Outlook message boxes that pop to the front of your screen when an item is due (often with a beep). Using this box is how you activate a reminder on a task. However, I do not engage reminders on tasks, and I recommend you don't either. I explain why at the end of Lesson 4, in the section "Managing Deadlines."

Notes Field

Perhaps 10 percent of the time, I enter text in the large text field at the bottom of the Task tab as shown in Figure 2.22 and 2.24. It's the task Notes field. This is a very good place to put task details and, most commonly, it's where the text of an e-mail that generated the task is displayed (you will see how to do that at the end of this lesson). Sometimes I also copy notes that I collected when the task was assigned to me in a meeting.

Status, Percent Complete, and Owner Fields (Windows)

I ignore the % Complete field (shown in the middle-right area of Figure 2.22). Later you will learn that tasks entered in this system are generally small, next-step style tasks, which should be relatively discrete and not subject to partial completion. That's also why I do not use the various values available in the Status field such as In Progress, Deferred, and Waiting on Someone. While these status values are used extensively in other systems, there are other ways in the MYN system that you can use to indicate status, in a much more useful way.

I also ignore the Owner field. This and many of these other fields are more useful when integrating Outlook tasks with other Microsoft products such as Microsoft Project, or if using the formal Assign Task button described in the Delegation lesson, Lesson 10.

Categorize Button (Windows and Mac)

In all versions, at the top of the open Tasks window, a Categorize button near the right end of the Task tab is displayed as shown in Figure 2.22 and 2.24. Clicking Categorize opens a dialog box, or menu, in which you can assign a category to the task. Why might you want to do this? With Outlook you can filter by category types when you view tasks in any of the task views. However, initially you will probably not use Outlook Categories with *tasks*. In subsequent lessons, you will discover many other ways to accomplish what using Outlook Categories might achieve for tasks. You *can* use Outlook Categories on tasks to track projects and goals, as I show in Lesson 12. And I use Outlook Categories extensively with e-mail in this system, which I describe quite thoroughly in Lesson 8.

Details Section and Other Tools (Windows)

The second major group of fields in the task entry dialog box is shown in the Details section. This is opened by clicking the Details button on the Show group on the Task tab at the top of the task window as shown in Figure 2.22). I completely ignore the Details section when working with tasks. This is another case where fields are useful only when integrating Outlook with other Microsoft applications, such as Microsoft Project, or perhaps when tracking billable time against a task.

There are many other tools and buttons on the tabs at the top of a Windows Task dialog box. Most are self-explanatory, so I don't cover them, but a few deserve more discussion and I will cover them to varying degrees as you progress through the lessons.

All About Using Flags in Outlook (Windows and Mac)

I've mentioned that flagging e-mail can be perilous to your task system. Maybe a bit dramatic, but it can be true. For example, do you have hundreds, maybe even thousands of items in your task list—and you don't remember putting them there? Those are old flagged e-mails, and your overloaded list is an example of how flagging mail can negatively impact your task system. Also, because those items are not *true* tasks, they introduce many challenges when managing your task list. For example, they do not display in many task lists. So, before going any further with Outlook tasks, you need to learn about these flags and how to use them safely.

To that end, following is a primer on using flags in Outlook. This will get you started so you can move forward with the MYN system. But using flags is a complicated topic, so I will revisit it in Lesson 7—there I show you a few more tips on using them. Then, at the end of Appendix A, I show you some subtle aspects of using flags and wrap the topic up completely. But let's get started with the basics.

Primer on Flagging Mail (Windows and Mac)

Ever since early versions of Outlook, a flag field has been present in all e-mail list views. It's called the Follow Up Flag, or the Flag Status field. The meaning of that field has evolved over time. The biggest change started with Outlook 2007 when Microsoft introduced a significant new philosophy on what flags on e-mail are for: Flagging an e-mail indicates that the mail needs *action*. In other words, these flagged e-mail items represent a kind of *task*. Microsoft even changed the functions of the Outlook task system to selectively display those special tasks in the same lists as true tasks. All Outlook versions since 2007 use this approach.

Flagged E-mail Can Show in Your Task Lists (Windows and Mac)

The last point—that flagged e-mail can be displayed in some task lists—is very important, because it can lead to both benefits and problems. Before I get to those, let me describe how this works.

When you set a flag at the right edge of an e-mail message, a copy of the mail item can be added to your task list. This item looks and acts very much like the true tasks that are in this list. You can recognize it because its subject line matches the e-mail's subject line. Whether you see them in the task list depends on a few factors.

You see them on the Mac's task list if you click the Flagged Items box on the Home tab of the Ribbon. You also see them by default in the Windows To-Do Bar task list (unless you filter them out as shown in Lesson 3). And when you enter the Tasks mode in Windows Outlook, you see flagged e-mail in the To-Do List folder, which is discussed next.

The To-Do List Folder Shows Flagged Mail (Windows Only)

This next topic is perhaps one of the most confusing parts of the task system in Windows Outlook. After you enter the Tasks mode in Windows Outlook (by clicking the Tasks button in the lower-left corner of the Outlook window), you can then select from a potentially large number of tasks folders and views. You pick folders from the My Tasks pane (Figure 2.26) in the upper part of the Navigation or Folders Pane (on the left side of the Outlook window). The first folder listed in that section is usually labeled To-Do List and it has a red-flag icon next to it. The primary purpose of the To-Do List folder is to consolidate all task types and sources in one folder-like view, and it's here where you'll see the flagged e-mail (along with all true tasks). The To-Do List folder is normally chosen by default when you enter the Tasks mode.

Figure 2.26
My Tasks pane in Outlook 2010 (similar in other Windows versions).

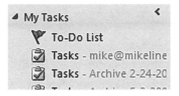

The folders in the My Tasks pane can be confusing because only the To-Do List folder shows flagged items. If you click any item *below* the To-Do List folder in the My Tasks pane (items labeled *Tasks*), those views exclude the flagged items. But that's also useful because there are times when you *want* to see only true tasks, so keep this distinction in mind. To learn more about the My Tasks pane and the items listed there, see Appendix A. I also discuss task views in Lesson 12 in the section "Understanding Outlook Task Views."

Flagged Mail Items Are Not Real Tasks (Windows and Mac)

A very important point about flagged mail you need to understand is that while flagged e-mails in your task list look very similar to tasks, they are not *real* tasks; rather they are only e-mails *displayed* in the task list. For this reason I call these items *flagged-mail tasks*, to distinguish them from real tasks.

Note also that these copied e-mails are not separate copies of the original e-mail, but *virtual* copies; that is, they are just *pointers* to the original e-mail. That means if you double-click a flagged-mail task in your task list, the corresponding e-mail opens. If you delete the original e-mail in your mail system, the corresponding item is deleted from your task list. If you delete a flagged-mail task from the task list, the corresponding e-mail is deleted from the mail system.

Many of us clean up our Outlook Inboxes by filing mail that we are done with into other folders. But note this: If you file a an e-mail with a flag on it in some other folder, and you forget to remove the flag, the flagged e-mail item *remains in the task list* even though you are done with it. This is one source of unwanted items in your task lists, so be sure to remove flags as you file mail.

Benefits of Flagged-Mail Tasks (Windows and Mac)

There are benefits to using flagged-mail tasks. First, they provide a very quick way to convert e-mails to tasks, which I will cover more at the end of this lesson and in Lesson 7. Second, flags also come in handy when using some mobile devices as a way to mark e-mails that need action. That's useful because if you are using Exchange Server with Outlook (most big companies are), that flag is transmitted back to the e-mail item sitting in your main copy of Outlook, and it's potentially added to your main task list, too. So using flags on a mobile device is a good way to highlight required later actions while on the road. Flagged-mail tasks are also an especially good way to mark deferred replies, as I discuss later in the lesson. However, you should use them sparingly, and here's why.

Use Sparingly—Flagged Mail Can Lead to Issues (Windows and Mac)

The main problem with flagged-mail tasks is if you forget to remove flags from old e-mail, these items can clog up your task lists. This is a common issue with users who start using tasks for the first time after years of using Outlook. They're surprised to find hundreds of tasks waiting for them in their lists. The section later in this chapter, "Cleaning Up Flagged Mail Tasks," shows you ways to clean up these old flags so you can start fresh.

Besides overwhelming your task list, flagged-mail tasks have a number of other issues. For example, they don't synchronize with many mobile task systems, they don't show in some task views, and more. (See a complete list in Lesson 7 section "Why Flagged Mail Tasks May Not Be Right for Converting E-mail to Tasks.") For these reasons, I recommend that you mostly avoid using flags on mail as a way to convert e-mails to tasks. Later in this lesson, and in Lesson 7, I'll show you a better way to convert e-mails to tasks.

Best Use of Flagged E-Mail: Deferred Replies (Windows and Mac)

There *is* one very appropriate case for using flags on e-mails. Use flags to mark mail that you cannot reply to immediately but that you intend to get to soon (within a day or so). Flag those items, and use the flags as a way to remind you to come back to them later in the day. When you write the replies, clear the flags.

When you use flags this way, however, you should commit to clearing them within a day or so. The idea is you don't want a lot of flagged e-mail to build up over time. To prevent that, in cases where you know it might be many days before writing the reply, *convert the e-mail to a true task* (using the methods at the end of this chapter) instead of flagging it. In Lesson 7, I'll give you more details on using flags for deferred replies.

Some Notes on Clearing Flags (Windows and Mac)

Because deferring replies on mail is fairly common, you'll likely be setting and clearing flags on mail repeatedly. How to clear flags seems pretty obvious—just click the flag again and the red flag goes away; however, there are some subtleties to this operation you should be aware of.

Acts Like a Completed Task

Let's say you are finished with a flagged-mail task listed in your task list, and you want to indicate that it's completed. If you click its flag in the task list, the outcome is similar to marking a task complete, and several things happen all at once.

First, the flagged-mail task disappears from any task list views that normally hide completed tasks (such as the Windows To-Do Bar task list, or the Mac Tasks window with completed tasks hidden).

Second, in task views that show both flagged mail and completed tasks (for example, the Simple List view if activated in the To-Do List folder in Windows, or the Mac Tasks window with completed tasks shown), the item remains visible, but it is marked as completed. How does that look? In Windows a gray line is placed through it, and the whole item becomes gray, just like on a completed task. On both Windows and Mac, a check mark is placed in the margin.

Third, if the red flag column is shown in the right margin (as on most Windows task views and nearly all Windows and Mac e-mail views), the flag there is replaced with a gray check mark. This last change happens both on the flagged-mail task *and on the original e-mail*.

You Can Clear Flags From Task Lists or E-mail Lists

All this happens whether you clear that flag on the item in the task list or on the corresponding e-mail item in the e-mail view. You can clear the flag from either location. This can be confusing, so let me say it another way. Removing the flag from a flagged-mail task in the task list removes the flag from the corresponding e-mail (whether it's still in the Inbox or somewhere else, such as filed in a folder).

Because these dynamics can be confusing, you might want to stop right now and practice setting and clearing some flags on various mail items in your Inbox. Notice how flagged mail shows up in your task list, and especially study what happens after you remove the flag.

Don't Accidentally Delete Saved Mail

One point I've mentioned is important because it can lead to a problem for you. Flagged-mail items with their flags removed look just like completed tasks in many task folder views. Due to this, you should be very vigilant when deleting what appear to be old completed tasks from your task folder lists. You might be deleting much of your old saved mail—mail that you perhaps wanted to save. There are usually warnings displayed when you do that, but you may dismiss them without thinking. And on the Mac they are not that clear.

One way to avoid making mistakes like this is to make sure you can identify your flagged-mail tasks more clearly, as I discuss next.

Identifying Flagged-Mail Tasks (Windows and Mac)

All Task-List Items Have Flags (Windows Only)

With default settings in Windows Outlook, it is often hard to tell the difference between flagged-mail tasks and true tasks. For example, when you look at the To-Do Bar task list, you'll notice that all items have a flag on them. That might cause you to think that all items in your entire task list are flagged-mail tasks. However, that's not true. Flags are shown on all *true* tasks, as well. In other words, *all* items in a task list have a flag at their right edge. That makes it harder to distinguish flagged mail from true tasks; however, you will often want to make that distinction, so let me show you how.

Note: *The reason Microsoft decided to show flags on all items in the Windows task list is described more thoroughly at the end of Appendix A in the section "Understanding the Flags at the Right Edge of All Tasks in Windows Outlook To-Do Bar."*

How to Identify Flagged Mail Tasks (Windows and Mac)

Luckily, there are easy ways to distinguish flagged-mail tasks from true tasks. One way is to double-click the item and see whether an e-mail window opens or a task window opens (a task window clearly displays start and due dates; an e-mail window does not). But if you are scanning a long list of tasks, opening each one takes time and is not practical.

A quicker way to identify flagged mail in a task list is to examine the icon at the left edge of each item. Flagged-mail tasks have an envelope icon on them. Such icons are shown by default on the Mac and in Windows Tasks folder views, but you have to activate that column in the Windows To-Do Bar (we'll do that in Lesson 3). Figure 2.27 shows how that icon looks in a mixture of flagged mail (at bottom) and true tasks in Outlook 2010. As in e-mail folders, the appearance of an e-mail icon in a tasks folder varies depending on reply status. For example, the bottom item in Figure 2.27 is an e-mail that has been replied to, and the second from bottom is one that has not.

Note: *Outlook 2013 has an odd twist on this. If you flag an item that has not been replied to, it displays no icon in the task list. But it does display an icon for any other type of flagged mail.*

Figure 2.27
Items that display an envelope icon in a task list represent flagged-mail tasks, as at the bottom of this list (Outlook 2010 shown).

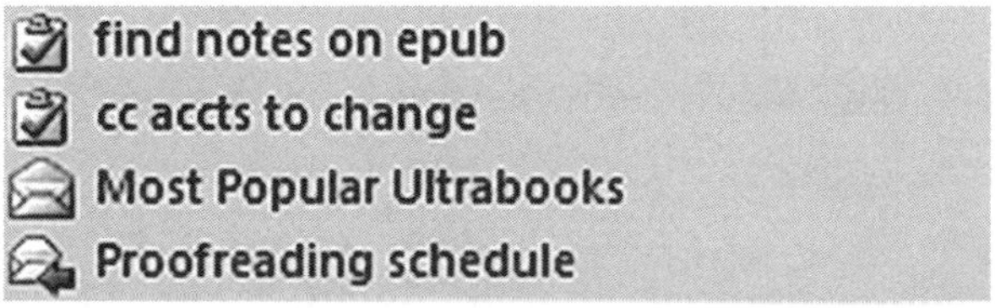

Cleaning Up Flagged-Mail Tasks (Windows and Mac)

As previously described, a somewhat unfortunate side effect of using flags on e-mail is that, if you have used flags a lot in the past, and then more recently decided to start using the Outlook task system, your task system will appear overloaded with flagged-mail tasks. They accumulate even if the mail is stored in older folders, even from years ago.

Clearly, listing all these items in your task list is not something you want, given how old most are, and if you have a lot of them, it can make the task list almost unusable. So you will want to clean this up, either by filtering them out, or by clearing them.

Filtering Out Flagged-Mail Tasks

Filtering out flagged-mail tasks does not remove the flags, it just prevents the flagged-mail tasks from appearing in your task list. On the Mac, filtering them out is easy. Clear the check box labeled *Flagged Items* (it's on the Home tab of the Ribbon). In Windows, you do this in the Tasks folders by choosing any folder *other than* the To-Do List folder. Remember, only the To-Do List folder shows flagged-mail tasks. However, in MYN we primarily use the To-Do Bar for managing tasks, and it *does* show flagged-mail tasks. Unfortunately, there is no easy way to filter these completely out there. I'll show you one way to do that in Lesson 3, which takes a few steps to do, but works fairly well.

Clearing Flagged-Mail Tasks

Alternately, you can clear and remove the flags from each item. You can do that one at a time by clicking each flag (either in the e-mail list or task list). Or you can SHIFT-select a number of the messages in the task list simultaneously, right-click the flag, and select Clear Flag (in Windows, if you select more than one, the right-click choice is Clear Flag/Delete Task—it leads to the same outcome). Clearing flags preserves the original mail, removes the flag from it, and removes the item from the task list, so it can be just what you want. If the old mail still has unique meaning to you, consider applying a color category to that mail as a way to mark it for later search. If there is some action still due on the flagged mail, you might even want to convert the e-mail to a task following the instructions at the end of this chapter.

Clearing flags like this, one at a time, is probably the best way to go, because it gives you a chance to evaluate each flagged e-mail. However, if you have hundreds of these scattered among hundreds of real tasks, then scrolling and selecting these can be hard to do. If they are really quite old, it might be best to make a decision to remove all old flags at once. The way you do that is to group all the flagged-mail tasks together and clear the flags in bulk. Here are the details.

How to Do a Bulk Flagged-Mail Task Cleanup:

1. Go to your Tasks folder. **Windows users:** Be sure the To-Do List folder is selected in the upper left of the Navigation Pane.

2. At the top of the list view, click the Item Type icon (usually the column at the far left) in the header. In Windows, its symbol looks like a dog-eared document; on the Mac it looks like a tiny *i* inside a circle. Again, click that symbol in the header at the top of the column, which sorts all items on that column.

3. Scroll through the task list to find where the icons that look like an envelope begin, and then use the SHIFT key to select them all. You've just selected all your flagged-mail tasks. If you were flagging e-mail recently to indicate tasks, then leave unselected any new flagged tasks you might have created on purpose.

4. **Windows users:** Right-click the flag column on any of the selected items, and choose Clear Flag/Delete Task from the shortcut menu.
Mac users: Find the Follow Up Flag button on the Home tab of the Ribbon. Click the small down arrow at its right, and select Clear Flag.

These steps clear out your old unwanted flagged-mail tasks from your task lists, and retain the original e-mail. They also remove the flags from all those mail items in whatever mail folder they are stored in.

Windows users who upgraded from Outlook 2003 will most likely find that all that previously flagged mail still has a corresponding color category assigned (probably red). Decide if you want to remove that, as well.

Do *not* delete these items with DELETE, because the corresponding e-mails are deleted. *And* do *not* select any of the true tasks during step 3, because those will be deleted, too.

I'll discuss flagged-mail tasks more in Lesson 7.

Other Places to See Tasks in Outlook

Outlook has other places to see tasks in both Windows and the Mac.

Daily Task List below the Calendar in Windows Outlook

There is one other task feature of Windows Outlook that I need to mention briefly. In the default Calendar data-type view, if you view by day or by week, you might see tasks listed under each day. Ignore this task list for now. It is another way to view the same task database you have been working with so far, but because of how it is configured, it can be confusing to MYN system users. I'll show one practical MYN use for this in Lesson 4. For more information about this feature, see the section "The Daily Task List under the Windows Outlook Calendar View" near the end of Appendix A.

My Day Window in Outlook for Mac 2011

In Outlook for Mac 2011, there is another task view called My Day. It's a small, separate, vertical window that looks somewhat like the To-Do Bar in Windows Outlook. But because of how it is configured, the tasks list on it is not useful to MYN system users.

That said, My Day does show your appointments for the day, so take a look at it and see if it that makes it useful to you. You access it by clicking the Tools tab (look at the left edge of that tab) or by selecting it from the Tools menu. In fact, My Day is a separate application that you can launch without opening Outlook, which makes it a possible quick-launch view of your appointments. Look in the Office folder inside the Microsoft Office 2011 folder for the icon to launch it.

Introduction to Converting E-mails to Tasks (All Outlook Versions)

There is one last skill I want you to learn before you complete this lesson: how to convert e-mails to tasks. I cover this briefly for Windows users in the Quick Start, and I cover it a bit more here including the Mac. I have an entire lesson on this topic, Lesson 7, which offers much greater detail.

Converting e-mails to tasks is at the core of the MYN system. If you learn one thing, it should be this skill. The following steps will get you started with an easy approach. If you like what you see here, and you want to skip ahead to do Lesson 7 now to learn more, feel free to do that. After you're done, come back and start Lesson 3.

Windows Outlook

Windows users, try this now. Look in your Inbox and find an e-mail that has notified you of some action you need to take, either explicitly or implicitly. Find one without an attachment for now to practice this easy approach. When you find one, close the e-mail (if you opened it) and do these steps:

1. From within your regular e-mail list view, click the e-mail item (a regular left-click) and drag it over to the Tasks folder icon or Tasks banner button in the Navigation (Folders) Pane.

2. After you drag it there, release the mouse, and a new task window opens, just like the window you saw earlier in this lesson when you used the full-entry method to create a new task. The beauty of this approach is that the new task window contains the entire e-mail text, and the task name equals the subject name of the e-mail. That means you have very little typing to do to complete the conversion. But you should at a minimum do the following steps immediately:

Alert: Outlook 2010 often displays odd behavior when creating a task from an e-mail like this. The new task window might flash for a moment and then disappear behind the main Outlook window. This happens if you leave your mouse for more than a second over the Tasks folder icon or banner button prior to dropping the e-mail there. To avoid this, quickly release the mouse button as soon as your mouse passes over the Tasks folder icon or banner button. If the new task window does disappear, just move the main Outlook window aside to find it. If you are unable to make a habit of releasing the mouse button quickly, see the section "Using Quick Steps (Windows Outlook 2010 and 2013)" in Lesson 7 to learn an alternate method of converting e-mails to tasks.

3. Change the subject of the newly created task to a title that describes the action needed. This is an essential step. You must extract from the e-mail text the core action it requires of you and *write that on the subject line*, overwriting the old e-mail title.

4. Set the start date and due date for this task to today for now. Do *not* leave it at None. Ignore the task priority for now.

5. Click Save and Close in the upper-left corner of the new Task dialog box.

That's it! Your task has been saved in the task database inside Outlook. You might be able to see the new task appear on your To-Do Bar right now — go take a look. However, if you have lots of other tasks in there, it might be buried under other tasks. Don't worry if you can't find it. In the next lesson you will clean up the configurations of the To-Do Bar such that newly converted tasks will jump to the top of your task list.

As I mentioned earlier, avoid for now flagging e-mails as a way to convert e-mails to tasks. Even though this places the e-mail in the tasks list, there are many disadvantages to doing that. In Lesson 7, I discuss at length the right and wrong ways to use flagged-mail tasks.

Outlook for Mac 2011—Use AppleScript

Regrettably, converting e-mails to true tasks in Outlook for Mac 2011 is not as easy or flexible as in Windows. It's just not built in to the software design. However, Microsoft added an AppleScript to enable the missing capability, and it works well. It's not really a command in Outlook; rather, it's an add-in script that should be automatically installed when you install Outlook 2011. Here's how to find and use it.

With a message selected in Outlook for Mac 2011 (either in the message list or as an open message), open the AppleScript menu (small icon that looks like a scrolled document) at the far right end of the Outlook menu bar at the top of the Macintosh screen and choose Create Task from Message from the drop-down menu. A new task opens with the e-mail title as the task name, and the e-mail body in the body of the task. Rename the task using an action-oriented phrase. Then be sure to set the start date, priority, and other fields, and save it.

Note: If the Create Task from Message command is missing from your script menu, go to www.myn.bz/MacScript.htm to learn how to install it. Link is case-sensitive.

As with Windows, avoid for now flagging e-mails as a way to convert e-mails to tasks. Even though this places the e-mail in the tasks list, there are many disadvantages to doing that. In Lesson 7, I discuss at length the right and wrong ways to use flagged-mail tasks.

Summary

Congratulations—you have completed the first step of your journey toward workday control. You now know where to find the task system in Outlook and how to enter tasks. You have learned many subtle task features in the various versions. Macintosh users have learned the different way Outlook 2011 displays and treats tasks. You've learned about the complications of flagged-mail tasks, and some of you have cleaned the flagged-mail tasks associated with old mail out of your task list. And you now know an easy way to convert e-mails to tasks in all versions.

Next Steps

I suggest that, as you start using the system after the next lesson, you begin converting important e-mails to tasks immediately. You will find such tasks are much easier to keep track of in your task list than in your Inbox. However, do not go through your whole Inbox yet, because this was just a brief lesson on the topic, intended only to get you started early. I devote an entire lesson to this topic in Lesson 7, where you will learn, for instance, how to include attachments with your converted tasks (Windows only).

In the next lesson you will change the configurations of the task lists to prepare them for using the core MYN task management methodology.

Lesson 3: Configuring Outlook for MYN Task Management

Introduction

Whether you are upgrading from the One Minute To-Do List (1MTD), or starting fresh with the Master Your Now! (MYN) system, it's time to make a number of changes to your copy of Outlook. That is the sole purpose of this chapter, to walk you through the steps to make those MYN changes. Then, in Lesson 4 and beyond, I'll explain how to use those new configurations.

Note: *This lesson is summarized in videos 8, 9, and 10 of the MYN-Outlook Complete Video Training (see beginning of the Quick Start chapter for more information).*

Going Beyond the One Minute To-Do List

If you made the One Minute To-Do List settings while using the Quick Start (or by using the book *The One Minute To-Do List*), you'll find the MYN settings in this lesson go well beyond those. With the MYN system, you can track far more tasks than 1MTD, and MYN gives you a wider set of powerful tools to keep you ahead of the deluge of new e-mails and tasks that busy professionals receive daily. It does this primarily by adding the use of the Start Date field in Outlook and by adding a set of new processes (shown in Lesson 4 and beyond) that optimize the use of that field. As a result, with MYN, you will gain much more control over managing your tasks and e-mail.

Note, however, if you are already accustomed to using the 1MTD system, these new MYN settings will cause you to *lose* a few features you might rely on. For example, with 1MTD in Outlook, you had the ability to prioritize tasks within urgency zones by dragging them into place. With the new MYN settings, that mostly goes away. Instead, in MYN you'll set the Outlook Start Date field to reprioritize within an urgency zone (you can still drag tasks within a given start date). Also, the ability to use the Due Date field to set

65

deadlines goes away. (We'll use other deadline approaches that are more powerful.) Don't worry about losing these, because the MYN processes are far superior to 1MTD.

Why the MYN Configurations Are Needed

Why are these changes to Outlook needed? Why can't you just use the Outlook task system as it is?

The out-of-the-box task configurations for Outlook are poorly configured for use in today's business world. That's because those configurations, like those in many other task systems, are based on 75-year-old principles of task management, and end up emphasizing old, dead tasks. Systems like that become unusable quite quickly in a busy office environment.

That was not Microsoft's intention, of course. They've merely used the same approach that nearly every other system today uses, an approach that sorts the oldest uncompleted tasks to the top of the task list, and marks them in bright red. That might still work in a home system, where tasks accumulate slowly and all chores are eventually done. But in today's business world where priorities change nearly every day, and high volumes of business e-mail can deliver us tens of new action requests per day, our business task systems need a vastly different approach. So you need to tweak Outlook to prepare it for the new MYN processes that handle that high volume.

Creating the MYN Task List

For this early lesson, you will reconfigure key Outlook task lists to create the MYN task list first shown in Lesson 1. In Windows Outlook, that means you will be configuring the To-Do Bar. In the Mac version it will be the main Tasks folder.

One great strength of Windows Outlook is that it is an extremely flexible application that can be reconfigured in numerous ways, and they work quite well for setting up the MYN task list. Outlook for Mac 2011 has far less configurability, but it can still be modified in ways you can use to create that MYN task list functionality.

To create this list in Outlook, you will be applying a custom filter to the tasks lists and adding some custom columns, formatting, and sorting. When finished, your Windows To-Do Bar will look roughly as shown in Figure 1.3 in Lesson 1. The Mac Tasks folder will look as shown in Figure 1.4 in Lesson 1. The Mac layout is less ideal compared to the Windows layout, but it still serves the purpose.

In either case, the following configuration steps take a beginner 15 to 30 minutes to complete. In future lessons, you might be optionally making additional configuration changes. But this is enough for now.

In this lesson I'll start with the complete Windows Outlook configurations (immediately following). If you are configuring a Macintosh, skip ahead to the section "Configuring Outlook for Mac 2011," which starts about two-thirds through this lesson.

Consider the Outlook Add-in Software ClearContext

The same Windows Outlook configurations made manually in this book are built in to the MYN Special Edition of the Windows Outlook add-in software called ClearContext, available through a link on my website: www.myn.bz/clearcontext.html. Should you install that software now instead of doing the configurations that follows? Doing so will not really save you setup time, because the software installation steps themselves take time. You'll also need to learn how to use the software. And most corporate environments discourage adding software (though ClearContext is usually not blocked even in locked-down environments).

The primary reason to consider this software is that the paid version adds many optional but useful new features to Outlook, features that simplify some MYN functionality described in this lesson and in the lessons ahead. I'll make notes in the book where advantage can be gained from the software. You can decide later if you want to install it. If you do, be sure to access the special version from my website. Other software options might be available on my website as well.

■   ■   ■

Configuring Windows Outlook for MYN

Sitting adjacent to your main Windows Outlook views, the To-Do Bar will be the primary command post for the tasks you use and look at several times a day. Ahead you will customize the To-Do Bar so that it will:

► Show the Start Date column and a few additional task columns.

► Show only tasks with a start date of today or earlier.

► Group on priority and sort within groups on start date, descending.

► Filter out completed tasks.

► Display some custom formatting.

► Clear a default settings in Outlook that turns all old tasks red.

Note: In case you are jumping directly from the first edition of this book to this fourth edition (and did not use the second or third editions), two major changes started in the second edition and continue to this day. First, I am now emphasizing the Outlook Start Date rather than Due Date field. Second, master tasks are no longer emphasized in this system. In fact, the new To-Do Bar configuration as follows will make your previous Master Tasks view no longer usable. Lessons 9 and 12 provide new options for this functionality, and a newly designed Master Tasks view is shown in Lesson 12, in case you still want to use it. For more information about these changes, see the preface in the third edition, as well as the note at the end of this lesson.

Before You Start, Close Any Other Open Copies of Outlook

Before you start these configurations, if you are in an Exchange Server environment and logged on to more than one computer, exit Outlook on all other computers first. Reason: All settings you are about to make are saved first in the Outlook client, and then in the Exchange Server profile. If you have multiple Outlook clients running, Exchange can get confused about which client's settings take precedence in the central profile.

Also, if you get halfway through the settings and need to pause, I recommend you save the progress of the configurations by closing whatever view you are working on (click OK all the way out of the configuration screens), and then exit Outlook and start it again. That saves the settings.

All these precautions are to prevent you from losing the configurations you make. That said, in some rare cases Exchange will still throw out some or all of your settings. I'll give you some tips on how to work around that if it happens.

Start the Configurations by Opening the To-Do Bar Customization Controls

It's now time to get started. Almost all configurations are started from one primary Outlook configuration dialog box.

1. Find the task list in the To-Do Bar. Note, you will be editing the To-Do Bar at the right of the Outlook window. *You are* not *editing the Tasks folder, or the To-Do List folder, a common mistake because the steps look the same. Make sure you are in the To-Do Bar.*

2. Right-click anywhere on the To-Do Bar task list header bar (the bar with the heading Arranged By, or Arrange By, or Task Subject on it). From the shortcut menu that pops open, you'll choose an item near the bottom that varies based on Outlook version. In Outlook 2010 and 2013 it reads View Settings. In Outlook 2007 it might read Customize Current View or it might read Custom instead. The dialog box shown next will open. You are going to set a few of the View attributes in this dialog box.

Note: In most figures in this lesson, I will show you Outlook 2010 images. I will call out any important differences from other versions, if they exist. For example, in the dialog box here, the Columns button at the top is called the Fields button in 2007 (but it does the same thing). Also, the label at the very top varies across versions. We'll be returning to this dialog box frequently, and because its name varies so much across versions, from now on I'll affectionately refer to it as "the large stack of buttons."

3. If the Reset Current View button at the bottom left is active, then click it to clear any previous To-Do Bar task list settings. Old settings can make the rest of the steps in this chapter difficult to follow. However, after you complete Lesson 3, be careful *not* to click that button because it will clear out all your settings.

Adjusting the Columns (Fields)

1. Start by clicking the Columns button (called Fields in 2007), which opens the Show Columns (Show Fields) dialog box.

2. Use the Add and Remove buttons to create a new field list in the right side of that dialog box, as shown in the following figure. To remove fields, select them on the right and click Remove. To add fields, select them first on the left and click Add. If you have difficulty finding these fields in the list on the left, see the instructions at the end of this step.

    Create this list: Icon, Priority, Task Subject, Start Date, Flag Status (match the right side of the following figure).

Use the Move Up and Move Down buttons to place the fields in the right order, or just click the field name and drag it to the desired position.

Note: *You must match these names exactly. If you have any trouble finding any of the field names in the list on the left, try selecting All Task Fields in the Select Available Columns From list box in the upper-left corner, and then look again at the scrolling field list. That should display the columns you need with two exceptions. The Task Subject and Flag Status columns (if you need to re-add them) are located in the All Mail Fields list.*

3. When you have all the fields and they are in the correct order in the right side of the dialog box, click OK and return to the large stack of buttons shown at the start of these steps.

Group by Priority

A core principle of the MYN configurations is to have high-priority tasks sort and group at the top of the To-Do Bar. To enable this:

1. Back at the large stack of buttons, click the Group By button, which opens the Group By dialog box (see following figure).

2. If checked, clear the check box in the upper-left corner that says Automatically Group According to Arrangement.

3. Choose Priority from the Group Items By list box. Ensure that Show Field in View is checked, and ensure that Descending is selected to the right, as shown in the following figure. Click OK.

Note: If you cannot find the Priority item, try selecting All Task Fields In the Select Available Fields From box at the very bottom of the window.

Sort by Start Date

Back at the large stack of buttons, you next want to have tasks with newer start dates sort to the top of each group of tasks. To enable this:

1. Click the Sort button, which opens the Sort dialog box.

2. Choose Start Date from the Sort Items By list box.

3. Select the Descending button to the right, as shown in the following figure. *This step is very important, so do not skip it.* Click OK.

Adjusting the Other Settings

You want to ensure that you can enter tasks directly on the To-Do Bar and that you can see all fields. To enable this, do the following steps:

1. From the large stack of buttons click Other Settings. The dialog box in the next figure is displayed.

2. Ensure that the three check boxes in the upper-right corner are selected, as shown in the next figure.

The Other Settings dialog box showing Column Headings and Rows, Grid Lines and Group Headings, AutoPreview, Reading Pane, and Other Options sections.

3. In the lower portion of the box, under Other Options, clear the check box next to Use Compact Layout in Widths Smaller Than.

4. Click OK.

Restart Outlook to Save and Confirm Your Settings (and Test Their Stability)

That was a complicated set of changes, so let's confirm that they are correct so far and save them if they are. After that we'll make some more settings.

Also, when used with Exchange, Outlook has a way of losing settings in some cases even when you make them correctly. You will notice this when you quit Outlook and restart it the first time after making the settings. This is usually rare, but during one seminar, I saw nearly half the users experience difficulties at this stage. It seems to be organization dependent. If the settings are correct, exiting and restarting Outlook saves them.

So, at this point I recommend you close all the configuration screens, and exit Outlook and restart it. That will hopefully secure this first group of settings, or at least challenge those settings, so you can resolve any issues. (Usually, if the settings fail at this point, they will remain on the second try.) Let's restart Outlook now as follows:

1. Click OK all the way out of the open dialog boxes.

2. Exit and restart Outlook. After Outlook restarts, examine the headings at the top of your To-Do Bar task list to ensure that your settings were preserved through the restart process (and that you made them correctly). Your To-Do Bar task list headings should look like the following figure.

Note: *In Outlook 2010, if you use the Black color scheme, some of the symbol labels in this header might be invisible. To fix this, go to the File tab and choose Options. At the top of the General option, under User Interface Options, change Color Scheme to Silver.*

If your headings are secure and look good, skip ahead to the section "Setting the Filter."

Fixing the Settings

In some cases due to the previously mentioned Exchange error, your settings will appear to have changed after restarting Outlook. There are two ways that bug can behave; 1) All settings might have reverted to the original ones, where the main label at the top is Arrange By, and there is no Start Date field, or 2) Everything is listed correctly except that the flag symbol at the right end of the headings is gone.

If there are other issues than these, you probably just missed a step, so try again from the start of this chapter. But if the issues match case 1 or 2, follow these steps.

Restoring Completely Lost Settings (Case 1)

Let's start with case number 1, where all settings appear to have reverted back to the original ones; that is, you've lost them. In fact, the settings are still there. They are just hidden due to the Exchange error. Here are a couple of quick steps you can take to recover them:

1. Follow the very first steps (1 and 2) in this lesson to bring up the large stack of buttons again.

2. Click the Columns (Fields) button.

3. Remove the bottom two column names on the right side of the field list dialog box. (It doesn't matter what they are.) I know this seems odd, but trust me, this will restore hidden settings in 99 percent of these cases.

4. Don't make any other changes. Click OK all the way out and restart Outlook. That should fix it.

Restoring the Missing Flag Symbol (Case 2)

The other common issue at this point is that the flag symbol is missing from the right edge of the To-Do Bar task list header, even though you know you put it in when following the steps at the beginning of this lesson. This is also the result of an error in Outlook. To fix this, repeat the steps in the earlier section "Adjusting the Columns (Fields)," and insert that field again (the Flag Status field). It usually remains permanently after the second try.

Exit and Restart Outlook to Confirm That Restoration Worked

If you made the corrections for case 1 or 2, exit and restart Outlook to make sure the settings stay this time. In 99 percent of the cases, they do. If so, move on to the next section, "Setting the Filter."

In some rare cases, however, the settings are lost again and the restoration steps don't work to restore those settings. If that happens, the only thing I have found to do is this: Start at the beginning again, and make a small subset of the settings (such as adjusting the fields only), and then exit and restart Outlook. If the settings remain, add another small subset of settings and exit and restart Outlook. For some reason, doing this incrementally usually allows the settings to hold.

Setting the Filter

Return to the large stack of buttons. (Follow the very first steps, 1 and 2, at the start of this lesson, but this time right-click the label Task Subject.) You are now going to create a somewhat complex filter to ensure that you see only certain tasks.

1. On the large stack of buttons click the Filter button.

2. The Filter dialog box opens. Click the Advanced tab. Most likely two filter conditions are displayed in the upper part of this window, as shown in the following figure. If so, leave those conditions there. If they're not present, you will add them in the following steps.

Note: Previously, MYN users who configured Outlook with the book's first edition (but not the later editions) might have a Due Date filter in there. If so, remove it.

The rest of these instructions assume you do not know how to create an Outlook filter, so the steps are very detailed. If you *do* know how to set a filter, examine the following dialog box and match it.

3. Start by clicking Field in the middle left of the dialog box.

4. From the Field list, choose Date/Time fields, and from its submenu choose Start Date.

5. From the Condition list choose On or Before.

Note: In some rare cases the Condition menu may be empty. If so, click Cancel to close the Filter dialog box, and then start again at step 1 above; that should fix it.

6. Type "today" in the Value box (no quotes); there is no *Today* list choice.

7. Click Add to List to place this condition in the criteria list at the top in the middle of the dialog box. This filter ensures that future dated tasks are hidden from view.

8. Leave this dialog box open. (Do *not* click OK.) You are going to create some more queries.

9. Click Field in the middle left of the dialog box again.

10. From the Field list, choose Info/Status fields, and from its submenu choose Status.

11. From the Condition list, choose Not Equal To.

12. In the Value box, select Completed.

13. Click Add to List to add this condition to the criteria list in the middle of the dialog box. This filter removes completed tasks from view; otherwise, they will clutter your list.

14. Click Field in the middle left of the dialog box again.

15. From the Field list, choose Date/Time fields, and from its submenu choose Start Date.

16. From the Condition list, scroll to the bottom and choose Does Not Exist. This filter enables tasks to stay in the list even if you forget to set a date for them; otherwise they will be hard to find.

17. Do *not* use the Value box. (It's grayed out.) Click the Add to List button. Your filter entries should now look like those in the previous figure. The top two items in the figure might not be present. If not, add them in the same way as the others. Note that to do that you will find the Flag Completed Date item under All Mail fields (one of the submenus you will see after you click the Field button). If you like, you can read near the start of Lesson 12, in the section "To-Do List Tasks Folder" to see why these two filters are needed.

18. (Optional) As we discussed in Lesson 2, if you have hundreds of flagged e-mails in your To-Do Bar task list, there is an optional filter you can add to prevent e-mail flagged in your Inbox from showing in the To-Do Bar by following these steps:

a. Click Field in the middle left of the dialog box.

b. Choose All Task Fields and from its submenu choose In Folder.

c. From the Condition box, choose Doesn't Contain.

d. In the Value box, type "Inbox". Click Add to List.

Because this filter is optional, it is not shown in the previous figure.

19. Click OK. Return to the large stack of buttons.

Now you know how to adjust the Filter settings. Next you will set some formatting rules that are required for MYN.

Disabling the Overdue Tasks Rule and Formatting Tasks Due Today

1. In the large stack of buttons, click the Conditional Formatting button (Automatic Formatting in Outlook 2007). The following dialog box opens.

2. Clear the check box next to the Overdue Tasks rule in the middle of the dialog box. This prevents tasks with an old Due Date field from turning red, which does not make sense in the MYN system.

3. Click Add to create a new rule and type "MYN Start Date Today" in the Name field. You will see it appear at the bottom of the scrolling box, as shown in the previous figure.

4. With the new rule selected in the scrolling box, click the Font button. In the Font dialog box, select the Underline check box. Click OK.

5. With the new rule still selected in the scrolling box, click the Condition button on the left side of the dialog box, and click the Advanced tab of the Filter dialog box.

6. Click Field in the middle left of this dialog box.

7. From the Field list, choose Date/Time fields, and from its submenu choose Start Date.

8. From the Condition list choose Today. Ignore the Value box.

9. Click Add to List. The filter should look like what's shown in the following figure.

10.   If your dialog box matches this figure, click OK. Click OK again, and then again, to close all configuration windows and return to the newly configured To-Do Bar.

Your configurations are now mostly done. Next, you will run a few tests to confirm that they were done correctly.

Confirming That the Windows Outlook Configurations Are Correct

You should stop and confirm that the configurations are correct. Do the following checks. If any fail, repeat the corresponding configurations.

1.   Examine the column labels of your To-Do Bar header, left to right, and ensure that they match the following figure:

2.   Create a new task and set the start date to today, priority equal to Normal. When you save it, that task should appear *underlined* near the top of your Priority: Normal section. I'll explain the purpose of the underline in Lesson 4.

3.   Create a new task and set the start date to today, priority equal to High. When you save it, that task should appear in the separate Priority: High section, near the top of the To-Do Bar. It is underlined.

4. Create a new task and set the start date to tomorrow, priority equal to Normal. It should disappear from the list when you save it. If you want to find it to confirm that it was created, just look in the Tasks folder.

5. Create a new task, set the start date to None, and set the priority equal to Normal. The task should appear near the bottom of your Priority: Normal group, with None in the date field.

6. Create a new task with the Task dialog box. Set the start date and due date both to yesterday, priority equal to Normal. When you click Save & Close, that task should appear in your Priority: Normal group, below the underlined items. Its text should not be red.

The reasoning behind many of these settings will be explained in Lesson 4.

Again, if any of these tests failed, you will need to reconfirm all the settings you just made. After all the tests are passed, there are a few more optional configuration steps to take.

Formatting the Date Column

You can fine-tune the formatting of nearly any column on the To-Do Bar. I like to reset the date format of the start date column to use a narrower scheme. This is purely optional, so feel free to skip this change:

1. Return to the configuration screen that looks like a large stack of buttons. (Follow the very first steps at the start of this lesson, but this time right-click on the label Task Subject.)

2. Choose the Format Columns button near the bottom of the large stack of buttons. The dialog box shown after step 5 opens.

3. Select Start Date in the list on the left.

4. In the Format box on the right, select the format shown here. Study this format. The date itself is different; for example, 1-Aug-13.

5. Ignore all other settings and click OK.

Adjusting the Width of the To-Do Bar and Start Date Column

Back at the To-Do Bar view, drag the left edge of the To-Do Bar to widen or narrow it so it is about 3 inches wide. Next, you will probably want the Start Date column a different width. Drag the left edge of the column *in the header* to the right or left until you can see just enough of the date to read it.

Turning Off the Task Reminders

By default, Outlook does not set the reminder check box (see the section "Reminder Check Box" in Lesson 2) on new tasks, but occasionally I find users whose Outlook is set to do that. Task reminders are not used in the MYN system, so if your copy of Outlook turns task reminders on by default when it creates new tasks, you should turn that setting off as follows:

In Outlook 2007, from the Tools menu select Options, Preferences tab. Click the Task Options button, and clear the bottom check box: Set Reminders on Tasks with Due Dates.

In Outlook 2010 and 2013, go to the File tab, choose Options on the left, and then choose Tasks on the left. In the Task Options section on the right, clear the check box Set Reminders on Tasks with Due Dates. I'll explain near the end of Lesson 4 why task reminders are not used in MYN.

■ ■ ■

Configuring Outlook for Mac 2011

Because of Outlook for Mac's unique design compared to Windows Outlook, setting up the Macintosh version of Outlook is quite different. The main difference is that you'll be making all the configurations in the Tasks folder, not a separate smaller view (there is no configurable To-Do Bar). Due to sorting limitations, you cannot show all MYN tasks in one list. Rather, you will be creating three different lists, one for each priority. To do that, you'll use an Outlook for Mac 2011 feature called Smart Folders.

Set Filter Check Boxes

To get started, go to the Tasks folder (click on the Tasks banner button or icon in the lower left of the Outlook window). Next, click on the Home tab of the Ribbon, and look at the right end of that tab. You'll see three check boxes. These are the filter check boxes. Select and clear those check boxes so they match the ones shown here.

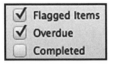

Select and Reorder the Tasks Folder Columns

Next, with the Outlook window active, click the View menu in the menu bar at the top of your Macintosh screen, and choose Columns. You'll see a submenu like the one shown here. This controls which columns appear within the Tasks folder. Use that submenu a number of times to clear and add check marks to match the list in the image below.

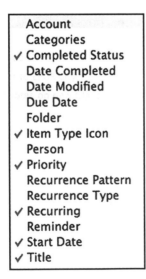

Next, you are going to reset the left-to-right order of those columns at the top of the tasks list. To do that, click and drag the column headings as needed to place them in the order shown in the following figure. Also, while there, confirm that all the column icons and names shown here appear at the top of your task list. If not, redo the last step. Adjust the width of the Start Date column as needed by dragging the edge of the column heading.

Sorting on Start Date, Descending

Click the Start Date heading as shown at the right end of the previous figure to force a descending sort. The arrow points down and the newest start dates should be at the top.

Note: *This sorting will apply to the Smart Folders that you will create next. When set as just described, I recommend you avoid changing the sorting of any columns in those Smart Folders; that is, don't click the heading of any column within the Smart Folders. If you do, due to an error in early versions of Outlook 2011, you'll lose the descending start date sorting and you will not be able get it back while the Smart Folder is open. You can get it back, but you'll need to navigate back to the main Tasks folder (click the Tasks icon at the top of the Navigation Pane) and re-sort it there to get the newest start dates back at top. Then reenter the Smart Folder. This error was fixed in later releases of Outlook 2011.*

Creating the Three Smart Folders

To group on task priority, you will be using a feature in Outlook for Mac 2011 called Smart Folders. You will create three separate Smart Folders to view each of the three urgency zones we use in the MYN task list as described in Lesson 1: a folder for High (Critical Now), a folder for Normal (Opportunity Now), and one for Low (Over the Horizon).

Note: *I wish you could do this in one folder as you can in Windows Outlook, but three separate folders are needed because subsorting on the start date, a key part of the MYN system and present in Windows Outlook, is not an available feature of the Outlook 2011 Tasks folder.*

To create a new Smart Folder, you have to first do an Outlook search and then save the search criteria as follows:

1. In the Tasks folder, click on the Tasks icon in the top of the Navigation Pane. Click once in the search box in the upper right of the Outlook window (labeled Search This Folder), which activates the Search tab of the Ribbon (shown in the following figure)—you might have to click on the purple Search tab title to truly activate it.

2. Click the Advanced button at the right end of that tab (shown in the following figure). After you do, you'll see an Item Contains button appear below the Ribbon.

3. Click the Item Contains button and change it to Start Date in the popup. In the new button that appears to the right, select Within Last. And in the field to the right of that enter 10,000 (this is simply a very large number to include all tasks with the past few years; feel free to change it if you'd like to include more or less). All this is shown in the following figure.

4. Click the plus sign (at the far right end of that search line) to start a new search line.

5. With these principles, create the next two search lines, duplicating exactly what you see in the following figure (Priority; Is; High; and Is Incomplete; Is Incomplete).

6. To turn this into a Search Folder, click the Save button that sits just to the left of the Advanced button in the Search tab. When you do that, a new Smart Folder appears in the Navigation Pane at the far left with Untitled selected. Type over *Untitled* with "Critical Now" and press ENTER. Your first Smart Folder is done.

7. Create another Search Folder by repeating steps 1-6 but when you get to step 5, change the Priority values in the priority search line (the second line) to Moderate. In step 6, title the folder *Opportunity Now*.

8. Create the third Search Folder by repeating steps 1-6 but when you get to step 5, change the Priority values in the priority search line (the second line) to Low. In step 6, title the folder *Over the Horizon*.

9. I suggest you delete the remaining predelivered Smart Folders so your three priority folders stand out by themselves. To delete a folder, press CTRL and click it and then choose Delete.

The left side of the following figure shows how your new Smart Folders list will look in the Navigation Pane. You can now click any of those folders to review your tasks in the three urgency zones. In the following figure, the

Opportunity Now Smart Folder is selected, displaying all Opportunity Now (moderate or medium priority) tasks to its right.

Due to the intelligence of these three Smart Folders, they will automatically populate based on task date and priority. For example, if you change a task's priority to High in any folder, it will move to the Critical Now folder. If you set the start date to the future, it will disappear and then reappear on its date.

Clicking the general Tasks folder icon above the Smart Folders (labeled Tasks in this figure) will show you future dated tasks. If you want to include completed tasks, you'll need to toggle the Completed filter check box you cleared in the previous Filter steps. In the next chapter, I'll show you how to use these folders.

				Title	Start Date
▶ ☑ Tasks					
				screenshot event	Jun 6, 2013
▼ SMART FOLDERS				new url possibilities	Jun 6, 2013
Critical Now				Find/get Rcpt HCH	Jun 6, 2013
Opportunity Now				Add to 1MTD full link	Jun 6, 2013
Over the Horizon				progress on OLbook4	May 22, 2013

Confirming That Your Outlook for Mac 2011 MYN Configurations Are Correct

You should stop and confirm that the configurations are correct. Do the following checks. If any fail, repeat the configurations.

1. Create a new task and set the start date to today, priority equal to Normal (that is, no priority set). When you save it, that task should appear near the top of your Opportunity Now Smart Folder.

2. Create a new task and set the start date to today, priority equal to High. When you save it, that task should appear near the top of your Critical Now Smart Folder.

3. Create a new task and set the start date to today, priority equal to Low. When you save it, that task should appear near the top of your Over the Horizon Smart Folder.

4. Create a new task and set the start date to tomorrow, priority equal to Normal. It should *not* appear in any of the three Smart Folders after you save it. (You will see it appear tomorrow in the Opportunity Now folder).

5. Create a new task and set the start date and due date both to yesterday, priority equal to Normal. When you save it, that task should appear in your Opportunity Now Smart Folder, below the items dated today. It

will appear red. (We will ignore that red color. There is unfortunately no way to turn off that setting in the Mac version of Outlook.)

Exit Outlook and then Restart Outlook

That completes all the configurations you will make in this lesson. After you have completed these settings, exit Outlook and then restart it. That saves the settings.

. . .

Next Steps

Your task system is now configured, and you are ready to apply the MYN processes to manage your tasks in an intelligent and effective way. You just need to learn how to use these new configurations.

The core processes for using these new configurations are all presented next, in Lesson 4. After that lesson, you will have all you need to manage tasks in a basic way. Subsequent lessons will expand on those skills.

Note: *If you were using Outlook tasks before doing these configurations, there is one other update procedure that has to do with recurring tasks. Any recurring tasks created prior to inserting these configurations now need to be deleted and recreated, this time making a point of saving the task with a start date set. Do not just try to edit an existing recurring task and add a start date; it won't work. You need to completely delete and recreate all your recurring tasks. Otherwise, they will not behave correctly. When you create the new task, set the start date to the next date you want the task to appear.*

Note: *If you are a longtime MYN user and configured your Outlook according to the first edition of this book, but you did not update to the second or third editions of this book, here is another important consideration.*

After adding the configurations in this lesson, you will see that all your old master tasks will now be visible in the To-Do Bar. That's because undated tasks now appear there. Here's what to do next to fix that.

Assign a priority of Low to all tasks with no dates. That will clean up the High and Medium portions of your list. Then read Lesson 4 all the way through, especially the section titled "Deferring by Converting Tasks to Over-the-Horizon Tasks." If you previously had a very large number of master tasks, and the Low priority section is now overwhelmed, I suggest you jump immediately to Lesson 9 to learn the Defer-to-Review method, which replaces the Master Tasks view approach. If, after reading all this, you decide you still prefer using a Master Tasks view, study the Lesson 12 section "The MYN Master Tasks View" on building a new Master Tasks folder and view which is compatible with this fourth edition.

Lesson 4:
A New Approach to Managing Tasks in Outlook

The Master Your Now! Methodology: How to Take Control of Your Tasks in Outlook

All the configurations in Lesson 3 were done for a reason: to set up a task list to match the principles described in Lesson 1, so you can succeed at managing tasks in Outlook. I call the resulting task list the MYN task list. The next step is to start applying the MYN system best practices of task management that this new task list supports. Let's go over those now.

Note: *This lesson is summarized in videos 9 and 15 of the MYN-Outlook Complete Video Training (see beginning of the Quick Start chapter for more information).*

The Now Tasks List

Tasks You Would Consider Doing Now

The first and perhaps simplest of these best practices of managing tasks in Outlook is this: From now on, the tasks you place in the High or Normal (medium) priority sections of your MYN task list should be *tasks you would consider working on now.* These tasks I label together as Now Tasks. They were first described in Lesson 1. I repeat a figure from that lesson below (Figure 4.1). It shows where Now Tasks sit on your newly configured To-Do Bar in Windows Outlook.

The Mac shows urgency zones separately as shown in Figure 4.2 . You cannot view the Now Tasks list in one list on the Mac, so the Now Tasks list corresponds to the top two Smart Folders.

What I mean above by "consider working on now" is this: They are relevant for current goals, events, and priorities and can be acted on now as stand-alone tasks. They include typical to-do's that need to be done as soon as possible. These might be tasks from yesterday you did not complete, or they might be new tasks. They might be Normal priority tasks that are due later this week, or High priority tasks that must be done today. All of them you could do today if you had the resources. The key point is that any and all Now Tasks are tasks that should be eligible to do *now* given enough time, the right location, or the right person.

Figure 4.1
The MYN task list and urgency zones in Windows Outlook, after being configured in Lesson 3.

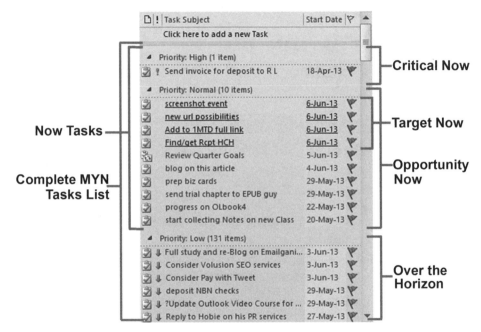

Figure 4.2
On the Mac, the three MYN urgency zones correspond to three named Smart Folders shown at left, as configured in Lesson 3.

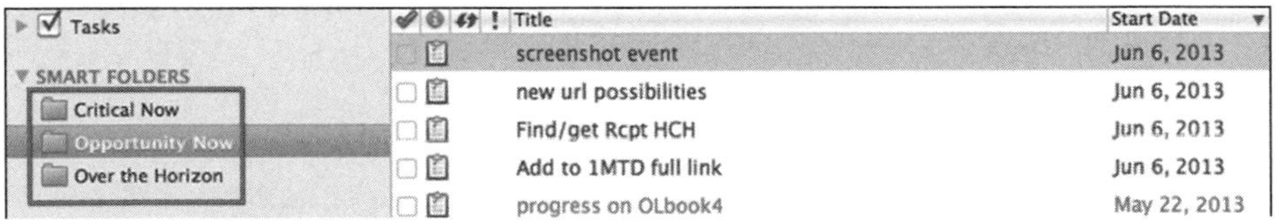

As a contrasting example, you would not list all the tasks leading up to the future completion of a project, because many are dependent on other actions happening first, so you cannot act on them now. Those dependent tasks would just clutter the list. Instead, use a separate way to plan and schedule future project tasks (see the section "The MORE Task" in Lesson 6 for one way). What you *would* put on the Now Tasks list is the very *next* step of that project that you *can* take action on *now*.

Note: More discussion of next steps and next actions is provided in Lesson 6. And more discussion of project management is provided in Lesson 12.

No Christmas Trees in August

Similarly, you would not display tasks on your Now Tasks list that only make sense to do on some future date, tasks that you would never consider doing now. You would not display "Decorate the Christmas Tree" on the list in August. More realistically, you would not place "Write the Friday status report" on the list the previous Monday. Tasks like this would only clutter the list and weaken it. You *would* include tasks you did not complete from previous days, if they still make sense to do now. Again, *Now Tasks are tasks currently eligible for action now* (I will discuss future-dated tasks below).

Note: This is one of the main ways MYN can be extended beyond the simpler One Minute To-Do List (shown in the Quick Start). In MYN, you can schedule tasks to appear in the future when action on them is appropriate. The configurations you made in Lesson 3 make that possible. More on how to do that in this lesson.

Figure 4.1 shows how the three built-in priorities for tasks in Outlook—High, Normal, and Low—map to the Now Horizon urgency zones discussed in Lesson 1. Tasks in the first of those priority sections, the High priority section, are called Critical Now tasks. Let's talk about that urgency zone and how best to manage tasks there.

Critical Now (Must-Do-Today) Tasks: Identify Them Early, Do Them Early

In this system there is a lot of emphasis on High priority Outlook tasks. This is important because, in this system, a High priority setting indicates what I call *Critical Now* tasks, as explained fully in Lesson 1 (in the first edition of this book they were called Must-Do-Today tasks, a term still viable today).

One of the first things you will notice in Windows Outlook when you start adding tasks to the newly configured To-Do Bar is that High priority tasks pop to the top of the task list, in their own group. That's to emphasize their critical importance. On the Mac they have their own Smart Folder.

Note: If setting priorities on Outlook tasks is new to you, review the Lesson 2 section "Three Ways to Set Priorities on Tasks." For the Mac, see Lesson 2 section "How to Set Outlook Priorities on Tasks."

You Can Shorten Your Workday

This High priority group is enormously useful. Establishing and using a Critical Now (Must-Do-Today) tasks list will actually *shorten your workday*. Why? Because it helps prevent a common problem that many very busy people experience, the working late syndrome. Let me explain this by sharing how it first helped me.

Back in 2002, just before I developed this system, I moved from a consulting role in a large company called Accenture into the role of Vice President of Technology for a new Accenture spin-off company. At that company I found myself consistently putting in 12-hour workdays, and I was not happy about that. After a little self-analysis I found one root cause was that I tended to start work on important actions only after I got out of all my daily meetings, usually around 5 p.m. Before 5 p.m., I did not really know all that was due *that day*. It was not until I finally examined my meeting notes from that day, my sticky notes, my various to-do lists (and maybe my e-mail inbox) that I usually discovered a number of critical deliverables for the day. As a result, a major portion of my workday actually *started* at 5, and I had to work late nearly every day to get those tasks done. Of course I wrote this off to the reality of all the meetings a senior executive tends to have. But actually, that was not the core problem.

Virtual Assistant

One way to illustrate the core problem is this. If I had an assistant who chased me around all day and collected my commitments, and then reminded me throughout the day of some key things I promised to complete that day, I probably would complete those tasks earlier. Knowing and seeing the list early and consistently, I would make the time to ensure that my promises were completed before my preferred departure time.

What I recognized is that without clear focus, I became a bit lazy about working tasks during the day. Instead I just went to meetings, reacted to phone calls and interruptions, and attended to my smartphone e-mail all day long. I consistently expected I would dig out of my task commitments later, after the hustle and bustle of the day had ended. By doing this, however, I was letting lower-priority items rule my day and ignoring my high-priority commitments. And I was extending my workday.

Without a fulltime assistant at my side, how might I have ensured a more appropriate focus? This sort of focus on current important commitments for the day is exactly what the Critical Now process and configurations give you: a way to clearly record and easily see at a glance what your critical list for today is and to facilitate getting items on that list done early. I cannot emphasize enough how useful this is.

The Critical Now (Must-Do-Today) Process

The Critical Now process is simple, deceptively so. From prior days, and then early in this day and throughout the day, identify urgent things that absolutely must get done today. Enter them as tasks in Outlook (configured as in Lesson 3), and mark them with a High priority and today's date in the Start Date field. Reserve the High priority only for these items. Then, throughout the day, glance at that list often, perhaps even hourly, and ensure that you get all High priority tasks done as early as possible. To work those tasks, use either dedicated task time or gaps in your day. If necessary, use part of your lunchtime or time freed up by skipping a low-value meeting. Just try to get them done early. That way, when the normal end of your workday arrives, your critical commitments are done. If you decide to stay late at that point, you do so only to work on *discretionary* tasks, not because you *have* to stay. With this new process, you will likely be able to leave work on time most days of the week, if you so choose.

Advantages of Using Critical Now

Knowing that using the system will get me out early is what makes this aspect of the system self-sustaining for me. When I look at my Critical Now tasks list I think to myself, "If I get these done I can leave work on time today." It is incredibly motivating. This also motivates me to find and write these tasks down. I become somewhat obsessive about identifying them because I know these are what may sabotage a reasonably timed exit later in the day.

When you do get these tasks done early, you have a sense of being ahead of the curve, which is a very nice feeling to have. It changes your whole work attitude and greatly reduces your level of stress at work.

Also, by creating this list early in the day and managing it throughout the day, you should be able to tell early if your critical list really will exceed your capacity to complete it that day. That gives you time to reach out to stake-holders early and get permission to extend their deadlines, or reach a compromise on the delivery. This avoids the sickening anxiety that can occur when the day's true deadlines tumble down on you late in the day, and it prevents an angry line of stakeholders from forming at your desk when you are trying to leave.

Do Not Abuse "High" Priority. Use the Going Home Test

But be sure not to abuse this High priority category. It is easy to move items into the High priority section just because you are enthusiastic about them. This category is only for urgent items that must be completed today. Give yourself this simple test (I call it the going home test). Ask yourself, "Would I work late tonight to complete this item if it is not complete by the normal end of the workday?" If the answer is no, then do not mark it High priority. Instead, mark it Normal (medium) priority. I'll explain use of the Normal and Low priority sections in a moment.

No More Than 5 Tasks in the Critical Now Section

Again, be conservative with High priority. If a High priority task remains in that section for two or more days straight, what does that tell you about how seriously you are taking the phrase "must do today"? I usually have only two or three items in that section, perhaps occasionally up to five. If you have more I suspect you have lost the point of the Critical Now section. That's one of the rules for the MYN system—no more than 5 tasks at a time should be listed in the Critical Now section. On many days it will be empty.

Task Importance

Maintaining the count small in the High priority section is essential. Overloading it artificially will destroy its utility. One reason many new users load up the High priority section with too many tasks is they confuse the must-do-today concept with the thought "This is important to me." Unless it is time-critical for today, keep it out of the High section.

Some tasks are important but not urgent, however, and that's good to know too. In this system those tasks are described as having high *intrinsic importance*. They link strongly to your goals and values. I have other ways to treat those, explained fully at the very beginning of Lesson 12; you'll get there soon enough. But for now, unless tasks have an urgent deadline of today, keep them out of the High priority section of the MYN system.

Critical Now Next Actions

Another reason people load up their Critical Now section with nonactionable items that linger from day to day is they fail to delineate a task's next action, and thereby put too large an item in the High section. You'll learn more about next actions in Lesson 6, but for now know that it is better to define for today only the small portion of a large task that you know you can and need to get done today. So instead of writing Quarterly Report Project, write Send E-mail to Team about Quarterly Report. That task you can knock off quickly and it really may be the only part of the project that is urgent for today. Again, in Lesson 6 I teach you more about this concept.

Fixing the Priority Group Sort Order (Windows)

If after using the To-Do Bar with the Lesson 3 configurations you find your Priority: High group is not above the Priority: Normal group, the priority group sort order is off. This is easy to disturb, because clicking on the To-Do Bar header can re-sort the list. To fix it, click once on the black exclamation point (!) at the left end of the header of the To-Do Bar task list (see figure).

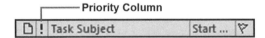

Clicking that black exclamation point should move the Priority: High group to the top. Be careful not to arbitrarily click that header bar from now on. If you do, however, a few well-placed clicks on the header should fix it.

Most Tasks Do Not Have Deadlines

Now that you have finished the configurations in Lesson 3, notice that the Due Date field is not displayed in the MYN task list, just the Start Date field. "What's up with that?" you might ask. Here's why that configuration is used.

Somewhere during the history of task management training, someone created a rule: If you do not assign a due date to a task it won't get done. That rule sounds good, doesn't it? It sounds so *proactive*. That is why nearly all automated task systems include a due date field. This rule makes sense for large project tasks. But this is not a good rule to apply to the small ad hoc tasks we routinely put on our to-do list. Why? Because the way the rule is usually used, which is to set *artificial* due dates on most tasks, it is an attempt to trick yourself—and you are not so easily tricked. It reminds me of the people I once knew who set their wristwatch ahead ten minutes thinking it would help them be on time to meetings. In reality, it only works for a couple of days and then the person just mentally adjusts and starts being late to meetings again. You do the same with artificial due dates. When they arrive you recognize their arbitrary nature and just start to ignore them. Inevitably, fire drills arise that pull you away to other things.

Artificial due dates can actually lead to more missed deadlines, because, as you start to skip deadlines that you know are false, you suffer from the Cry Wolf phenomenon. Because most of your tasks have fake due dates, you get used to skipping them. Then you might not recognize a true due date when you see it, and you might skip it. You may get eaten alive, but in this case by missed deadlines.

That does not mean you shouldn't apply a true deadline to those tasks that really have them, particularly those imposed from the outside (from your client or boss, for example). There *are* appropriate times to set true deadlines. But, as will be explained, due to technical issues, you will not be using the Outlook Due Date field for this. You will use other approaches. I will show you how to do that near the end of this lesson in the section "Managing Deadlines." For now, note that the kinds of tasks you should put on your Now Tasks list are small next-step, or next-action, tasks. These are small actions toward larger goals, and these kinds of intermediate-step tasks usually do not have hard deadlines. So don't set deadlines artificially. Instead, use the next technique to set a *start date*.

Always Set a Start Date

While most next-step style tasks do not have hard deadlines, most *do* have approximate time frames for when they are best acted on. As part of the MYN system I want you to use the *Start Date* field in Outlook to indicate that approximate time frame, and that's why the Start Date field is exposed on the MYN task list in this system. In fact, I want you to apply a start date to *all* MYN Tasks. Do not leave any tasks on the MYN task list with a date set to

None. Setting a start date on all tasks is a primary distinction between MYN and the simpler 1MTD system shown in the Quick Start. Setting start dates adds enormous power to your ability to manage tasks. Here are the two main advantages to putting a start date on all tasks:

▶ To tell you when to *first start considering* the task, so you can schedule it to appear on your task list at about the right time.

▶ To support something I call the FRESH Prioritization approach to Opportunity Now (Normal priority) tasks, by showing how *old* the task has become.

I'll talk about the first of these immediately next. The FRESH Prioritization technique is addressed in its own section further ahead.

Using Start Dates to Show When to Consider Doing a Task

I wish I could do most tasks immediately when I think of them, and I would, if only I had infinite available time in the day. Why do I like to do tasks immediately? There is an energy associated with a task the moment I think of it that helps define it, that helps me start it, and that helps me complete it. If I put the task off, I lose that momentum. And like many people, I enjoy instant gratification; I want to do it now.

But while *sometimes* I can do tasks as soon as I think of them, *usually* my workday world doesn't support that sort of spontaneity. Rather, I have promises to keep that day, or higher-priority items to do first, so I need to focus on those. Instead I put the new, inspired task on my task list for later action. Or maybe the task was imposed by someone else and I really do not want to do it now, so I mark it for later action. On the task list I indicate approximately when I hope or intend to get to it. Sometimes it's later today, but often it is some later day or week.

By "when I hope or intend to get to it," I usually mean the day I want to consider doing it, or first start thinking about doing it. Wording it that way recognizes this: I am not committing to doing it on that day. It's not that I am afraid of commitments. Rather, I feel commitments should be used only with true deadlines. I don't make a firm commitment on a task like this because I know I cannot "do it all." I know I'll always think of more to do than I can do, I will always bite off more than I can chew. Or new emergencies will arise that reorder my priorities. I expect your world is like that as well. As professionals and dynamic individuals, that is natural to us. And as a result, you will often be delaying nondeadline tasks to later, as other more important or more inspired items drop in ahead of them. I feel it is okay to delay tasks without hard deadlines. Priorities and inspirations change and you should react accordingly to the new priorities. Feel no regrets when you delay such a task (again, I'll discuss how to schedule tasks with true hard deadlines in a moment; these are treated differently in this system).

So from now on when you create a task, think of approximately when you would like to consider doing the task, and write that in the Start Date field. If it's today, then just put today's date in the Start Date field. I find that for most new tasks I set the start date to today. (I do that out of hope and enthusiasm to get to them soon; but I often change that date later.) Luckily, Outlook automatically populates today in the Start Date field of all tasks you create manually, so this works out well. If I do not get to it today, it will still be on the list tomorrow.

And if you set a future start date on the task, due to Lesson 3 settings it will be hidden until that date arrives. Then when you work your tasks that day you will weigh it against the other things on your list and see if, given the shifting priorities and urgencies of the day, it makes sense to do it. If not, it will forward on to the next day.

Don't Use the Outlook Due Date Field in MYN

Unfortunately, there is a poorly designed feature in Outlook that impacts all MYN users and prevents us from using the Outlook Due Date field. Let's do an exercise together to demonstrate this. Create a new task in Outlook and enter today's date in the Start Date field. You should notice that after you enter it, Outlook automatically populates the Due Date field with the same value. Next, try setting that Due Date field back to None, and notice doing that clears the Start Date field. In other words, the Start Date and Due Date fields are inextricably linked in all Outlook tasks. If you populate one, you must populate the other.

The reason this does not work for MYN users is that MYN users set start dates on *all* tasks, so with the auto-populating Due Date field, it appears that all the tasks have deadlines, which we know is not true. There is no way to tell if the contents of the Due Date field were set by you or set automatically. As a result, the Due Date field is unusable for MYN users as a way to set deadlines, and unfortunately, we must ignore the contents of the Due Date field from now on.

Another reason to ignore it is this: If you change the start date of a task, the due date changes by the same number of days. Let's say you set the Start Date field of a new task to Tuesday, and the Due Date field to its actual deadline of Friday. Then when Tuesday comes let's say you decide you are too busy with other things, so you want to hide the task until Thursday, when you know you'll have more time. If you change the Start Date field to Thursday to hide it until then, behind the scenes Outlook changes the Due Date field to Sunday (also two days later). You will now miss your Friday deadline!

So do *not* use the Outlook Due Date field to set deadlines. I'll show you other ways to set deadlines. In the meantime, just ignore the contents of the Outlook Due Date field.

The Growing Opportunity Now Tasks List

In an environment with constantly changing priorities, it is likely that when you try to work items on your Opportunity Now task list (the Normal section in Outlook), other urgent events may take over part or much of your day and you will not get many done, and that is okay. In our Lesson 3 configurations, tasks not completed automatically forward to the next day. This is expected; it happens a lot in real life, so it is an important design element in this system. That's why it is best to think of the start date not as the day you *must* do the task, but rather the day you want to *first consider* doing the task, knowing that it is likely to forward on after it appears. Again, this is not primarily a guilt-driven system (such systems usually don't work).

Of course, as uncompleted tasks remain on your list from day to day, and you add new tasks each day, your list will grow. Particularly after you start converting action e-mails to tasks, your list will grow very rapidly. You will quickly reach a list size that is larger than what you can possibly consider in a given day. And that is good, to a point. It is good because you want your Opportunity Now list to be a reasonably large-size list of tasks that you can pick from with your business intuition about what is best to do that day. Having a choice like that increases the likelihood that you are picking the highest-priority things to do that day. This works well as a way to allow you to get the most important work done each day, by having your prioritized list of top *candidate* tasks visible at all times and reviewed daily.

Keep the Opportunity Now List to 20 or Fewer Tasks

But you do not want your Opportunity Now list to get *too* large. If you have too many tasks there, you will not scan the whole list every day and some important tasks may get dropped. And you may find the large size demoralizing. You need to keep the size of that list reasonable enough that it is not impossible to review and consider in one brief scan. I have found 20 tasks is the ideal upper limit for an Opportunity Now list.

Prioritize by Keeping Your Opportunity Now List at a Reasonable Size

So that raises a question. After I reach 20 items do I stop adding tasks? No, absolutely not. You have to keep moving forward in business and in life, keep the momentum of new ideas and passions going. So instead of stopping new tasks and ideas, you now need to start prioritizing your current and new tasks so that the 20 items left on your Opportunity Now list are your *best* ones, given current work priorities. You need to shorten it back down to 20 or so. Comprehensive strategies to keep it at about 20 are discussed in Lesson 9 about Strategic Deferrals. A simple approach to use now is this: Delete, Delegate, Defer.

Deleting Tasks

If a task has lost all life, certainly delete it. But don't spend a lot of time fretting over whether it is dead or not. If you cannot decide, keep it. I do not delete tasks unless I am confident they are dead.

Delegating Tasks

Obviously, if you have staff or team members to delegate to and can do so, take advantage of them as a way to lighten your workload and reduce your effort on tasks. But note this, you still need to track delegated tasks and you are ultimately responsible for them, so delegating does not really remove an entry from your list, it just reduces the amount of work you need to expend on it. Techniques for tracking delegated tasks are discussed in Lesson 10.

Deferring by Converting Tasks to Over-the-Horizon Tasks

Using the "Low" Priority Section

The primary form of deferral to use at this point in your studies is to convert tasks to Over-the-Horizon tasks for periodic review as a group. In the first edition of this book I instructed readers to use a *master tasks list* to do that. As you will see in Lesson 9, I now teach a number of other processes to accomplish the same goals that are much better. But before you get there, for now, I want you to use the *Low priority section* of the MYN task list to store tasks that you do not need to think about for a while, tasks without a specific future action date. Referring to Lesson 1, this is the same as tossing the tasks over the Now Horizon. And you'll see in Lesson 9 this is pretty close to the remainder of the Strategic Deferral process, but not quite. This is simpler and sufficient for now.

Over-the-Horizon Task Process

Here is how you do this. When your Normal priority list (the Opportunity Now list) exceeds 20 tasks, identify tasks in the that section that you do not need to think about again for a week or more, and move them down to the Low priority section. Due to the FRESH Prioritization system, described ahead, these are likely the tasks at the bottom of your Normal priority section.

Then, once each week review the Low priority list to see if anything in that section has escalated and now needs greater attention. If it does, move it back up to the Normal or High section. This means that the Low priority section should be *reserved* for longer-term tasks like this. Don't put tasks you intend to work today or this week there.

This process should serve you well for a while, but it is really a temporary solution. Eventually the Low priority section will become too large to easily review weekly. No worries. In Lesson 9 you'll replace this process with an approach that easily handles a virtually unlimited number of tasks.

Deferring Tasks: Setting Task Start Dates in the Future (Simplified)

As I just demonstrated, moving tasks to the Over the Horizon section is our main way of deferring tasks and shortening the Opportunity Now list. But another way to defer tasks is to keep them in the Opportunity Now section and schedule them in the future.

This works because a key part of the system configurations you made in Lesson 3 is this: If you set a start date in the future on a task, the task will disappear from the MYN tasks list and remain out of sight until that date arrives. This is a great way to keep your Now Tasks list small, focused, and doable. Schedule in the future those tasks that you can postpone to a day best suited to work on them. The task will appear at its appropriate date. I call this a Defer-to-Do task, and it is covered completely in the "Strategic Deferral" section of Lesson 9. For now, a simplified version of this is to set the start date ahead for any task you know is best worked on a *specific* future date, keeping the priority at Normal (or High if it *must* be done on that future date). Change the start date by editing the date in the Start Date field.

Windows: Viewing Future-Dated Tasks

When you defer a number of tasks, you might want to view what's coming in the future occasionally. Unfortunately, you can't see them by clicking a future date on the mini-calendar above the To-Do Bar—that does not change the tasks displayed (in 2007/10 that takes you to the calendar view, and in 2013 that changes the appointments preview list). Instead, if you want to see future-dated tasks, there are two methods.

One is go to the Tasks folder and sort on Due Date by clicking Due Date in the header. This forces tasks with future due dates to the top. You can see all tasks there, and the due date is usually equal to the start date, so this is a good estimate. However, it is not entirely accurate and the view is a bit messy, so I provide instructions for a custom view in Lesson 12 that is better and uses the Start Date field. It's called MYN All Now Tasks.

Note: For now, if you know how to add fields, feel free to add the Start Date field to the default Tasks folder view that's called Simple List.

Another way to see future tasks that are not too far in the future is to activate and use the Daily Task List, which sits below the week view in the Calendar. (To activate it, use the View menu or tab, Daily Task List, Normal.) It's good for glancing ahead at future tasks when you're in the week view, but don't try to use it for today's tasks—that part of the list is not sorted correctly for MYN. I discuss the Daily Task List in detail at the end of Appendix A.

Mac: Viewing Future-Dated Tasks

On the Mac, the way to see future-dated tasks is to simply click on the Tasks icon in the Navigation Pane above the Smart Folders section. Then sort on the Start Date field by clicking the heading of that column.

Why the Underlined Tasks in Windows Outlook

When a deferred task's start date arrives and it appears on your list, it appears at the top of its priority section and in Windows Outlook it is *under-lined*. This is a result of the configurations you did in Lesson 3, when you stipulated that all tasks with a start date of today should be underlined. One reason for that configuration is this: When a deferred task pops into your list, you might not notice it. By underlining all tasks with a start date of today, you are more likely to notice a deferred task that pops in fresh that day. There is another reason for that underlining rule, and that is to indicate Target Now Tasks, an optional feature I will describe in Lesson 9.

Don't Defer Too Many "High" or "Normal" Tasks

You do not want to defer all excess tasks to the future as High or Normal (medium) priority tasks, as they will just catch up with you then and load up your Now Tasks list again. Reserve this approach only for tasks that have a fairly firm day when they will become important or more easily done. That won't be too many. So instead, use the Over the Horizon setting—the Low priority setting—as your primary way to defer lower-priority tasks.

Summary of Managing Your Now Task List

Here is a summary of the steps you will take as you add to and edit your Now Tasks list.

▶ Place only those tasks on the Now Tasks list (the High and Normal priority sections) that you could consider working on now. That usually means tasks with a deadline of today (High priority, Critical Now tasks) and tasks you would like to consider working but know you may not get to for up to ten days (Normal priority, Opportunity Now tasks).

▶ If the Now Tasks list (the High and Normal priority list) gets too large, try deleting or delegating first. If that is not possible, move tasks without specific future action dates (probably most of them) that you can put off for a week or more to the Low priority section (just reset the priority; they will move automatically). Do that until you have five or fewer High priority tasks, and 20 or fewer Normal priority tasks.

▶ Defer any tasks with logical specific future dates by setting the start date to the future.

▶ Review Critical Now tasks every hour or so. Review Opportunity Now tasks at least once a day. And review the Low priority section once a week.

Moving excess tasks to the Low priority section is also a key part of the FRESH Prioritization approach, covered next.

The FRESH Prioritization System

Prioritizing within the Opportunity Now Section

High priority or Critical Now (must-do-today) tasks always take precedence and presumably are completed each day, so they do not tend to build up. In contrast, Normal (medium) priority tasks (also called Opportunity Now tasks) are discretionary and *do* tend to build up from day to day, and that's okay as long as you keep that list to about 20 tasks total, using the techniques I just described. But even with a list of 20, you probably need a way to indicate which ones are most important so you know which ones to do first. And if you let your list grow longer, you definitely want to prioritize it (so you know which ones to *remove* first). That is where the FRESH Prioritization system comes in—to prioritize the Normal priority or Opportunity Now section of your task list with a system that keeps newer, fresher, more energized tasks at the top of your list. The word FRESH spells out this approach: Fresh Requests Earn Sorting Higher. More on that ahead.

As you will see, the FRESH Prioritization system is nearly automatic; there is very little for you to do. But it is one of the things that make the system usable and successful day after day, week after week. It's also one of the things that help keep this system from being guilt-driven. Let me show you how it works by first discussing an older way of tracking to-do's.

The Advantage of a Paper Journal To-Do List

You've probably seen or even used one of those paper journal to-do list systems in which you use a new page at the start of each day, and list your latest tasks on that page. As you start to list your tasks each day, you may even flip back a few pages and copy forward some of the more important incomplete older tasks. But you do not copy *all* your older tasks forward because you know you can flip back in the pages and find the lower-priority ones later. Because of that, the old tasks you lose interest in "disappear;" that is, in your mind they fade into the old pages of the journal. As a result, those systems are essentially self-cleaning—the page you look at today has a relatively short list, and the tasks on that list tend to be your most recent and energetic tasks. This is a good thing.

Older Tasks Are Usually Less Relevant

In contrast, as I have stated earlier in the book, nearly all computer to-do list systems place the *oldest* tasks at the top of the list. But those tend to be dead, unconnected to recent priorities, and guilt laden. And while a case might be made that *if you wrote it down you should do it, even if it is old*, that is not how you, as a dynamic individual, really work. Rather, as a professional and busy person, you know by now that you will never get it all done—that you or your boss will always think of more to do than you can possibly do. You know that many of things you wrote down last month, or even last *week*, are no longer very important.

Why do many tasks decrease in importance so quickly? Because you live in an environment with constantly shifting priorities, interests, and preferences. This abundance of new things and changing priorities is a good thing. It keeps life dynamic, interesting, and active (and as an employee it keeps you employed).

Your newer tasks tend to reflect those latest priorities and interests. You advance beyond old ideas quickly, so your older tasks tend to become less meaningful. One way to say this is that *the half-life of a task is very short*, and you need to recognize that.

Two Roles of the Start Date in MYN

Given this is how we work, if you are using a computer system that emphasizes old tasks, and not the newer and more energetic ones, you are likely to give up and switch back to paper. So we want a computerized approach that mimics the advantages of paper. That's what FRESH Prioritization does. How? By using the Outlook Start Date field to sort newer tasks higher and older tasks lower. In Lesson 3, you configured the task list such that older tasks sort lower in each group. In other words, if you did those configurations, FRESH Prioritization is already in place.

The start date really has *two* roles in MYN. Remember, in the MYN system the start date, if in the future, is used to determine when the task appears on your list. This is one important role of the start date—to schedule tasks to the future by hiding them. That behavior is made possible by the *filter* settings you made in Lesson 3.

However, after a start date arrives and a task shows up on your Now Tasks list, or when you enter a new task with today's date, the start date's role completely changes. Now the date's purpose is to show, as tasks age, how *old* the task is and to allow older tasks to be sorted lower in your list. That behavior is made possible by the *sorting* settings you made in Lesson 3. These are the two roles of the start date in the MYN system.

It's this second role of the start date that implements FRESH Prioritization. By sorting the older visible tasks lower in the Normal (medium) priority section you end up directing most of your attention to your newer tasks, the ones at the top of the list. This keeps the task list fresh, energized, and relevant to your latest priorities, just like the paper journal systems I described a moment ago. But doing this in Outlook is better than using paper because you have all the advantages of a computerized list: You can copy e-mails to tasks, see your to-do's synchronized on mobile devices, easily reprioritize items, and so on.

You Can Promote Older Tasks

When using FRESH Prioritization, older tasks scroll lower in the list. If your list is long, they eventually scroll off the page and out of sight. You could stop prioritizing at that step if you really wanted, working from the top of your list down. But some of those old tasks are probably still important, and some might even become more important than your newer tasks. So as part of the system, I ask you to scan your whole list every day, and if you see anything important that has scrolled too low, set the start date back to a recent date. That will move it back to near the top. In other words, feel free to promote old tasks if needed, using the start date as the mechanical way to do that.

Note that even after prioritizing a task higher, as new tasks are added, it starts to drift down again. That's a good thing. It causes you to re-ask how important that old task is. In other words older tasks need to *earn* their position near the top of your list—you must continue to promote them to keep them there. Otherwise, newer tasks take precedence. Eventually you might decide to move an older task to the Over-the-Horizon tasks list (the Low priority section), especially if you have 20 items that seem more important in the Normal priority section.

This system allows the task list that you look at daily to be time-tested as to its real value. This also serves as a reminder to strictly adhere to that 20-item limit. If your Opportunity Now list reaches 30, 40, or even more tasks, you are unlikely to do the type of daily reprioritization I recommend.

Keep a Date-Sorted Task List

There is one thing you need to do to support this FRESH Prioritization approach. You need to ensure that your MYN task list remains *date sorted*, with newest start dates at top (as shown in Figure 4.1). Unfortunately, this sorting is easy to mess up, especially in Outlook 2011. All you need to do is accidentally click the task list header bar and the sorting is gone.

To demonstrate, try this: Click the Start Date label in the task list header, and notice that the sorting reverses, with oldest dates on top, within a given priority group. What this demonstrates is how easy it is to undo the MYN sorting on the Outlook task lists.

To fix misplaced sorting, click Start Date in the header once; that will re-sort the list. You might need to click a second time to ensure that the newest dates are at top. You can do that on any list in Windows Outlook. But on the Mac, if you have not updated your copy of Outlook 2011, due to an old bug you may need to click on the main Tasks icon first and then click the Start Date column heading to sort it.

In Windows, one way to determine, at a glance, if your sorting is correct is to notice whether your underlined tasks are at the top of each section (as shown in Figure 4.1). If not, the sorting is off, and you should fix it by clicking the Start Date field heading. You will get in the habit of noticing this, and after a while you will make a habit of avoiding stray clicks on the task list header bar. Also ensure that the High priority group is always at the top. If it is not, click on the black exclamation point in the task list header.

Managing Deadlines

How to Indicate Tasks with True Hard Deadlines

As discussed earlier, most small, next-step tasks do not have hard deadlines. They are intermediate steps to larger goals or projects, and it's those larger end points where the deadlines usually reside. And short of making a formal project plan, say in Microsoft Project, which maps out detailed task dependencies and dates for each, I have not found much value in trying to identify firm deadlines for small independent next-step tasks. The start date system described above usually works best.

But occasionally a task needs to be entered on your list that does have a firm deadline. How should you show that? Well, as you now know, the Due Date field is useless in MYN, so we need to use other ways. Luckily, there are quite a few other ways to indicate deadlines in MYN.

Five Ways to Indicate Hard Deadlines in MYN

I teach five alternate methods to indicate hard deadlines. Pick one or more that works best for you and each task.

1. **Set Priority to High.** If the deadline is today, just set the Priority field to High. After all, the definition of a High priority task in this system is that the task must be done today—no deadline date is needed. Also note, if the deadline is in the future and you do not need to start work on it till that day, set the start date to the future and mark the task's priority to High. It will be hidden until that date arrives, and then it will pop into the High priority section, indicating it is due today.

2. **Put Deadline in Subject Line.** If the deadline is some day in the future, but you want to start work on it before the deadline day (say, you want to see it on your task list starting today), then you should enter today's date in the Start Date field—that makes the task visible today. But you cannot set it to a High priority as in the first method—that would imply it is due today. Instead, set the priority to Normal and enter the deadline day or date at the beginning of the text in the subject line with the word DUE in all caps. So, for example, if a final year-end report is due Friday of this week, enter "DUE FRI Final Year-End Report." If due more than a week out, enter the date itself like this: "DUE Dec 29 Final Year-End Report" as shown in the next figure. Set the start date to today so you can start working on it now. In this sample the start date is December 19.

> ☑   **DUE Dec 29 Final Year-End Report**   19-Dec-12

By definition, these will be in the Opportunity Now list, and because you will be checking that complete list daily, you will notice the DUE tasks each day. On the day they are due, if not completed yet, move the task to the High priority section to ensure that you complete it that day. This is one reason it makes sense to review your Opportunity Now list in the morning, so that you have time to react to deadlines like this when they arrive.

Note: *One word of caution, use the word DUE only if the date is a true deadline; not if the date is merely a soft deadline or a preferred date. You do not want to get into a Cry Wolf routine and end up watering down the meaning of the word DUE, because you might start ignoring it.*

Although typing a deadline in the title of the task might seem like a rather low-tech method, this is the deadline method I routinely use. It works surprisingly well as a way to keep the deadline in sight. If the deadline is this week or early next, this should be all you need to do. However, if the deadline is farther out, do this *and* consider adding the following method.

3.   **Add Duplicate Task.** Occasionally, using the previous method alone can be problematic, especially if the deadline is several weeks or more away. That's because that task might scroll off the bottom of the task list and out of sight as newer tasks are added on top, and you might miss the actual deadline if you don't review the whole list each day. So in cases of long-term deadlines, in addition to doing option 2, try adding this optional bit of insurance: Create a duplicate task with the Start Date field set to the deadline date, and the Priority field set to High.

Here's how you would do that using the example in the option 2. First, create the task as described in that option. Second, copy that task and change the start date to the deadline date (Dec 29) and set the Priority field to High. This second task causes a task to pop into your Critical Now section on the day of the deadline. It's a fallback in case you lose track of the first task.

Note: *In case the task has a lot of text or attachments and you do not want to create it from scratch again, in Windows Outlook there is a quick way to create a duplicate task in the To-Do Bar: right-click and drag the original task from the To-Do Bar to the Tasks icon on the left side of your Outlook window. Choose Copy from the shortcut menu that pops up when you drop it. You'll see the duplicate task appear in the To-Do Bar.*

4. **Add Deadline Column.** The above three options, used together, are sufficient for the rare times that you need to set deadlines. But if you tend to have a lot of next-action tasks with deadlines, the above actions will start to feel like a lot of steps, particularly having to create duplicate tasks. In that case, Windows Outlook users should consider adding the optional Deadline column to the To-Do Bar, following my instructions in Lesson 12 in the section "The To-Do Bar Deadline Column." This field does not have the problems of the Due Date field. Here is how that looks after it is added.

🗋 !	Task Subject	Start Date	Deadline	🏴
⊿ Priority: High (2 items)				
🗓 !	Add to 1MTD full link	6-Jun-13	6-Jun-13	🏴
🗓 !	Send invoice for deposit to R L	18-Apr-13	None	🏴
⊿ Priority: Normal (9 items)				
🗓	screenshot event	6-Jun-13	6-Jun-13	🏴

This makes life much simpler, but I recommend only adding the Deadline column if you have many true deadlines, because it occupies valuable screen real estate. Unfortunately, Mac users cannot add this field.

5. **Place on Calendar.** If the deadline is a major one, you might want to place the task as an entry on your Outlook calendar so that it stands out more. You can do this one of two ways. Make it an all-day, nonblocking appointment (at the top of the appointment box set the Show As field to Free). This causes it to sit at the top of the day for that day on the Outlook calendar, but it doesn't block your entire day for other appointments. For an example, see the following Finish Quarterly Report task.

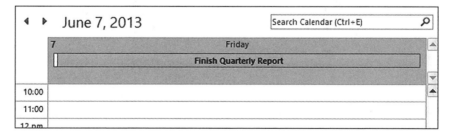

Alternatively, if you think you might need an hour or two of final action to finish the task, schedule it as a two-hour *blocking* appointment during business hours on your calendar. That way you have time locked in for final actions. Feel free to use an Outlook reminder on these appointments.

If the source of the task is an e-mail, you can convert an e-mail directly into a calendar item by dragging it to the Calendar icon or label in the lower-left corner of the Outlook window.

These are the best ways to indicate hard deadlines for Outlook tasks when you use the MYN system. Do *not* use the Outlook Reminder feature on tasks to mark such deadlines. It's okay to use reminders on appointments as mentioned in the fifth option. In the next section we'll look at reasons why.

Do Not Use Reminders on Outlook Tasks

You may be tempted to use the Reminder capability of Outlook tasks to emphasize their deadlines. It is good to use Outlook reminders on Outlook calendar *appointments* but not on Outlook *tasks*. They cause problems when used with tasks. That's why in Lesson 3, I suggest you confirm that the default reminders setting for new tasks is turned off.

Reminders cause an alert window to pop up on your computer screen on a specified day at a specified time. "What could be wrong with that?" you might ask. Well, while reminders work well on Outlook appointments, here's the problems they cause with tasks:

▶ The reminder date is unstable in the same way that the due date is unstable. How? If you later change the start date, the reminder date changes by the same interval, and you might miss your deadline. As you recall, I encourage you to change the start date frequently as a way to prioritize Now Tasks. So if you use task reminders, you might miss a lot of deadlines.

▶ The reminder feature is not the right approach anyway. Reminders should only be for time-of-day-specific items like appointments. The idea behind using a task list is that items on that list should be worked when the right moment, energy, situation, people, and so on, present themselves in the day. Having an alert pop up in the middle of other activities does not make that moment the right time to do the task. It is likely that you will ignore it anyway. At a minimum, the reminder distracts you from other things you might be doing. Instead, examine your High priority list often, perhaps hourly, and work your tasks off your list. If an activity is very time sensitive, make an appointment out of it, and set a reminder on the appointment, as in option 5 above.

■　■　■

Summary: Your Task Management Steps

This lesson explained the theory and practice of how you should manage tasks in the days ahead, now that you have configured your MYN task list following the MYN System principles. Let's put this all together into a clear set of steps and rules. These steps are copied in Appendix C.

From now on, as you create tasks in your task list, from e-mail or other sources, do this:

1. Assign a High and Normal priority only to tasks you must do or would consider doing now. These are your Now Tasks. Give must-do-today tasks a High priority (your Critical Now tasks), and all other tasks a Normal (medium) priority (your Opportunity Now tasks).

2. Set the Start Date field of all new tasks to today or to a future day you would like to start seeing the task on your MYN task list. If it is in the future, the task will not appear on your list till that day. Do not leave any tasks with a start date of None.

3. Do not set Outlook reminders on tasks (*do* set them on appointments if the task is time-of-day sensitive).

4. Keep the High priority (Critical Now) list to five or fewer items. Work those tasks early, and complete all your High priority (Critical Now) tasks by end of day.

5. If a task has a future deadline, but you'd like to start work on it before that deadline, set the start dater earlier, use a Normal priority, and enter DUE and the deadline date in front of the task title. Or use the Deadline field taught in Lesson 12 instead.

6. Review your Critical Now tasks about once an hour. Review your Opportunity Now tasks once a day (morning is best).

7. When reviewing your Normal priority (Opportunity Now tasks) section, if you find tasks near the bottom of the list that are important, and so need to be promoted in the list, set their start dates to a date near today. This moves them to near the top of the list. This is part of the FRESH Prioritization approach.

8. Keep the Opportunity Now section of your MYN task list no larger than about 20 items. If it gets much larger than 20, first try deleting or delegating. If that is not possible, set some tasks to a future date you really intend to do them, or better, move tasks to the Low priority section by setting their Outlook priority to Low. This is the same as tossing them over the Now Horizon as described in Lesson 1. Review your Low priority section once a week in case any tasks there become more important over time.

That's it! You have learned the core task management principles of the Master Your Now! system. Follow these principles and you will find your workday starting to come under control.

Exercises

Create in your To-Do Bar five types of tasks as described below, paying attention in particular to start date and priority, and whether a deadline is needed.

1. Enter a task you would like to start today (but that has no deadline).

2. Enter a task absolutely due today.

3. Enter a task you would like to start working on tomorrow (no deadline).

4. Enter a task you would like to start working on next Wednesday and that is absolutely due next Wednesday

5. Enter a task absolutely due next Wednesday that you'd like to start working on today.

Exercise Solutions

1. Enter a task you would like to start today: *Start Date equals today, Normal priority, no deadline needed.*

2. Enter a task absolutely due today: *Start Date equals today, High priority.*

3. Enter a task you would like to start working on tomorrow: *Start Date equals tomorrow, Normal priority.*

4. Enter a task you would like to start working on next Wednesday and that is absolutely due next Wednesday: *Start Date equals Wednesday, High priority.*

5. Enter a task absolutely due next Wednesday that you'd like to start working on today: *Set Start Date field to today, Normal priority, and then indicate a deadline in one of several ways: Enter "DUE Wed" at beginning of subject line, and optionally, create a duplicate task with Start Date equal to next Wednesday, High priority. Or, use the Deadline field added in Lesson 12. Or place the task as an appointment on your calendar for next Wednesday (and set a reminder).*

Next Steps

Start entering tasks in Outlook now, both by converting e-mails to tasks (as taught at the end of Lesson 2) and by entering them manually, say from tasks received in meetings. If you have task lists from an older paper system, start copying them into the Outlook task system now. In general, I encourage you to use the MYN task list as your main to-do list from now on; you have learned all the basics.

One more thing. This lesson contains more core principles of MYN task management than any other in this book. As such, it is worthy of periodic review. At minimum, periodically reread the Summary section. I recommend you put a Normal priority task on your list right now for that, and set a start date on it for a relatively close future date. That itself is good practice for the principles in the chapter.

In the next lesson, I will focus on e-mail and on how to empty your Inbox.

Lesson 5:
The Bliss of an Empty Inbox

Introduction

I am about to describe an action whose benefits are almost magical. I say magical because whenever I do it, I cannot really explain why it works so well, but it always leaves me in awe. This magical thing is emptying my Outlook Inbox. Even today, every time I do it, I am left feeling amazed. Amazed at what a difference it makes. Amazed at the refreshed feeling I experience each time, the reduction in Inbox stress, and at my resulting eagerness to move forward with my work and even to get new e-mail.

All that joy really does not make sense. After all, all I am doing is dragging a group of e-mails en masse from one folder to another. I usually don't even classify or file it into different folders. I really haven't done anything with that mail other than having previously extracted tasks from it when I first read it, and making one last scan of titles to ensure that I didn't miss anything.

And yet a remarkable change occurs as soon as I drag the mail. All the tension and uncertainty associated with e-mail I've been getting all day instantly disappears. Questions like Have I read it all? Did I forget to reply to anyone? Is there a time bomb in here? Am I leaving something undone? All those are gone when I glance at my empty or near-empty Inbox. It clears my psyche by clearing one big block of my day's open ends.

That is such a refreshing feeling, to know there is nothing lurking in there. Emptying your Inbox (after extracting tasks) provides that very clear, almost symbolic statement: "I am done with this e-mail, and I can move on."

Note: *This lesson is summarized in video 16 of the MYN-Outlook Complete Video Training (see beginning of the Quick Start chapter for more information).*

The Real Purpose of the Inbox

There is some history here. There is a reason why Microsoft called the place where Outlook stores your incoming mail the "Inbox." You may recall the old two- or three-level tray systems office workers used on their desks to process incoming paper mail. Some still do. While these systems varied, they were often box shaped and made out of wood, and the top box was always called the "In Box" or "In Tray." The meaning of this top box was simple: It was where new, unprocessed paper mail and memos were placed. And the rules of most of the systems were this: As soon as you picked up and read an item from the In Tray, it never went back to the In Tray. Rather, it was filed, or disposed of, or placed in one of the lower boxes indicating that the item was "in process" or "ready to be filed." There was great value to these systems and they generally worked well if you knew how to use them.

This idea of using the Outlook Inbox in a similar way, as a place only to receive new unread items, has unfortunately been lost by most users of e-mail. The Inbox now not only has that receiving function but has also become the place to store previously read "in-process" mail that you have additional actions in mind for, as well as being a bulk filing location for old mail. No wonder the Inbox has become so useless for so many people. You just cannot mix all these functions together and hope to make sense of your e-mail.

Don't Use Your Inbox as a Task Management System

Of the misuses described in the previous section, the worst one is leaving e-mail with to-do's in your Inbox, saying to yourself "I'll come back to that later." But *later* usually never comes, and those unreconciled action e-mails actually jam your Inbox, preventing you from emptying it. Instead, convert those e-mails to tasks, and get them out of your Inbox immediately. As for e-mails with no actions inside, after you determine that, move those out as well.

As I stated in Lesson 1, you really want to get the Outlook Inbox back to the receiving-only function; otherwise your Inbox becomes hopelessly cluttered. A cluttered Inbox represents a congestion of unattended responsibilities. Emptying the Outlook Inbox every day using MYN relieves that congestion in a very noticeable way. It also makes you more efficient, because without clearing your Inbox you'll be constantly glancing through old mail in search of passed over to-do's and unfiled information. Emptying your Inbox helps prevent responsibilities buried in e-mail items from getting away from you. It saves you time because it allows you to clearly delineate between the mail that needs further processing and mail which you no longer need to read.

Note: Having less mail in your Inbox also helps when later using a mobile device, because it synchronizes faster and leaves you less mail to scroll through when finding new mail.

Like an Emergency Waiting Room

One way to highlight the proper role of the inbox in any e-mail system is to compare it to the waiting area of a hospital's emergency room, the ER. If you were the administrator in charge of the ER, you wouldn't leave 400 to 1,000 people in the room, all in various states of health. Rather, you'd want to triage them quickly, and then move them to the appropriate parts of the hospital for the right attention. Otherwise, you'd be continually revisiting waiting patients and asking them, "Tell me again, why are you here?" Some patients with serious conditions might get much worse as you waste time circling the room. Someone could even die. Triage them once and then move them.

In the same way, consistently rehashing and rereading hundreds of mail messages in your inbox leads to wasted time and dropped important items. That's also why it leads to so much stress. Instead, use your inbox as a triage area to scan your mail once, make a quick decision on what to do with it, and then move the mail out of your inbox immediately.

Four Ways to Maintain an Empty Inbox

After you've converted an e-mail to a task, or decided it has no task, there are four ways to remove it from your Outlook Inbox and maintain an empty Inbox daily. I cover only one of these in this lesson.

▶ The first is to toss it all. This most likely is not an option for you, but I mention it for completeness and because for many people it is a partial solution.

▶ The second is to do what most people who file do, and that is to distribute mail among multiple topic-named Outlook folders. It is neat, logical, and matches what we do when we file physical papers in manila file folders. But as you'll see in Lesson 8, it is a problematic solution.

▶ The third is to file all mail out of your Inbox in one bulk folder, and either ignore topics or optionally apply topic-like tags (called Outlook Categories) to the mail in that location. Doing the first part of this is the focus of this lesson. The latter I save for Lesson 8.

▶ The fourth is a combination of some or all of the previous three points.

Focus on Filing in Bulk

In this lesson, I am only going to teach you the third of these methods, and only the first part of that: how to file in bulk. I feel this is the simplest and most practical way to empty your Inbox. Filing in bulk is a method that nearly everyone can do, and it is the quickest way to maintain your Inbox near empty every day. It also can be combined with topic filing into multiple folders, the method that many of you are doing now. In Lesson 8, I'll show you a different topic approach that uses topic-named Outlook Categories added to the bulk-filed mail. But that comes later. The very first step is simple: Empty your Inbox every day, and declutter your life.

If You Are Already Filing Mail Successfully

If you have an existing filing system and it is working for you, *and you are emptying your Inbox every day,* you can skip the rest of this lesson and begin reading Lesson 6. You should be proud that you have mastered this and you should stick with it — there is no need to change.

Unfortunately though, many people with seemingly good filing systems find it nearly impossible to empty their Outlook Inboxes daily, usually because their filing systems are too slow. So if you are unable to empty your Inbox every day with your filing system, I encourage you to give this new approach a try. The benefits of achieving that empty Inbox every day are just too good to pass up.

A Very Simple System: Drag All Mail to the Processed Mail Folder

A Simple Solution

The first step of the Master Your Now! (MYN) e-mail filing system, the step covered in this lesson, is so simple it is almost silly. Create one folder called Processed Mail. Then, after you have extracted tasks from your mail and read or replied to those you want to, drag each mail item from your Inbox to that folder. That's it! I'll discuss how to create the folder in the next section.

In its simplest form that really is it; you merely leave all the mail in the Processed Mail folder, and you are done. There are exceptions and complications, of course, which I will mention later in this lesson and in Lesson 8, but they are not so bad. For most users, what I just described — simply dragging all mail to one folder — is all you need to do. It is a very quick and simple system. Now let me explain why this is so powerful.

▶ It's simple and easy to do. It gets you quick results. This ensures that you will do it every day.

▶ After you master using the Outlook search tools (discussed later in this lesson), you can find mail faster than hunting through multiple folders.

▶ When you leave all your old mail in the Processed Mail folder, you have all the benefits of a single date-sorted storage location for your e-mail, just like the Inbox (more on that ahead).

▶ It sets you up well for applying Outlook Categories, covered in Lesson 8.

▶ You can stay ahead of the flow of events in your work. *Nothing* drops through the cracks.

► Best of all, you receive a very positive psychological boost each time you empty your Inbox. That positively impacts your whole day.

Three Other Reasons to File Mail

Let's step back a moment. I have emphasized filing mail out of your Inbox primarily to achieve a clean and refreshed Inbox and to enjoy the benefits of that. Here are three additional reasons to file mail:

► To encourage you to do a final triage of your Inbox at the end of every day. This is important. Just before I file my mail in the Processed Mail folder, I take one last scan of my e-mail titles. I do this to see if I missed anything: when I read new mail on and off during the day it is easy to skip some, and I often do. This scan prevents me from dropping important items, whether task conversions, important replies, scheduling events, or anything else important that might arrive by e-mail. The bliss of an empty Inbox is dependent on that scan, so I make certain to do that scan.

► To solve any space limitations you may be reaching in your Inbox. This is the reason most people want to file or toss mail, and this simple approach makes it easier to do that.

► To make it easy to find the mail you file, if you need to see it again. This is the reason most people get serious about choosing a good filing system; otherwise they would just toss away all their previously read mail. Let's talk more about this point—finding mail after it is filed—as it's a big topic.

Four Ways of Finding Mail After It Is Filed

I am a pack rat—I tend to save nearly all my business e-mail that is clearly not junk. My theory on saving most mail is this: Storage space is much cheaper than the time it takes me to confidently decide that I can throw an e-mail away. Sure, if the mail is obviously spam or junk, I delete it immediately. But if I have any hesitation about tossing a business-related item, I retain the mail and move on. My time is just too valuable, and I suspect yours is too.

This means when I go looking for mail I have quite a bit of mail to sort through. However, with the Processed Mail single-folder system, I can actually *find mail easier*. With this single-folder system, there are four different ways you can find your mail:

1. **Visually.** You can find it the same way you find mail now when you leave it in your Outlook Inbox: visually. One great advantage to the Processed Mail folder system is that it gives you one long list of all your mail, just like the Inbox, so you can visually scan down your e-mail list, searching backward in time. This is not such a bad way to search for mail, particularly for mail less than a month old, which is the mail you

are most likely to search for on any given day. You can use dates and adjacent e-mail titles to reconstruct events and determine approximately when the mail arrived, and usually find it fairly quickly. Or you can sort on the From column (just click the column heading) and search for all mail sent by a sender; that's another way we often search for mail.

The utility of a single list of mail is one reason why I think many people do not file mail out of their Inbox. Even if they want to file it, they unconsciously know leaving it in the Inbox is a pretty good means of keeping recent mail searchable (it is just a bad place to leave mail for other reasons). Losing the power of a single list is also the main reason multiple topic-named folders for filing mail is not my preferred method; they preclude me from doing these sorts of visual one-stop searches (I list other disadvantages of using multiple topic-named folders in Lesson 8).

2. **Using Search Tools.** In addition to doing a visual search, you can use the Outlook search tool on the Processed Mail folder. For all versions of Outlook since 2007, Microsoft has integrated a fully indexed search engine into Outlook (called Instant Search in Windows and Spotlight on the Mac). What this means is that searches can be made blindingly fast. However, you need to be sure that it is fully installed and that its indexes are set appropriately; for many users that is not true (more on that later in this lesson).

3. **Using Folders.** If you are firmly set on using multiple topic-named folders, you can periodically file mail from the Processed Mail folder into those folders. Later you can search visually in those folders. Presumably, you know exactly which folder to go to when you need to look for mail.

4. **Using Categories.** Finally, if you know you need to file by topic, I hope you will consider using the Outlook Categories filing system I teach in Lesson 8 as an alternative to using multiple topic-named folders. With this, you essentially "tag" mail items in the Processed Mail folder with topic-named categories. The categories system allows you to keep all your mail in the Processed Mail folder, thereby maintaining the visual date-based or sender-based searches described in point 1. But it also allows you, when needed, to view all mail in virtual category groups that you can open and close, as if they were in a folder system. And you can store one e-mail item in multiple categories. To view this mail in category groups you merely click the Categories column heading. You will learn all this in Lesson 8.

More on Topic-Based Filing

Of the techniques I just listed for finding mail, two rely on topic-based filing; that is, identifying a keyword to associate each mail item with, and either filing it in a folder with that name or tagging it in a bulk location. But recall that filing by topic is optional. And given the large ratio between the time consumed filing mail by topic and how often you probably search for mail, I think topic-based filing all your mail is of questionable value for most users. Given the power of e-mail search tools, especially the newer ones discussed in the previous sections (and again later in this lesson), I think most people can get by with just dragging all their mail to one folder (the Processed Mail folder) and then using a search tool on it as needed. This saves a huge amount of time, time otherwise spent on topic-categorizing all the mail you get; some people spend an hour a day filing their mail, which just doesn't make sense. And in case you need help with these search tools, I'll show you how to use them at the end of this lesson.

But some people or organizations need topic-based filing. And there are ways to speed up topic-based filing and make it more practical, at least for some of your mail. You can use Outlook rules to automatically tag e-mail with categories based on, for example, sender, subject, or body text keywords. And add-in software can do more intelligent tagging and filing, allowing you to auto-file entire "conversations," for example. All of that I describe in Lesson 8.

And if perhaps you like to store only a small portion of your mail by topic, by all means do that filing either before or after you store the rest of the mail in the Processed Mail folder. That can be a good compromise for those of you who have just a few key topics that need special attention. Again, that too is discussed in Lesson 8.

Completely Empty My Inbox?

When I present this concept in my seminars, I almost always get the question "Do I really completely empty my Inbox? What if I am not done reading a lot of that mail?"

The answer is essentially yes. Completely empty your Inbox. There are a few exceptions (for example, mail flagged for reply, which we discuss more in Lesson 7), but very few. Here's why this works:

► The name of this folder is Processed Mail. That means you've made one pass on the mail to triage it, mainly looking for tasks. After you convert a mail item to a task, why keep it in your Inbox? And when you determine there is no task, you are finished with the first pass on this item, so it's easy to move it out of the folder.

► The folder is not called *Deep Archive* or *Mail I Never Look at Again*. You can easily go in the Processed Mail folder and read some mail more thoroughly. The Processed Mail folder is adjacent to your Inbox, so it's easy to open and restudy recent messages if you need to. I find I do that often.

► After determining there is no task, if you know you want to read an e-mail more, I suggest you tag it with the category name Read Later before moving it to the Processed Mail folder. Later, you can group on that category and catch up reading your mail. This Read Later category makes emptying your Inbox easy. For more details on the Read Later category, see the end of Lesson 8.

For all these reasons, I think you'll find emptying your Inbox each day is easy to do. So let's get started. The first step is to create the new Processed Mail folder.

Emptying Your Inbox—Step 1: Creating the Processed Mail Folder

The first step in emptying your Inbox is deciding where to create the Processed Mail folder. For now I suggest you make it a subfolder of your Inbox so it looks like this:

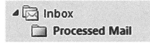

Note: *If you are using Exchange Server with your Outlook, that means this folder is on your server, and you may be tempted to put it instead in a local file to help manage space on your server. But keep in mind, your smartphone or non-Windows tablet cannot see mail that's not on your server, so leaving it on the server is the best plan. You can archive out of it easily, as discussed in Appendix B. And Appendix A presents other location options for the Processed Mail folder.*

Here are the steps to create the folder:

Windows Outlook

1. Go to the Navigation or Folders Pane and click the Mail banner button or icon.

2. Right-click the Inbox.

3. Choose New Folder from the shortcut menu.

4. In the dialog box that opens type "Processed Mail" as the folder name. Leave all other settings as is, and click OK.

Outlook for Mac 2011

1. Go to the Navigation Pane and click the Mail banner button or icon.

2. If you have a small arrow to the left of your Inbox, toggle it so you can see account names or locations below. Find your main account (it's probably the top one) and use it in the next step. If no account names are below the Inbox, then focus on the Inbox itself in the next step.

3. CTRL-click the item in step 2.

4. Choose New Folder from the shortcut menu.

5. A folder is created with the name Untitled selected; replace that with the name "Processed Mail" and press ENTER or RETURN.

Note: *Windows 2007, 2010, and Mac 2011 users, if you have many other Inbox subfold-*
ers, consider placing an underscore in front of the P, to drive it to the top of the list:
"_Processed Mail." Or use some other symbol. This is needed because folders position
alphabetically in the folder list. The exception is with Outlook 2013 – with that ver-
sion you can simply drag folders into the order you wish.

The previous sections showed a quick way to get started with the Processed
Mail folder. For advanced users or those with more time, I invite you to
read a full discussion of Outlook folders in Appendix A. There you will find
complete coverage of strategies for the best place to put your Processed Mail
folder, ones that include getting mail off the Exchange system to beat any
space issues you might have there. But try this quick solution for now and
start emptying your Inbox into the Processed Mail folder following the points
in the sections ahead. I think you will like it. You can always study Appendix
A later. And if you currently have Exchange space issues, see the Note in the
next section; that may work for now.

Next, you need to move mail into this new folder. Here's how.

Step 2: Filing in the New Processed Mail Folder

The workflow for moving mail to the Processed Mail folder follows.

As you read the mail in your Inbox, follow these steps:

1. If the mail is obviously junk, delete it. If not junk, plan to save it; your
   time is too valuable to spend much time deciding.

2. If the mail has an action (or appointment) associated with it, copy it to a
   task (or appointment).

   You saw a quick way to do that at the end of Lesson 2. I cover it more
   fully in Lesson 7. However, if the action is quick (under a minute), such
   as a quick reply, do it now instead. In both cases, immediately file the
   item in the Processed Mail folder

3. If you have read enough of a message to determine it is not a task and it
   needs no reply, then drag the mail to the Processed Mail folder.

4. If an item needs a reply – and you don't have time to reply now – set
   an Outlook flag on it. Then, by end of day or early next, write the reply,
   remove the flag, and drag the item to the Processed Mail folder.

5. (Optional) If you are using Outlook Categories (Lesson 8), apply categories to your mail before dragging it to the Processed Mail folder.

That's it. Your mail is filed and, other than mail flagged for reply, your Inbox
is empty! *Do this every day.* I do it several times a day.

Note: *Because you created the Processed Mail folder as a subfolder of your Inbox, here's an*
important point: If your Exchange mailbox has size limits, you must periodically drag

mail from the bottom of the date-sorted Processed Mail folder to some off-server location. You can create a folder there called something like Old Processed Mail. Do this just as you are doing now for your Inbox. For more information about more complete archive solutions, see Appendix B.

Assuming you do want to use this single-folder filing system (with or without categories), how do you transition from what you are doing now? Let's look at that now.

Transitioning to Using the Processed Mail Folder

From a Multiple-Folder-Based Filing System

If you are already using a multiple-folder-based filing system for e-mail, you may wonder what my recommendations are for transitioning to a single folder–based system. My primary recommendation—start fresh. There is no reason you can't add a Processed Mail folder to your existing multiple-folder system and start using it with mail that is currently in your Inbox. Then retain your current system for the old mail you've already filed. Just try to put the Processed Mail folder near your Inbox, as described in the earlier section, so it is easy to find. Don't bury it among your old folders.

I realize adding it to your existing folders splits your stored mail for a while, but the useful life of most old mail passes quickly. In no time the only old mail that you'll be looking at will be the mail filed in the Processed Mail folder, and your old multifolder-based filing will be a rarely touched system. At some point you'll feel confident to archive that system and refer only to your Processed Mail folder.

That said, you can also move your old folder-filed mail out of those folders and into a Processed Mail folder. However, if you use Exchange, do this only if your old folders are on Exchange Server. Be careful to confirm this, because if your old filed mail is stored *off* Exchange Server, then dragging it to the server-based Processed Mail folder will cause the server to overfill almost immediately. If you feel strongly about consolidating old mail like this, move that mail to the Old Processed Mail folder described in the note in the previous section. The Old Processed Mail folder is not on the server and so is less likely to overfill. But it is better done in conjunction with Outlook Categories, as described in Lesson 8. For more information, see the section "Transitioning to a Categories System" near the end of that lesson.

From No Filing System or From an Overflowing Inbox

If you do not have a filing system (or even if you do and you haven't been using it for a while), chances are good that your Inbox is quite overcrowded with months or even years of old mail—and you'll want to empty it. How do you get started? Do you need to commit to extracting tasks from all of your months of old mail before dragging it to the Processed Mail folder? My answer is no.

Again, what I recommend is to take a fresh start. In this case, I recommend picking a date one week ago and dragging all mail older than that to the Processed Mail folder immediately. Then, commit to processing all mail left in your Inbox into your Processed Mail folder immediately, extracting tasks as you do so. That should only take an hour or two to do. Now you have an empty Inbox! Make a note of that processing cutoff date.

Then, as time allows in the days ahead, dip into the older mail in the Processed Mail folder and extract more tasks, doing at least one entire day at a time. Notice the date on which you stop again each day, so you can start below that the next time you come back to this task.

But doing this additional processing is purely optional. It's likely that embedded tasks older than a few weeks have diminished in importance anyway or have been communicated again.

These steps enable what is most important: emptying your Inbox quickly and extracting tasks, so you can start experiencing the benefits of an empty Inbox. Then empty your Inbox *every day*.

One last point. If you are going to process much of your older mail, you might want to skip ahead and study Lesson 7 completely before spending too much time. There you'll find thorough coverage of all the various ways to convert action e-mails to tasks. Also, study the end of that lesson for more transitioning suggestions. Then come back here and read the next section to see how to *search* your newly filed mail.

Start Emptying Your Inbox into the Processed Mail Folder Now

I cannot emphasize enough how important and powerful it is to empty your Inbox every day. Get started on this today. If after doing that you are eager to include a topic filing system, feel free to skip ahead to Lesson 8 to learn how to use Outlook Categories as your topic-based filing system in the Processed Mail folder. You can also read about other approaches there. Then come back and study the rest of this lesson.

If instead you want to save time and use a search tool approach within the Processed Mail folder (my current favorite method), read on. If you already know how to use the search tools in Outlook and are happy with them, you can skip the remainder of this lesson and move on to Lesson 6.

Using Search Tools with the Processed Mail Folder

We've looked at four ways to find mail after you store it in bulk in the Processed Mail folder. For most of us, using a search tool will be all you need to know. The tools in Windows and Mac Outlook are nearly perfect. So for the rest of this lesson, I am going to describe how to use Outlook search tools: Instant Search (Windows Outlook) and Spotlight (Outlook for Mac 2011).

Using the Windows Outlook Instant Search Tool

Let's start the Windows Outlook Instant Search tool. For Mac users, this section on Windows Outlook is long, so skip ahead to the description for your version.

Outlook Instant Search is the name of the search tool in Windows Outlook. However, you won't see the name Instant Search anywhere in Outlook. You will see the search box above each folder (see Figure 5.1), and you'll see a few search controls in the menus and on the Ribbon. All of that is Instant Search. It's a powerful tool you should learn to use effectively.

Figure 5.1
Outlook 2010 Instant Search box; 2007 and 2013 are similar.

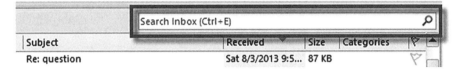

Note: *If you can't find the search box, or if Instant Search is not working correctly in your copy of Outlook, see the section ahead "Troubleshooting Windows Instant Search."*

Getting Started with Windows Outlook Instant Search

In Outlook 2007, the tool sits inconspicuously to the right of the folder name at the top of the current folder contents. You might not even notice it.

In Outlook 2010 and 2013, Instant Search sits above the current folder contents, and depending on how wide your Outlook window is, it can occupy the entire width of that space.

Like all good modern search engines, the tool works by first indexing your mail, which means it builds invisible tables of the locations of every word in every e-mail. (That's why searches are so fast.) Building this table ahead of time takes time though, so when you first install the program, it spends hours indexing in the background. If you save much of your old mail, it can take almost a day to finish. Don't worry, this won't slow your computer significantly, and it automatically stops when you start using the computer. After it is complete, as you add more mail, it indexes only the new mail almost instantly as it comes in. However, if you rearrange all your folders one day, it takes a long time to reindex everything in those new locations.

Using Instant Search for Basic Searches in Windows Outlook

In Outlook 2007 and 2010, when you click inside the search box, the entire folder header lights up in orange, indicating the search tool is ready for you to use (in 2013 clicking in the box just highlights the box). In Outlook 2010 and 2013, after you've clicked in the search box, the Ribbon's Search tab becomes visible and usable for advanced searching; however, ignore that for now. I'll discuss more about that later.

After clicking in the box, type your search term in the box, and depending on the settings (discussed ahead), the results are displayed immediately when you pause typing, or when you click the magnifying glass icon at the right end of the search field, or when you press ENTER. The results *replace* the mail previously displayed in the folder. To clear the results and see all your mail again, click the Close button (x) that replaces the magnifying glass after a search. The orange coloring or highlighting goes away to confirm that you are back to your entire folder contents again.

Narrowing Your Search Results

If all you do is type a word or phrase in the search box, you can get a very wide search with too many hits. That's a problem people often have with Instant Search: They can't find the e-mail they are looking for on the first try because too many items are listed. So they give up. But you can easily narrow the results of the search by using some of the same simple search tricks and commands that are available in most online search engines.

For example, putting quotation marks (" ") around a phrase ensures that you'll get better results. Why do that? Well, you probably know by now that if you enter Tim Jones in the search box, you'll get all e-mail with *Tim* and all e-mail with *Jones*. Typing *"Tim Jones"* gives you e-mails containing only that exact two-word phrase.

Using OR and AND is useful, too. Let's say you are looking for a bill you received, so you want to find e-mails that have either *Accounting* or *Billing* in them. To do that you'd merely type *Accounting OR Billing* in the search box. If you wanted to see e-mails that had *both* terms in the same e-mail, you'd type *Accounting AND Billing*. Later in this lesson. I'll show you even more sophisticated ways to narrow your search with field-based searches. But first, let's look at some ways to change some of the fundamental ways that Instant Search works. Be sure to type OR and AND in all caps.

Changing Search Options

Outlook Instant Search has many settings you can use to alter how it works. You might want to explore these settings to customize how you use the tool. The Search Options dialog box is the best place to start because it has quite a few settings that impact how you search. How you get to that dialog box varies by version.

In Outlook 2007, click once in the Instant Search box and then click the small black drop-down arrow at the right edge of the search box. At the bottom of the drop-down menu you'll see Search Options. Click it.

In Outlook 2010 and 2013, click in the Instant Search box to activate the Search tab on the Ribbon, and then click the Search Tools button at the right end of the tab, as shown in Figure 5.2. At the bottom of the drop-down menu, you'll see Search Options. Click it.

Figure 5.2
Outlook 2010 Search Tools menu and Search Options; 2013 similar.

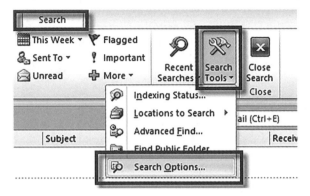

Among the settings in Search Options is a command to turn on and off the Search While Typing feature. (Look for the check box with that phrase or the phrase Display Results As Query Is Typed.) What this does is display search results immediately, even after you type only a few letters, narrowing your results as you type more characters. Experiment selecting and clearing that check box to see whether you like it. I find that given how much old mail I have, if I include too many data stores in my scope of search (described later), I don't like having the search-while-typing feature on. It makes the search a bit "jumpy." But with simple, one-folder-at-a-time searches, it is usually a nice feature.

Changing Which Mail Stores Are Indexed

If you have lots of old mail in many different local folders (PSTs), one thing you might want to do is expand or restrict the local folders being indexed. Restricting it can save time during the initial installation, which can help you get started on searching more quickly that day. Restricting it will also help return fewer results, making searches easier, and it reduces subsequent indexing efforts if you move folders around.

To do that in Outlook 2007, go to the Search Options dialog box as described in the previous section, "Changing Search Options." Then, at the top of that dialog box (in the Indexing section), you can control which data files are indexed.

In Outlook 2010 and 2013, click in the Instant Search box to activate the Search tab on the Ribbon, and then click the Search Tools drop-down menu at the right end of the tab, as shown in Figure 5.2. From that menu select Locations to Search and select the mail stores you wish to include in all your searches.

Controlling Search Scope Default Settings

Selecting which stores are *indexed,* as described in the previous section, does not mean that all indexed files are automatically *searched* when you actually do a search. Do you recall seeing a message after a search asking if you'd like to search all mail items? You might think to yourself, "Yes, and why didn't it do that in the first place?" That's because, by default, the search scope is usually limited to the currently open folder. This default is reasonable for our MYN Processed Mail folder system, where all mail is stored in one folder and we are usually searching there. But what if you always want to search all folders from the outset? You can change that default in the Search Options dialog box: Open that box with the instructions in the earlier section "Changing Search Options," and then in 2007 change the controls in the portion of the dialog box called Instant Search Pane. In 2010 and 2013 that portion is called Include Results Only From.

Controlling Search Scope at Time of Search

Instead of changing the default search scope settings applied to all searches, as described in the previous section, you can override the current defaults *at the time of a particular search.* The common case for this is when you do not find what you are looking for on the first search because the search is by default limited to the current folder, so you want to repeat the search beyond the current folder.

To do that in 2007 and 2010, if you see the link Try Searching Again in All Mail Items at the bottom of the results list, click the link. The search is expanded to other folders. In 2013, you can change the scope from the drop-down menu just to the right of the search box. You can also change those settings *before* you do the search. Here's how.

Controlling Scope Prior to Each Search in Outlook 2007

In Outlook 2007, you can control what mail is searched prior to each search with a control near the top of the Navigation Pane. It is separate from the main search box, so you might not notice it. Figure 5.3 shows how it looks when Mail is the active data type in the Navigation Pane. Notice the All Mail Items banner in the middle of that figure.

That might look like a label, but it's actually an Instant Search control. Also notice the magnifying glass icon to its left. That's how you know this control is associated with Instant Search. Also, it lights up in orange when you start using Instant Search. Notice that as soon as you click this control, whether you open it or not, you immediately expand the scope beyond the currently active folder. Your search speed slows noticeably if you have lots of other mail. That also changes the title at the top of the search results window on the right (for example, to All Mail Items if the Navigation Pane is in Mail mode), reminding you of your search scope.

Figure 5.3
2007 Instant Search control on the Navigation Pane.

If you click the solid down arrow at the control's right edge in the Navigation Pane, the list of data stores is exposed (see Figure 5.4). You can select or clear those you want included in the upcoming search. If you do this *after* running a search, it starts the search again and updates the search results in the search window.

Figure 5.4
2007 search scope control.

In 2007 you can also search beyond mail—that is, in other Outlook data type folders—by clicking at the bottom of the Navigation Pane is. For example, if you want to search across *all* Outlook data types (Mail, Contacts, Calendar, and so on), click the Folder List button (Lesson 2) at the bottom of the Navigation Pane, which changes the mode of the Navigation Pane to show all Outlook data types. *Then* click that new control. It's now labeled All Outlook Items. If you want to search on all contacts (only), click the Contacts banner button or icon first in the lower portion of the Navigation Pane to enter Contacts mode, and so on. For a discussion of the Navigation Pane and its various data type modes, see the second half of Appendix A.

If you find all this a bit complicated, I agree. In Outlook 2010 and 2013 Microsoft simplified these search controls greatly.

Controlling Scope Prior to Each Search in Outlook 2010 and 2013

In Outlook 2010 and 2013, you can control what mail is searched prior to each search with the controls located on the Search tab in the Ribbon. Look a the left edge of the Search tab and find the Scope group (see Figure 5.5), which you can change before running individual searches. As you can see, this is much simpler than the Outlook 2007 interface.

Figure 5.5
2010 Search tab; 2013 is similar.

In 2013, an alternate control is even easier. Notice the scope selector located in a drop-down menu just to the right of the search box. You can change that before or after a search.

Next, I want to cover how to enhance the logic for the item terms you are searching on.

Using Field-Based Instant Searches in Outlook 2007, 2010, and 2013

I showed you earlier how to use AND and OR to narrow your search results. An even better way to narrow your results is to use field-based searches. I find if I use these I can nearly always find an item I am looking for, even if my first simple search yields far too many results.

For example, let's say you are looking for a bill you received and Instant Search returned too many results on the word Invoice. It occurs to you that you know this particular vendor probably puts the word Invoice in the subject (title) of all its e-mails. Wouldn't it be great if you could search only on e-mails with Invoice in the Subject field? You can.

In Outlook 2007 you do that by opening the Query Builder; you reach it by clicking the down-pointing chevron at the right of the search box—that results in Figure 5.6 (notice the chevron highlighted in that figure).

Figure 5.6
Instant Search Query Builder.

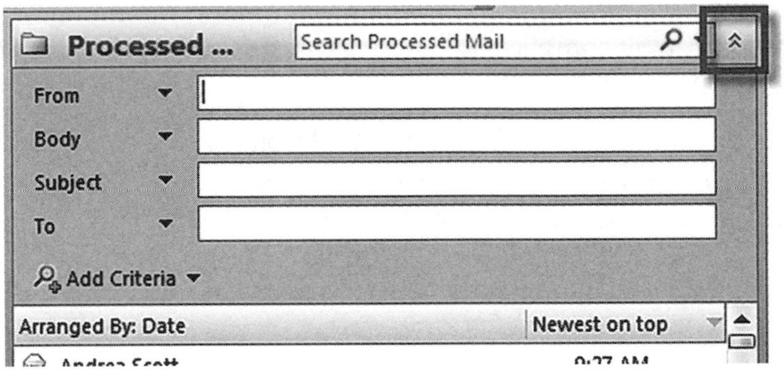

Here you can limit the search by entering additional search terms specific for various e-mail fields. For example, in Figure 5.6, you could enter person's name in the From box and a keyword in the Subject box. The default field list you see may be different from that in Figure 5.6. You control that either by using the Add Criteria button at the bottom, or by changing the title of any existing field with the drop-down arrow next to each. I recommend you play with this query tool and teach yourself how to search on various field combinations; it's fairly intuitive.

Note: *If the extra fields just described for Outlook 2007, or the More button in 2010 (which I describe ahead), are grayed out, see the section ahead "Troubleshooting Windows Instant Search."*

In Outlook 2010 and 2013, you can pick specific field values with the commands in the Refine group on the Search tab (see Figure 5.5). You can indicate that you want to search on the From field, Subject field, on particular date ranges, and so on. But I don't like the way these buttons work because the design forces you to edit the values in the search box and that can be confusing. I prefer using the older Outlook 2007 interface that gives you a separate box for each search criterion (as in Figure 5.6). You can get to that in Outlook 2010 and 2013, too, by clicking the More button at the lower right of the Refine group on the Search tab (it should have a green plus sign next to it as in Figure 5.5) and selecting a field name from the context menu. You can click that More button several times to add multiple fields to narrow the search even more.

Note: *If you use More fields often in Outlook 2010, I recommend turning off Search While Typing because that feature can lead to frustrating behavior when entering field values. For example, if you pause too long, the cursor jumps out of the box you are entering.*

Narrowing the search as just described (with Query Builder in 2007 or the More fields in 2010 and 2013) actually edits the search phrase itself in the search box. You'll see a phrase like "iPad received:this week" where *iPad* is the search term, *received* refers to the date field, and *this week* is the date value. What you are doing is building a text-based query. The various fields and controls you click are just helping you do that. You can then edit that query directly. In fact, you can build that entire query manually, by typing the query directly in the search box, with the Instant Search query syntax. Let's look at that now.

Outlook Instant Search Query Syntax

Let's say you're an experienced search-tool maven and are starting to think the interfaces described in the previous sections seem a little lightweight. You can make your searches as elaborate as you want with a very sophisticated query syntax. With it you can find almost anything. To understand all the possibilities, study Microsoft's documentation on search syntax. Figure 5.7 shows the first seven commands in one of the query syntax documentation sets; the complete list of commands stretches to several pages in length, so there's a lot of power here if you want it. To find this documentation, open a Google search and enter "query searches in Outlook". Find the article "Learn to narrow your search criteria for better searches in Outlook." Other documentation is available, as well.

Figure 5.7
Query syntax, sample documentation.

TYPE THIS	TO FIND THIS
bobby	Items containing *bobby*, *BOBBY*, *BoBby*, or any other combination of uppercase and lowercase letters. Instant Search is not case sensitive.
bobby moore	Items containing both *bobby* and *moore*, but not necessarily in that order.
bobby AND moore	Items containing both *bobby* and *moore*, but not necessarily in that order. Note that logical operators such as AND, NOT, and OR must be in uppercase letters.
bobby NOT moore	Items containing *bobby*, but not *moore*.
bobby OR moore	Items containing *bobby*, *moore*, or both.
"bobby moore"	Items containing the exact phrase *bobby moore*. Note the use of double quotes so that the search results match the exact phrase within the quotes.
from:"bobby moore"	Items sent from *bobby moore*. Note the use of double quotes so that the search results match the exact phrase within the quotes.

Troubleshooting Windows Instant Search

When first learning about Instant Search, some users say they can't find a search box above their folders. Even if it is there, when using it some mail is not being found, or not all the search features are working. Here's why these things can happen and what to do about it.

If you are missing the search box, or it appears inactive, look for the command Click Here to Enable Instant Search just below the Search box in Outlook. If it's not there and you see no search box, then your installation was incomplete, and you'll need to check with your IT department to activate the complete Instant Search capability.

If you do see the search box, but the extra fields described in the earlier section "Using Field-Based Instant Searches in Outlook 2007, 2010, and 2013" are grayed out (or if the plus sign next to the More button in 2010 or 2013 is not green), it's likely Windows Search needs to be installed on your computer. Windows Search provides many of the tools for the search engine in Outlook. Your IT department can help you with that (it's a separate installation from Outlook), or search the Internet for Windows Search and download it from Microsoft.

Because Outlook Instant Search uses the same indexes as Windows Search, make sure you have not turned off Indexing Service on your computer. This disables Outlook Instant Search.

Even if all of the tools I just described seem to be behaving correctly, it is fairly common that the indexes in Windows Search can be set incorrectly or become unstable, which can cause your Outlook searches to run slowly or to not find things. There are a variety of problems and ways to fix them—too many to list here. Ask your IT department to help you, or search the Internet for terms such as "Reset Outlook Search Indexes".

Using Search in Outlook for Mac 2011

The indexed-search capability in Outlook for Mac 2011 is based on Spotlight—the search tool used throughout the Macintosh. Compared to Windows Outlook, the user interface is much simpler in Outlook for Mac 2011, but it is just as powerful.

To start a search in Outlook for Mac 2011, click in the Search This Folder box above your e-mail list. Type your search term. After you stop typing, the results are displayed in place of the current folder contents.

Narrowing the Search

By clicking a choice in the popup shown in Figure 5.8, which automatically appears after you type the search term, you can narrow that search to a particular Outlook column name, or you can ignore the popup.

You can get even more control over those column name searches if you click the buttons in the middle of the Search tab (see From, Subject, Sent To, and so on, in Figure 5.9). That activates the Advanced Search panel just below the Ribbon, as shown in the lower half of Figure 5.9. Each time you click a button on the Ribbon's Search tab, you add a line to the Advanced Search panel.

Figure 5.8
Narrow your Outlook for Mac 2011 search by choosing a column name just after typing.

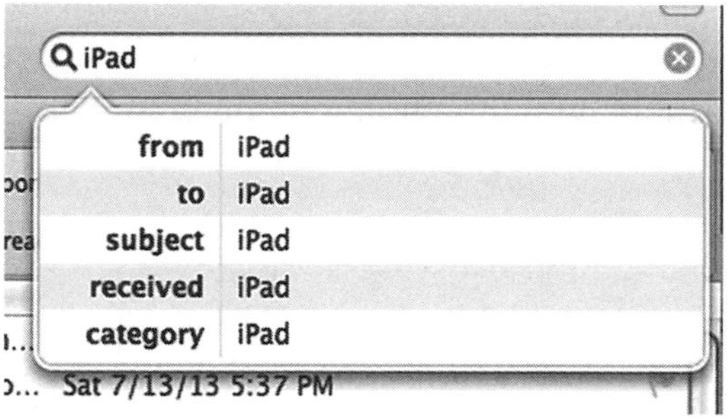
iPad
from iPad
to iPad
subject iPad
received iPad
category iPad
Sat 7/13/13 5:37 PM

Figure 5.9
Outlook for Mac 2011 Advanced Search column controls.

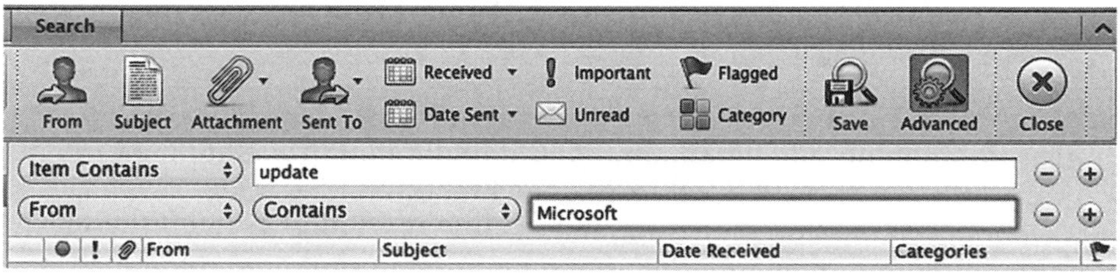
Search
From
Subject
Attachment
Sent To
Received
Date Sent
Important
Unread
Flagged
Category
Save
Advanced
Close
Item Contains
update
From
Contains
Microsoft
From
Subject
Date Received
Categories

You can also add or remove lines in that section by clicking the plus and minus signs at the right end of each search line. And you can change the search logic by changing the values in the popup column names and search verbs; the latter usually defaults to Contains. You can show and hide that entire Advanced section by clicking the Advanced button near the right end of the Search tab in the Ribbon.

Adjusting the Search Scope in Outlook for Mac 2011

Controlling the scope of the search is possible as well. By that, I mean controlling what folders or Outlook data types are searched. You do that by using the four buttons at the far left of the Search tab (Figure 5.10).

Figure 5.10
Outlook for Mac 2011 Advanced Search scope controls.

Home
Organize
Tools
Folder
Subfolders
All Mail
All Items

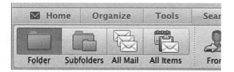

For example, if you choose All Mail, the search expands to multiple mail files or mail accounts (if you have those). If you choose All Items, Outlook searches through mail, tasks, contacts, calendar, and notes for your search term.

As with Windows Outlook, you can gain even more search control by typing complex search criteria directly into the Search box. Do a Google Internet search on "Spotlight Search Syntax" to find documentation on available commands.

Summary

▶ Using MYN methods to empty your Inbox every day is an important way to increase workday control because it captures unattended responsibilities that may otherwise haunt you. It removes clutter from an important area of daily focus. It signals you are ready to move on to new work.

▶ The easiest way to empty your Inbox is to first extract tasks and then drag everything to one folder (called the Processed Mail folder). I recommend you create that as a subfolder of your Inbox and use it from now on for all your filing.

▶ If you'd like to get started quickly, drag all mail older than a week from the Inbox to the Processed Mail folder now. Then immediately process the mail left in your Inbox into the Processed Mail folder as well, extracting tasks as you go. Make a note of the cutoff date, and when you have time later, extract tasks from mail in the Processed Mail folder that's older than that date.

▶ If you are in an Exchange Server environment with tight mailbox size restrictions, create an Old Processed Mail folder in an off-server location (for example, a PST file on a PC or an ON MY COMPUTER folder on the Mac). As you reach your server limits, drag your older mail there from the bottom of your Processed Mail folder.

▶ Consider studying Appendix A for other Processed Mail folder location suggestions (such as using a local folders file).

▶ Try using Outlook built-in search functionality as your way to find older mail in the Processed Mail folder. It's much easier than hunting through multiple folders.

Next Steps

Congratulations on finishing Part I! You are now using all components of the system in a basic way. You can stop here if you like, and start to enjoy the fruits of your labor. This book was designed so you can do just that: get a relatively speedy start, and then take a break from study if desired.

But better is, if you have time, to plunge ahead into Part II. You have more to learn. For example, if you intend to empty a relatively full inbox now and extract tasks, you may want to skip ahead and study Lesson 7, which is the full lesson on converting e-mails to tasks. That way your task creation will be most productive. And if you are eager to apply topic-based filing to the mail stored in your Processed Mail folder, feel free to jump ahead and study Lesson 8 now as well. In both cases come back to Lesson 6 to continue your core training. Lesson 6 will help you understand task management even more.

PART II

Advancing the MYN System

Lesson 6:
When and Where to Use
Outlook Tasks

Introduction

You've come a long way learning how to use tasks. In Lesson 2, you learned how to use the basic task system in Outlook and a quick way to convert e-mails to tasks. In Lesson 3, you learned how to configure Outlook for the Master Your Now! approach to tasks, and in Lesson 4 you learned the MYN best practices for managing tasks. Now let's step back a moment and think a little more deeply about using tasks in Outlook.

Let's consider what we really mean by *tasks* and what kinds of tasks are best to place in Outlook. While most belong there, some do not. We'll look at the very important concept *next actions*. I'll also describe the idea *follow-up tasks* and how they can improve your work life.

As to the *where* in the title of this lesson, I'll discuss taking your tasks mobile with various approaches. I'll discuss which mobile devices make sense, and what software approaches to consider.

There are some situations where, even if you use Outlook for e-mail, I do not recommend using Outlook as your task solution—I recommend other products. I'll tell you why and what to use instead.

But first, let's start with the basics—what a task is and why knowing that matters.

Note: *Portions of this lesson are summarized in video 14 and parts of video 20 of the MYN-Outlook Complete Video Training (see beginning of the Quick Start chapter for more information).*

What Is a Task?

Tasks Compared to Appointments

A question I often get is, Should I enter an action in Outlook as an appointment on my calendar or as an item in my task list, and if I put it on my calendar is it still a task? To help answer this, let's start with defining appointments.

Appointments

Appointments are time-defined events, usually meetings, which have distinct stop and start times. To most, this is obvious: You should manage appointments by placing them on your Outlook Calendar. The MYN system uses Outlook appointments occasionally as a technique to complete tasks (see the section "Managing Deadlines" at the end of Lesson 4 for an example), but appointments are only a peripheral focus of this system. Virtually all our tasks go on the MYN task list. If there is a specific time of day that a particular task must be done, yes, make an appointment out of it. And, in general, whenever you need to delineate a certain part of a day for an activity (or, for example, block out the entire day), use an appointment on the calendar, not a task on the task list.

Tasks

Tasks, then, are activities that do *not* need a specific time of day identified. They are the types of things you would normally write on a to-do list. They may have a specific *day* as a deadline, but as long as they are not *time*-specific, then in general keep them on your task list.

That said, there are times I move a task to the calendar; for example, if a deadline is coming up and I want to delineate some specific time to work on it. But that is the exception rather than the rule.

Ad Hoc Tasks Compared to Operational Tasks

The distinction between ad hoc tasks and operational tasks can be important, too. Many companies have stable operational environments with daily repeated tasks and work steps that are best managed by dedicated workflow systems, either manual or automated. For example, if you process a hundred invoices a day, I hope you're using an invoice management system (a specialized application to process invoices). I don't want you to think I'm recommending the Outlook task system for high-volume work processes like this that have better automated systems available.

Note, though, you might be assigned a related task *outside* such a system. For example, if you are a manager and do not routinely use the invoice management system but occasionally are sent invoice-approval e-mails generated by that system, the Outlook system described in this book *can* be useful for you to track these one-off requests as Outlook tasks.

The Place for Goals

Do I Need to Identify My Goals First?

Nearly all teachings on time and task management start with a discussion of goals. The general line of thought is this: How can you work on any tasks unless you know what your own goals are? The message is usually that you should not focus on tasks unless you have first mapped out your personal mission, vision, and goals and have ensured that your tasks link to those goals through planning.

This is sage advice. However, my experience is this: Most people cannot get even their minimal daily tasks off their plate effectively enough to have time to focus on visualizing and planning tasks to meet their goals. They have no system for doing so. In the heat of the business day, inspired goals are usually the first things that they abandon as they scramble to stay ahead of the freight train of urgent work. There is nothing more frustrating than seeing your favorite goals crushed under the wheels of out-of-control urgency at work.

But goals do have an important place; let me explain where they fit.

The Workday Mastery Pyramid

In my 2010 book *Master Your Workday Now!* I identify three levels of work focus: Control, Create, and Connect, and I show them graphically in a pyramid (see Figure 6.1).

Figure 6.1
The Workday Mastery Pyramid.

The Control level, at the base of the pyramid, is all about keeping urgency managed, and tracking tasks appropriately so that the right things get done first. It's what this Outlook book is about. The result is that you accomplish more with less stress, and your mind is free enough to start focusing on your larger goals in the layers above.

Goals are what the Create layer is all about—visualizing and managing larger outcomes. You have a different mindset when working at this level, one where your attention is on achieving more in your work and life. This is where you consider the bigger things you want to accomplish and how they pull you forward and even excite you. Broader thinking occurs here in the Create Layer, as does creative thinking and visioning.

After you spend adequate time at the Create layer, then the Connect layer comes next. The Connect layer is all about connecting the entirety of your work to who you really are. It is about deciding that most or all of your work activity should be spent on activities that support your core higher motives. It is about seeking work that inspires you, and it is about constantly expanding toward that in your career. Ultimately, it is creating a career by doing what you are passionate about—doing what you love.

A key premise of this three-layer model is that you cannot rise successfully to the Create or Connect levels until you have the Control level fully mastered—Control is the basis of creating the time and mental space for your higher-level work. If you are constantly distracted by out-of-control urgency, or if you are constantly feeling behind and always fighting fires, you can never reach the more passionate and creative mindset that higher-level goals are based on.

So, while there is a major place for goals in the overall skill of mastering your workday, this book is about mastering the control level first so you can get beyond it. And of course it uses Outlook as the tool to do that. Therefore, you won't find my theories about creating and achieving goals in this book—read my book *Master Your Workday Now* for that emphasis; about one-third of that book is all about goals and how to succeed with them.

That said, in Lesson 12 of this book, I do cover mechanical ways to track and work your own goals into your task stream; I show you ways to do that in Outlook.

Do I Put Goals on My Now Tasks List?

The next question I get is, When I do identify my goals, should I place them on my task list? For instance, should I put the statement "Practice an Exercise Program" or "Increase Sales" on my Outlook To-Do Bar? The answer is no; this is too broad a statement to put on your to-do list. There are practical reasons not to. For instance, when you see this on your list in the heat of the business day, you will skip right over it—it is too big to do. And there are logical reasons not to as well; successful goal management requires a much different mindset than task management. Instead, what you should put on your Now Tasks list is some next step or action that you intend to take to reach that goal. For instance, "Make appointment with Jake the personal trainer" is a good task to put there, or "Register for Sales 101 class." I'll talk extensively about the concept of next actions a few pages ahead.

The Place for Projects

Similar to the question in the previous section about whether goals should be listed on the Now Tasks list, you might ask if *projects* should be listed there. For instance, should you make an entry like "Rebuild garage" on this list? As before with goals, the answer is no, because this is too broad a task to place on your Now Tasks list; you will skip over a task like this in the heat of a busy day. Rather, once again, any *next steps* due against a project can and should be listed on your Now Tasks list. For example, "Call Jim for an estimate on garage" is a good task to list on your Now Tasks list. Some fine points of this will be discussed in the section about next actions. And a full discussion of making project lists and tracking tasks against projects is provided in Lesson 12.

Significant Outcomes

Finally, there is something that sits between next-action tasks on the one hand and projects or goals on the other: Significant Outcomes, or SOCs. These are the big things you want to accomplish this week. They aren't as big as goals but they are too big to be called tasks. Because they don't list well on the MYN task list, you need another way to show them. I'll talk more about SOCs later in this lesson.

Put Nearly All Your Tasks in Outlook

What's left is everything else: all ad hoc tasks, all next steps on projects and goals, actions from e-mails, actions from meetings, and actions from phone calls. The very first and most important thing you can do to get ahead of your workday is to track all these ad hoc tasks in the MYN task list in Outlook. What you should *not* do is try to use Outlook task tools in combination with other formal or informal ad hoc task tracking systems. This applies to obvious external task systems such as paper to-do lists, yellow sticky notes on your computer monitor, journals, and so on. Sure, use those as collection spots while on the move or to plan out projects, but as soon as you are back to Outlook, copy specific tasks into the Outlooks task list.

Note: *If you have a separate system to track operational tasks, like those described earlier in the section "Ad Hoc Tasks Compared to Operational Tasks," or if you have a system to plan and track future project tasks (like Microsoft Project), continue to use those. I am only referring here to multiple ways to track ad hoc tasks, daily to-do's, or current next steps on projects.*

Why One Location Is Important

Why is having one place for all tasks so important? If you don't have one place to look, you will not know where to look for your next-highest-priority to-do. You will not get the benefits of being able, at a glance, to know what is on your list for today (and what isn't). More important, at the end of the day, you won't have a clear picture of whether all your critical tasks are done and whether you can leave the office in comfort. You will gain a huge sense of relief by having one and only one task list that you get in the habit of using.

This can also lead to rather subtle distinctions. For instance, something we all tend to do is leave important e-mails in our Outlook Inbox with the intention of returning to them later to act upon them. By doing this, however, you have created a second home for storing your to-do's. Similarly, we all tend to leave important voice mails in our voice mailbox with the intention of following up later on them as well.

So one subtle but important discipline is to get in the habit of immediately transferring both explicit and *implied* tasks to the MYN Outlook system as soon as you receive them from all their various locations.

Keeping Tasks Out of Your Head

One more place you should not store tasks—your head! All good task management experts recommend getting out of the habit of trying to rely on your memory for tracking to-do's. This was a personal epiphany for me, when I finally accepted this lesson years ago. You might think you have a good memory—and you might, but that's not the point. Until you spread out your task list in front of you visually, it is impossible to adequately prioritize, filter, defer, and dismiss tasks that are bouncing around in your mind all day. You should use your mental cycles for strategic thinking, planning, analysis, appreciating life, and so on—not for constantly tracking and trying to recall your responsibilities. If you are currently experiencing any anxiety about the number of tasks you seem to have on your plate, then storing them only in your mind increases that anxiety.

It's the tasks that you cannot remember, but you know are there, that have the most destructive effect. In the Introduction I mentioned long-standing research that shows the human mind cannot clearly remember a list of more than six or seven items at once. Beyond that, items become a blur, and it's that blur that increases mental stress. That nagging feeling that you are ignoring important responsibilities has a negative effect on your attitude, your sense of well-being, and your self-esteem. For some, it can be hard to relax in the evening after work or on the weekend when they sense that they have much work left undone. What a tremendous relief my clients report when they finally get all of their to-do's out of their head and into one visible and trusted location.

And if you maintain that approach—recording to-do's immediately in one location as they come up rather than holding them in your head—you will be amazed at the sense of freedom this provides.

Getting Tasks Out of Physical Piles

One of the common sources of tasks is stacks of paper on your physical desktop, bookshelf, cabinet, or in a desk drawer. A primary benefit of implementing an effective task management system is no longer feeling haunted by piles of paper that you know contain things you need to work on. So from now on, as you receive physical documents with things for you to do in them, rather than using a pile as a to-do system, immediately enter the required action in Outlook before you drop the item on your desk. Then when Outlook tells you the time is right to work it, go find the item as required.

If you find you are currently overwhelmed by an out-of-control pile of materials on your desk or an overflowing physical in-basket, David Allen, in his book *Getting Things Done*, has some great techniques to get you past that (see Chapters 5 and 6 of that book). He describes a system that will get rid of your piles and create very simply organized and highly usable file cabinets. His techniques will help you get those tasks out of your piles, and they dovetail nicely with transferring them into Outlook.

Voice Mail

Think of your voice mailbox as a big pile of paper with buried to-do's in it; it is adding to your sense of your workday being out of control. From now on, whenever you listen to a voice mail, immediately determine the action needed and place that in an Outlook task. Write as many details as possible into the body of the task and delete the voice mail. If the voice mail is too long to write all the details, save it and reference the time and date in your task so you can listen again when you take action. Even better is if your organization has unified messaging, covered next.

Unified Messaging

Regarding work voice mail, one of the greatest recent inventions in voice mail technology is unified messaging. This is an intelligent link between your voice mail system and the Exchange e-mail server, which places entries into your Outlook Inbox for each voice mail you receive. From there you can convert them to tasks as needed using what you learned at the end of Lesson 2 and will learn in Lesson 7. Most systems include a recording of the message attached as a file you can play and listen to on your computer, so when you are ready to work the task, you can listen to the message again right from the task. If your company does not have unified messaging and you receive many voice mail messages, encourage your management to get it.

Note: *Unified messaging is available from a variety of vendors, usually from your corporate voice mail vendor. This is a major upgrade to a company's voice mail and e-mail system, so do not expect this to arrive overnight.*

If you use your cell phone voice mail a lot for business, there are services that will move voice mail out of your cell-phone carrier's voice mail box into your Outlook Inbox or some other text-based system. Some even transcribe the voice mail for you and put it in the text of the e-mail. I describe those solutions more in the section ahead titled "Mobile Voice Mail."

Personal and Work Tasks: Separate or Merged?

I get this question often: Should I mix my business tasks with my personal tasks in the same system? Unfortunately, the answer is "It depends." If you have a separate Outlook system at home and use it a lot there, I would not want to oblige you to boot up your business system just to look up tasks. Rather, what I commonly do is transfer tasks between the two systems by e-mail. For instance, if I am at work and I think of a home task, I'll send an e-mail to my home address with the task in the subject line. Then when I get home I convert that e-mail to a home task. I do the same in the other direction.

If you do not have a home Outlook system, by all means use your business system for home tasks and access it from home. And if you are self-employed, the choice is easy: one system for both.

Summary of Using Outlook for All Tasks

▶ Do not store tasks on paper at your desk: not slips of paper, not note-pads, not notebooks, except for initial collection while away from your computer.

▶ Do not try to track to-do's by leaving them in e-mails or voice mails.

▶ Do not try to track and work tasks from meeting notes and journals (although you certainly can initially record them there).

▶ Do not try to track tasks in your head.

▶ Do not try to track to-do's in stacks of paper.

▶ Rather, immediately transfer all tasks from e-mail, voice-mail, paper memos, paper slips, meeting notes, journals, incoming physical memos, and your mind into the Outlook task management system.

▶ Consider services that move voice mail automatically into your Outlook Inbox, where converting them to tasks is easy.

▶ Feel free to mix personal and company tasks together or to keep them separate, whichever works best for you.

Going Mobile with the MYN System

iPads, Android tablets, Windows 8 tablets, and other midsize mobile devices are making inroads into corporate environments. And smartphones are growing in computational power—even Microsoft Office documents are being edited on these small screens. Furthermore, cloud computing, which is a new term for the old concept of working from servers, is gaining steam as a viable work approach—one that makes mobile computing much more feasible. So, you are probably wondering how the MYN system might fit in to this rapidly changing mobile landscape. After all, getting organized and having all tasks and e-mail under control clearly means finding ways to do that while on the road. These days, many of us read more than half our e-mail on such devices, away from our main copy of Outlook.

Considerations When Choosing a Mobile Solution

The MYN system plays very well into the growing mobile footprint. But deciding which mobile strategy to use, and even which device to use with MYN, requires some forethought. The right solution really depends on what form your travel takes and the nature of your work when traveling.

Consider your form of travel. Is the extent of your mobility walking across the hall to a conference room? Or do you travel to other office locations where you sit and work for extended periods? Or are you often working in transitional locations (an airport gate, an office lobby, or a taxi) where you need to do small, quick, segments of work?

Next, consider how and why you are using e-mail and tasks when on the run. Are you simply reviewing e-mail and perhaps inputting tasks for later work at your desk? Or are you doing the actual task work when on the road?

Finally, consider your connectivity options. Has your IT department enabled access to your company data while on the road such that you can access company servers or documents? In what way have they done that?

All of these considerations help determine which device and approach to use for your mobile solution. With these in mind, let me start with the simplest mobile solution—paper—and work from there to laptops, tablets, and smartphones.

Printing Your Tasks Instead of Using a Mobile Device (Windows)

I know you might be eager to obtain a sexy new smartphone, tablet, or laptop, but if the extent of your mobility is inside an office building, say between your desk and a conference room, you can often get by with much less. If your IT department has not given you the appropriate connectivity methods, this might be your only choice.

When I worked in a large corporate office environment years ago, I found I was quite successful with just printing out my Outlook task list and appointments for the day on one page and taking that to meetings (see Figure 6.2). In my experience, it trumped the complications of a handheld device. I found using a full-sized sheet of paper preferable to navigating through the tiny screens on a handheld device during a meeting.

Figure 6.2
How a printed Outlook schedule and MYN task list looks. This is probably your simplest mobile solution.

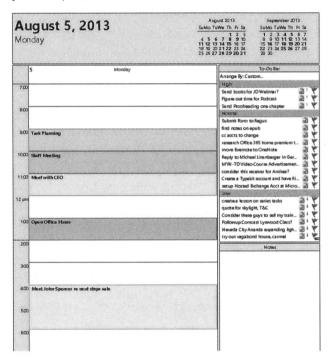

If you want to do this, you need to first find the Print Options dialog box and change some settings as detailed at: www.myn.bz/PrintCalendar.htm.

Unfortunately, printing the MYN task list with Outlook for Mac 2011 like this is not currently possible because each urgency zone is in its own folder.

Using this paper approach as my mobile solution worked well in other ways. In meetings, I made notes right on the sheet of paper to indicate task changes or additions, and I entered them in Outlook later when back at my desk. At times I would print a week or month calendar view each morning, as well, so I could check future appointments when needed in meetings. Because it's so simple, sometimes paper really is better than fancy new technology.

Laptop (Windows or Mac) or Windows 8 Tablet

Using a desktop copy of Outlook on a Windows laptop, on a Windows 8 tablet, or on a MacBook (all with Internet access to your work servers), is your best mobile solution. The new Windows Ultrabook laptops are incredibly lightweight, very powerful, and jump in and out of standby mode quickly. The same is true for the new MacBook Air laptops. The new Windows 8 tablets are even lighter and quicker to start and stop.

Using these with your desktop copy of Outlook, plan to sit for extended moments throughout the day to do some serious e-mail and task management. Spend some time converting e-mails to tasks, replying to messages, and filing mail in your Processed Mail folder.

In this scenario, if you also have a smartphone, iPad, or Android tablet, I'd plan to use these primarily as a quick way, when standing or on the run, to *read* e-mail and *view* high-priority tasks. Perhaps you can make short replies to important messages. Why just that? You will find that none of these solutions are as nimble as a laptop or Windows 8 tablet with Outlook installed. With most you can usually view only a subset of your saved mail, and many have trouble accessing your company servers. And they usually do not allow converting e-mails to tasks.

Your most powerful solution is to use your laptop or Windows 8 tablet with a desktop copy of Outlook. You want to use the right tools for the right job, and sometimes access to a desktop copy of Outlook is the only way to go.

To make this feasible, the laptop or tablet you use needs to be a reasonably updated and lightweight model that you feel good about carrying whenever you travel. My laptop weighs 3.5 pounds, launches out of standby in seconds, and uses a good broadband solution (the Ultrabook and MacBook Air laptops mentioned earlier are like this). If instead you are using a seven-pound or heavier monster that crashes a lot, or does not handle standby well, or that has poor Internet connectivity, you should get a new laptop or Windows 8 tablet.

Even if you have the best laptop, however, I doubt you will fish it out of your briefcase for a 60-second glance at your e-mail or tasks. Rather, you will probably check your mail and tasks on your smartphone or tablet. And as of this writing, iPads and Androids dominate the tablet world. So next, let's look at how these fit into the MYN system.

Using a Smartphone, iPad, or Android Tablet

Smartphones and non-Windows tablets make up the next group of devices to consider. In this world, you need to find ways to use MYN without a desktop copy of Outlook.

Smartphones like a BlackBerry, an iPhone, an Android, or a Windows 8 smartphone are in common use today. Many people are using an iPad or an Android tablet. All of these are powerful and handy, and all have many business strengths. However, using these means you can't use a desktop copy of Outlook. Instead, you will have to settle for a mobile mail app, and you'll need to manage tasks another way. You might think a browser version of Outlook for tasks would work in this situation, particularly on a tablet, but it won't. OWA (the browser version of Outlook) does not have the task functionality you need to support MYN. So, how can you go mobile with the MYN task system?

How a Mobile MYN Task Solution Works

If you're using Outlook on your PC or Mac for all your tasks, as I encourage in this book, then you should plan to synchronize those tasks with your mobile device. Do *not* keep a separate mobile task list. I've described earlier in this lesson the problems caused by having multiple to-do lists. The best synchronization setup is the one available in many corporate settings where the tasks (and e-mail, calendar, and contacts) on your corporate Outlook Exchange Server can be synchronized wirelessly with your mobile devices. And make sure you configure the mobile app to display the MYN task list. What I just described is the ideal. But there are currently several barriers in the way.

Barriers to Mobile MYN Task Solutions

The first barrier is finding a mobile device that will *synchronize* tasks with your corporate Outlook servers. Older versions of iPhones, iPads, Android, and Windows Phone devices suffered with this. That's because ActiveSync, which is the standard Microsoft Exchange interface in these devices, for some reason was not enabled for easy *task* syncing (mail, calendar, and contacts synced fine on these; just not *tasks*). Nearly all these devices *do* synchronize tasks now, but you need to make sure you are using the latest operating system on your device to ensure that.

The second barrier is, even if your device or app does have task synchronization with your corporate Exchange Server, it is hard to find task software that can be configured to create MYN views anything like the ones you created in Lesson 3. When your mobile device cannot show those views, it makes it hard to use the complete MYN system from that device. The BlackBerry suffers from this. Most BlackBerry devices can sync with Outlook Exchange tasks, but the standard tasks software on the BlackBerry can't sort or filter tasks flexibly. Add-in software offers some help here, and we'll look at applicable apps ahead.

The third and final barrier to easily using your Outlook tasks on a mobile device is that you usually cannot easily convert e-mails to tasks on these handhelds. You can't drag or move your e-mail to the tasks folder in their built-in systems. This is troubling because, currently, the primary use of corporate handhelds is to check e-mail on the run. Without a good way to convert action e-mails to tasks, you might read an e-mail indicating an important work task for you to do, and then skip to the next message, possibly losing track of the action as a result. You can stop and enter a new task by hand in the device, but rarely do you have time to do that when you're on the run. Workarounds do exist, so let's look at these solutions now.

Mobile Solutions

I just painted a fairly bleak picture for mobile devices, but there are workarounds, and even some very bright spots, on the mobile landscape. The best solution is to get one of the new lightweight Windows 8 tablets and use a desktop copy of Outlook. But if for some reason that is not an option, here are some solutions for the other platforms. Let's start with some simple compromise solutions, and then work up to some full-blown MYN mobile solutions with third-party add-in software.

Note: All the solutions in this section assume you use Exchange Server with Outlook. If you do not, then I recommend you use the Toodledo solution described later in this lesson.

Using "Native" Task Software on Your Mobile Device

If you do not want to purchase add-in software (or can't), you might be able to use native, pre-installed apps to view and enter tasks. These days, if your device can sync with your Outlook e-mail, then in most cases your tasks are also synced. As mentioned, however, none of these native tasks apps sort in MYN order, but you can still get some use from them. Which native app to use is, of course, highly dependent on which device you have.

▶   If you are using a BlackBerry, where you see your Outlook tasks on it depends on what version of BlackBerry you are using. The brand-new BlackBerry 10 was just coming out at the time of this printing, and reports are that it can sync Exchange-based tasks into its Remember application. We haven't tested it, but I suspect tasks will not be sorted to match MYN needs. In the previous versions of BlackBerry, you could see your Outlook tasks imported into the included app called *Tasks*. (You can find that app in the Applications folder.) However, the tasks sort incorrectly in that app; that is, you cannot see them in MYN order. In the Tasks app you should, at minimum, use the Options menu to sort by Priority and to hide completed tasks. That way, at least you can see your upcoming High priority tasks at the top. Because High priority represents your must-do-today list, this may be all you need to see when on the run. However, because the app cannot filter out future-dated tasks, your list becomes unusable after you collect many of these. Still, any tasks you enter in this app will show up in your synced Outlook task list back at your desk. So entering new tasks while on the run is still a good reason to use the task tools built in to the BlackBerry. Better, though, is to purchase the add-in software, described later in this lesson.

▶ On newer iPhone and iPad devices, the Reminders app syncs with your Exchange tasks. One big advantage of the newer iPhone is that with Siri, you can easily input tasks on the run. All you need to do is tell Siri to "set reminder," and it interactively collects the action, date, and time for you. The task will then be imported to your desktop Outlook. However, when viewing tasks in the Reminders app on the iPhone, note that you can't see the tasks in anything close to an MYN view; they are completely out of order. So it's better to purchase and use add-in software (TaskTask, discussed ahead) that syncs with your desktop Outlook through Exchange.

▶ On a Windows 8 tablet, the best task solution is a desktop copy of Outlook. But without a keyboard and mouse, manipulating desktop Outlook with a tablet's touch interface can be unwieldy, so another solution is to purchase and use app-style software (such as TaskTask). The simple user interface of app-style software is easier to use with touch.

▶ On a Windows 8 phone, Exchange tasks sync into the to-do section of your calendar, in the Day, Agenda, or To-Do view. But to sort them correctly for MYN, you'll need to use add-in software such as TaskTask.

▶ Android users can sync Exchange tasks into the Calendar app (with proper settings). But to sort them correctly for MYN, you'll need to purchase add-in software such as TouchDown (discussed ahead).

Converting E-mails to Outlook Tasks on the Run

As to converting e-mails to tasks on your mobile device, the best solutions are with add-in software. Android has a good third-party app solution with the TouchDown app, and iPhone and iPad have an app solution called eMailGanizer. Both are described ahead.

Without adding software, other strategies can be used. For example, on newer smartphones, you can set the e-mail's Follow Up flag on your smartphone. When synchronized back to your desktop copy of Outlook, the e-mails are copied automatically as flagged-mail tasks in your To-Do Bar (assuming you did not make the optional setting in Lesson 3 that prevents that).

If your device does not have a way to flag an e-mail, one strategy is to forward the e-mail back to yourself, inserting *TASK:* at the start of the subject line. Then, when you're back at your desk, you can do a proper conversion to a task. You can also create an Outlook rule in your desktop Outlook that looks for *TASK:* to insert a Follow Up flag on such e-mails and convert them to flagged-mail tasks.

Using Add-In Software for MYN Tasks and Exchange

One reason for the huge success of smartphones and tablets is the abundance of third-party apps and the ease with which these are installed, updated, and used on your mobile devices. There are lots of third-party *task* apps in this collection. However, the same issues I described earlier in the section "Barriers to Mobile MYN Task Solutions" greatly limit what you can use. Most of these apps either do not synchronize with Exchange or do not sort and filter to match the MYN task list. That said, some do stand out, and I list those here. There are even products that convert e-mails to tasks.

Keep in mind that for each of these, some post-installation configuration will be required to make the task list look and act like the MYN task list. Also, because the smartphone app world is a rapidly changing environment, the recommendations I list here can change over time. Check my website— www.myn.bz/Software.html (link is case sensitive)—to confirm that what you read here is still what I consider the best.

iPhone, iPad, and Windows 8 (and Windows Phone 8): TaskTask

On the iPhone, iPad, and Windows 8 tablets, I recommend an app called TaskTask (called TaskTask HD on the iPad and Windows 8). It's an excellent tasks app, and its tasks view can be sorted to match the MYN task list. It also recognizes flagged-mail tasks in Outlook and displays them in your task list—something very rare to find.

Keep in mind, however, that because this has no e-mail module, there is no way to convert your mobile e-mails to tasks. So, you'll still need to flag or forward e-mails back to yourself as a reminder to convert e-mails to tasks later, when at your desk or laptop.

The TaskTask app is also your best bet on Windows Phone 8. As of this writing it was not quite MYN compliant, but work was under way to change that, so check my website for its status.

To see my articles about TaskTask, including how to configure it for MYN, go to: www.myn.bz/TaskTask.htm (link is case sensitive).

iPhone and iPad: eMailGanizer

If you are willing to switch from the standard Mail app on the iPhone and iPad, then you should consider eMailGanizer as a way to convert e-mails to tasks. eMailGanizer is a full-featured mail app that is a worthy replacement to the Mail app. It has tons of extra functions and features. The feature I like the most is that inside each open e-mail is a button that converts that mail item to an Exchange task (it does not pick up attachments, however). This is a mail-only app, so you'll want to use TaskTask to see your tasks. For more information, go to www.myn.bz/eMailGanizer.htm (link is case sensitive).

Android: TouchDown

The Android platform (smartphone or tablet) has probably the best solution of all the devices listed here: an add-in app called TouchDown that interfaces well with Exchange and can display the MYN task list. The product installs a suite of apps that include an e-mail client that works well with Exchange. And best of all, that e-mail client has a command to convert e-mails to tasks (or even to appointments). Of all the solutions I've seen on any platform for managing your Outlook tasks while on the road, the TouchDown solution is the best. To me, this is an excellent reason to migrate to an Android device. However, you cannot pick up *attachments* in tasks created this way. For instructions on how to configure TouchDown for MYN tasks, go to www.myn.bz/TouchDown.htm (link is case sensitive).

BlackBerry: ToDoMatrix

The BlackBerry is traditionally the most business-focused mobile tool, and yet, while it syncs tasks with Exchange natively, its task applications are still the most limited from an MYN perspective. A number of BlackBerry add-in task solutions are available. It's just that for those that interface with Exchange tasks, the sorting is usually not right for MYN and they do not include start dates. For those with relatively good sorting, the interface with Exchange is lacking. That said, if you are using the pre-BlackBerry 10 models, the application called ToDoMatrix works relatively well and syncs tasks with Exchange. (At the time of this writing this app had not been updated for the new BlackBerry 10. Check with the ToDoMatrix website for updates.) For instructions on how to use and configure ToDoMatrix for MYN tasks, go to www.myn.bz/TDM.htm (link is case sensitive).

Non-Outlook Task Solutions

Reasons Not to Use Outlook as Your Main Task Solution

The solutions listed in the previous section provide options to take your Outlook-based, MYN tasks mobile. They assume you use Outlook, of course, and they also assume you use Exchange server; that's because the connectivity tools in Exchange are the best way to go for over-the-air synchronization of Outlook tasks.

However, in some cases, usually due to the mobile limitations of Outlook, I recommend solutions other than Outlook and Exchange as your main MYN task application. I don't mean to abandon Outlook entirely—Outlook remains my first choice for e-mail, calendar, and other purposes. It's just that there are times when Outlook is not your best *task* solution. There are a number of situations where I feel this is the case, and I'll cover each next. Then I'll discuss my recommended replacement.

Here's where Outlook may not be your best task manager:

If You Use a Macintosh

If you are a Mac user, you've noticed by now that Outlook for Mac 2011 provides a relatively weak task solution; and that's true whether you are using it on your main computer or with a mobile solution. I discussed the issues with Outlook for Mac 2011 tasks in earlier lessons, but as a reminder, here are a few again. Because date sorting within priority groups is missing, you cannot see or print one view of your MYN tasks (you need three separate lists). The ability to create custom views is greatly limited. You cannot turn off the red color on overdue tasks, even though we ignore the due date field in MYN. And you cannot attach files to tasks. So you may want to use another task solution, and one that is server based so you can also use it while on the road.

No Remote Exchange Access

To go mobile with Outlook tasks, you need to be able to connect to your Exchange Server tasks from outside your company's firewall. Many companies do not have that connectivity. That's because some companies have not turned on ActiveSync or OWA access, or provided any other remote access suitable for mobile devices. If you lack such connectivity, you'll need another server-based task solution.

No Exchange Server

Or perhaps you are not working in a company with Exchange Server (or a comparable IMAP server with tasks), so you use Outlook with an Internet mail service. In that case your tasks are stored on your computer's hard drive and you lose the easy over-the-air sync of Outlook tasks with your smartphone. Sure, you can use a local wired or Wi-Fi sync with some smartphones, and there are other solutions, but none are very good if you travel a lot. Rather, my first suggestion is to switch to a hosted Exchange account so you can get all the benefits of Exchange and remote access wherever you go (see Appendix A for a discussion of hosted Exchange). But if that is not practical for you, then using an alternate server-based task solution may be your only choice.

Mixed Mobile Devices

If you use a lot of different mobile solutions, you may have noticed that none of the solutions I've just listed work across *all* platforms. Perhaps you have an Android phone, and an iPad tablet, or maybe some other mobile device. If so, a multiplatform task solution may be the best way to preserve a uniform approach.

Recommended Non-Outlook Task Solution: Toodledo

The best way to conquer the mobile and platform limitations just described is to use an Internet server-based (also called cloud-based) task management product that is not limited by platform. That way you can view your tasks in any device that has a compatible app; or use one that has a good Internet browser capability and a screen large enough to read a web page.

The question is, which Internet-based task management product to use? Whichever one you choose, it needs to meet the MYN task list requirements. That means it needs to support start dates and it needs to have very flexible sorting and filtering. I have looked at many products on the market and very few meet those requirements. For example, as mentioned earlier, the web version of Outlook does not pass the test. Another popular product called Remember the Milk does not get close enough either. As of this writing, the only Internet server-based task product that I have found that does the job is called Toodledo.

Toodledo is an Internet server-based task application that meets all the task requirements of MYN. And you can access Toodledo on just about any device, either from a browser or from a wide range of compatible mobile apps. So, Toodledo meets MYN mobile needs as well.

Toodledo's Browser Mode

In its browser mode (its primary mode), Toodledo can be run on any computer that supports a web browser, such as a PC, Mac, Linux, or Chrome OS, as well as most tablet and smartphone operating systems (iOS, Android, BlackBerry, Windows 8, and more). The browser solution is ideal for a tablet because of the tablet's large-screen view. A large-screen smartphone works as well.

Note: The preinstalled browser app on some older Android phones may not work right with Toodledo. You can fix that by choosing other browser apps off the Android Market; for example, the Dolphin browser app works great.

Toodledo Mobile Apps for MYN

If you don't like using a browser on a smartphone or tablet, there are easy-to-use dedicated apps that connect to the Toodledo Internet servers and so give you full synchronization of your tasks across all your devices. Toodledo has created apps for the iPhone and iPad that work great and configure well for MYN. Third-party developers are creating apps for Android and other devices, and quite a few are available now.

Toodledo Features

Toodledo has nearly all the features that Outlook has for tasks. And in many ways, after being configured for MYN, Toodledo even goes beyond Outlook tasks. How? As a web application it is well implemented with no task feature degradation across platforms or clients (unlike the web or Mac versions of Outlook, which have limited task capabilities). Furthermore, you can convert e-mails to tasks from any e-mail system on any device, which offers a huge advantage. It uses start dates correctly and it has a correctly implemented due date field (the Outlook due date field is hamstrung after you use the start date), and it has multiple views to track impending due dates. It has newer types of task features that Outlook does not; for example, the iPhone version has location awareness for tasks (for example, a pending field office task could ring an alarm on your iPhone if you are driving by that office). So, if you cannot use Outlook for tasks, Toodledo is the software to use.

Toodledo Self-Study

My book *The One Minute To-Do List* shows, at a simple level, how to use Toodledo with MYN. I've also released a full MYN-Toodledo video training that parallels the MYN-Outlook video training and goes well beyond any of *The One Minute To-Do List* book material. For more information, go to this link: www.myn.bz/FullTD-MYN.html (link is case sensitive).

Paper-Based (Non-Outlook) Solution

Some of you may prefer a nonautomated solution—many people like to use paper for tasks. My book *The One Minute To-Do List* shows how to use the simple 1MTD system with paper. For more power, in my book *Master Your Workday Now!* I show you how to implement much of the MYN task list on paper. Read more about this at: www.myn.bz/MYWN-Book.htm. You can download free templates to print out at this link: www.masteryourworkday.com/tooldownloads.

Mobile Strategies for Capturing Tasks

Even with the perfect mobile solution, a number of mobile scenarios complicate collecting tasks in Outlook; they may require some thought to keep them worked into your system. And if you do not have an MYN mobile device like those described in the previous sections, you may need to get creative. The scenarios I list next represent common situations where you might receive tasks while between meetings, or away from the office, with some suggestions on how to deal with them. The goal of the points I list next is to prevent you from falling back into the habit of trying to keep tasks in your head. Many of them rely on the skill you learned at the end of Lesson 2: converting e-mails to tasks.

Entering Tasks on a Mobile Tasks App Directly

In all cases in this section, if you have a mobile device with a synchronized tasks app, you can enter a new task that you receive on the run directly into the app. However, I find few people take the time to do that because there are usually too many steps. You need to open the task app in the handheld device, create a new task, and then type all the fields in that task. Most people avoid these steps if they are moving fast.

One solution that does work well is if you are using Siri on an iPhone and have a task system linked to its Remember app (Exchange is linked by default). In that scenario, tell Siri: "Remind me to finish sales report on Tuesday." When it asks for a time just say "No time." If you use Exchange, after a few moments a Normal priority task named Finish Sales Report will appear in your Outlook task list with a start date of Tuesday. If you are using Task-Task, the new task will appear there as well.

If you do not have an easy way to enter tasks directly in your mobile device while on the run, you need to find workarounds. Here are some ideas.

Entering Tasks on a Mobile Device from E-mail

As mentioned in a previous section, if you have an Android device, Touch-Down software has tools to convert e-mails to tasks while on the run; it's a simple menu choice. The iPhone and iPad software called eMailGanizer has this feature as well. But not many other mobile systems allow that. So, here's the alternate solution I mentioned earlier. If you get an e-mail on your mobile device that has an action for you in it that you cannot do now, just forward the message back to yourself and put the word "TASK:" (all caps) at the beginning of the subject line (or some other easy to spot word). That way you will know to convert it to a task when you see it back at your primary computer.

Hallway Conversations

If a colleague or supervisor stops you in the hall and dumps an *unwanted* to-do on you, put the onus back on them by stating: "Hey, could you send me an e-mail on that? Otherwise I will forget this." Then, back at your desk, if they have sent it you can convert it to a task. Again, only do this with tasks you'd rather not be responsible for—there is a good chance the person will forget to send it.

Other Methods for Capturing Tasks

For mobile scenarios where you *do* want to remember a task that someone gives you verbally (or if you think up one on the fly), a small pocket notepad that you carry with you is a good option. Alternatively, use one of the many voice recorder apps built in to your smartphone. The voice recorder built in to the Evernote smartphone app is my favorite because it syncs to my main computer. Or use your smartphone's voice-to-text converter with apps like OneNote.

Home Computer

As mentioned earlier, if you are working at your home computer when an office task is identified, you can send an e-mail to your work address with the e-mail title identifying the task. Back at the office, convert the e-mail to a task. The reverse is also useful: For things you need to remember to do when you get home, send an e-mail from work.

Mobile Voice Mail

Often you receive and listen to a voice mail on your mobile phone that contains a to-do that you later forget is saved there. There are a couple of ways to handle this. You can leave the message in the message queue unsaved. On many phones, this leaves the message icon active. So when you see this icon at your desk, you can listen to the messages again and record it in Outlook.

Or, after listening to the message, you might leave yourself a voice note in Evernote or OneNote (described in this section, in the subsection "Other Methods for Capturing Tasks"), or instruct iPhone's Siri to create a reminder (described at the start of this section, in the subsection "Entering Tasks on a Mobile Tasks App Directly").

Sending Your Cell Phone Voice Mail to Outlook

The best solution for voice mail, however, is to use a service that collects your voice mail and sends it into your Outlook Inbox (like unified messaging, described earlier in this lesson). You then later convert these e-mails to tasks. There are several such services. Some provide just the sound file to play at the touch of a button, while others transcribe the message into text. Some replace your carrier's voice mail system, and others leave your voice mail system as is, but periodically copy messages off it. I used to keep up with all the various product solutions, but these days I steer everyone to Google Voice. That's because it provides a compelling full-featured solution—and it's free. Google Voice has apps for all smartphone platforms.

Writing Only Next Actions on Your Now Tasks List

Next, let's move away from mobile computing and return to the main topic of this lesson: when to use Outlook tasks and which types of tasks are best to record in Outlook.

To this end, I encourage you to apply the *next-action* concept to your Now Tasks list. This practice I highly recommend because it helps ensure that your tasks actually get done. There is nothing worse than having a task list full of items that sit there without completion; using this technique helps you avoid that and get more tasks done each day.

I first saw this concept in the book *To Do... Doing... Done*, by G. Lynne Snead and Joyce Wycoff. Lynne describes a system of top-down task creation where a small project is planned out as a whole, and then periodically the next action for each project is "time activated" and moved out to the daily tasks list or appointment calendar.

David Allen, author of the book *Getting Things Done*, is probably the most prominent voice for using next actions these days, and his perspectives are worth studying. David attributes his next action ideas to one of his mentors from 20 years back: Dean Acheson (no relation to the former US Secretary of State). Sally McGhee is a productivity writer who also promotes next actions in her books (Sally and David Allen used to work together).

Nearly all writers on next actions emphasize this lesson: Examine tasks you have on your to-do list and to ask yourself "What is the very next physical action I need to do to accomplish this task?" They encourage you to identify the most discrete and significant next action possible, and write that on your task list. This stimulates action more effectively and unsticks tasks that tend to remain uncompleted (more on that later in this section).

Here are some examples of well-written next-action tasks:

▶ Call Fred and ask for new meeting date

▶ E-mail James about proposal

▶ Review Ted's summary notes

Note that each of the examples just listed has a verb in it; you really want to identify the action, specifically the *next* action needed to achieve an outcome. Make sure the action is as small and discrete as possible.

Similarly, your Now Tasks should not consist of generic nouns such as "James's proposal" or "Ted's notes," because these general descriptions leave you, on cursory review, uncertain of what to do. Reading these poorly written tasks in the middle of the busy day, it may take you a minute or two to decide what the action really is, and that delay can prevent you from acting on the task.

Also, only put the *very* next action task on your MYN task list; don't enter as tasks all sequential steps to a goal. Recall that your Now Tasks list shows only things eligible to do now. So if you list future dependent steps, you will clutter your list with unusable tasks.

The MORE Task

If, after you extract a next-action task, you end up needing more steps to reach the outcome, you now have a multistep task, so do this. Put the first step in the task subject name, and list the subsequent steps inside the body of the Outlook task item. Then place the phrase "…MORE" at the end of the subject name, to indicate there is more to this inside the task.

When you complete each step, read the text in the body of the task, identify the next step, and re-label the item with this new task name (thanks to Don Morgan for this suggestion). This and similar approaches are discussed more in Lesson 12 under the subheading "Series Tasks" in the section "Tracking Goals and Projects in Outlook."

Next Actions of Projects

The next-action concept applies to projects as well. Plan and manage your projects using whatever project tools you like. Then, to execute specific tasks when their time has come, put *only* the next-action task for each project (or each parallel work stream within a project) on your Now Tasks list. In Lesson 12, in the section "Tracking Goals and Projects in Outlook," I show some ways to use Outlook to track small projects.

Solution to Stuck Tasks

The next-action approach helps you clear stuck tasks. How many times have tasks sat on your to-do list for weeks or months? Many stuck tasks get stuck because you really haven't thought through and identified the very next action needed on the task. Instead, you often end up writing midstream outcomes that in reality require further dependent actions before you can get to them. Or you write higher-level goals with no indications of next steps needed to get there. In the midst of a busy day, when you see the item, you get stuck; the task description does not ring true as something that you can do immediately. So it is essential that you clearly think through what the very next action is to achieve a task, and write only that on your Now Tasks list. This keeps that list action-oriented and focused on the immediate.

Identify the Very Next Action

One way to ensure that you are writing the *very* next action on a stuck task is to ask yourself several times, "Is there anything else I need to do first?" If you find something, it becomes your very next action. This is also a useful exercise with new tasks, if you have time.

For example, I once received a request to assist the planning department of a client with a project proposal they were developing. I started to write "Assist planning dept. with project," but then I thought, "No, there's something ahead of that. Of course—I need to call up the planning specialist to discuss the project." I imagined myself doing that and realized I knew nothing about this project and if I got questions during that call, the call would be counterproductive. I knew we had some material on their planned project somewhere, so really the first thing to do was to review the project material. I started to write that. Then I thought, "Where is the material?" I remembered that Tom last worked on the project and had the file on it. So what I finally wrote was this: "Call Tom and get planning dept. project file." When I saw that on my list later, it was easily accomplished, and doing it got the project moving. If I had seen my original task, "Assist planning dept. with project," in the middle of a busy workday, as I paused trying to figure out how to do that, I probably would have skipped over it. Take a look at your task list now and decide if any of your current tasks can be replaced with more actionable next actions.

However, what I just described can be a lot of steps. So if you are on the run and don't have time to think this through, get the task recorded as best you can and use the tips I list next to create a placeholder for later consideration.

Helpful Next Action Bridges and Placeholders

Sometimes, when you enter a task, you cannot decide what the next action on a task is or you do not have time to decide. That's okay. Just write "Determine next step for [task name]." That creates a bridge to further activity when you can later identify follow-up steps. Other useful bridges: "Plan work on [task name]"or "Start work on [task name]." Sometimes just getting started on a task allows you to think it through, and by writing it that way you do not commit yourself to a large block that you might skip over when you see it on a busy day. Small-effort tasks like this are often useful as must-do-today (Critical Now) tasks to get you moving on a project that may be stalling out.

Using MYN with Getting Things Done

As you learned in the next-actions section, one current proponent of using next actions is David Allen and his popular Getting Things Done (GTD) program. While MYN and GTD are two completely different task systems, next actions is one place the two systems overlap, and there are other ways you can use the two systems together. So if you are a GTD user and are looking for more ways to integrate MYN with GTD, here are some ideas on how to do that.

First of all, the two systems are completely compatible—there is nothing in MYN that conflicts with GTD, and nothing in GTD that I find unusable with MYN. Even better, they are fantastic when used together. In fact, many GTD users say that adding MYN principles on top of GTD solves many issues that come up in GTD if it is not used with care. And MYN's intelligent integration with Outlook provides one way to marry GTD with Outlook, and in a very powerful way.

Here are some points on how to integrate MYN, Outlook, and GTD.

▶ Treat MYN's Now Tasks list (the Critical Now and Opportunity Now lists combined) as your GTD next-action list. MYN's smart way to manage tasks there gives you much more control and solves the common problem of the GTD next-action list getting too long to easily review. Used correctly, MYN gives you the tools to keep the next-action list well controlled and well managed.

▶ Treat the Low priority section (Over the Horizon) as the GTD Someday Maybe list. Like the GTD next-action list, many GTD users complain their someday maybe list quickly becomes too long to review, and tasks there just disappear, never to be seen again. As a result, they stop using the someday maybe list. You'll see in Lesson 9 how MYN's Defer-to-Review process solves that problem quite elegantly. It gives you a very intelligent way of deciding what low-priority entries to review, and when to review them. The result is that your GTD weekly review is not overwhelming, and tasks still get the appropriate attention they need. If you are a GTD user, you are going to love the MYN Defer-to-Review process in Lesson 9.

▶ Use the Follow-Up Task process (discussed ahead and in Lesson 7) to replace the GTD waiting-for list. It accomplishes the same thing as the waiting-for list in a way that I think is easier to use because it places the item right in your Now Tasks list at exactly the right time. It keeps you from having one more list to review.

▶ GTD's definition of a project is much different from that in MYN. In GTD, any task that requires multiple steps is defined as a project, so even very small efforts are called projects. In MYN, only large efforts that require formal project management skills are called projects. However, both systems recognize the need to create a project list, and Lesson 12 shows you various ways to make a projects list in Outlook that meets the needs of both GTD and MYN. As with GTD, you can then use the list to feed next-action tasks into the MYN Now Tasks list.

▶ GTD uses the concept of Context to define where and when to focus on particular tasks. It identifies tags like @Computer and @Phone that you can sort on to show you candidate tasks to work on when you are in those settings. MYN does not have a similar concept. In fact, in these days of smartphones, tablets, and other mobile devices, I do not see a strong need for identifying Context. But that said, if you find the Context approach to be useful, you can easily add GTD Context tags to tasks in the MYN system by placing them in Outlook Categories that are then tagged on your MYN tasks. You can then use the skills you learned in Lesson 3 to add a category column to your MYN tasks lists. That way, you consider Context when you work your tasks. You can even sort on that column to work similar tasks together. Before you do that, read the section "Adding a Categories Column to the To-Do Bar — Use Caution," in Lesson 12. It tells you how to do this safely.

Those are the obvious ways that GTD and MYN can be used together. I think you will find that MYN solves the common challenges people have with GTD, but still lets you implement all of GTD's principles. And I think you will find that GTD principles help clarify how best to use MYN. Feel free to use as many or as few of these ideas as you like to merge the two systems.

Significant Outcomes (SOCs)

The recommendation I stated earlier to put only next-action tasks on your Now Tasks lists may lead to the following question: "How do I show bigger things I am working on?" It could be you are in the middle of a larger effort that you need to focus much of your free time on this week, and just listing next actions doesn't seem enough — you want to give it more prominence.

I call these larger items "Significant Outcomes," or "SOCs" for short. These are usually the bigger deliverables you want to create (for example, a large report) that you are actively working on, in between meetings and other ad hoc tasks. They might also be a large and less tangible accomplishment (a cleaned-up and organized office, for example) that you would like to get done as soon as possible, and you want to highlight it somehow on your list.

You often have no specific time you intend to work on it. Rather, you intend to fit some work on them into your schedule when you can. Or you may have smaller tasks on your Now Tasks list that are leading toward the larger outcome, and you want to track that overall outcome.

SOCs Are Smaller Than Goals or Projects

SOCs are not significant enough to be called goals—*goals* implies something beyond the task level (see my book *Master Your Workday Now!* for extensive coverage of how to set and manage goals). I do not like calling them projects either—to me the word *project* implies a much bigger activity, often employing formal project management methodologies.

SOCs are just very large tasks, and as with most tasks, typically you focus on these when you have time and it feels right. For example, you may decide, "During this week my major effort between meetings will be to get the quarterly report done." Or you may think, "This week I want to finish the BigCo proposal."

It is especially satisfying to complete a few important SOCs each week, as it leads to a significant sense of forward momentum. I call this "knocking your SOCs off." So I encourage you to list a few each week and track them.

Deciding how to record SOCs in your task system can be a quandary. Just listing them as Opportunity Now tasks seems too small because they may get lost; you want them in your awareness all week. And they are not Critical Now tasks for any given day, so putting them there does not make sense either. And scheduling specific time for them on your calendar may not feel right either, because you may not be sure when during the week you want to work on them; these are often background activities.

So you need a way to give these Significant Outcomes a general but prominent focus—to keep your attention on doing them during a given week or two.

How to Show SOCs

I recommend two ways to indicate SOCs in Outlook using the MYN system.

If you use a monthly or weekly calendar, you can place them as a banner appointment across a period of time, such as a week, or even longer. In Outlook, that means creating a nonblocking banner appointment on the Outlook calendar for the week, and then listing one or more SOCs in that banner appointment. I give it a distinctive category color like green so it stands out. Figure 6.3 is an example of how this might look in the monthly view.

Another way to do this in Outlook is to list it as a Critical Now task with the letters SOC: in front like this: "SOC:Finish Quarterly Report." That way you see it many times a day. This is the only Critical Now item that makes sense to carry over from day to day.

And finally, after you create an SOC, don't forget to put any appropriate next action tasks for these SOCs right in your Now Tasks list.

Figure 6.3
Significant Outcomes (SOCs) shown in calendar.

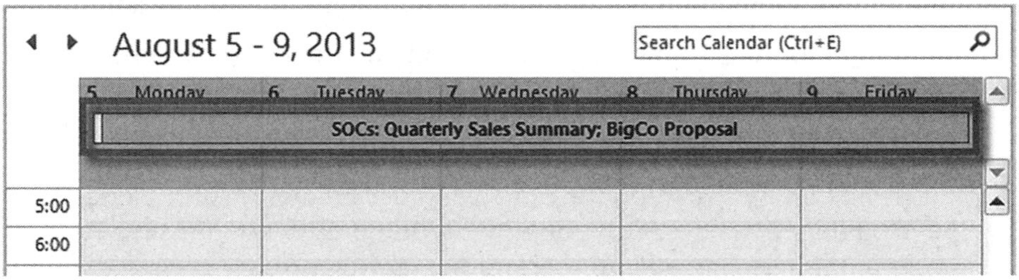

SOCs: Quarterly Sales Summary; BigCo Proposal

SOCs Are Excellent for Deadlines

SOCs are excellent items to put deadlines on. Do you recall how I said that I rarely put deadlines on the typical small next-action tasks I place on my Now Tasks list? That's because they are usually smaller steps on the road to a larger outcome, and the larger outcome is the thing that usually has the true deadline. Well, a SOC is perfect for this because it is usually the larger thing that I am working toward—it is exactly the right place to put the deadline.

Use the deadline approaches I listed in Lesson 4. For example, write the deadline date directly on the SOC subject line: "SOC: DUE Fri Mar 7, Quarterly Report."

Use Follow-Up Tasks for Actions You Are Waiting On Others For

Here is a technique that can protect you from fire drills caused by colleagues or staff who don't deliver. How often in your organization does someone promise to deliver something but never follows through? Perhaps you're in a meeting and a promise is made to fix something. Or you direct someone who works for you to complete some work by a certain date. The trouble is, you usually forget that the promise was made until well after the item is due. Then you kick yourself for not doing something earlier to usher the task forward. Whether this is a formal delegation or simply a promise made in a meeting, if you want to make sure it gets done, you need to follow up with the person who promised it at some point before the deadline, to encourage them on. Sometimes people say they will do something and really intend it, but just forget. Other times they say they will do it only to get you off their back. In either case, wouldn't it be nice if you had an automatic way to remind yourself to check in with these people to make sure the promised activity is being done?

Instead of a Waiting-For List

Many task management systems use a "waiting for" list to track items like this. It is one long list of all the things that you are waiting on others to get to you. The idea is to check that list every day or so and then follow up with those items that seem urgent. Outlook has a status value called Waiting On Somebody Else that can be applied to tasks, just to accomplish this.

I don't like using a waiting-for list, and I do not use that Outlook status setting. The problem with this approach is there is no way to tell by examining the list which waiting-for items need urgent follow-up and which can wait. You need to think about each item, consider when you last checked in on it, decide if now is a good time to do another follow-up, and then move to the next item. I find this way too much work to do every day on a long list. Plus, keeping a separate list to check is one more process you need to remember to do each day.

Create a Follow-Up Task

Instead, my recommended approach to items that you are waiting on is to create follow-up tasks for each item at the time the promise is made; here's how. As soon as someone promises you something, at that point decide when an appropriate time to follow up would be. Then create a task on your own list with a start date of that day. Put an F: in front of the subject line and perhaps the name of the responsible person; for example, "F: Tom–Send me Planning Dept. file." Then, on the date that task pops into your task list, do the follow-up; call the person or write them an e-mail.

This is so much better than a waiting-for list because it removes any ambiguity as to when an action is needed. You decide this when you make the entry, and the actions appear in your task list exactly when needed. Otherwise, examining a waiting-for list can be a painful and uncertain activity. What's worse, you may be examining items that do not need to be followed up on for weeks at a time; this can extend the review unnecessarily and lead you to review less often. The result is that you might miss some important follow-up activities. Follow-up tasks appear right in the same task list you use every day, so you are more likely to do the follow-up. For these reasons, I feel using follow-up tasks is the best method for tracking items that you are waiting for.

Two Types of Follow-Up Tasks

There are two ways to do this. The first way I just described: You are in a meeting or have a verbal discussion with someone, a promise is made, and you note the need to track the promise. Just create the task manually in your task list, with a future date. The key here is to select a good follow-up date. If it is a Monday and you need something by Friday, perhaps you should set the follow-up for Wednesday, to give them time to respond to your reminder. When Wednesday comes and the task appears, give the person a call. With tight timing like that, give that task a High priority; that way it appears in your Critical Now list and you do not delay on your follow-up activity.

The other way of creating a follow-up task is useful when you make your original request for action through an e-mail. I have a few tools you can use to automate that process, but you will need to wait to Lesson 7, where I give a much more complete discussion on how to convert e-mails to tasks (in section "Create Follow-Up Tasks for Important Requests You Make by E-mail"). And in Lesson 10, I expand on this concept considerably when I cover the topic of delegation.

But for now, start creating future-dated follow-up tasks whenever someone promises an action that you really want completed. I think you'll find this to be very useful.

Summary

So as you can see, there are a wide variety of tasks that you should enter in Outlook. Here are some key points from this lesson:

▶ Make sure you record all your current tasks in one place: Outlook. Do not keep multiple to-do lists.

▶ Use appointments instead of tasks when appropriate, but reserve appointments only for those items that have specific times during the day they need to be done. Otherwise use the tasks list.

▶ You have many options for viewing your MYN task list on your mobile devices, and for collecting tasks while on the move.

▶ Don't list goals or projects on your Now Tasks list, because these broad items are not actionable during a busy workday. Rather, write all your tasks only as next actions; write the next physical action needed to achieve an outcome.

▶ If you are a GTD user, consider using GTD and MYN together. There are many ways they complement each other.

▶ Use Significant Outcomes to track and manage larger efforts that do not warrant formal project management techniques.

▶ Create follow-up tasks when waiting for promises others have made you.

Next Steps

In the next lesson I will enlarge on the technique you learned earlier for converting e-mails to tasks.

Lesson 7:
Cure "Inbox Stress" by Converting
E-mails to Tasks

Introduction

Inbox Stress Can Be Cured

You need a cure for what I call "Inbox stress" — that sinking feeling you have when you glance at an overwhelmed Outlook Inbox. It's the stress you feel when you know your Inbox is full of unreconciled requests that will come back to haunt you. It's the dread you feel as you realize you are going to have to sort through and reread weeks or months of mail to find e-mails you promised yourself to come back to or skipped over and never looked at.

Note: *This lesson is summarized in videos 6 and 11 of the MYN-Outlook Complete Video Training (see beginning of the Quick Start chapter for more information).*

Beyond Quick Start and Lesson 2

In the Quick Start and at the end of Lesson 2, I introduced how to convert action e-mails to tasks. The reason I started you so early on this practice was to give you an early taste of how powerful this action really is. When used correctly, it is the solution for Inbox stress. It allows you to remove the tension from your Inbox by moving unreconciled actions into the task system, where they can be prioritized, scheduled, delegated, worked, or deferred, all with appropriate tools to do so effectively. It allows you to work through your Inbox much more quickly by giving you a way to process action e-mails without stalling on them. And it allows you to fulfill the Lesson 5 steps of emptying your Inbox. If you are doing that now and emptying your Inbox following Lesson 5, I suspect your Inbox stress is nearly cured.

There are some fine points, however, to converting e-mails to tasks that you need to know as you do this more, so I am now going to devote a full lesson to the topic. And in case you have not yet started converting e-mails to tasks, I want to fully convince you here how important this is.

For those who *have* started using this practice on their own Inbox, you probably have noticed how, after you did this, it was much easier to move mail out of your Inbox. Converting e-mails to tasks is the primary enabler of reaching an empty Inbox. In addition, after you do it regularly, you will complete the processing of your Inbox much faster. You will also get important e-mail actions moved into your MYN task list where they can be better managed. Ultimately, you will get much closer to being in full control of your workday. Converting e-mails to tasks is the number one most important skill you will learn in this book.

What's in This Lesson

In this lesson you will learn:

▶ More ideas on why converting e-mails to tasks is so critical to getting e-mail and tasks under control.

▶ How the Mac and Windows versions vary in this action.

▶ How to include or access attachments in converted mail so that files you need are at hand when you do the task.

▶ Three other ways to convert e-mails to tasks.

▶ More about flagged-mail tasks: what they are and when to use them. Although flagged-mail tasks are another way to convert e-mails to tasks, they need to be used with caution.

▶ How to create follow-up tasks from e-mail you send in a way that makes tracking your requests to others much more powerful.

Let's start with a bit more background on why this skill is so powerful.

The Trouble with E-mail

Learning how to use e-mail effectively is essential to succeeding in the modern work environment. Why? Because e-mail, which was supposed to *improve* work, actually makes us work *harder*. And I am not referring to just the time it takes to read or respond to e-mail. Rather, the real reason e-mail makes us work harder is that e-mail leads to many more *business interactions* per day than we ever could have with only live phone calls or in-person meetings. Both of those were limited by the hours in the day, but the e-mail inbox knows no such limits.

Business interactions almost always lead to required action. Think about it. If someone sends you a business e-mail these days—tag, you're it. "I sent you an e-mail on this. Didn't you read it?" You are now on notice, either to process the information or, more commonly, to take some additional action. You can get dozens, even hundreds of these per day.

And while more business interactions per day can multiply our business success (more sales, more clients, and so on — the upside of e-mail), the added actions represent added work. So yes, we are busier at work, due to e-mail, than ever before. Using e-mail intelligently and managing it efficiently is essential to succeeding in the modern work environment.

Strategies to Fix E-mail in Today's Office

Most people don't think in terms of the potential for greater business success when it comes to e-mail. Instead, they see an overloaded inbox and the hours spent thrashing through their mail. People have tried lots of strategies to get around the e-mail problem and optimize its use. For example, some people suggest you control when you read e-mail so as to decrease its impact on your workday. There is even a book titled *Never Check E-mail in the Morning*. And some well-known personalities have posted "e-mail bankruptcy," declaring null and void all old e-mail. A governor of New Jersey several years ago announced to his staff and the world that he was quitting e-mail altogether — he directed them all to other means of communication.

But you do not need to quit e-mail, you just need to be smart in how you use it. The first step to that is to recognize that the problem is not with *reading* e-mail but rather with *doing* e-mail.

For example, deleting spam or wasting time on unneeded cc'd mail (colleague spam) is not what bogs down our ability to get through the inbox. Both of those are irritating, but they don't actually lead to our major inbox problems.

Rather, it is the way we handle (or don't handle) *important* e-mail, e-mail with potential actions for us to do, which skids us off track. It's this mail that kills a huge chunk of our day. The trouble is, we do not have a natural way to prioritize our reactions to mail like this, so our inbox and workday spin out of control.

The Solution

The solution is to use the following core principle of my training and this book:

Unless it is time-urgent, don't take significant actions on an e-mail when you first read it. Instead, quickly convert an action e-mail to a prioritized, date-assigned Outlook task, and continue to read or scan all your new mail to the bottom of your Inbox. File that mail out of your Inbox, and work all your tasks off your Now Tasks list.

This is an important, powerful, and *simple to implement* rule. Here's why it's important. What many of us do is try to work action requests as they arrive in the Inbox, thinking we are being proactive. The trouble with this is that these days we all get too much e-mail—way too much to act on everything each day. If we attempt to act on every e-mail as we get it, we miss other important work. By acting on mail as it comes in we are likely working our lowest-priority tasks first. No wonder our important work is not complete at the end of the day. And we'll never get to the bottom of our Inbox that way.

Some of us, after reading an e-mail, skip even an important action—leaving it in the Inbox with the promise to get to it later. Later, we spend hours trying to find the important stuff in our Inbox. This is especially difficult because the titles of e-mail rarely match the request inside. So we are forced to open and reread each e-mail looking for those actions. What a mess and unnecessary churn this creates.

Instead, Speed Through E-mail

Instead, you will speed through your mail by spending only a few seconds converting such action e-mails into *prioritized, dated tasks in Outlook*, without taking action first, and moving on. You will use simple Outlook techniques for converting e-mails to tasks detailed in this lesson. You will then work these tasks later along with your other work, *in priority order,* using the task system you learned in Lessons 1, 4, and 6. As a result, you end up purposely deferring or deleting many e-mail actions that do not make the priority cut, and that is a good thing in today's overloaded work and e-mail environment. By doing this, you ensure that current commitments on your task list get attended to along with e-mail actions just moved there. The important items get first action, and many requests get prioritized downward. What a novel concept, working your highest-priority actions first! That's what you can do by converting e-mails to tasks.

Shouldn't We Just Use E-mail Less?

Some people say the solution is for organizations to use e-mail far less often for business communication. I disagree. I certainly believe the Reply All button should be used much more sparingly, as we all suffer from colleague spam as a result of overuse. But mistakes like that should not mean using e-mail less for business communications. E-mail has a huge number of advantages when used and managed correctly:

▶ E-mail can allow batching up of communication processing, which allows you to focus for longer periods of uninterrupted time on dedicated work.

▶ Sending e-mail prevents you from interrupting or distracting yourself and your coworkers with an in-person call or meeting every time you need to pass on information or seek it out.

▶ It speeds communications because you can send a message without starting a live discussion, which usually takes longer.

▶ It speeds communications because you do not need to wait for appropriate times to deliver a communication.

▶ E-mail tracks communications by creating a record of every sent and received e-mail.

▶ It clarifies communications because the well-written word leaves little room for misunderstanding, and the reader can reread a message as often as is needed to fully understand the communication.

All of these advantages, when fully realized, will contribute to the goal of getting your tasks done more quickly and achieving greater accomplishments at work.

So no, don't use e-mail less often. Rather, learn how to use and manage e-mail more *intelligently*. Converting action e-mails to tasks effectively (and sometimes into appointments), and emptying your Inbox daily, are two primary ways to do this.

Note: In Lesson 11, I'll show some other e-mail management tips that will help you and your company or organization become more productive with e-mail, including ways to make the e-mail you send more useful.

Using Outlook Tools to Convert E-mails to Tasks

When you find an action item in your e-mail, you could create a new task by hand—that is, create a blank task—and copy and paste the e-mail into it. However, as we've seen, some easy tools are built in to Outlook to *convert* e-mail messages directly into tasks. When using these tools, the entire text of the mail is stored in the new task, and the subject line of the task takes on the subject line of the e-mail (which in most cases you will then want to edit). You can optionally include attachments in Windows Outlook. And there is additional Outlook add-in software that makes the conversion even smarter.

Multiple Ways to Convert E-mails to Tasks

In the Quick Start, and at the end of Lesson 2, I showed you a simple way to convert an e-mail to a task. But there are really more ways to do this, and many subtleties to how you can do it.

For Windows, there are five ways to convert e-mail messages to tasks. The primary way is what you've already learned—a simple drag and drop operation. This is best for e-mails without attached files. The second method, a modified drag and drop, is best for e-mails *with* attached files. Third is to use the flag tool. Fourth is to use the Move menu, and fifth is to use a Quick Steps button.

For the Mac, there are two methods: using an AppleScript to create a true Outlook task, and using the flag tool.

Note: *In their simplest form, all these methods maintain a copy of the original e-mail in the Inbox, which is what I recommend; more on that point later.*

Let's go over all of these in the order I listed them. Windows Outlook gets more coverage here because it has more options for converting e-mails to *true* Outlook tasks compared to the Mac, and that leads to a number of opportunities for refining the ways you manage tasks.

Converting E-mails to Tasks in Windows Outlook with a Drag-and-Drop Operation

One of the Windows Outlook features that makes it so powerful is that you can convert *any* data type to any other data type with a simple drag-and-drop operation. (This feature is not present in the Mac version of Outlook.) You use this capability extensively for converting e-mails to tasks, as I describe next. You might also use this drag-and-drop procedure for converting e-mails to calendar appointments or for converting tasks to e-mails; I'll talk about those optional capabilities, as well.

Note: *In the following steps for converting e-mails to tasks in Windows Outlook, you always drag the e-mail to the Tasks icon (or Tasks label in 2013) in the lower-left corner of the Outlook window. You should not attempt to drag the e-mail directly into the To-Do Bar task list (dragging to the right). Why? In recent versions of Outlook, you might get an error message. But even if it appears to work, notice that it creates a flagged-mail task, not a true task. You always want to create true tasks, so do not drag to the right.*

The methods I showed you in the Quick Start and at the end of Lesson 2 just scratched the surface of the drag-and-drop technique. Let's look at some more details starting with the basic operation of creating tasks without attachments.

Detailed Steps: Creating Tasks Without Attachments

Here are the detailed steps behind the drag-and-drop method in the Quick Start and at the end of Lesson 2. This procedure creates tasks with a copy of the e-mail text in the notes section of the task. But it does not pick up attachments from the e-mail.

After you decide that an e-mail contains a task that is important to you (and it has no attachment you want to include with the task), close the e-mail and follow these steps:

1.   From your regular e-mail *list* view, click the e-mail item and drag it to the Tasks folder icon, banner button, or label in the bottom-left corner of Outlook. Depending on which version of Outlook you have and how you have configured it, the Tasks folder icon is located at the bottom of the Navigation Pane (2007 and 2010) or as a label or icon in the bottom-left corner (2013). For a complete description of where to find the Tasks folder icon or banner button, see Lesson 2.

2. A new task window containing the entire e-mail text opens, and the task name is the same as the subject name of the e-mail. That means you have very little typing to do to complete the conversion. But do the following steps immediately:

Alert: Outlook 2010 often displays odd behavior when dragging and dropping an e-mail like this. The new task window might flash for a moment and then disappear behind the main Outlook window. This happens if you leave your mouse for more than a second over the Tasks folder icon or banner button prior to releasing it. To avoid this, immediately after your mouse passes over the Tasks folder icon or banner button, release the mouse button quickly. If the new task window does disappear, just move the main Outlook window aside to find it. If you are unable to make a habit of releasing the mouse button quickly, see the section "Using Quick Steps (Windows Outlook 2010 and 2013)" later in this lesson to learn an alternate method of converting e-mails to tasks.

3. Change the title of the task so that it is in next-action format. This is an essential step: You must extract from the e-mail the core next action it implies and write that in the subject line, overwriting the old e-mail title. Lesson 6 covers next actions and how to write them.

4. Set a start date for this task. Set it to today, or earlier, if you want to see it in the To-Do Bar now, or defer it to a later date. Do not leave the date at None. If you are undecided on the date, then set it to today. Allow the Due Date field to match the Start Date field (that's automatic). Recall that the Due Date field is ignored in the MYN Outlook system due to the unfortunate linkages in Outlook. Decide on and set the task Priority field according to the principles in Lesson 4. Click Save & Close in the upper-left corner of the new Task dialog box.

That's it! Your task has been saved in the task database in Outlook. If the Start Date field was set to today or earlier, and you made Lesson 3 configurations, the new task appears on your To-Do Bar.

Converting an e-mail to a task by this method does not save any e-mail attachments to the new task. If you want to do that, follow the steps in the next section.

Creating Tasks with Attachments: Detailed Steps

The second drag-and-drop method allows you to pick up attachments in your task. It does this by converting the e-mail itself into an attachment and placing it in the notes section of the task, as shown in Figure 7.1. This is a complete and fully functional e-mail, and if you open it all its original attachments are inside.

Figure 7.1
Result of creating a task with the e-mail saved as an attachment.

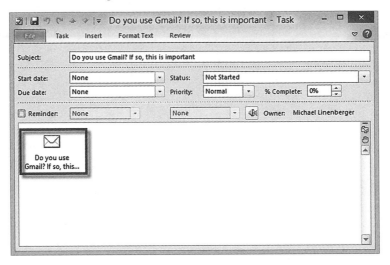

There are three reasons to use this method. First and most obvious is if your e-mails to be converted to tasks have attachments that you wish to save within the resulting task item. Second, if you think you might want to easily convert the task back to an e-mail someday (perhaps to reply to it after the task is done), this method allows that. Because the attached e-mail is a complete and fully functional e-mail, you can reply to it, forward it, and so on.

The third reason is a bit more subtle. When Outlook converts an e-mail to a task using the text-only method, it sometimes reformats the text layout in the task in undesirable ways—in some cases it even makes the message unreadable. This is especially true with HTML e-mail messages. Using the attachment method provides a way to see the correctly formatted message.

Here are the steps for conversion:

1. Right-click the mail item to drag it to the tasks folder. When you release the mouse button over the tasks folder icon, a four-item shortcut menu opens. Choose Copy Here as Task with Attachment, the second item in the menu (see Figure 7.2).

Figure 7.2
Shortcut menu when dragging an e-mail to create a task.

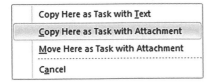

Note: *This right-click operation can be difficult. If you do it incorrectly you do not see the four item shortcut menu but a different, longer menu. If that happens to you, keep trying. The trick is to make sure you right-click and <u>hold down</u> the right mouse button and then drag the item with that button still held down.*

   2. A new Task dialog box opens. (If the dialog box flashes and seems to disappear, a solution can be found in the alert after step 2 in the previous section.) The complete e-mail is an attachment in the notes section of this Task dialog box (see Figure 7.1). Any attachments to the original e-mail are left intact and nested in this attachment.

   3. Immediately retitle the task to indicate the core next action, and set the start date and priority. If you are undecided on the date, then set it to today. Allow the Due Date field to match the Start Date field, which is automatic. (Recall that the Due Date field is ignored in the MYN Outlook system due to the unfortunate linkages built in to Outlook.) Decide on and set the task Priority field according to the principles in Lesson 4. Click Save & Close in the upper-left corner of the new Task dialog box.

Later, when acting on the task, to open the original e-mail, just double-click the e-mail icon in the task item. The e-mail that opens is a fully operational e-mail with all its original attachments. You are able to reply to this e-mail, which makes this right-click technique useful even for e-mails without attachments. That way, you don't need to search for the original e-mail in your mail system. It's right in your task when you need it.

Copying as task with attachment is a great way to create follow-up tasks for important e-mail responses you're waiting for. That's described in the section "Create Follow-Up Tasks for Important Requests You Make by E-mail" near the end of this lesson.

Another advantage of this method is that it gives you the choice to delete the original e-mail at the same time you create the task. Use the third item in the shortcut menu (Move Here as Task with Attachment; see Figure 7.2). I don't normally recommend doing that, as discussed later, but there might be times when it is appropriate.

Disadvantages of the Right-Click Method

There are a few disadvantages to using this technique, so consider these when deciding whether to use this or the normal left-click method. First, because this is a complete copy of the original e-mail, if the attachments are large, using the right-click method doubles the impact of this message on your mail storage. If your mail storage is limited, this might be a factor.

Second, when examining the task later, you need to double-click the e-mail icon in the notes section of the task to read the original e-mail. Some might see this as an extra step. This trivial step is usually not a problem. But if you really want to see the text of the e-mail when you first open the task and have the attachments there too, do this: Create the task with the text-only method, and then open the original e-mail and drag the e-mail attachment from the e-mail to the newly created task window. This way, both the e-mail text and the attachments are visible when you open your new task. Even better, install the ClearContext add-in software and use the special Task button. It creates a task that includes both text and attachments automatically.

Converting E-mails to Tasks in Outlook for Mac 2011

In Outlook for Mac 2011, the drag-and-drop conversion features that have been in Windows versions of Outlook for years do not exist. So to convert an e-mail to a true task on the Mac, you need to use an AppleScript utility provided in the script menu at the right end of the Outlook menu bar. Here's how.

Creating Tasks

1. With a message selected in Outlook for Mac 2011, simply open the AppleScript menu at the far right end of the menu bar (see the very top of Figure 7.3—it looks like a small scrolled document) and choose Create Task from Message.

    Figure 7.3
    Outlook for Mac 2011 AppleScript menu to create a task from an e-mail.

    Note: *If the Create Task from Message command shown in Figure 7.3 is not present in your software, go to this link to fix that: www.myn.bz/MacScript.htm (link is case sensitive).*

2. A new task window containing the entire e-mail text opens, and the task name is the same as the subject name of the e-mail. That means you have very little typing to do to complete the conversion. But do the following steps immediately:

3. Change the title of the task so that it is in next-action format. This is an essential step. You must extract from the e-mail the core next action it

implies and write that into the subject line, overwriting the old e-mail title. Lesson 6 covers next actions and how to write them.

4. Set a start date for this task. Set it to today or earlier if you want to see it in the MYN task list, or defer it to a later date. Do not leave the date at None. If you are undecided on the date, then set it to today. Allow the Due Date field to match the Start Date field (that's automatic). Recall that the Due Date field is ignored in the MYN system due to the unfortunate linkages built in to Outlook. Decide on and set the task Priority field. Click Save & Close in the upper-left corner of the new Task dialog box.

That's it! Your task has been saved in the task database inside Outlook. If the Start Date field was set to today or earlier, and you made Lesson 3 configurations, the new task appears in your MYN task list.

Note: *Step 1 in the steps I just listed works both if the e-mail is selected in a mail list view and if the e-mail itself is open for reading. This is an advantage over Windows Outlook.*

What About Attachments on the Mac Version?

Unlike in the Windows versions of Outlook, tasks in Outlook 2011 cannot hold attachments—which is a real shame. I am not sure why they cannot, because e-mails can. I especially miss this feature when converting e-mails to tasks. Often the e-mail has a file attached that I will need to refer to when I work on the action in the e-mail later. Or I may want to reply to that e-mail later, so I'd like to attach it to the task. This is one big disadvantage compared to Windows Outlook.

You can work around that, however. Assuming you save or file your mail as discussed in Lesson 5, you can use the search tool in Outlook 2011 (called Spotlight) to easily find that e-mail and its attachments later. Here's how:

With the task open, select and copy a unique phrase or sentence from the notes section of the task (text in the task notes section came from the original e-mail). Next, activate the Processed Mail folder and paste the text in the Spotlight search box. Doing that search should allow you to find the original e-mail almost instantly. You can then either reply to it or access the attachments inside.

Note: *If the e-mail is filed somewhere other than the Processed Mail folder, select All Mail at the left edge of the Search tab on the Ribbon to help you find it.*

Other Methods to Convert E-mails to Tasks (Windows)

The drag-and-drop methods are not the only ways to convert e-mails to tasks in Windows Outlook. There are three more. One is to use the Move menu, and another is to create two Quick Step commands to automate the process. The third method is flagging the mail, although it does not create a true task. Let's start with that third method.

Use Flags on E-mail to Mark Deferred Replies, and When Mobile

In Lesson 2, we learned that flagging a mail item, while it appears to create a task, does not create a *true* task. Rather, it creates a flagged-mail task. I discourage using such flagged-mail tasks in Outlook; however, there are two cases where using flags makes sense.

▶ Flagged-mail tasks are good for marking deferred replies. In other words, use them when you see an e-mail whose only action is a reply (and you can't write that reply now). Remove the flag after you write the reply.

▶ Flagged-mail tasks are also good for marking tasks in e-mail that you're reading on a mobile device — one that does not have the tools for converting e-mails into true tasks (see Lesson 6).

Later in this lesson, I'll give you more details on how to use flags.

Using The Move Menu (Windows)

You can convert an e-mail to a task with the Move menu in Windows Outlook. There are three ways to access this menu:

▶ Select the e-mail in the folder list and click the Move button at the top of the Outlook window (in Outlook 2010 and 2013 look in the Home tab), then choose Tasks. Or choose Other Folder and find Tasks in the folder tree.

▶ Use the same steps as in the previous bullet, but find the Move menu by right-clicking the e-mail in the folder list view.

▶ Click the Move menu at the top of the open e-mail (the same choices described in the previous bullets are displayed).

Use caution when using the Move menu because this deletes the original e-mail from your Inbox or other folder where you are selecting the e-mail. Even if you cancel the operation partway through, it still deletes the e-mail, and you might not notice that. If you do that accidentally, you can restore the e-mail by finding it in the Deleted Items folder and dragging it back to your Inbox.

To avoid deleting the e-mail from your Inbox or other folder, when you use the menus described in the previous bullets, look at the bottom of the Move menu for the command Copy to Folder. With this you can create the task and leave a copy of the e-mail in the original folder. This is my preferred approach when using menus to create a task.

Note: *When you use the Move menu you can only convert the task as text. There isn't a way to use it to convert the e-mail as an attachment.*

Using Quick Steps (Windows Outlook 2010 and 2013)

Starting with Outlook 2010, Microsoft added a new feature to Windows Outlook called Quick Steps. With Quick Steps, you can automate a number of commonly used functions in Outlook, and it can be an excellent time-saver. One good use of it is to create a few one-click buttons that convert e-mails to tasks.

There are three advantages of doing this. First, using it is quicker than the drag and drop technique. Second, it eliminates the 2010 bug that causes the task window to disappear. Third, it places a copy of that button right in the open e-mail window, so it enables you to convert an e-mail to a task without returning to the Inbox list view.

The disadvantage is that it does not work on multiple selected e-mails — only one e-mail at a time can be converted. So you'll want to retain your drag-and drop-skills for such cases.

I am going to show you how to add two Quick Steps buttons: one to create tasks with attachments and one to create tasks without. Because the steps to add those buttons are complex, I prepared a video that teaches you how to do this. To watch this complimentary video, go to www.myn.bz/mvc.htm, and select video #24.

Note: *Similar to Quick Steps, the Outlook add-in software ClearContext also adds a button to all e-mails to convert them to tasks. It has one advantage: it can insert the e-mail both as text and as an attachment — the best of both worlds.*

Tips for Converting E-mails to Tasks (Windows and Mac)

Header Information at Top of Task Notes Section

In Windows Outlook, after you convert an e-mail to a task, you will notice at the top of the notes section of the task, just above the e-mail text, that Outlook has inserted some useful header information about the source e-mail. This includes the sender, the date of the e-mail, and the original e-mail subject line. Later, when you work the task, this provides you some context about the original e-mail that led to the task.

On the Mac that's not true. Using the Outlook 2011 script described in the previous section does not insert that header information, so later you might be confused about the context of the task. To fix that, here's a workaround. Before using the Create Task from Message command, first create — but don't send — a reply message to the original e-mail. Then apply the command with that reply message window open. This creates the header, inserts it in the body of the new task, and gives you the context you need. Then delete the reply without sending it.

Converting Text Tasks Back to E-mails

In Windows, copying as a task with attachment is not the only way to enable replies to converted tasks. If you create a task as text and later decide you want to reply to the original e-mail, there are ways to convert it back to an e-mail. The easiest is to drag the task from the task list to the Mail banner button (the Mail label in 2013) or to the Inbox icon. You'll need to edit the resulting e-mail to remove the old header information and put an address on it. For more details, see Lesson 11.

You can't do this with the Mac. However, if you are in the habit of using Spotlight to find the original e-mail as described in the earlier section "What About Attachments on the Mac Version," the method in that section is all you need. Just find and reply to the original e-mail.

Dragging More Than One E-mail Simultaneously (Windows)

Let's say there are three e-mails in your Inbox that pertain to a task you want to create, and you want to save all three of them in a single task. In Windows, you can create one task by pressing CTRL or SHIFT, and selecting the three e-mails in the list view. You can then drag them all at one time. If you create a task as text, the text of all three e-mails is placed in the notes section of the task, one below the other. If you create a task as an attachment, three attachment icons appear in the task notes section. You can also add another e-mail to an existing task later: Open the task and drag the e-mail to the notes section of the task. Unfortunately, on the Mac these approaches do not work.

Turn Off Message AutoPreview and Reading Pane

I find it easier to scan through messages and quickly convert e-mail to tasks if I turn off the message AutoPreview and Reading Pane features of Outlook. Give it a try. You might find this helps you, as well.

Reading Pane is a Windows and Mac feature you can use to see the contents of the currently selected message displayed in a separate segment of the Outlook window, usually to the right of the Inbox. AutoPreview is a Windows-only feature that shows you two or three lines under each message in the Inbox.

I find both of these distracting. They also reduce the number of e-mails I can see at one time in the Inbox list. So I turn them off. When I do, I can move faster through my mail by scanning titles and sender information alone and only occasionally opening a message. Try this yourself and see what you think. Here is how.

To turn off the Reading Pane, in all versions of Windows and on the Mac, go to the View menu or tab, choose Reading Pane, and from the submenu select Off (Windows) or Hidden (Mac).

To turn off AutoPreview in Outlook 2007, go the View menu and find Auto-Preview. If there's a check mark next to it, clear it by selecting it. To turn off

AutoPreview in Outlook 2010 and 2013, it's more complicated than in 2007. At the top of the Inbox, right-click any column label, such as From. Then choose View Settings from the context menu, and click the Other Settings button. In the AutoPreview section of the resulting dialog box, select No Auto-Preview. Then click OK all the way out. I think you'll now find that scanning e-mail to identify tasks is much easier.

Don't Convert Actions That You Can Do in One Minute

Needless to say, if you can actually do an action faster than you can convert an e-mail to a task, common sense says to just do it immediately. Typical for this would be a quick one-sentence e-mail note or reply. But be careful: If that act turns into a 20-minute discourse, you've gone off the track.

Why You Should *Copy* and Not *Move* the E-mails (Windows)

As mentioned earlier, when you right-click and drag a task, and then open the shortcut menu over the task icon, you'll see as in Figure 7.2 that the third item down in that context menu is the command Move Here as Task With Attachment. This means you can choose to *move* the e-mails to a task rather than *copy* it. A move operation removes the e-mail from your Inbox. Some users may be eager to do that, thinking, "Hey, I processed that e-mail so now let's get rid of it."

I do not usually recommend doing that, though. Why? Because there are *two* components of most action e-mails and both are important. There is the *action* component, which is what the task represents, and there is also an *information* component that you might need to reference separately from executing the task. Most of us are used to looking in saved e-mail for the information component. Years ago I used to *move* instead of *copy* during task creation, but not anymore, because I often spent hours looking in the wrong place (saved e-mail) only to recall that I had converted it to a task. Now I always *copy* when I create tasks from e-mails. There are just too many times I search my saved mail for things. If you are dragging all mail to the Processed Mail folder each day, it's soon out of your Inbox anyway.

Creating Appointments from E-mails (Windows)

Nearly everything I have described in the previous sections for creating Outlook tasks also applies to creating Outlook *appointments* on the Outlook calendar. Just drag an e-mail to the Calendar icon or banner button. In addition to setting the date, you'll need to set the time, of course, but all else is similar.

The times you will want to do this should be obvious: whenever an action e-mail leads you to create a calendar appointment. For example, Jon Brown sends me a note saying a meeting is needed and asking me to set it up. His e-mail has details of what will be discussed. I just drag the e-mail to the calendar icon, an appointment item dialog box opens, and in that I set the date and time and change the title. If I have a second Outlook window open, I can drag directly to the intended date on the calendar. All I need to do is set the time.

Next, I send Jon an Outlook meeting invite generated from that item. Later, when I am about to go to the meeting, I can open the calendar item and all the original e-mail details from Jon about what will be discussed are right there.

Creating appointments from e-mails is needed much less often than creating tasks, particularly because many such e-mails arrive as an Outlook meeting invite already; all you need to do is accept it to place the meeting on your Calendar. But that said, this may come up occasionally. As mentioned before, however, do not get in the habit of placing all your tasks as appointments with yourself on your calendar. I will give more details about why this is not a good idea later in this lesson.

Flagged-Mail Tasks (Windows and Mac)

Near the end of Lesson 2, I spent quite a few pages discussing flagged-mail tasks and how to use them. Flagged-mail tasks are difficult to understand and often lead to issues, so make sure you have read that section in Lesson 2.

Here in this lesson, I want to review a small amount of that material, and then take it further.

Review of Flagged-Mail Tasks

As I discussed at the end of Lesson 2, one of the major changes in all the Outlook versions covered in this book, compared to earlier versions, is the promotion of flagged mail to near-task status. What I mean is this: When you activate a Follow Up flag at the right edge of an e-mail, a virtual copy of the e-mail is placed in the task list. It looks very much like a real task, so I call it a *flagged-mail task*.

Why are these so important? As you know by now, my number-one assertion about how to get control of mail is to convert action mail to tasks (and then manage them in your task system). So anything that makes this easier I highly welcome. Particularly because this new feature will lead thousands of people who normally would never do this to start converting action mail to tasks.

But don't celebrate yet, because this feature will initially introduce some con-fusion for MYN system users, enough so that I recommend limiting the use of flagged-mail tasks. Why? Because these flagged items, even though they show up in the task list, are not true Outlook tasks and therefore lack some important task features. For example, after it is flagged, if you open a flagged-mail task from your task list, you won't see date fields, a priority field, or the reminder field as you would in a task; it's still an e-mail. You can find equivalents of those in various places (in the e-mail Ribbon menus and the flag shortcut menu), but setting them is inconvenient compared to a true task window. And I have identified a long list of other limitations (see the next section, "Why Flagged-Mail Tasks May Not Be Right for Converting E-mail to Tasks in MYN"). These have led me to conclude that a more limited use of this feature is in order for MYN users. That said, it will play an important role, described after the next section.

Why Flagged-Mail Tasks May Not Be Right for Converting E-mail to Tasks in MYN

Here are the major limitations of using flagged-mail tasks as a comprehensive way of converting action e-mails to tasks for MYN users:

▶ Recall that you should always change the e-mail subject to an action phrase after converting to a task. With flagged-mail tasks in Windows Outlook, you *can* change the subject without changing the original e-mail subject, which *is* good. However you need to go find the new task in the To-Do Bar and change it there, which is inconvenient. In contrast, during conversions of mail to true tasks, the window that opens upon conversion is the right place to change that wording, and it is right in front of you. It is a much smoother set of steps. And on the Mac you cannot change the title.

▶ You can't easily edit or add additional text to the flagged mail, say for describing thoughts about how to execute the task. There is a way to enable that in Windows, but as in the previous point, you need to find the new task item, open it, and enable the editing there. Again, it is an awkward set of steps.

▶ As mentioned in the previous point, you won't see date fields, a priority field, or the reminder field when you open a flagged-mail task as you do in a true task; it's still an e-mail (though you can find e-mail equivalents by searching the e-mail Ribbon menus and the flag shortcut menu).

▶ If you connect handheld devices to Exchange Server, flagged mail items do not show up in the synced task lists of most devices. So you may not see all your tasks when mobile if you use flagged-mail tasks.

▶ In Windows, when working in the Tasks folder views, you need to select a special To-Do List folder to see flagged-mail tasks, and your existing Tasks folder custom views may not be visible there at first. This can be confusing.

▶ A flagged-mail task is a Search Folder item, so if you delete it, you delete the original e-mail as well. Awareness of that is needed as you handle these items.

Recommended Use for Flagged-Mail Tasks: Tagging Delayed Replies

Flagged-mail tasks are still useful, though, because in one very good way they fit nicely in the MYN system: marking e-mail replies you want to delay for a few hours or a day. Although I mentioned this earlier, it is so important I want to repeat it in more detail here.

For example, let's say you read an e-mail and realize that to reply adequately would take several minutes, and that time is not available now. It is silly to convert it to a task, which takes several steps and will be gone in hours. Rather, I recommend you flag this message so you can find it easily later in the day to do the reply.

Flagging an e-mail item works quite well for delayed replies because it is quick, it leaves the e-mail intact as an e-mail, and it is very easy to reply to. Many more reasons are listed in the following section.

Why Flagged-Mail Tasks Are Excellent for Tagging Delayed Replies

Here is a complete list of reasons why flagged-mail tasks are especially well suited for delayed replies:

▶ After flagging a mail item, if while emptying your Inbox you drag that flagged e-mail out of your Inbox, the corresponding task remains in your task list (assuming you skipped the optional setting in Lesson 3 that prevents that). This is a good thing because I often find that I am reluctant to empty my day's worth of mail when I recall mail items are in there that I intend to reply to. Now, after flagging them, I can select all mail in the Inbox and file it if I want, knowing my deferred replies are still neatly displayed and marked in my task list (however, I still recommend you leave them in the Inbox if you can).

▶ With default Outlook settings, when you create a flagged-mail task it sets a hidden start date to *today* for you. That's good; you usually want to reply the same day. And due to our Lesson 3 task list configurations, it sorts the copy of the item in the To-Do Bar to the top of the Normal priority section (nicely underlined in Windows). This makes them stand out.

▶ Flagged-mail tasks turn red in your Inbox the next day (assuming you allowed the default date setting of Today). That's appropriate because I feel you should reply within 24 hours to delayed replies; this reminds you to do that.

▶ A flagged-mail task puts a mail icon on the item in the MYN configured task list, so you can get in the habit of visually scanning for those first; replies are usually the first thing you should do (after must-do-today tasks), and this makes them easy to spot.

▶ In Windows, you can change the subject line to match the action name (with a little effort), and if you make that edit within the To-Do Bar list (not in the open flagged-mail task window), any later reply to that mail still carries the original subject line with it.

Other Impacts of Using Flagged-Mail Tasks

Here are few more impacts of using flagged-mail tasks.

The One Exception to Emptying Your Inbox Daily

One impact of flagging for deferred reply is this: When you collect and move your e-mails into the Processed Mail folder, you want to avoid the flagged items and leave them in your Inbox temporarily. Later, after you write the reply, immediately clear the flag and then file the mail in the Processed Mail folder.

Now, I know in Lesson 5, I strongly encouraged you to completely empty your Inbox daily. However, this is the one exception. Leaving such pending reply mail in your Inbox ensures that you will see it often throughout the day and get to the reply soon. When these are the only items left after clearing your Inbox at the end of the day, it reminds you that the replies are still in play. It's a good way to highlight their presence before you leave your office.

If a Flagged E-mail Persists, Convert It to a Task

But watch out. When you flag a deferred reply, try to keep the commitment to return to and reply to those messages *before the end of the day* (or early the next). I try to reply to all mail within 24 hours. You or your organization might want to set a similar standard for maximum reply times.

If you wait too long, too much flagged e-mail builds up and becomes hard to manage. Because flagged mail items do not have easy-to-use date and priority fields, they do not work well for long-term action management. Also, all mail needing a reply should be replied to in a reasonable time, even if the note is just to say, "Got your message. Busy now, will get back to you soon." Otherwise, team members might lose trust in e-mail as a reliable communication tool and revert to less efficient methods.

So to prevent the buildup of flagged mail, in cases where you know it might be many days before writing the reply, convert the e-mail to a *true* task instead of flagging it. Or if you know there is some other action needed before you can write the reply, convert the e-mail to a true task and *identify that action in the subject line*. In any case, if you see a flagged e-mail that has been sitting in your Inbox for more than two to three days, convert it to a true task and move it out of your Inbox. In all these cases, the element of time is becoming prominent, so you should start using the date fields on a *true* task to manage that timing.

Flagged-Mail Tasks Are Good for Marking Tasks On Smartphones (Windows and Mac)

Another good use for flagged-mail tasks is with smartphones that have no software to convert e-mails to tasks. Most smartphone mail apps don't allow task conversion but *do* allow flagging mail. So, if you see an e-mail on your smartphone that requires later action, flag the item on your smartphone. Then, when you are back at your desk or laptop, you'll see those flagged items and be reminded to convert them to true tasks.

In Lesson 6, we learned that there are two third-party apps that do support converting e-mails to tasks, so use them if you can (instead of using flags for tasks). On Android it's the app called Touchdown; you can read more at: www.myn.bz/TouchDown.htm, and on the iPhone it's the app called eMail-Ganizer (www.myn.bz/eMailGanizer.htm). (Links are case-sensitive.) If you read a lot of mail on your handheld, these are useful. However, neither allow picking up e-mail attachments in the converted tasks, and both require you to migrate off the native e-mail app on your smartphone.

Other Features of Flagged-Mail Tasks (Windows and Mac)

Here are some other, less-important features and implications of using flagged-mail tasks:

▶ On the Mac and Windows, you can set the start date and due date of a flagged-mail task by opening the item, choosing Follow Up from the Ribbon menu at the top of the mail item, and then choosing Custom from the drop-down menu (Custom Date on the Mac). Or in Windows, right-click the flag at the right edge of the list view. Doing that in Windows changes the intensity of the red color on the flag. I don't generally recommend making those settings, however. It's better to use true tasks if you intend to manage by date.

▶ In Windows, it's not just flagged *mail* that gets shown in the To-Do Bar. If you flag an Outlook contact item, it also pops into your To-Do Bar. With proper linkages, you can see tasks from SharePoint, OneNote, and Project Server.

▶ In Windows, with a minor configuration change, you can prevent mail you flag in your Inbox from showing in the To-Do Bar. (For that configuration, see Lesson 3). If you did not make that setting and want to know more about it, see my complete discussion of it at www.myn.bz/FlagFilter.htm (link is case-sensitive).

Create Follow-Up Tasks for Important Requests You Make by E-mail (Windows and Mac)

Let's move on to something different: the topic of follow-up *tasks* (not to be confused with our previous topic about follow-up *flags*).

In Lesson 6, we learned something about follow-up tasks. They are tasks you set in your own task list to remind you to check on something you are waiting on from someone else. You often do this if another person promises you they will do something, and you want to remind yourself to check in on that later.

One way to create a follow-up task that is best used if your request is made live with the person (or if you think of it later after the meeting) is to create the task *manually*. However, if your request is made by e-mail, there is a better way to do this, which I will show you now. During my seminars this is often the most popular section, so I know many people share this need. Some background first.

The Problem to Be Solved

Before I created this process, I found I was often frustrated by colleagues and staff who failed to respond to simple requests in e-mails. Often their one-minute effort to respond would have advanced my small project immeasurably. But their reply never came.

The trouble is, to be polite I usually give staff or colleagues a few days to respond to these requests. By then I've often forgotten that I am waiting. It's often not until the day my project is due that I realize I received no response. It's too late by that time, and then the blame game starts. ("Bill never got back to me" or "I would have completed this if Bill hadn't dropped the ball." and so on.)

But the blame really rests with me. Many of the staff I send these requests to don't work for me, so they deprioritize my requests, perhaps rightly so. And if I am juggling five or ten background projects, as many workers and managers are these days, it's impossible to manage in my head all the loose-end requests that are hanging out there. So I should manage these requests better.

The Answer

Here's the solution. If you make an e-mail request for something important—and you want to ensure that the request is fulfilled by a certain date—do the following. The moment you send the e-mail request, create a follow-up task to yourself from the sent item telling you to remind that person later in case they don't reply. By using the sent item, you retain the original e-mail request in the task. Set your task to appear on your Now Tasks list by some reasonable number of days in the future—but well before your absolute due date. That way, if they drop the ball on getting back to you, you are reminded to escalate this while you still have time to get your work done.

How to Create the Task

To create such a follow-up task easily in Windows Outlook, do this: Immediately after you send the e-mail, open the Sent Items folder and find the item (at the top of the date-sorted list). Then convert it to a task. In Windows, use the right-click-and-drag method. In the popup menu that appears, choose Copy Here as Task with Attachment, as described near the beginning of this lesson. On the Mac create it with the AppleScript menu command. Or instead of going to the Sent Items folder, bcc yourself when you send the message and convert it out of your Inbox.

In either case, set the start date to a reasonable day to send them a reminder. And set the subject text to start with *F:* to signify this is a follow-up task, such as *F: Tim Jones-Request for Report Copy.* If the timing is tight, also set the priority to High to ensure that you make the reminder the day it appears.

Note: For a similar, but more complete, follow-up task system that helps track assignments to subordinates, see Lesson 10.

Effective Next Step: Send the Original Note Back

Here's why this operation is so useful. When the reminder date arrives and the follow-up task appears in your task list, if your request is unfulfilled, it's easy to find the original e-mail you sent and *resend it* as part of your escalation with the recipient. In Windows, you can open the message from within the task, and on the Mac you can search for it as I described in the earlier section in this lesson titled "What About Attachments on the Mac Version." Then, write a new sentence above the old note, such as "Wondering if you received my e-mail below and had any thoughts," and send the message.

There are two advantages to this method over starting a brand-new e-mail. First, it saves the time needed to reiterate the details of your request — all the text of the original request is in the lower part of the message. Second, the reply action inserts a header above the old mail that clearly shows the recipient that the message was originally sent addressed to them and indicating the date it was sent, presumably some time ago. Showing this history (and the fact that a response is way overdue) is usually very effective at eliciting some action.

Note: Here's a small time-saver when you create the reply. When you open your own original message, click Reply All instead of Reply. That inserts the recipients address automatically and you don't need to readdress the message. Also, in Outlook 2007, you'll need to adjust the To field back to the recipient only, by removing your name.

Alternative to Waiting-For List

For those of you who have used a waiting-for list in the past to track items like this, I find the follow-up approach much better because the follow-up item does not appear until it has aged an appropriate interval. There is nothing worse than bugging a recipient about a request without giving them time to work on it. This also eliminates your mental calculation of looking at a waiting-for list to decide whether action is needed on the items in the list. And it means you have only one task list to track. The follow-up task appears directly on your Now Tasks list and at just the right time and priority level.

Flag on Send Feature of Windows Outlook

This ability to create a follow-up task to e-mail that you send is built right into Windows Outlook, so you can do it in essentially one step. It's called *flag on send*. It's a well-designed feature and quite simple to use. However, I do *not* recommend using it compared to the follow-up task method. Here's why:

▶ It creates a flagged-mail task, not a *true* task. We looked at the many limitations of flagged-mail tasks earlier in this lesson.

▶ You need to remember to set it *before* you send the mail or it does not work, and you'll often forget.

▶ The control to create it is a redesign of a previous control, and so you might find it to be a little confusing.

Let me explain the feature and these limitations, starting with the third point first.

Note: *The Outlook add-in software ClearContext adds a Followup button that creates a* true *task, which makes this tool more viable. But you still need to remember to use it before sending the e-mail.*

Retooled Follow Up Flag Control

If you used versions of Outlook prior to Outlook 2007, you could flag an outgoing message. Do not confuse this with setting a high-importance marking on the item; that is different. Rather, this was a true Follow Up flag so that, when the e-mail arrived in the Outlook Inbox of the recipient, it already had an Outlook Follow Up flag attached to it and possibly a reminder alarm.

This pre-2007 feature was a pretty cool capability, but honestly I and many others found it a bit intrusive. Why intrusive? Because it enabled you to control someone else's Outlook to pop up an alarm window on their computer against your e-mail deadline. I found that to be too pushy when others did it to me, so I rarely used it on others. When I teach seminars and ask how people as recipients feel about getting such alarms, they unanimously say they find it obnoxious.

Regardless, the way you could use it in pre-2007 Outlook was simple: You just clicked the flag symbol at the top of the outgoing e-mail before clicking the Send button.

Newer Windows Outlook In-Message Flag Controls

In Outlook versions newer than 2003, that flag button is still there on outgoing messages, but it now looks different (see Figure 7.5) — and it *works* differently. Its main purpose now is to create a flag on *your* copy of the mail, specifically, in your own Sent Items folder.

Figure 7.5
Setting Flag on Send in Outlook 2010 (2007 and 2013 are similar).

At first that might seem silly. Why put a flag on a mail item hidden in the Sent Items folder that you might never see? But here's the key. This creates a flagged-mail task and consequently places a copy right in your Now Tasks list (To-Do Bar), along with all your other tasks. It's even marked with a special task icon indicating it is an e-mail follow-up (see flagged envelope icon in Figure 7.6). The net result — you have a tool that can create a follow-up task from an outgoing e-mail in one click.

Figure 7.6
Special icon on flagged-mail task created with Flag on Send feature.

Again though, it only creates a flagged-mail task. Because I encourage you to rely mostly on *true* tasks, not flagged-mail tasks, I do not encourage use of this tool very often.

More About Flag on Send: Setting Follow-Up Dates and Reminders

When you use the flag on send feature to create a follow-up task like this, the Outlook interface also allows you to pick a follow-up time frame from the flag drop-down menu. Using that menu, you can set the flag and pick a date like Today, Tomorrow, This Week, or Next Week, all in one step, which can be useful. If you choose Custom or Add Reminder at the bottom of that menu, you get the dialog box shown in Figure 7.7. Use the top portion to set dates and reminders for yourself. Use the bottom portion to set flags or reminders in your recipient's mailbox, as I describe next. (Notice you can set both simultaneously.)

Figure 7.7
Flag on Send date and reminder settings.

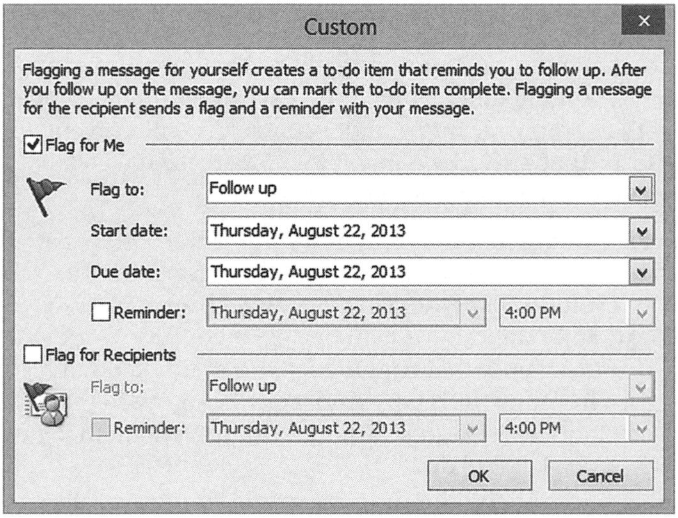

What If I Still Want to Set a Reminder Flag in the Recipient's Mailbox?

If you enjoyed the old pre-2007 way (where the outgoing Follow Up flag placed a flag and reminder alarm in the recipient's mailbox), it's still there in newer versions. In Outlook 2007 and beyond, it's an option called Flag for Recipients. To activate it, select Custom or Add Reminder from the Follow Up drop-down menu and then click the Flag for Recipients check box in the bottom of the dialog box that opens (see bottom of Figure 7.7). In Outlook 2007, Flag for Recipients is also listed at the bottom of the Follow Up drop-down menu; using that pre-selects that check box when it opens the dialog box.

But again, I discourage you from using this feature because it is irritating for the recipients.

One More Bonus of Flag on Send Tasks

There is one more bonus of using these flag on send tasks. If the recipient in fact replies to your original e-mail request, the Infobar at the top of that reply tells you that this is a reply to a flagged message. You can click that bar and automatically open the related flagged-mail task, and then mark it complete.

Note: *The Infobar is the message bar sometimes displayed in opened Outlook items, just below the Ribbon. Typically it displays messages such as "You replied on [date, time]").*

In Summary: The Cure for Inbox Stress

Immediately converting e-mails to tasks as soon as you see an action in them removes the primary cause of an out-of-control Inbox. It is the cure for Inbox stress. If that is done consistently, the majority of your Inbox woes evaporate.

Establishing a repeatable e-mail processing habit that includes converting e-mails to tasks is essential for creating a successful task-management system, and essential for keeping your Inbox under control. It will prevent you from losing track of tasks that arrive by e-mail. It will increase the collaborative flow of productive work within your team.

You will be amazed at the sense of relief and control that you get after you have a sustainable e-mail workflow in place that allows you to stay ahead of your Inbox. Your attitude about e-mail will change dramatically. You will begin to appreciate fully the value e-mail brings to you as a work tool, and you will no longer experience that nagging feeling of unattended responsibilities every time you look at your Inbox. And, after being mastered, it may even allow you to leave work at a reasonable hour without feeling that you have a stack of unfinished work left to do.

Exercises

Convert e-mails to tasks as follows:

1. Convert three e-mails to tasks as text only.

2. Convert three e-mails to tasks as attachments (Windows only).

3. Create a follow-up task for three items currently in your Sent Items folder. Pick items you know you may need to follow up on later.

Next Steps

Now that you have learned how to convert e-mails to tasks, next you will learn how to topic-file e-mail with more powerful filing tools. That is the subject of Lesson 8.

Lesson 8:
Topic-Based E-mail Filing

Introduction

I consistently refer to many of my old e-mails as I work through my day, even mail many months old. So I appreciate having a good way to find my stored e-mail. As mentioned in Lesson 5, if you retain old e-mails, I feel you should not store them in your Inbox. Old e-mail stored there will clutter both your Inbox and your workday. You'll end up missing some important items in the clutter. And you'll unnecessarily rehash old mail as you look for things. So some filing system, even very simple, is needed to get old mail you are done with out of your Inbox.

In Lesson 5, I showed you how to empty your Inbox into a single folder called the Processed Mail folder. I hope you tried that, or one of the variants, because I want you to have that incredible experience of emptying your Inbox daily.

Note: *This lesson is summarized in videos 17 and 18 of the MYN-Outlook Complete Video Training (see beginning of the Quick Start chapter for more information).*

There were two fundamental directions you could go from there to enable you to find individual mail later:

▶ Use a visual search for recent mail in that new folder. Use a search engine for the rest as described at the end of Lesson 5.

▶ Use topic-based filing in one of two ways. Moving mail into multiple topic-named folders is the old standby. Tagging mail with Outlook Categories and using a view that shows your mail grouped in those category collections is a newer way.

Many people combine these two approaches. They topic-file an important subset of their mail and use search engines on the rest stored in bulk.

In this lesson I review both of these methods but focus primarily on the second: tagging mail with Outlook Categories and activating a view that shows your mail grouped by category.

Let me be perfectly clear, though: This lesson is purely optional. If you are content with how your mail-filing and searching needs were met as of the end of Lesson 5, then skip this lesson. It's long and a bit technical. And because topic-based filing takes so much time, if you can possibly avoid it, you should.

Mac users, this lesson is also for you; it fully applies to Outlook for Mac 2011.

Topic-Filing Your E-mail (Windows and Mac)

Some people, due to business requirements in their organizations, need to do topic-based filing. They need distinct collections of all mail associated with various dimensions of work. Here are some of the different dimensions people use when creating key words to file against.

► projects

► clients

► client groups

► cases

► initiatives

► persons

► business entities

► departments

► business process or function

► activities

► message type

► time periods

Sometimes the need to file is industry specific. Legal organizations usually need to create case files so there is a crystal-clear identification of all mail associated with a case. Organizations with distinct client groups often need to be able to trace all client mail. For situations like this, topic-based filing of e-mail may be the only way to go.

However, topic-based filing is not for everyone. It takes a lot of time. For many people, given the ratio of time actually using old mail compared to the time spent filing, the tradeoff is not worth it. For them, bulk filing as in Lesson 5 may be sufficient.

And by no means is topic-based filing a requirement for regaining workday control. Why? Because after you have extracted explicit or implicit tasks from incoming e-mail with the techniques in Lesson 7, what you do with that mail after that is, by comparison, low priority, as long as you get it out of your Inbox. Compared to taking action on e-mails or converting them to Outlook tasks, filing e-mails by topic is way down the scale of importance. And, certainly, if you are happy with the powerful Outlook e-mail search tools covered in Lesson 5, topic-based filing is almost unnecessary. All you need to do is move the mail to another folder and apply the search tool.

All that said, if you determine that you definitely need topic-based filing, you have three choices to implement it:

▶ Move mail into multiple topic-named Outlook folders.

▶ Move saved mail into one folder and tag it with Outlook Categories.

▶ Use a combination of both.

Moving Mail into Multiple Topic-Named Outlook Folders

The most common way to file by topic is to create a series of custom Outlook topic-named folders and move your e-mails there. I suspect you have tried this before. Years ago I did this, but it is no longer my favorite approach and research has shown it to be very slow. But for those who need to do it, or like it, here is some advice to help you set it up.

Decide Where to Put the Set of Folders

In Appendix A, I discuss considerations to make when deciding where to store the Processed Mail folder. Use those same factors when deciding where to put your multiple file folders. If your organization is using Exchange Server, does it impose size limitations for your Inbox, and does your IT department provide file server storage in place of local storage? Does your IT department even allow local storage? Do you have a backup system for your local storage? Based on questions like these, Appendix A can help you decide where to put your folders.

Decide How to Name (Categorize) the Folders

The naming or categorization system for your file folders can take several dimensions, as the list earlier in this section shows. If your reason for using file folders is merely to empty your Inbox, date-based folders are a good solution. If you are truly looking for topic names, then use business priorities to guide you. Clearly, you should think about how these names will help you find the mail or use it later.

Decide Whether to Use Nested Folders

I really do not like nested folders (also called subfolders or hierarchical folders) because they greatly complicate filing and searching for mail. They also greatly increase the number of folders you have, which can make searching harder. But sometimes they are the only way to match the most logical filing system for your business needs. If you use them, try to keep their depth and count to a minimum.

Decide What to Do with Mail That Does Not Fit in a Particular Folder

How should you handle mail that doesn't fit in any of your existing folders? Should you just keep creating new folders or is there another approach? I strongly recommend keeping your folder count low. Otherwise filing and searching will become very cumbersome. So create an Other or Miscellaneous folder for all mail that doesn't fit any other topic.

Consider Using Add-In Software to Help: ClearContext

The Outlook add-in software ClearContext has a number of tools to help with filing mail into multiple Outlook folders. For example, you can configure the tool so that after you file one member of an e-mail thread into a particular folder, all other items in that thread will automatically be moved into that folder. You can also auto-tag e-mail with topics as it comes in but not move it into the matching individual folders until later, when you are sure you are done reading the mail. And ClearContext has a good, simple rules engine for picking topics automatically. So if you like filing in multiple folders, take a look at this software as a way to speed your filing. See this link for more information: www.myn.bz/clearcontext.html.

Problems with Filing into Multiple Outlook Folders

I have mentioned several times that moving mail into multiple topic-named folders is not my favorite topic-filing method. Though I used to do this, I now realize it is not the way to go; here is why.

► Whenever I tried this in the past, I regretted no longer having one view of all my collected e-mail. I often locate an e-mail by approximately how far in the past it arrived and by proximity with other events. I missed the ability to scan through my entire Inbox, sorted by date. Having my saved mail split among multiple folders precluded that.

► Along these lines, I often like to view all e-mails sent from one individual. Again, having my saved mail split among multiple folders precluded that. (There is now a workaround for these two problems, you can create a custom All Mail Search or Smart Folder, which I show in Lesson 11. It doesn't solve all the downsides to topic-filing, however.)

▶ Sometimes it seemed that an e-mail item belonged in several different folders. Using folders required me to decide on one and only one folder to file it in. In my indecision, I'd leave the item unfiled or waste time and get frustrated with the process. Then, when I searched for the mail, I would often look in the wrong folder first.

▶ After an item was filed, I would often forget which folder I stored it in and would become annoyed with having to hunt through multiple folders to find it.

▶ Because of how long it takes to file, I would often not finish filing for days or weeks at a time. In the meantime, when I needed to look for mail, I would not know whether to look in the folders or in my Inbox and would waste time searching both.

▶ I use an offline archive storage area where I transfer my oldest saved mail. But when my mail was split among tens or hundreds of folders, I found it harder to do that because I had to open each folder and find the oldest to move.

For these reasons and others, I have given up on filing e-mail into a collection of various topic-named Outlook folders. Perhaps you have had similar problems. You'll see in this lesson that Outlook Category tagging, and putting tagged mail all in one folder, solves nearly all the above problems.

That said, many people have no problem with filing into multiple topic-named Outlook folders, and they are able to empty their Inbox nearly every day. If that is you, fantastic; keep doing what you are doing. However, if due to slowness of filing you go weeks at a time without filing or if any of the above symptoms sound familiar, read on and try these next approaches.

Better Filing Solution: Place Mail in One Location and Tag It with Outlook Categories

There is a better filing approach: Place the mail in one location (the Processed Mail folder created in Lesson 5) and tag it with Outlook Categories. This solution provides the best of both worlds for finding important e-mails. You can store your e-mail in a single date- or sender-sorted folder yet also view all mail in a folder-like structure grouped by category names. You can tag one e-mail with multiple categories and see it in multiple category groups with no impact on storage space. With this solution, all the shortcomings previously described are eliminated, and a fluid system of filing and finding e-mails is made possible.

My recommended process is simple. You just add the category keyword to the mail item in your Inbox with a variety of simple tools in Outlook and then drag the mail from your Inbox to a single folder—the Processed Mail folder.

Categories in One Folder Compared to Filing in Separate Folders: Easier to Find Mail

Later, when you want to find an e-mail, you can take advantage of the category tags. With the single Processed Mail folder open, you just toggle to the view that groups mail by categories by clicking the top of the Categories column (see Figure 8.1 for an example), scroll to the group you want, and then scan the items in the group.

Figure 8.1
Category groups in Outlook.

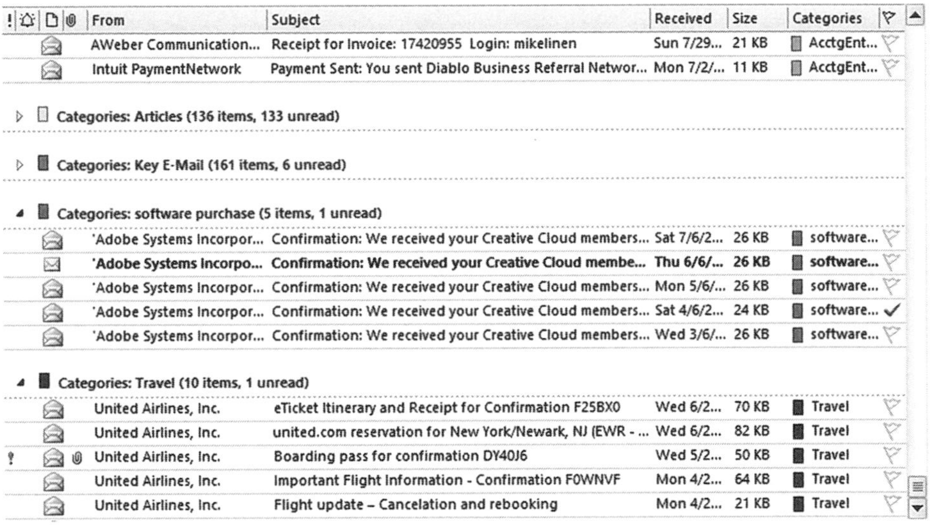

But even more important, because, with MYN, you store all mail in one folder, you can use three other nontag ways to find mail. That's the beauty of using categories in Outlook. You can store all the mail in one folder with all its advantages and still enjoy the advantages of seeing mail in folder-like groups with a category view.

Here's a list of four methods of finding mail with this MYN filing system. For more information on methods 1 to 3, see Lesson 5. Only the fourth method in this list uses categories, and it is the focus of this lesson.

1. If you know approximately when the mail arrived, do a visual search in the Processed Mail folder of your chronologically sorted mail (as many of you do now in your Inbox).

2. If you know who sent it, sort on the From column by clicking the heading of that column, scroll to the person's name, and visually search across titles and dates in the mail from that person (again, many of us do that already in the Inbox).

3. With a search engine search the mail in the Processed Mail folder. (See Lesson 5.)

4. Tag mail with categories and group your Processed Mail folder with category names as shown in Figure 8.1.

Categories Compared to Separate Folders: Why It's Faster

Even with the relative advantages described previously, I am sometimes asked: "Doesn't assigning categories take just as long as moving items to separate topic-named folders because I need to touch the same number of items in either case?"

There are a number of reasons why using Outlook Categories is better.

Leads to Fewer Topics

When you are using a single folder and the search tool more to find items, you tend to use fewer topic names than you did when using separate folders. With fewer topic names, filing becomes simpler and faster. For example, when I transitioned from folders to categories, I started with 40 or 50 category names that matched my old folders. But over time, as I came to use the search tools more, I slowly cut back on my category count because the search tools worked so well. Now I routinely use only three or four category names and I trust Instant Search to find everything else. You will probably reduce the number of categories over time. After that happens, your filing effort will be greatly reduced using categories.

One of the topics you will no longer need is an Other or Miscellaneous folder. As you will see, untagged mail is put in a None category automatically for you. This saves a lot of time.

Using Outlook Rules with Categories Is Much Faster

If you start using Outlook *rules* to automatically set categories, setting categories is much faster than using folders.

The multiple-file folder user responds: "Aha! But I can create Outlook rules for automatically filing in folders, too!"

Yes, but there is a huge difference between auto-categorizing and auto-filing. With auto-categorizing mail, the tagged mail stays in your Inbox until you drag it somewhere else. So, you can still read it day by day, hour by hour, as it comes in. In contrast, with auto-filed mail (filed in folders), because the mail goes directly to the folder, you don't have a chance to read new mail that day (unless you hunt through all your file folders several times a day, which I doubt you will do). That means you are very unlikely to use auto-folder-filing rules on important types of mail. Rather, I find that most people who use auto-filing directly in folders do so only with mail they rarely read anyway (junk mail, newsfeeds, specialty mail subscriptions, and so on). So you will need to file most of your true business mail by hand.

So, category tagging comes out way ahead in this comparison. Using rules, you can ensure that most of your *business-critical* mail is auto-tagged, and you can read as much of that mail as appropriate right in your Inbox before dragging it all to the Processed Mail folder. I'll show you how to create these rules in Lesson 11.

Note: *If you absolutely must use separate folders for each topic, Windows users should consider using a tool like ClearContext. It tags mail but leaves it in your Inbox — filing it later in separate folders when you click the File button. With ClearContext you can read your mail before you file it.*

Tagging Compared to Separate Folders: Solves the Problem of Where to File

One of the other big advantages of tagging with Outlook Categories is that with it, you can apply more than one category to a mail item. This solves the common problem of not knowing where to file an item when it appears to fit two or more topics. For example, say you get an invoice for the marketing project. Do you file that in the Accounting folder or in the Marketing Project folder? With categories you can easily apply both, and the item will appear in each of the groups, making it much easier to find. Outlook does not actually duplicate the item, it merely shows it virtually in both places, so there's no extra space required.

In Outlook for Mac 2011 this works the same and then goes even further. It also shows an extra group for each combination. More on that later in this lesson.

Some Disadvantages of Outlook Categories

With all the advantages I've just described, you might think using Outlook Categories as opposed to multiple folders is a no-brainer. In most cases it is. But there are a few cases where you might think using categories leaves you at a disadvantage.

No Category Hierarchy

Notice that you cannot create a hierarchy of Outlook Categories; that is, there is one list at one level. Some users worry about that. However, I feel that's not a problem because it forces a simple approach, which is always better. And because you can assign more than one category to an e-mail, that will often replace the need for a hierarchy.

Limited Smartphone Support

Smartphone e-mail software rarely includes mechanisms for assigning categories. So if you do most of your e-mail management on a smartphone, you'll need to delay filing until you can get back to your desktop Outlook application. This also applies to viewing mail in category groups. That's hard to do on smartphone software.

However, most traveling Outlook users *can* return to their desktop version of Outlook at least once every day or two, whether at their main office or by using a laptop. That's usually adequate for cleaning up your Inbox using categories.

Also, third-party smartphone apps are starting to add category assignments. At press time, the Android app Touchdown (described in Lesson 6) was just releasing this capability. Others say they have it planned.

Finally, category filing provides another reason to consider purchasing one of the new very lightweight Windows 8 tablets like the Surface RT or Lenovo Thinkpad Tablet 2 (or equivalent). Because they are nearly as nimble as a smartphone, and can run a desktop version of Outlook, they enable complete MYN Outlook management while on the road.

How to Use Outlook Categories (All Outlook Versions)

If I convinced you to try Outlook Categories, there are some detailed skills you'll need to learn. In this section I cover how to view, assign, and group by categories.

How You See Categories in Windows Outlook and Outlook for Mac 2011

In all versions of Outlook covered in this book, it is hard to miss categories. Look at the right side of your Inbox and you should see the Categories column. You might even see mail with colored rectangles in that column (circles are used in Mac 2011). That column may be very narrow, so widen it if needed.

However, the Categories column can be hidden. One reason for that is if your Inbox mail list is too narrow. You can widen your Inbox by minimizing the To-Do Bar (Lesson 2). You can also widen your Inbox list view by moving the Reading Pane to the bottom or turning it off (use View menu or tab, Reading Pane, Bottom or Off or Hidden).

In some rare cases, the Categories column is really missing in your Windows Outlook configurations, and the steps I just described won't reveal it. If so, use the instructions for adding it that follow.

To Add the Categories Column in Windows Outlook:

1. Open your Inbox, right-click any of your column headings, and from the bottom of the shortcut menu choose View Settings or Customize Current View (it might say Custom).

2. I recommend you click the Reset Current View button. This is to clear out any odd settings you may have inadvertently made to the Messages view.

3. Click Columns [or Fields].

4. In the next dialog box (called Show Fields or Show Columns) click Categories in the list on the left to select it. Then click Add (in the middle of the dialog box) to add that field to the bottom of the list on the right side as shown in Figure 8.2.

Figure 8.2
Adding the Categories field.

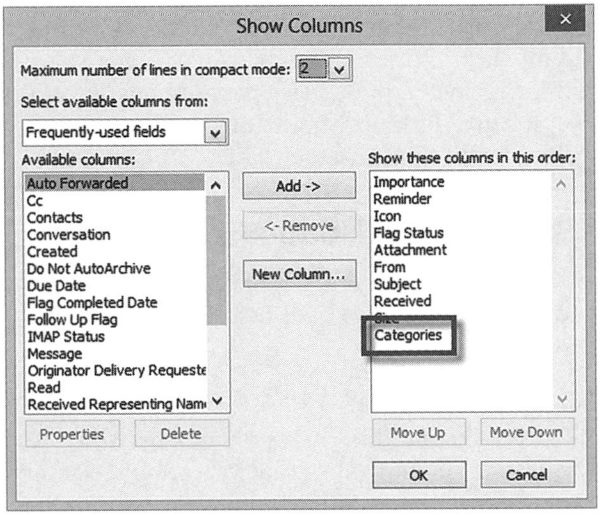

Note: *If you have trouble finding the Categories field in the list on the left, try selecting All Mail Fields in the list box titled Select Available Fields [or Columns] From, and then look again at the scrolling field list. That should display it.*

5. Click OK, and then OK again.

When back at your Inbox, you may need to resize the width of the new Categories column to make it more readable. Do this by dragging the margin of the Categories column heading.

You probably won't see anything currently in that column if you have not been using categories. But you might. Outlook Categories can travel with e-mail messages (sent from pre-Outlook 2007 users), so if others are using Outlook Categories on their mail you might see them in your Inbox.

Now let's see how to tag mail with these categories.

Note: *If you are currently using a multiple-folder filing system or no system at all and you would like tips on how to transition to this new category-based system, see the section at the end of this lesson titled "Transitioning to a Categories System."*

Note: IMAP servers do not support Outlook Categories. The category lists shown in the sections ahead will be empty if using an IMAP server. Check with your IT department to confirm what type of server you are using.

How to Tag Mail with Outlook Categories

Now that you know how to view categories, next you need to learn how to apply them to e-mail. There are a number of ways to do this, and each has its advantages and disadvantages. Let's start with the easiest methods.

Using Categorize Buttons or Menu Items (All Versions)

Here's the easiest way to assign categories to e-mail. Select the e-mail in your Inbox, and then click the Categorize button at the top of the Outlook window and choose a category from the drop-down menu (as shown in Figure 8.3). After you pick a category, you'll see the name appear in the Categories column next to the e-mail.

Figure 8.3
Categories drop-down menu in Windows Outlook (left) and Mac (right).

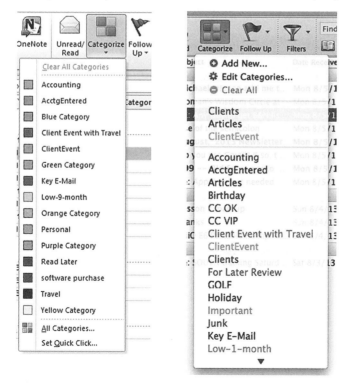

However, where that Categorize button is, what it is named, and how it looks all depend on which version of Outlook you use.

In Outlook 2010, 2011, and 2013, look on the Home tab (in Windows it's in the Tags section of that tab). You'll see a Categorize button. In Windows, depending on how wide your Outlook window is, it will either be a large button (left side of Figure 8.4) or a small one (right side of Figure 8.4).

Figure 8.4
Categorize button in Ribbon menu.

On the Mac, it will look like the left side of Figure 8.4.

Note: *Windows 2010 and 2013 users, don't get that Categorize button confused with the Categories button that resides on the View tab. While the spelling is different, it looks the same — but does something very different. So make sure you're on the Home tab when looking for the Categorize button.*

This Categorize button is also available in an open mail message, which can be useful if categorizing while reading mail.

In Outlook 2007, the Categorize button is on the Standard toolbar, which is the default toolbar just below the menu bar. The button looks like the one on the right side of Figure 8.4, but it's unlabeled. In 2007, you can also reach the Categorize command by going to the Edit menu or the Action menu. In Outlook 2011, you also have the option of using the Categorize command under the Message menu.

No matter which of these buttons or menus you use, you'll see a shortcut menu open with a list of categories (Figure 8.3).

The Right-Click Method of Assigning Outlook Categories (All Versions)

Instead of using the Categorize button or menu item, there is a quicker way to assign categories, and you'll want to use it if you are categorizing much mail. From the Inbox list view, right-click in the Categories column (CTRL-click on the Mac) *next to the mail item* and select a category from the shortcut menu (similar to that shown in Figure 8.3, left). The category is immediately applied to the adjacent e-mail. This method saves one click per item, and that can add up when assigning categories to a large number of individual e-mails.

However, if you have trouble right-clicking, then don't use this method. You may accidentally left-click and assign the default category. More on assigning a default category later in this lesson.

Using the Categories Dialog Box (All Versions)

In both Windows and Mac Outlook you can view a more detailed list of your categories in a special dialog box. Here you can add to and edit your categories list, and in Windows even assign categories. Let's start with the Windows version.

The Windows Outlook Color Categories Dialog Box

The Windows version of the Categories dialog box is called Color Categories (see Figure 8.5, top).

Figure 8.5
Category editing in Windows Outlook (top) and Mac (bottom).

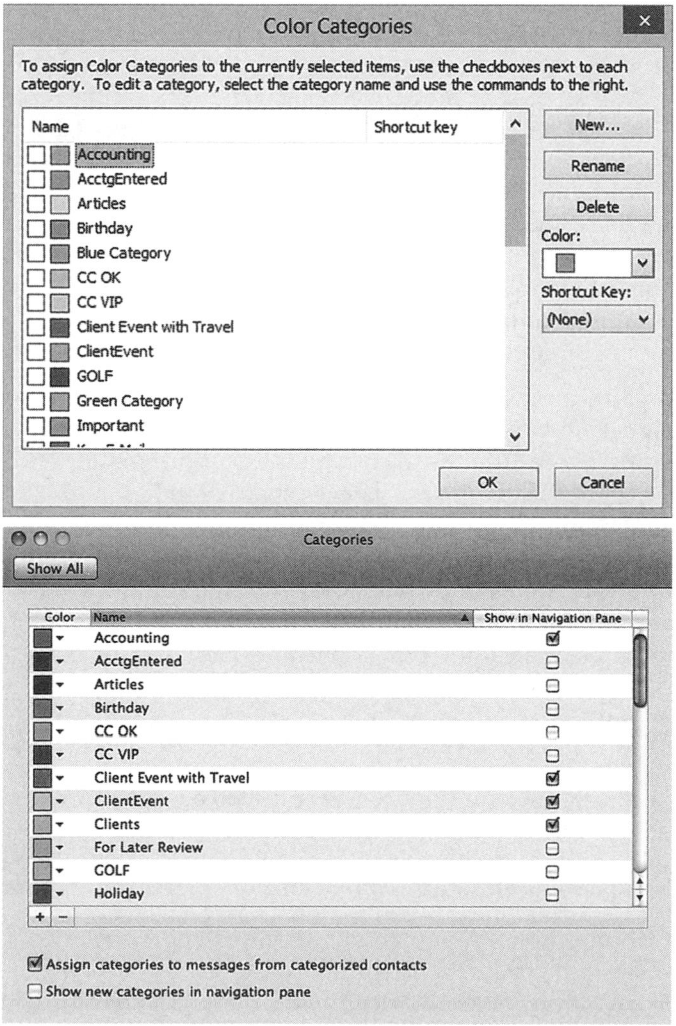

To open it, choose All Categories at the bottom of the Categorize shortcut menu (see bottom of Figure 8.3, left). One reason you need this dialog box is because when using the drop-down menu in Windows Outlook (the one shown in Figure 8.3) you'll find that it shows only the most-used 15 categories. If you have more than 15 categories in your category list, the excess ones seem to be gone. They aren't gone, you'll just need to use the Color Categories dialog box and scroll to the other categories. As you can see in Figure 8.5, top, the Color Categories dialog box displays a scrolling list of Categories; this is your complete list.

You can assign one or more categories to selected mail by clicking the check boxes on the left. This is also where you add, delete, or rename categories. (Before editing your list, however, read the cautions in the section "Editing and Adding to the Category List" later in this lesson.) You can also set keyboard shortcuts here for up to 11 categories; the control to set those is shown in Figure 8.5.

The Mac Categories Dialog Box

On the Mac, if you choose the Edit Categories command on the Categories shortcut menu (shown at the top of Figure 8.3, right), you'll see the Categories dialog box shown in Figure 8.5, bottom. Why might you need this? Unlike Windows, it's not needed to assign from a long list of categories. That's because the shortcut menu in Figure 8.3 (right) shows *all* categories; just use the scroll arrow at the bottom to reach any categories that have scrolled off the bottom. (It's not limited to 15 as in Windows.)

No, the reason you want to use the Categories dialog box on the Mac is solely for editing your category list. You can rename, add, or remove categories here. (Before editing your list, however, read the cautions in the section "Editing and Adding to the Category List" later in this lesson.)

Adding and Removing Multiple Categories (All Versions)

One of the powerful features of Outlook Categories for filing mail is that you can assign more than one category to each mail item. This solves the typical folder-filing dilemma of deciding how to file an e-mail that logically fits in more than one folder. An e-mail with multiple categories is repeated in each folder-like category group, but takes no extra storage space. How do you assign multiple categories to an e-mail?

When using the shortcut menu (Figure 8.3) to assign a category, if you repeat the process on the same e-mail item, each newly assigned category is *additive*. That is, it is added adjacent to any existing category rather than overwriting it. That's the simplest way to assign multiple categories.

But this leads to a question. What if you have one category assigned to an e-mail and you want to *replace* it rather than add to it? You need to choose the existing category again from the shortcut menu, which removes it. Then go back and assign the new category. Or in Windows click All Categories and select or clear the check boxes at the left side of the Color Categories dialog box. On the Mac you can choose Clear All as shown at the top of Figure 8.3, and then add your new categories.

The Six Special Color-Named Categories in Outlook

In all recent versions of Outlook since 2007, you will likely see a number of items in the categories list identified only by colors (Red Category, Green Category, and so on). New users of Outlook Categories often wonder why these exist. The reason is historical. They are the six colors from the Outlook 2003 Follow Up flags. They exist now mainly to transition old mail to the new way Follow Up flags are used in all versions of Windows Outlook after 2003.

Here's some background. In Outlook 2003, the various colored flags were intended as a way to classify types of mail. Perhaps you used a green flag for all accounting-related mail, or a red flag for topics of high importance. However, starting in Outlook 2007, the core purpose of flags in Outlook was redefined. They are now to be used for marking *action* only. That's why flagged items are copied into the To-Do Bar task list. If you want to *classify* mail, Microsoft now wants you to use Categories; not flags. So the rainbow-colored flags of 2003 no longer exist in versions of Outlook since 2007, just red ones.

But what if you upgrade from Outlook 2003 and you have rainbow colored flags assigned to your mail? Microsoft did not want you to lose that color information. So the color information is retained by transferring the color to a corresponding *category* of each e-mail. The Red, Green, Blue, Purple (and so on) Outlook Categories exist mainly to enable that transfer. Any mail that previously had a green flag on it will, after an upgrade from Outlook 2003, now have a green *category* on it.

But naming categories based only on colors doesn't tell you what those colors mean. So, the first time you use one of these predefined color categories for a new assignment, Outlook might ask you if you want to rename it to something more meaningful, as shown in Figure 8.6.

Figure 8.6
Result of first use of a color-named category.

This dialog box gives you a chance to record what you intended when (if) you used the rainbow-colored Follow Up flags on Outlook 2003 mail. If you *do* have such a specific meaning for each color in mind, indicate it now in this dialog box by giving it a new name and clicking Yes. If you do not care about the meaning of the rainbow-colored flags on old 2003 flagged mail (or never used them before), click No. If you find no use for these color categories, feel free to delete them (see the section "Editing and Adding to the Category List" ahead); but before doing that, make sure you have not used them elsewhere in Outlook.

Quick Click to Set Categories in Windows Outlook

With a feature in Windows Outlook, you can assign a default category to your mail when you click in the Categories column next to an e-mail. Here I am referring to a left-click (don't confuse this with the right-click method of assigning categories I described earlier in this lesson). This default category assignment feature is called the Quick Click assignment. I found this confusing at first, because I set a every time I accidentally left-clicked in that column. After I got used to Quick Click, however, I decided I liked this feature a lot. I renamed the Red Category to Key E-mail. Now I click and categorize this way any e-mail that contains important reference information I know I'll want to search visually for later. That takes the place of using flags to mark important e-mails, something I did prior to Outlook 2007. I now only use e-mail flags for deferred replies (Lesson 7).

Out of the box, the default Quick Click is set to Red Category. This setting can be changed by right-clicking any e-mail and choosing Set Quick Click from the bottom of the shortcut menu (shown in Figure 8.3, left). This opens the dialog box shown in Figure 8.7. Or, instead of changing the default category, you might want to rename the Red Category to something more meaningful as I did (Key E-mail). Use the Color Categories box for that.

Figure 8.7
Setting the Quick Click choice in Outlook 2007/10.

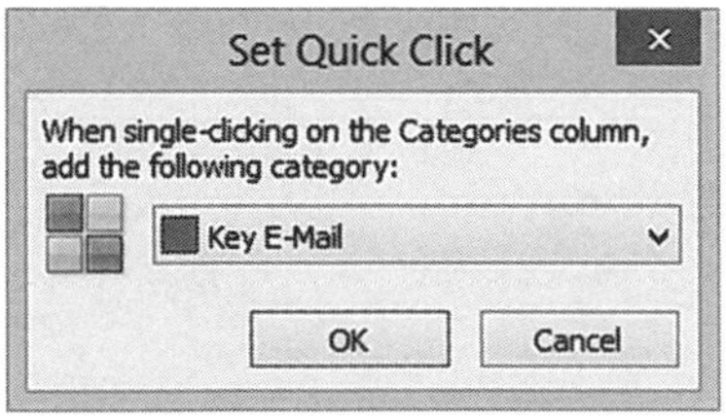

If you have one category you tend to use a lot, this is a nice feature. If you do *not* have a favorite category, you probably want to turn Quick Click off to avoid accidentally assigning categories. Do this by choosing No Category from the drop-down list in Figure 8.7.

Editing and Adding to the Category List (All Versions)

If you want to use the category method of tagging e-mail, you'll soon want to edit the default categories that come with Outlook. Most are not useful for the business world. You do that editing using the category dialog boxes shown in Figure 8.5.

Before you edit the category list, however, be aware that categories can be assigned to the multiple other data types used in Outlook: Calendar items, Contacts, Tasks, Notes, and Journal items. All these data types share the same master list of Outlook Categories to pick from when you tag e-mail. You might already be using categories in different places in Outlook and not realize it. So don't delete category names you might be using elsewhere, and keep the cross-functional use of categories in mind as you create new ones.

Adding to or deleting from the category list in Windows Outlook is easy. Open the Color Categories dialog box shown in Figure 8.5, top (select the All Categories command shown in Figure 8.3, left) and use the New and Delete buttons there. Use the Rename button to change an existing category name.

Adding to or deleting from the category list in Outlook for Mac 2011 is also easy. Open the Categories dialog box shown in 8.5, bottom (to open it, use Edit Categories shown in Figure 8.3, right) and then use the plus and minus buttons there to add or remove categories.

Note: *Maintaining and changing category names can sometimes get complicated. For more details on how to do this, see in Lesson 11 the section "Maintaining Category Names Quickly and Efficiently."*

Some Points about Creating Outlook Categories (All Versions)

Here are some important points you should keep in mind when creating and using Outlook Categories.

The None Category

You might be tempted to create a category called Other or Miscellaneous to file e-mail that doesn't fit other categories. However, don't bother creating one of these catchall categories. The reason: Outlook automatically creates, assigns, and (at the top of groups) displays a category called None for all uncategorized e-mail. So for any e-mail that does not fit a category, just leave it uncategorized. This is a great time-saver!

Do Not Create Too Many Categories

In the old days of using multiple topic-named folders, when I came across an e-mail that did not fit any of my existing folder names, I'd often create a new folder. But that led to folder proliferation and slower filing. The same is true with categories—you don't want too many. I recommend you keep your category list very short to keep filing fast. Favor using the Outlook search tools over tagging with categories. However there are times you really do need to use categories. So how do you decide? Here's my rule of thumb for when to (and when not to) create a new category:

If an entire group of e-mail must be retrieved all together, then create a category. For example, if you work in the legal department and know you might need to find and transfer *all* e-mail related to a given case to another attorney, then create and assign a category to all that mail as it comes in.

However, if you know you will search for e-mail items only one at a time, then don't create a category. Rather, bulk file the mail in the Processed Mail folder without a category, and use search tools when you need to. You'll save a lot of time filing and still be able to find the mail.

Setting Category Standards

If multiple individuals in your organization intend to adopt this category-based e-mail filing system, and you are using an older version of Exchange Server, I recommend you consider adopting common category names for similar subjects. The reason: E-mail arriving from colleagues using this system can occasionally (pre-Exchange 2007) display your colleagues' categories. You might need to change the category to match one of yours. You all will save time if you agree to use the same category names. For more information, including how to block migration of categories with e-mail, see Lesson 11.

Viewing and Grouping Mail by Category (All Versions)

Now that you know how to tag mail with categories, you're probably curious how you are going to use those tags to find specific mail you've dragged to your Processed Mail folder. In most cases, it's very simple, and I already showed it to you earlier in this lesson. You just click the top of the Categories column in the mail list view. Then immediately collapse the None group by clicking the symbol button next to that category heading. (You might need to scroll your Inbox to the top to see the None group category heading.) The reason you collapse the None group is because that group tends to be very large, so it dominates the view and prevents you from seeing the other groups.

Or you can collapse *all* groups using a special menu command. Doing this makes it easy to see your group names and to scroll to the group you want to open and view. In Windows, use the View menu or tab, choose Expand/Collapse, and then Collapse All Groups. On the Mac, go to the Organize tab and then choose Arrange By, and then Collapse All Groups.

Grouping gives you a virtual folder-like view of categories, such as those in Figure 8.1, which shows the Windows version of Outlook with some categories expanded and some collapsed. All mail with the same category is grouped together, and any mail item that has more than one category applied to it will be repeated in each category group. On the Mac you'll see that and a little more, which I describe in the following section. When you are finished viewing the category groups, click the top of the Received column to revert to the standard date-sorted list view.

Unique Category Features on the Mac

In both the Windows and Mac versions of Outlook, any mail item that has more than one category applied to it is repeated in each category group. But the Mac version expands on this feature. You'll also see a group for each category name *combination*. For example, if you have applied the two categories Accounting and Marketing to an individual mail item, you'll see a group called Accounting, a group called Marketing, and on the Mac a third group with the phrase *Accounting, Marketing.* This third combined group lists only mail that has both of those categories applied.

This combined category group emulates the function of nested folders and is quite handy. But it also makes a mail list grouped by Categories much larger. If you have many categories, or a large amount of mail in your category groups, it can be difficult to scroll through them to find the start of specific category groups. To help with that, you can collapse all groups. Go to the Organize tab and then choose Arrange By, and then Collapse All Groups.

Using Search Folders to View Categorized Mail (Windows)

Another way to view categorized mail is with Search Folders. Search Folders are an optional Windows Outlook feature you can use to create virtual folders in your folder list. The Macintosh has an equivalent feature called Smart Folders (described in a following section). Search Folders can be used to create category folders directly in your Navigation or Folders Pane. They appear in and under the Search Folder group (see Figure 8.8). In this example, six Search Folders are shown. Using Search Folders is optional but often useful.

Figure 8.8
Search Folders in the Navigation or Folders Pane.

Search Folders Defined

Search Folders are virtual folders that are populated with copies of e-mail that match search criteria defined at the time the particular Search Folder is created. You create one folder for each set of search criteria. For example, you can create a Search Folder that shows a copy of all mail in the Processed Mail folder (or other folders) tagged with a certain category. Another example is a Search Folder that shows you all unread mail across all folders (Outlook includes that one by default). Many other search approaches are also possible, but I think creating them to view mail assigned to specific categories might be their most useful application. In Figure 8.8, the Accounting, Key E-Mail, Read Later, and Travel folders are examples of category-based Search Folders.

Features of Search Folders

The advantage of using Search Folders to view categorized mail are many. They look and act nearly identical to regular Outlook folders. If you are accustomed to using a folder view in the Navigation or Folders Pane for manipulating saved mail, Search Folders create a very similar view for your collection of category-assigned mail. When you double-click a Search Folder, it opens just like any other folder, displaying its mail. So there is a familiarity factor at work here, which many find appealing.

Also, they take no extra space and leave the original copy of the mail in the Processed Mail folder. So you can scroll through your date-sorted mail as you normally do in the Processed Mail folder or look at mail grouped by category in the Search Folders.

Disadvantages of Search Folders

There are, however, two primary disadvantages. One is that you cannot drag mail items to the Search Folder, as you can with real folders. Rather, you need to assign categories as described earlier. Only then does the item appear in your Search Folder.

The other disadvantage of Search Folders is that you must explicitly create a Search Folder for each category you are using, and as you will see, that takes a few steps. So if you consistently create new categories, Search Folders might not be for you.

Also, you cannot create nested Search Folders (no subfolders), and you cannot share Search Folders over a network. Furthermore, Search Folders are usually limited to one mail store; you cannot collect mail across multiple accounts, for example.

Learning How to Use Search Folders

Even with those disadvantages, Search Folders have a certain elegance. Their folder-like appearance right in the Outlook folder list is quite satisfying. If you have a relatively small and stable set of categories, you might prefer this approach.

Starting in this edition, all my instructions on how to use Search Folders are on my website: www.myn.bz/SearchFolders.htm (link is case-sensitive).

Creating Category Smart Folders in Outlook for Mac 2011

The Mac's equivalent to Search Folders is called Smart Folders. They have been available for years in the Mac operating system, and they are also in the Outlook for Mac 2011 application. There they can be used to collect categorized mail just like the Search Folders described above for Windows Outlook. In Lesson 3 you learned how to create Smart Folders for tasks. The same principles apply in the Mail folder.

You may not need to manually build these for categorized mail because, in theory, Outlook for Mac 2011 will do this for you automatically. Here's how this is supposed to work. In the bottom image in Figure 8.5, if you look at the right side, you see a check box column titled Show in Navigation Pane. Checking this is supposed to list the indicated categorized mail in a group on the Navigation Pane (in the equivalent of a Smart Folder). If this were functional, it would replace a lot of manual work and I applaud Microsoft for this excellent design.

However, the reason I just said "in theory" is that I could not get this feature to work on my installation (the folders never appeared), and I have heard similar complaints from others. Give it a try; if it does not work I suspect it will be fixed in a future software update. In the meantime, follow Lesson 3 principles to create them manually.

Deleting a Search or Smart Folder and Mail Inside (All Versions)

Search and Smart Folders are a virtual view of your mail. The actual mail sits in real Outlook folder(s) such as the ones you defined above as the source of your search (Processed Mail, most likely). So if you are done using a Search or Smart Folder, you can delete the *folder* and the mail itself is not deleted but is retained in the Processed Mail folder.

However, when viewing *individual mail* inside a Search or Smart Folder *the opposite is true*. If you delete an individual e-mail item from within the folder, the actual mail item is *deleted* from its source folder (in this case, the Processed Mail folder). Any operations that you perform on individual e-mail items (delete, change category, or edit item, for example) within a Search or Smart Folder are made on the actual item wherever it is located.

Tips on Using Categories (All Versions)

Now that you have learned how to apply and use categories, you are ready for the next step—learning many fine points about using categories. Here is a collection of tips that will help you take category filing to the next level.

Transitioning to a Categories System

When I teach Outlook users about using categories, they are almost always concerned about how to use categories in their own collection of mail. In particular, their concern is usually about how to transition from an existing filing system.

From a Multiple-Folder-Based Filing System

If you are already using a multiple-folder-based filing system for e-mail, you might wonder what my recommendations are for transitioning to a category-based system. My primary recommendation is this—start fresh. You can add a Processed Mail folder to your existing multiple-folder system and start using the category system with mail that is currently in your Inbox. In this scenario you retain your current system for the old mail you have already filed.

Or you can pick a date a reasonable period back in time and then categorize and drag mail newer than that date from each of your folders to the Processed Mail folder. That way, you have some continuity with recent old mail.

Note: *Be careful in an Exchange environment. If you are dragging mail from local folders to Exchange-based ones, you can exceed your Exchange limits. For folder strategies to prevent that, see Appendix A.*

Of course, the useful life of most old mail passes quickly. In seemingly no time, the only mail that you look at often will be the mail filed by category in your Processed Mail folder, and you'll rarely touch your old folder-based filing system. At some point you'll feel confident to archive that system and refer only to your category-based Processed Mail folder. And this is a good way to try out the Category filing approach. If you don't like it, you can always drag the mail back to your old folders.

Note: *If you do combine the Processed Mail filing system with an old folder system, you might want to name your Processed Mail folder something like "_Processed Mail" so that it sorts to the top of your folders. You can also store your older folders as subfolders of one other folder next to the Processed Mail folder. Call it "Before_MYN," or something similar.*

If You Are Tempted to Consolidate Old Folder-Filed Mail

In case you are tempted to categorize and move all old filed mail out of your old folders and to the Processed Mail folder, here are some considerations before you do that.

▶ Do *not* do it right away. Rather, make emptying your Inbox your highest priority. Why spend time consolidating old filed mail when you still have months of unfiled mail in your Inbox? So empty your Inbox first *before* thinking about consolidating your old mail.

▶ If your Processed Mail folder is on Exchange Server, do *not* move mail there from locally stored folders. Otherwise, as I just mentioned, you will exceed the storage limits of your server.

With these two considerations in mind, go ahead and consolidate that old mail. Just select all the old mail in one folder, apply a category to it in bulk, drag it all to the Processed Mail folder, and delete the old folder. Done!

Transitioning from No Filing System or From an Overflowing Inbox

If you have no current filing system, you most likely have many months of mail in your Inbox. So the question is: Do I need to commit myself to classifying all that old mail? My answer is no.

Make a fresh start. As discussed in Lesson 5, pick a date about one week ago and drag all mail older than that to the Processed Mail folder *immediately*. Mail newer than that (still in your Inbox) you should commit to processing into your Processed Mail folder immediately, extracting tasks and applying categories (make generous use of the Read Later category, discussed ahead). That should only take about an hour or two. Now you have an empty Inbox! Make a note of that process cutoff date. Then, as time allows, dip into the older mail in the Processed Mail folder and process it, doing at least one complete day at a time. Keep track of the date you stop each time, so you can continue with unprocessed mail the next time you come back to this task.

Processing that older mail, however, is optional. It's likely that mail older than a few weeks has diminished in importance anyway, and because everything is in the one Processed Mail folder, you can find mail by other methods. What is important is that you empty your Inbox quickly so you can experience the benefits of doing so. And then keep emptying it daily.

Tips on How and When to Assign Categories

Now that you know how to categorize mail, next you should study some practical tips on doing this.

Should You Categorize Everything in Your Inbox?

Is it necessary to categorize every piece of mail in your Inbox? Absolutely not. In fact, I encourage you to categorize very little mail and use the search tool to find mail when you need to find it.

And even if you do intend to categorize a lot of mail, don't get obsessive about it. If you stare at a piece of mail for more than a second or two and no category jumps out at you, waste no more time on it. You need to balance the advantages of the system against its imposing on your time. One of the goals of this system is to get you out earlier at the end of each workday. You won't do that if you spend too much time using the system. I find I can assign categories to two full screens of mail in about five minutes or less. After you get good at this, if it takes you longer than that, you are probably spending too much time choosing your categories. It may be better to leave more mail uncategorized (and/or reduce the number of your categories). Recall that mail in the automatic None category is still easy to search by eye or using search tools.

Should You Categorize Sent Mail?

I get this question a lot: Should I categorize sent mail? I generally don't categorize sent mail, primarily to save time, but it is certainly useful. You can assign categories in the Sent Items folder after you have sent the mail using the usual Outlook tools. And you would think there would also be easy ways to assign a category to a message before you send it, but there are not. Rather, you need to perform three or four menu or button operations, and that's just too many.

One strategy is to bcc yourself and process the mail out of your Inbox with other mail, categorizing as you go. Another is to keep an extra window open showing the Sent Items folder. Then, each time you send a message, quickly click the sent item in that folder and categorize it.

How Often to Categorize?

Try to categorize at least once a day. If you are very busy or traveling, this step can be put off for a few days, but any more than that and it starts to become painful.

The problem with putting off categorizing is that when you come back to it later, you will have forgotten the contents of some of your mail and you may need to reread them to classify them. Plus, this may discourage you from emptying your Inbox every day. So it is better to include the categorization step whenever you engage in an extended session of e-mail reading. After you get ahead of your Inbox, looping back at the end of each e-mail reading session to categorize and completely empty your Inbox becomes easy. And the smaller the amount of mail you need to process simultaneously, the easier this becomes. When you do categorization just after reading and acting on a block of mail, there will be no need to reread any e-mails. Just quickly go through your Inbox and categorize in blocks, based on titles (see below). The crisp decision-making process and read-once policy are what makes this Inbox workflow so speedy.

But if you must skip categorizing, I still recommend you drag the e-mail (after extracting tasks) to the Processed Mail folder at the end of each day, following Lesson 5. Then, when you can, categorize the new mail in the Processed Mail folder later to catch up. Do not use categories as an excuse for not emptying your Inbox daily.

Use the Read Later Category to Empty Your Overloaded Inbox

I recommend you create and use a Read Later category. It's especially useful if your Inbox is heavily overloaded and you want to clean it up. After you extract any tasks, you apply the Read Later category to any e-mail that you think you might want to read more of, and move the mail to the Processed Mail folder. Keep doing this until your Inbox is cleaned up.

When you have more time later in the week or next, you can group mail by the Read Later category in the Processed Mail folder and catch up on your reading. You might even want to create two such categories, Read Later High and Read Later Low, to delineate the relative priority of each message. You can even put time limits on how quickly you attend to each category. Remove the Read Later category from each mail item after you've caught up on reading.

By using one, or more such categories, you remove nearly all excuses to not clean your Inbox. You should your Inbox as a triage location to find tasks, not as a long-term processing or reading area (see Lesson 5). Keep in mind that the Processed Mail folder sits just below your Inbox, so you can easily open it to study recent mail that needs more attention.

Speeding Up Category Assignments

You will discover many ways to speed up assigning categories to tasks. Here are a few suggestions.

Assigning the Same Category to Multiple Messages at One Time

Prior to assigning a category, select multiple e-mails simultaneously in an e-mail list. Whatever category assignments you make are then assigned to all the selected e-mail items.

For example, if I see a number of messages scattered about the Inbox that fit the Personal category, I will press CTRL to select the group (hold down the CTRL key and click noncontiguous items with the mouse. Use the CMD key on the Mac), then set the Personal category on *one* of the items. This operation sets the category for *all* the selected mail. (Instead of CMD, I use the SHIFT key for e-mails next to each other.) Then, while the group is still selected, I drag the group to the Processed Mail folder. I then repeat this operation for other groups of categories I might see. After the obvious groups are done, I pick off and categorize the single items that are left in the list. This works for me. You will find your own preferred way of batch-processing your mail.

What might make this even quicker for you is this: Try sorting on the From column before you apply your categories in batches. Often e-mails from the same person all categorize the same, so you can select adjacent items together (by holding down the SHIFT key) before setting the category.

Categorizing by Conversations

Another way to take advantage of block-categorizing is to group all mail items in a *conversation* and categorize them together. In Outlook 2007, you can do that by clicking the Subject column label. In Outlook 2010, 2011, and 2013, you can also use a formal Conversation view. The control to activate that in 2010 and 2013 is under the View tab and called Show as Conversations. The control in Outlook 2011 is under the Organize tab and it's called Conversations.

There are advantages to using this formal conversation view (over just sorting on the Subject column). It has a cleaner grouping appearance, and in Windows Outlook it can include items from the Sent Items folder. That way you can see and categorize the entire conversation. The biggest advantage, also only in Windows Outlook, is the ability to delete redundant items in a conversation. To use this feature, right-click the top of a conversation group and select Clean Up Conversation. This deletes any earlier message in the conversation group that is repeated in a later message. It also intelligently saves branched messages that contain unique material. If you are short on storage space, this is a great way to clean up your Inbox before categorizing and saving your mail.

Consider Creating Category Assignment Rules

As we learned at the beginning of this lesson, you can easily create an Outlook rule that automatically assigns a category to all incoming mail from a particular sender, or to mail with particular keywords in the subject line or body of the message. For example, I have created a rule to assign the Personal category to mail from family members. I have many more like that.

In Lesson 11, I describe how to do that—how to set rules in Outlook so that mail arrives in your Inbox precategorized. After you've been assigning categories to your mail for some time, I recommend you take a look at that section and give it a try. It takes a little work to set it up, but it speeds up your Inbox processing tremendously. When I was using categories extensively (before I switched primarily to using Outlook search tools), nearly 70 percent of my filed mail was automatically categorized due to my frequent use of this feature, so it can be quite useful.

Auto-Categorizing Based on Sender in Outlook for Mac 2011

On the Mac, if your intention is to categorize incoming mail based on sender, a feature makes this very easy. You don't need to use the rules feature, you just assign the category to the sender's entry in your Outlook Contacts list. Then select the Assign Categories to Messages from Categorized Contacts check box at the bottom of the Categories dialog box (see Figure 8.5), and it is all automatic for all mail you receive after that. (To open the Categories dialog box, press CTRL and click any e-mail in its Categories column. Then choose Edit Categories from the shortcut menu.)

Summary

Filing e-mail by topic is an optional activity you may want to do. Over the years, filing by using categories has proved to be an effective way to topic file mail without using multiple folders. Category groups, Search Folders, and Smart Folders are excellent ways to create folder-like structures from a collection of categorized e-mail. After you gain a little practice, using categories to file mail will become second nature.

Next Steps

The next lesson revisits the theory underlying the MYN system and teaches you a few more core tools to help manage tasks.

Lesson 9:
MYN Target Now, MYN Strategic Deferrals, MYN Summary Flow Chart

Introduction

You've come a long way! You've learned how to use powerful task and e-mail management tools. You're tracking your important tasks and moving actions out of e-mails to your task system, where they can be properly managed. Congratulations! You're gaining control of your workday.

Now it's time to learn even more ways to fine-tune those techniques. That's what this lesson is all about. I build on the MYN Now Horizon theory (Lesson 1) to show you more task management tools you can use to better manage your workday. And I show you additional ways to take the MYN system beyond the simple 1MTD system you might have learned in the Quick Start.

Note: Portions of this lesson are summarized in video 13 of the MYN-Outlook Complete Video Training (see beginning of the Quick Start chapter for more information).

What's in This Lesson

After a brief review of core MYN principles, I cover how to use the Target Now portion of the Now Tasks list to indicate which noncritical tasks you want to target each day. Using this fourth urgency zone can be a powerful way to focus your work on specific nonurgent tasks, after you complete your Critical Now tasks.

Then, building on what you learned about MYN Strategic Deferrals in Lesson 4, I'll show you the more advanced elements of that tool, specifically the Defer-to-Do and Defer-to-Review processes. If you are having trouble keeping your Now Tasks list short, or if the Low priority section of your task list is growing too large to review every week, now is the time to take this more advanced lesson.

At the end of this lesson you'll find a series of useful flow charts that help you visualize the core elements of the MYN system. All of these skills are from the MYN Now Horizon theory, so I'll start this lesson with a brief review of that theory and then provide a deeper analysis of some key aspects. If you skipped Lesson 1, I encourage you to read it before taking this lesson.

Review of the Now Horizon Work Model

The Now Horizon work model is best represented by an employee walking on the left end of a moving treadmill-like conveyor belt at a speed that just keeps him or her in place. The person's workday and workweek tasks approach on the belt from the right, and the person works those as they arrive, occasionally working ahead on the belt.

At the far right end of the conveyor belt is the limit of the work stream that the person can easily see coming; this is called the Now Horizon. Work beyond that point is out of sight and therefore out of mind, so the person is not anxious about it. All this is shown in Figure 9.1.

Figure 9.1
Review from Lesson 1: the Now Horizon conveyor belt workload model, ideal state.

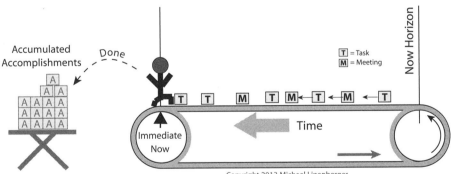

Copyright 2013 Michael Linenberger

Most knowledge workers report that horizon being about ten days out. Nearly all attention is normally placed on work inside that horizon and inside that time frame.

If the rate of work entering the Now Horizon and exiting it completed is the same (as in Figure 9.1), the person feels good. If the person complains about being overloaded with work, he or she is most likely complaining about pile-ups of work inside the Now Horizon (see Figure 9.2). Even when overloaded, though, the person does not think much about work outside, or "over," the Now Horizon.

Review of Urgency Zones of the Now Horizon

In Lesson 1, I described the Now Horizon's four urgency zones — Critical Now, Target Now, Opportunity Now, and Over the Horizon; see Figure 9.2.

Figure 9.2

Review from Lesson 1: the Now Horizon model showing various "urgency zones" and an overloaded state.

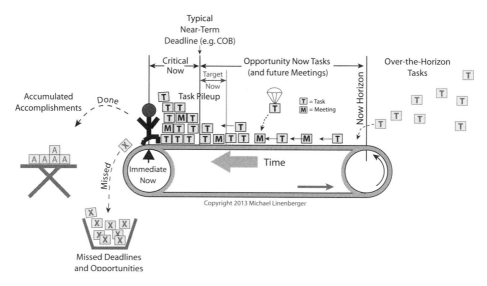

I showed how the zones map to the Outlook configurations made in Lesson 3 (see figure 9.3 for Windows example). In Lessons 4 and 6, I showed how to manage your tasks with these zones. Let's review them briefly.

Two Main Urgency Zones

Two of these zones you are already using extensively when you manage tasks in Outlook: the Critical Now and Opportunity Now zones.

Critical Now Tasks = "High" Priority in Outlook

Critical Now tasks are due within the typical deadline of close of business (COB). They are your must-do-today tasks. They probably have most of your attention and cause most of your feelings of urgency. It is here the typical task pileup occurs, leading to missed deadlines and opportunities. MYN users identify tasks in this zone by giving them a High priority in the Outlook MYN tasks list, configured with the steps in Lesson 3. They manage them by tracking them well and giving them extra attention throughout the day.

Figure 9.3

How urgency zones map to the Windows Outlook task list configured in Lesson 3.

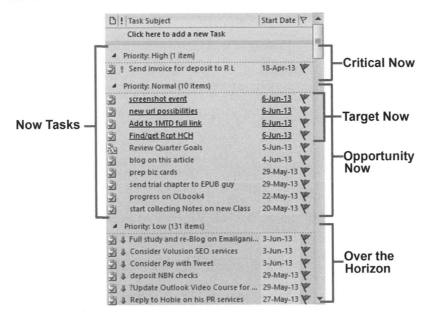

Opportunity Now Tasks = "Normal" Priority in Outlook

Tasks to the right of the Critical Now deadline but to the left of the Now Horizon are tasks that users are aware of and that need to be done as soon as is practical, but users will only do them *now* if the right opportunity arises. These map to the Normal priority section of the Outlook MYN tasks list, configured using Lesson 3.

Critical Now Tasks + Opportunity Now Tasks = Now Tasks List

One final reminder: These two groups together (High and Normal, or Critical Now and Opportunity Now) make up your Now Tasks list first described in Lesson 1. Now Tasks are those you either must do now or would *consider* doing now if you could. They form the list you review every day.

How these zones map to Windows Outlook is shown in Figure 9.3 (repeated here from Lesson 1).

Two Other Urgency Zones

The other two urgency zones, which we covered only briefly in Lesson 1, are the Target Now and Over the Horizon zones. Drilling down on these reveals two more powerful task management tools you can use. Let's look at these zones now.

Target Now Tasks: the Fourth Urgency Zone

I only briefly covered Target Now tasks in Lesson 1 and did not discuss how to implement this optional feature. Let me cover that here with some additional information, so you know how to implement it. Doing so is purely optional, and the Target Now zone does take some energy to maintain, but I think you will find it very useful.

Target Now tasks refer to noncritical tasks that you would *like* to do today but that are not urgently due. Getting them done now might make a client happy or ease the timing on downstream tasks. Or perhaps you are just very enthusiastic about the task. In essence, they are your most important Opportunity Now tasks. My recommended way to show these in Outlook is to *set a Normal priority task with today's start date* on it. This, with Lesson 3 configurations, causes the tasks in Windows versions of Outlook to be underlined and placed at the top of the Normal priority section, where they stand out nicely (see Figure 9.3 for an example). On the Mac they sort to the top of the Opportunity Now Smart Folder.

Optional Target Now Task Process

This leads to an optional process change to the MYN system, and it works as follows. Currently you might be setting tasks to today's date somewhat randomly as new tasks come in. Now do this instead: Set new tasks to today's date only if you really want to do them today. Otherwise date them to the future or to the past (the latter will place them lower in your task list).

Then, each morning, identify which noncritical tasks on the Normal priority list you would like to target for today, and set the start date to today for those tasks. That places them at the top of the Normal section and adds an underline to them. If any items there are already set to today's date that you *don't* intend to do today, you should change the start date for those. Each day, you'll need to repeat the morning routine, because that section resets itself every day at midnight (more on that ahead).

That's it. These Target Now tasks will be your next action focus after you get your Critical Now tasks done.

Some Implications of Using the Target Now Task Process

This optional process fits nicely with many other processes you may currently be using in the MYN system and with Outlook. For example, if you defer a Normal priority task to a specific day you want to do it, when it arrives that day it pops into the Target Now zone of your task list, which is just what you want because you intend to work that task today.

If you have a large number of Target Now tasks, in Windows you can show priority within that list by dragging individual tasks up and down. Outlook repositions the tasks where you drag them, allowing you to create an ordered list inside that zone (such dragging only works in Windows, and with Lesson 3 configurations only on tasks with the same date).

Maintaining the Target Now list takes a little attention, however, so you may decide you do not want to use this process. For example, you may be in the habit of setting all new tasks to a start date of today to get them on the Now Tasks list quickly. But stop and think about that. Do you really want to target them for today? If not, set the date for, say, yesterday, which places it lower in the Opportunity Now list. That's a little less automatic. One shortcut is to type "yesterday" in the Start Date field when you create the task (this works in Windows Outlook only). You may want to make a habit of that so you do not water down the Target Now list.

And as stated earlier, you will quickly see that due to the MYN configurations you made in Outlook, this Target Now designation clears itself each morning and you need to choose your Target Now list again each day. This is good, because it ensures that your target list is fresh and matches your current priorities each day. This is similar to an old paper-based system where you had to rebuild your target list as you started a new page every day. It worked well then and it works well in this system. But it does take some energy to maintain and you may find yourself unable to keep up with it.

Note: *If you want to set the start date of a group of tasks to today (to place them all on the target list at once), press SHIFT or CTRL (CMD on Mac) and select them all, then right-click (CTRL-click on Mac) one of them, choose Follow Up, and choose Today.*

Summary: Four Urgency Zones on the Task List

In Figure 9.3, I show all four zones mapped into an Outlook task list, configured as in Lesson 3. Naturally, your highest-priority attention is placed on the Critical Now tasks. If you have time after those are done, you work the Target Now tasks next. And then if you have more time, you would pick from the remainder of the Opportunity Now tasks, presumably starting at the top. You may of course mix up your order of attacking these.

Using the Now Horizon Model to Keep Your Workday Balanced

One advantage of reviewing the Now Horizon model is that it helps you get the most out of the MYN system to keep your workday balanced. It gives you a picture that helps you see how to use Outlook to keep urgency impact small enough, and at all times visible enough, to prevent a chronic feeling of overload. Here are some ways this model might influence how you manage your tasks to add balance to your day.

Which Tasks Go Directly to the Opportunity Now List?

When people first start using this system, they often ask, "Which tasks should I put directly into my Normal priority task list? Should I pile every nonurgent task there and then just clean it later? That seems to be the process." Their concern is that the list will get too big if everything goes there and it is not cleaned constantly.

My answer is "Study the model." The model shows that you put tasks there that need to be in your current awareness. That's what the Now Horizon defines, and that's what the limit of the Normal priority section should be. We've stated that for most people the Now Horizon is about ten days out. So if a task does not need your attention in the next ten days, don't put it directly on the Now Tasks list. Rather, schedule it out for future attention, using one of the Strategic Deferral approaches shown in more detail in the next section. This keeps the churn out of your list. And don't forget the 20-item limit in the Opportunity Now Section.

Too Many Critical Now Tasks?

Without this system, many people feel frustrated by fighting too many deadlines at the end of each day. The model shows that you should try to eliminate the pileup of tasks shown on the left side of Figure 9.2, inside your Critical Now. You want to prevent a constant state of near-term overload that can lead to unnecessary work anxiety. To do that, early in the day, make sure the list of items in your Critical Now really can be done today. If not, clean up the list so it is achievable and so you feel good about your day.

Recall that you should review the Critical Now list often, even hourly. Perhaps in a late-morning review you realize that there are too many things on the list to possibly complete by end of day. If so, you may need to eliminate some tasks that you owe others, perhaps contacting stakeholders to get permission for delayed delivery. Then move the tasks out of the Critical Now section of the list to make that section reasonable again. After that list is clearly defined and doable, your stress level will drop dramatically.

And again, the overall review cycle that I recommend is to review the Critical Now section about once an hour, the Opportunity Now section once a day, and the Over the Horizon section once a week.

Tossing Tasks over the Now Horizon Revisited

If the Opportunity Now section of the conveyor belt grows larger than 20 items, and starts to pile up such that you cannot easily review it every day, you need to find lower-priority tasks that you can safely toss over the Now Horizon. In Lesson 4, you placed most excess items in the Low priority section. Now you review that Low priority section once a week. If on that review you find anything that has become more urgent, you can move it back up to the High or Normal sections.

The "Low" Priority Section Becomes Too Long to Review

When you first start using either the MYN or 1MTD system, you'll find that the simple method of tossing excess tasks over the horizon and reviewing that section once each week will work well for a while. But if you're a very busy individual, you'll find that, after about two to three months, this approach will stop working. Why? The Over-the-Horizon list becomes too long to review. One day you'll sit down to do your weekly review and find that the list is demoralizingly long—so long you'll skip the review. Perhaps nothing unfortunate will happen that week as result of skipping the review, so the following week you will skip it again. And then it's likely that you'll *never* review it again as it gets bigger and bigger and bigger.

Finding a Better Method

Eventually though, after a few items in that unreviewed list fall through the cracks and blow up on you, you'll start to feel uneasy with that list. You'll regret not managing it better. You might even become reluctant to move tasks to that Low priority section because you know it has become a black hole—items placed in there are never seen again. But if you don't move tasks there, you'll leave them in the Opportunity Now list, and that list will quickly exceed 20 items. When you do that, that section will become uncontrollable, as well. Eventually, the MYN system breaks down.

Assuming you are experiencing some degree of that now, this is the time to learn a more sophisticated version of tossing items over the horizon. Even if you're not experiencing that yet, it make sense to learn a better method now—*and create a habit of using it.* That way the MYN system never drifts out of control. This better method of managing your growing list of tasks is called MYN Strategic Deferral. It's not complicated—it's just a small adjustment to what you are already doing.

I predicted you would get here in the Quick Start, where you learned that if you're juggling fewer than 100 tasks you can use the 1MTD system indefinitely. When you start juggling more, you'll want to graduate to MYN. That 100-item threshold is what I am highlighting here. Let's say you have five Critical Now tasks and 20 Opportunity Now tasks. That means after you reach about 75 Over-the-Horizon tasks (for a total of 100 tasks), you'll want to start using the expanded methods of MYN. The MYN Strategic Deferral method in this lesson is one of the most important MYN methods to learn when your list gets too long.

Why It Is Hard to Delete Tasks

One last point before we learn how to use MYN Strategic Deferral. Sometimes I'm asked about the need for a new method to control long lists. Why not instead just ask people to *delete* tasks whose priority is very low? Wouldn't that be a way to keep the list short?

The answer is simple: Deleting is good—but not sufficient—as a strategy to keep your list short. Sure, you *should* delete old, useless tasks. But ask someone to identify tasks that are "no longer important and are ready to delete," and I guarantee you that they will find very few.

Why? As responsible adults, we all tend to feel that if something was important enough to write down, it's important enough to do. We have trouble
letting go of written tasks, even old ones, so our Low priority list gets bigger
and bigger. Then we no longer review it. So yes, you need a new approach to
keep your list under control — one that goes beyond just deleting tasks.

MYN Strategic Deferral (Windows and Mac)

In this section you learn how to tweak your current MYN process so you
can easily manage a long list of tasks. It involves setting a future date on *all*
deferred tasks that you toss over the Now Horizon (see Figure 9.4), and using
the more advanced MYN Strategic Deferral tools. By doing that, you not only
lower the number of tasks within the Now Horizon to a reasonable level, but
you also ensure that you have a reasonable way to track those deferred items.

Figure 9.4
Using Strategic Deferrals and scheduling reviews.

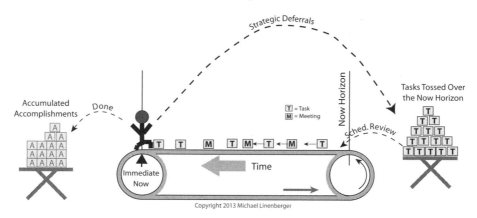

Use the CEO Approach

Some people hesitate postponing a lot of tasks, thinking they are just procrastinating. But don't feel bad about doing this. Even CEOs postpone tasks, and
they often receive big raises when they do. Let me explain.

Sometimes you hear about CEOs who decide to postpone projects or products
their company is currently working on. The CEO often says, "We're doing
this to allow the company to focus better on current primary priorities," or
maybe, "We need to return to our company's core competencies." The CEO is
usually hailed as "strategic," "decisive," or "practical," or as being capable of
"making the hard choices." The CEO is not usually called a procrastinator.

Similarly, when you postpone focus on certain tasks in your list because you
honestly have too much on your plate, *take pride* in your decision. Don't think

of yourself as weak or procrastinating. Think of yourself rather as making strategic choices. Just be sure to use the new MYN Strategic Deferral tools to do it in an accountable way. Let's go over how to do that.

Two Ways to Defer Tasks Strategically

When you defer a task to the future, past the Now Horizon, how you set the Outlook *priority* on that task leads to a very important distinction. If you set a High or Normal (medium) priority on that future-dated task, you've just created what I call a Defer-to-*Do* task. These are tasks you intend to *do* on the future date.

In contrast, if you set a *Low* priority on that future-dated task, you have created what I call a Defer-to-*Review* task. These are tasks you only intend to *review* on the future date. You're not committing to do them at that time. Let's discuss both. The distinction between the two is subtle yet very powerful.

Defer-to-Do Tasks

Defer-to-Do tasks are High or Normal priority tasks that you hide until a future day. This should sound familiar because we went over scheduling tasks in Lesson 4. Now, however, I want you to be very diligent about restricting these High and Normal priority deferred tasks to *only* those you really intend to do *on the day they appear in your Now Tasks list.* In other words, on the day it appears, the task is either a Critical Now task or a Target Now task.

Think about the name Defer-to-Do. You are deferring this task to *do* it on a specific day. There is something special about that day that makes it perfect for that task.

So, for example, let's say you want to call Jon on Friday. That happens to be the perfect day to reach out to him to check on the progress of a shared work item, and there's no need to think about it until then. Today is Tuesday, so you enter the task now and set the start date to Friday, hiding the task until that day. If you do this, and set the priority to High or Normal, you have just created a Defer-to-Do task. It's a task you intend to do on Friday, the first day it arrives.

This is a great way to schedule tasks, but I don't use it as a general way to clean up a long list by setting random future dates on tasks. Instead, I use Defer-to-Review to clean my list when it gets too long.

Defer-to-Review Tasks: Your Main Deferral Solution

In contrast to tasks that you defer because you know you want to do them on a specific day are tasks you defer just to get them off your current list. For example, what if you have many more tasks than 20 visible in your Normal priority section and you want to shorten that list? A good way to do that is to hide some tasks in the future and get them off the visible portion of your list.

But in this case, the specific day you pick to hide each task is relatively unimportant, so you'll pick a general time frame to consider each one again.

The Defer-to-Review process says this: You should place a task like this in the *Low* priority section and assign it to various relatively distant start dates. Don't place these review-only tasks in the Normal or High section; otherwise, they'll just overwhelm that section later.

Think about what this does. By placing them all in the Low priority section, you are telling yourself: My only commitment is to *review* tasks in this section when they appear there. I'm not committing to *do* them on the day they appear. In other words, these are Defer-to-Review tasks, not Defer-to-Do tasks. This is usually the reason I defer items—just to get them off my list to reconsider later. As tasks build up, you, too, will likely see that this will become your main deferral solution, one that you can use all the time.

Set the Date to a Monday as Far in the Future as Possible

When you use Defer-to-Review, I recommend you always set the start dates to a future *Monday*. I also recommend that you set the dates as far in the future as possible for each task. The reason for using Mondays is that as a number of tasks appear each week on that day, you'll be inspired to plan your week ahead on what to do with those tasks. Plus, you'll have to do that planning only once a week. I even set an appointment on my calendar to do that.

The reason to set the dates as far in the future as possible is so that, on each Monday, you see only tasks that really need consideration. This solves the common problem of long *unmanaged* low-priority task lists. Typically with such lists, we review and dismiss the same tasks over and over again each week. Because their status rarely changes from week to week, we gain nothing other than frustration by that repeated review. We eventually stop reviewing the list. But by setting the next review date as far in the future as is reasonable for each task, when that task next appears for review it feels appropriate to review it again, and might even yield results. It's more likely to be the right time to do something with the task.

The other reason to set dates as far in the future as possible is that it makes the Monday processing easy to do. That's because, with a typical spread of distant future dates, only five to ten tasks will appear in the Low priority section each week (see Figure 9.5). The review of a short list like this normally takes only five minutes or less. You're not deluged by a large list of tasks to review each week.

Figure 9.5
Every Monday a new list will pop into your previously empty Low priority section. Process those out as soon as possible; keep that section empty.

Processing Defer-to-Review Tasks: Four Options

In each Monday morning review session, your job is to *empty* the Low priority section. How do you empty it? There are four alternate ways you can process these tasks out of the Low priority section.

1. Set start dates to some other future Monday, and thus defer tasks over the Now Horizon again (as in Figure 9.4). Select a Monday as far in the future as is safe, practical, and appropriate. Because I have so many deferred tasks whose status rarely changes, this is my most common choice.

2. Set the Outlook priority to Normal or High so that these tasks are promoted immediately to your current Now Tasks list. Do this if their importance has recently increased or if your workload has diminished enough now to get to them. Surprisingly, I find I do this rarely.

3. Do the task right now and mark it complete. (If you have too many tasks in the list, this is a less likely choice.).

4. Delete the task. If you take the first option on a task repeatedly, eventually you'll realize that you have little commitment to the task, and you can finally delete it.

Try to do this review first thing Monday morning. You can even set a Monday morning recurring appointment or recurring task to remember to do this. That way you don't allow these tasks to sit in the Low priority section during the week or beyond. Plan to completely empty the Low priority section when you process it.

Using this method, I can usually empty the Low priority section very quickly. I've never found this hard to do or a burden. It's almost a pleasure, because I often find things there I now really want to do, because of more favorable circumstances. More likely I find that the contents of my indistinct list of future to-do's, which can haunt my subconscious at times, are not so bad now that I see them again. Most can be deferred even longer this time — or even deleted. It's satisfying to do that because it feels so good to empty that section. It clears my psyche of concern about postponed items.

Why Defer-to-Review Works

Many new users worry that Defer-to-Review just causes hundreds of urgent tasks to fall back onto the main part of their list later, and they'll feel overwhelmed. However, the reason it does work so well is due to the following truism: Nearly all tasks become much less important over time. Why? Because, due to rapidly changing business conditions, people's priorities change quickly. Yours do, your client's do, your boss's do. That means older tasks fade in importance over time, and that's why Defer-to-Review works. (It's also why FRESH Prioritization, described in Lesson 4, works so well.)

As a result, of the four review options I listed earlier, I find that 95 percent of my tasks make sense to defer to the future again (option 1 in previous section). They have not yet become more urgent. A few I might defer only one week, but most I defer much longer, often six months or more. That is the beauty of this system. It gives you a way to apply appropriate deferral periods to each task, according to their built-in time frames.

Note: *For anyone moving to this edition directly from the first edition, in the first edition I recommended using none-dated Master Tasks to track low-priority actions. Defer-to-Review replaces that. The first edition process of using the Low priority section of the Master Tasks view for tasks that you review very rarely is also incorporated in this new process. The Low priority section of the master tasks list held your ideas, inspirations, and long-term Low priority tasks, none of which you have any near-term intentions to act on. I now recommend you make Defer-to-Review tasks out of them, too, and schedule their review out 6 to 12 months. You really should review everything eventually, and this enables you to do that in an orderly way.*

Getting Started with Defer-to-Review

After you start using Defer-to-Review, the Low priority section should be reserved for only these long-term review tasks. When you first start using this process, I recommend you empty the Low priority section. Do that either by moving some items to High or Normal priority, or by keeping them at Low and setting the start dates to future Mondays.

The next time you clean your Opportunity Now list by moving items to the Over the Horizon (Low priority) section, assign a future start date at the same time. The task will disappear and your Low priority section will remain empty until the following Monday.

If you are doing Defer-to-Review correctly, the Low priority section should be completely empty Tuesday through Sunday. That leads to a nice compact Now Tasks list as the only list you see each day. The result? The Defer-to-Review process will lower your stress level throughout the week.

An Optional Tasks Folder View: Defer-To-Review Tasks (Windows)

You can manage these tasks right in the To-Do Bar. That's what I usually do—I review and reset the task dates right there. But you might also want to build a new optional Tasks Folder view that gives you a way to do some proactive management (see Figure 9.6). This suggested view groups tasks by their deferred-to Monday.

Figure 9.6

Optional Defer-to-Review Tasks folder view where all defer-to-review tasks are displayed grouped in their scheduled future review week (or month). Next-month's tasks are at the bottom; tasks at top are farther out. Today is July 29.

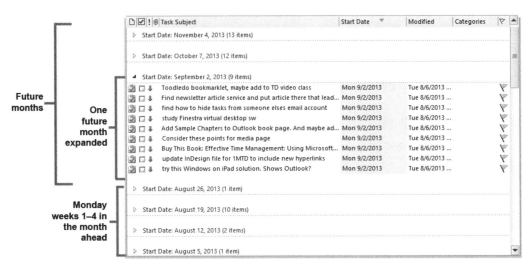

One benefit of this view is to see what week or month tasks are piling up in so you can avoid putting too many tasks into the same review period. If you use this view, you should make one adjustment to the Defer-to-Review process as follows. If your defer a task one month or longer, then set the start date to the first Monday *of the month*. Consistently using the first day of the week and the first Monday of the month as target dates is what makes this view work. It creates distinct groups that are easier to track and manage. Perhaps most useful is you can drag multiple tasks from group to group in that view to reset their start dates en masse. I'll show you how to build that view in Lesson 12, when I cover optional custom Tasks folder views. This view is also delivered with the MYN-enabled version of ClearContext.

Summary of MYN Strategic Deferral Steps

MYN Strategic Deferrals are a way to reduce the size of your Now Tasks list to make it easier to use and better focused. Here are the basic operations.

▶   Set Defer-to-Do tasks: for any task that you intend to do on a specific future day, just set the start date ahead to that date. Leave the Outlook priority at either High or Normal as appropriate. Only do this if you really intend to do the task on that date.

▶   Set Defer-to-Review tasks: for any task that you merely want to put off for a while, set the Outlook priority to Low, and set the date ahead to some Monday in the future (beyond the Now Horizon) on which you want to review the task again.

▶   Every Monday, as Defer-to-Review tasks mature and appear in the Low priority section of your To-Do Bar, process them out immediately using the four options listed in the earlier section "Processing Defer-to-Review Tasks: Four Options." You will most likely use option 1 in that list.

If you use Defer-to-Review correctly, and if you also apply the MYN maximum limits to your High and Normal sections, you will have a short, compact, and low-stress Now Tasks list to work from each day.

MYN Strategic Deferral FAQs

Here are some questions I sometimes get about Defer-to-Do, and their answers.

Q: Isn't this just procrastination?

A: No, absolutely not. You are proactively managing your dynamic and busy work life. Remember, you will always think of more things to do than you have time to do, so you need to prioritize and do the things that are right for the moment. You then need to come back to all those other creative ideas and tasks periodically to see if their time has come. This is merely a management tool to accomplish that effectively.

Q: Why hold on to tasks so long? Why not just delete them when you first see them fall "below the line"?

A: You never know when the ideal time to revisit a good idea or moderately important task may come. Even though you may only reactivate a small portion of your deferred list, even if only one out of 20 offers high value later, you still come out ahead. Furthermore, what I find is that without this tool, I would never delete many of my Low priority tasks. I would not have the confidence to do so. I would be too concerned that they may actually become important later. But if I retained them in my Now Tasks list, it would quickly get too big. This tool gives me a competent way to confidently move Low priority tasks off my Now Tasks list, thereby keeping that list well focused.

Q: Isn't the Monday review just another burdensome "should" I need to do and will probably skip?

A: Granted, that is a risk, but it is my experience that, compared with all the other "shoulds" in the time-management world, this one is pretty darn easy to do and keep up with. As I mentioned earlier, it is almost a pleasure to do because it works so well. Plus, if you do skip it, the tasks sit rather prominently at the bottom of your list, urging you to do something.

Q: Over time, won't this list of Defer-to-Review tasks grow huge every month and become unusable?

A: No, and the reason is, as tasks get older you will eventually delete them. Think about it. The only reason you maintain these tasks on the list is that they had some near-term relevance at the time. In my experience, the half-life of a task is relatively short. Business and personal priorities tend to move on and eventually the very old tasks on the defer-to-review list will stand out and you'll delete them, particularly after reviewing the same tasks many times.

Q: I used a previous version of this system, with the master tasks approach. In that system I was able to assign various levels of priority to master tasks. If everything is now a Low priority, how can I indicate various levels of priority?

A: The time frame settings are a form of prioritization. But if you are talking about core importance (regardless of time), use the intrinsic importance approach described in Lesson 12 for this.

Q: Isn't it possible that my entire collection of tasks with deadlines within the Now Horizon is so large that reducing that list to 20 Opportunity Now items (and up to 5 Critical Now items), by deferring them, is impractical?

A: Sure, that's possible. But I want you to study the exercise in Lesson 11 titled "Doing the Math on Your Workweek" first before you decide that. If after that exercise you still conclude you are overloaded, yes, now you will have confirmed that and you need to do something about it. Strategies to correct the problem are discussed there. I suspect, however, that most people who think they are hopelessly overloaded really do have more options for remedy than they think, and Strategic Deferral is one.

How do you put this all together with all the other techniques you have learned to date? The following workflows answer that question.

． ． ．

MYN-Outlook Flow Charts: Summarizing Parts I and II of the Book

In the management consulting world, we often use flow charts to present work process flows. I like to say that there are two kinds of people in this world. The first are those who prefer or even *demand* to see flow charts to help explain their world. The second is those who don't.

While I usually say that as a joke, I am often approached by the first kind requesting, even demanding, that I meet their flow chart needs in my writings about the MYN system. I do sympathize a bit, so I have finally acquiesced.

New to this edition is this final section of Part II—a set of flow charts that help explain how MYN works. If you are of the second type and can't stand flow charts—well, just move along, there's nothing to see here!

Actually, even if you don't enjoy flow charts, I encourage you to take a look at the charts in this section and to read the accompanying descriptions. Together they summarize everything in the book through the end of Part II (which ends with this lesson). Because the remaining material in the book (Part III and the Appendixes) represents a collection of add-on concepts, this is the appropriate point for a summary of the core MYN processes. Studying these can help you understand all the core MYN processes and how they relate to one another.

The High-Level, Overall Workflow

The first chart that follows—the overall workflow—looks complicated. But don't worry. I divide that workflow and describe it piece by piece in the subsequent charts, making it much easier to understand. Let's look first at the overall workflow.

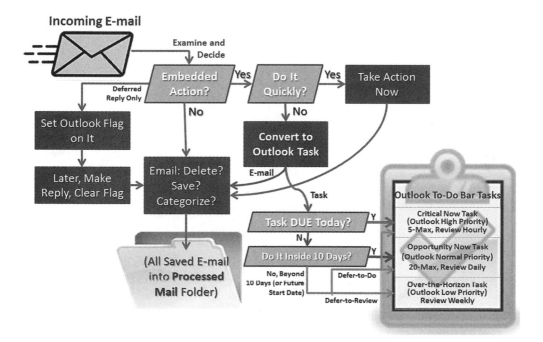

An E-mail to Task Workflow

In today's business world, most of our tasks arrive by e-mail. For many of us, 90 percent or more arrive that way. With that in mind, nearly everything starts in the upper-left corner of the chart with the arrival of a business e-mail with a potential action for you to do. The workflow ends with the e-mail possibly being moved to the Processed Mail folder in the bottom middle, and the option of a task being created in the lower right.

Of course, some tasks do not arrive by e-mail. In that case you should start in the middle right of the workflow at the box labeled Task DUE Today?

Four Workflows in One

The previously shown workflow is the high-level view. But let's break it down. The overall workflow is a combination of four distinct workflows. The first three of these workflows are simple processes. Let's start with the first one.

Workflow 1: No Action, Just File

This is the very simple case in which you get an e-mail and see that there is no action for you to do. Here's how that looks:

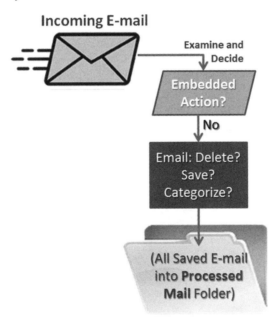

Notice the middle box that is labeled E-mail: Delete? Save? Categorize? Its role in an incoming nonaction e-mail you've just examined can be summarized as follows: Do you want to save the e-mail for later? If not, delete it. But if you decide to save it, you also should decide if you want to categorize it (Lesson 8). To save it (categorized or not), you move it to the Processed Mail folder.

The Read Later Category

There is one important but subtle aspect of this. If you decide there is no action, but you cannot completely read the e-mail today, you might want to assign to it a Read Later category when you move it to the Processed Mail folder. That way, when you are not as busy later, you can group recent e-mail in the Processed Mail folder by that category and catch up on your reading. You can empty your Inbox each day even if more reading of today's mail is needed. (For more information about the Read Later category, see the end of Lesson 8).

Workflow 2: Do it Quickly and File

Workflow 2 is also a very simple case. You get an e-mail and see that there's an action in it that is very quick (under a minute or so), and you decide to do it immediately. You know there is no point converting it to a task because you can probably complete the task just as fast as you can convert it. This might also be the case where an urgent longer action comes in and you *must* do it now. After taking action, you'll use the same delete, save, categorize decision block used in workflow 1. Here's how this looks:

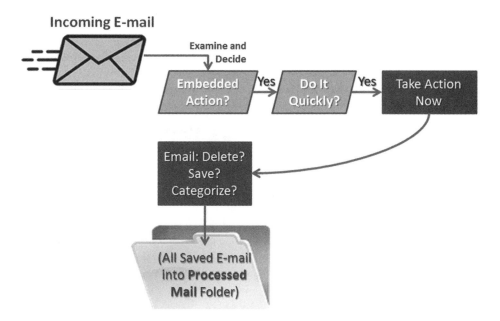

Workflow 3: Flag and Reply Later

Workflow 3 is also very simple. This is where you get an e-mail and see that the only action required is to write a reply to the e-mail. But you realize you can't write that reply immediately. There's no point converting it to a task because it's just a reply.

The correct action here is to simply mark the e-mail with a Follow Up flag and reply later (see Lesson 7). Here's how it looks:

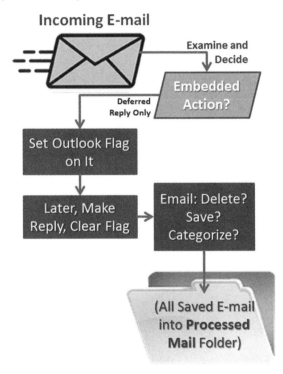

One key point is this: If you use a Follow Up flag, you should commit to writing that reply *later today* or *early tomorrow*. If you know you can't write the reply for some time, then convert the e-mail to a task (instead of using a flag). That's because flags do not work well for longer-term action management. If you see a flagged item sitting in your Inbox for more than a few days, convert that item to a task.

The last three blocks in this workflow demonstrate its important final steps. After you write the reply, immediately remove the flag and either file the e-mail into the Processed Mail folder, or delete it.

Workflow 4: Convert to Task and File

This next workflow is the last and by far the most complex case. In fact, it's what the bulk of this book is about. This case is where you get an e-mail that has an action for you to do that you cannot, or will not, do now. So you need to convert the e-mail to a task and then probably file the e-mail out of your Inbox to the Processed Mail folder.

The reason this workflow is more complex is that it shows many of the decisions you will make when converting the e-mail to a task.

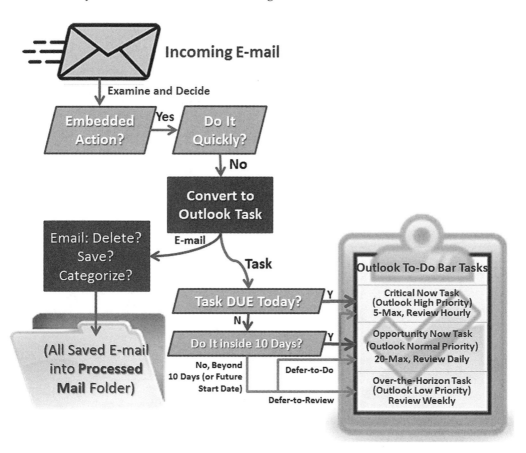

Decisions When Converting E-mails to Tasks in Workflow 4

The complex part of workflow 4 is in the lower-right corner—how to convert the e-mail to a task. The reason it is complex is due to the material you learned in this lesson on Strategic Deferrals. Let's take a look at the convert-to-task decisions shown in the workflow, starting with the block labeled Task DUE Today?

Critical Now and Opportunity Now Tasks

If a task is absolutely due today you simple make it a Critical Now task. That's straightforward (see Lesson 4).

But if the task is not due today, then ask the next question: Do you want to do the task within the next ten days? If so, then (with an important exception) you make it an Opportunity Now task—set the priority to Normal—and you probably set today as the start date. (For more information, see Lesson 4.)

Defer-to-Do

There's an important exception to setting the start date to today. That's if you want to use Defer-to-Do and hide the task to a specific future date (either within the next ten days or beyond). By *specific date* I mean a date on which you *must* do or *strongly want* to do the task. To do that, follow the workflow down to the lower right and make it a Defer-to-Do task according to the principles you learned earlier in this lesson. That means set a future start date as needed, and set the priority by following the two branches on the Defer-to-Do flow chart, which are 1) set the priority to High if you *must* do the task on the day it appears, or 2) set the priority to Normal if you *strongly want* to do the task on the day it appears. (Case 2 meets the definition of a Target Now task. For more details on Target Now, see the beginning of this lesson.)

Defer-to-Review and Over the Horizon

Another option for a task that follows the No branch below the box labeled Do it Inside 10 Days? is described by this question: What if I just want to *delay* the task and get it off my list for a while? Then use the Defer-to-Review process (bottom arrow), which states the following: Set the priority to Low (Over the Horizon) and set the start date to a future Monday that is as far in the future as is practical. On the Monday that it appears, either do it then or move it up in the list or redate it to the future again. To review these steps, see the Defer-to-Review section earlier in this lesson.

Set a Future Deadline?

Not shown in the flow chart: If a task has a future firm deadline, you should show it using one of the four methods described at the end of Lesson 4. The simplest of those is to place the word DUE and the deadline date right at the start of the task's subject line.

Delete, Save, Categorize the E-mail

After converting an e-mail to a task, you are left with the e-mail still in your Inbox. So next, move your attention back to the middle of the flow chart to where the e-mail branch flows out of the *Convert to Outlook Task* box. Follow it down to the left. At this point use the same steps you used in the earlier workflows, deciding whether to delete or save the e-mail and whether to categorize it. If saved, move it to the Processed Mail folder. Notice that nothing stays in your Inbox in workflow 4.

Larger-Sized Image in Appendix C

That's it! That's the complete MYN workflow. A somewhat larger-sized version of the overall workflow image is shown in Appendix C, where you can cut it out, copy it, (or print it out of an e-book version). You can tape it next to your computer, which might help you succeed during the first weeks of using the MYN system. Good luck!

Don't Forget the Review Cycles and Urgency Zone Maximums

Summarized in the tasks portion of this workflow are the other two sets of MYN rules, the review cycles and urgency zone maximums:

▶ Review the Critical Now section approximately once per hour, and keep it to five or fewer tasks.

▶ Review the Opportunity Now section at least once a day, preferably in the morning. Keep it to 20 or fewer tasks.

▶ If the Opportunity section exceeds 20 tasks, reduce the list by deleting and delegating if you can, but primarily by using the two MYN Strategic Deferral tools in this chapter. The most important of those two is Defer-to-Review, which places tasks in the Over the Horizon (Low priority) section with a future Monday start date. Review that section once a week as tasks appear there.

Enjoy the Benefits of the System!

With this complete MYN workflow in practice, and with these review cycles and maximums in use, you will quickly reach the point where you feel the extensive benefits of the system. You will not feel overloaded or anxious about your work. During your workday, you can add more and more of your important but not urgent items, thereby reaching more of your goals. Instead of being buried by, and reacting only to urgent matters, you can advance your important projects and life priorities, making headway in your career. You'll develop a completely different attitude about your work, and possibly for the first time start to enjoy your job. That's what the MYN system can do for you.

▪ ▪ ▪

Summary

The Target Now and MYN Strategic Deferral tools provide a way to reduce workday overload and the feeling of anxiety by giving you a practical tool to focus on your top tasks. The latter, Strategic Deferral, gives you a clean and accountable way to toss tasks over the Now Horizon, where the perceived impact on your workday is minimal. Of the two MYN Strategic Deferral tools, Defer-to-Review is the most important for managing down the size of your workload, so learn it well and use it often.

The entire MYN system can be depicted in an easy-to-use flow chart. Study that flow chart often when first starting the system.

Next Steps

You have now completed Part II of the book, focused on advancing the system. This completes the core trainings of the system.

The next part, Part III, contains mostly optional components of the MYN system that can make your work life easier, more efficient, and better focused, but that you can postpone implementing if you wish. The first lesson is on Delegation. If you have staff you delegate tasks to, I encourage you to study Lesson 10 now. Lesson 11 is on time management and various ways to save time with this system. Lesson 12 is a collection of optional techniques and custom Windows Outlook task views that you may find useful. Feel free to jump around these next lessons and take them out of order if you wish, as they stand fairly independently of one another.

PART III
Mastering the MYN System

Lesson 10:
MYN Delegation in Outlook

Introduction

Delegating tasks effectively is an essential means for clearing tasks off your list, which frees up time to focus on activities that are more important and more appropriate to your role. It is also good for the staff you delegate to because, as you assist them through increasing levels of skills, they learn. It can and should be a win–win arrangement.

However, many new and even experienced work managers have trouble delegating effectively. As a result, too many tasks that should be delegated end up remaining self-assigned.

Failures with delegation often stem from lack of good systems to assign, track, and follow up on delegated tasks. When a deadline arrives and the delegated task has not been completed, too often managers blame the delegated staff: "That person can't seem to get things done for me. If I need something done I'd better do it myself," and tasks end up back on the manager's list. It's highly likely that the failure was due to the delegation methodology, not due to the staff the task was delegated to.

Delegation of tasks can represent handoffs to subordinates or "requests" to colleagues. Both can be managed the same way.

Note: *There is no video summary of this lesson. (For more information about MYN videos, see the note at the beginning of the Quick Start chapter.)*

Successful Delegation

It's amazing how much respect and attention staff will give you and the tasks you assign if you provide three elements in your requests:

▶ An honest and thoughtful discussion of the reasons the task is important and why this person may be the right one to work on it.

▶ Plenty of lead time on the deadline of the task.

▶ Consistent and reasonably spaced check-ins while waiting for the task to be completed.

It's when you manage assigned tasks *without* providing these elements that tempers get short and staff feel overburdened.

It's no wonder managers are so bad at delegation. They have a large pile of their own tasks to manage, so how can they be expected to correctly assign and consistently track the task list of others? In the earlier lessons of this book, you have learned best practices for getting your own tasks under control. In this lesson you will learn best practices for delegating tasks to others.

The Task Delegation Approach

My delegation approach is an extension of the follow-up task system I taught you in Lesson 6. Extending it is a three-step process:

1. **Identify**: At the moment the task and the need to delegate arises, enter and annotate it in your task system as a task to be delegated and indicate to whom to delegate it. Do not actually communicate the task until the next step.

2. **Get Buy-In**: Use a face-to-face or phone meeting to gain buy-in and acceptance from the staff or colleague and to set an agreed deadline for the task. Update the system to indicate acceptance (if achieved), to record the deadline, and to schedule your first check-in time frame.

3. **Follow Up**: At the scheduled check-in, follow up on the assigned task, provide help if needed, and set subsequent follow-up time frames. Escalate only after several follow-ups.

I like this approach because the staff manages the task in their own way, and I use my task system to initiate regular personal follow-up activities. This prevents me from forcing my task management approach on other staff, yet it allows me a personal touch in my follow-up. I cover logistics for each of these steps next.

Step 1: Identify and Annotate a Task for Delegation

In step 1, when I identify tasks that I intend to assign to others, I enter the task *in my own task list*, and annotate the subject line to indicate I intend to delegate it. This helps me plan and initiate the assignment process. My assignment annotation system is simple: I place the initials of the staff member I intend to assign the task to in the very front of the subject line, followed by a colon, then the subject itself. So a task I intend to assign to Jon Smith to provide network performance resolution would have the subject line "JS:Resolve network performance." This is for my use only. I do not give the task list to Jon. I may give Jon a heads-up e-mail that something new is coming to be discussed in the next meeting. For big tasks, the more warning the better. And I set the start date to the day I intend to meet Jon to discuss the task assignment.

By using this annotation system, on the day I intend to meet with Jon I am reminded to make this assignment. Or if I meet with Jon early, I can sort the subject field alphabetically within the Tasks folder of Outlook (in Windows use the MYN All Now Tasks view described ahead in Lesson 12. On the Mac just use the unfiltered tasks folder), scroll down to Jon's initials, and collect the tasks that I propose to hand off in person.

Step 2: Gain Buy-In for the Task

A Valuable Step

Assigning a task to someone without prior discussion is largely discouraged by management experts. An important element of delegation is achieving buy-in from the staff member you plan to delegate to. During one-on-one meetings, I spend time discussing the value of the task. I try to share the vision behind it. And if the task is an interesting one, I try to share my excitement. If the task is urgent I make sure the staff member shares my feeling of urgency and the reasons behind it. I then make a point of asking if he or she is interested in the task and feels it can be added to their list. And very important, can they complete it by the intended deadline? One hopes the answer is yes to all of those questions. If working this task may cause other delegated tasks to be late, now is the time to discuss that. You may have to make some tradeoffs in your list of delegated tasks for this individual.

Gaining buy-in like this is incredibly important. It builds your staff's respect for you and your management techniques. It creates a sense of ownership for the task. And it goes a long way toward ensuring the successful completion of the delegated task.

The Outlook Assign Task Feature (Windows)

Skipping the buy-in step leads to bad morale and incomplete assignments. There are hundreds of ways to do this wrong. For example, dropping a task assignment in someone's Inbox without prior discussion is inadvisable.

This specific example is why, even though Windows Outlook has an automatic way to delegate tasks, I recommend that you do not use that capability. Let me explain.

If your organization has a Microsoft Exchange Server implementation, you can use windows Outlook to assign tasks electronically to other staff. Automatic assignment of tasks is activated by clicking the Assign Task button at the top of the task entry dialog box (see Figure 10.1). This feature is also available by right-clicking a task in the task list view.

Figure 10.1
Windows Outlook Assign Task buttons.

When you use the Assign Task feature, your copy of Outlook actually sends a special e-mail with the task attached, asking the recipient to formally accept or reject the task assignment. If it is accepted, the task is added to the recipient's own Outlook task list, and you automatically get back a message saying the task was accepted. At that point your copy of the task is modified to show that a formal assignment has been made and to whom it was assigned. Subsequently you can request special Outlook-based status reports from those recipients (sent using the button just to the right of the Assign Task button shown in Figure 10.1). And when you receive those status reports back, the status fields (Status and % Complete) will be updated in your own task list to reflect the progress of work that your staff has made on the task.

This is a great concept and a great technical implementation. However, every time I've tried to use it I've found that for various reasons, usually people-related, the team stops or never fully starts using this approach. There are two main problems:

▶ If not used carefully, it encourages the classic "dump and run" approach to delegating tasks. Dropping a task assignment in someone's Inbox is not consistent with gaining staff buy-in.

▶ Many of your staff may prefer not to use the Outlook task system to manage their tasks, or may not know how to. So such tasks go into a black hole.

That said, it is a well-implemented technology. One scenario where it could be used effectively is this: Your entire staff is already using Microsoft Outlook to manage tasks with MYN principles, and you agree not to use the Assign Task button until *after* you've had your discussion with your staff about a task assignment. You may want to try that. But it is rare that this combination of factors exists. So, the following discussion assumes that you do *not* use the Outlook automated assign task functionality.

Step 3: Follow-Up

There are a number of possible ways you can follow up with your staff.

Meeting with Your Staff to Review Assignments

I have one-on-one meetings weekly with all my key staff to discuss and assign tasks and to check the progress of previously assigned tasks. But if the next one-on-one is too far off and the task urgent, I set a separate short ad hoc meeting to have the discussion. Before that meeting, I use the Tasks folder and, in Windows Outlook, I use the MYN All Now Tasks view (see Lesson 12) to sort on tasks for that staff member. Mac users should just use their unfiltered Tasks folder. I review all tasks that are outstanding and all tasks that I intend to assign. I sort alphabetically on the subject line so that all tasks with that individual's initials sort together. I bring that list with me to the meeting for review. The best way to do this is with a laptop or tablet. Or you can instead print that list and bring the paper copy.

I discuss with the staff member tasks that they have not yet agreed to and, if needed, reprioritize and redate the outstanding ones to reflect newer priorities and meeting outcomes. I input those changes immediately or when I return to my computer. Again, this is even easier if you bring the laptop or a tablet with you to the meeting. Having a PC with you is an effective way to keep up with a rapidly changing landscape of assigned tasks — particularly if you have many staff. And assuming that during your discussion about the status of each task you may have changes to make to those tasks (for example, marking the subject for follow-up, extending the deadline, or marking the task as complete), you can edit the tasks right in this window, in the meeting. If you are not using any mobile devices you can mark up your paper printout of tasks and make the changes when you return to your computer.

Following Up on Delegated Tasks

After the task is accepted, it is essential to schedule and engage in regular follow-up activities. Consistent and reasonable follow-up is the key, often-overlooked point. We are tempted to think that after a task is assigned, the recipient "should" do it. Even if we agree that check-ins are needed, it is easy to forget to do this well before the deadline. New managers are often afraid to disturb their staff about assigned work.

This is an essential step of task delegation. It is good management practice to track delegated task assignment progress regularly, well before the task is due. It is bad management practice to wait until the task is due for the first check-in.

The solution is to adopt a system whereby the next "fair" date for the check-in is negotiated at the assignment and clearly scheduled in your task system as an activity for you to do. And then you take a very proactive follow-up when that time arrives. With Outlook tools, this is an easy operation. You simply create a dated follow-up task for each outstanding delegated item.

I discuss later in more detail various ways to follow up with your staff. But first, let me show you how to notate such a task.

Creating the Follow-Up Task

Creating follow-up tasks is made very easy if you do the following: Convert your task entry for the intended assignment into a follow-up task at the time the task is accepted.

Here is how this works. Recall the task that I intended to assign to Jon Smith to resolve network performance issues. Remember that at the time I decided to assign it I marked it "JS:Resolve network performance." This notation indicated I intended to assign this task to Jon but that Jon had not yet accepted it. After I discuss this assignment with Jon and he accepts it, I immediately modify the annotation by simply adding a F: in front of the task as follows: "F:JS: Resolve network performance"; the added "F" stands for follow-up. That way, before or during my weekly one-on-one with Jon, I can sort separately on those tasks he's accepted already and on those that still need discussion to establish buy-in.

And at the same time I add the "F" for follow-up to my task I also change the Outlook Start Date field of the task to the day I want to be reminded to check in with Jon (see "Summary" sidebar for examples). I usually set the priority to High (Critical Now). This priority level ensures that I take action on the day the task appears on my Now Tasks list. Again, I avoid using Outlook reminders or alarms for tasks (I only use them for appointments). Rather, the appearance of a brief check-in task at the top of my Now Tasks list nearly always leads to my taking action on that check-in the same day it appears. In fact, check-in tasks are among the quickest tasks to accomplish, so engaging them is a great way to knock a number of tasks off your list for that day, which always feels good.

Because the next check-in date in the Start Date field is usually before the actual final deadline, you'll want to input the agreed-to final deadline in the subject line of the task. So, for example: "F:JS:DUE Aug 16: Resolve network performance" (see end of Lesson 4 for a discussion of using the subject line for deadlines). If that deadline day is approaching and the task is still not done, on my morning review of open tasks I convert it to High priority (a Critical Now task).

Better Than a Waiting-For List

For those who may have used a "waiting for" list in the past to track items like this, I find this approach much better because the follow-up item does not appear until it has aged an appropriate amount. There is nothing worse than pursuing someone about a request that you just gave them without letting them have time to work on it; this keeps that from happening. And it keeps you from having to do a mental calculation every time you look at a waiting-for list to decide whether action is needed on the items in the list. Instead, the follow-up task appears on your action list at just the right time. Also, a separate waiting-for list is one more list you have to remember to check daily. It is so much easier if your follow-up tasks appear automatically in your single Now Tasks list on the day that they are due.

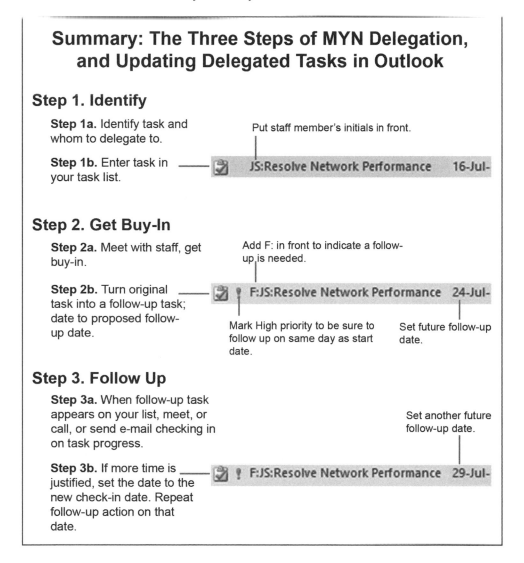

Summary: The Three Steps of MYN Delegation, and Updating Delegated Tasks in Outlook

Step 1. Identify

Step 1a. Identify task and whom to delegate to.

Step 1b. Enter task in your task list.

Put staff member's initials in front.

JS:Resolve Network Performance   16-Jul-

Step 2. Get Buy-In

Step 2a. Meet with staff, get buy-in.

Step 2b. Turn original task into a follow-up task; date to proposed follow-up date.

Add F: in front to indicate a follow-up is needed.

F:JS:Resolve Network Performance   24-Jul-

Mark High priority to be sure to follow up on same day as start date.

Set future follow-up date.

Step 3. Follow Up

Step 3a. When follow-up task appears on your list, meet, or call, or send e-mail checking in on task progress.

Step 3b. If more time is justified, set the date to the new check-in date. Repeat follow-up action on that date.

Set another future follow-up date.

F:JS:Resolve Network Performance   29-Jul-

Assign Partial Deliverables for Check-In Points

You may also wish to negotiate a specific partial deliverable on a follow-up date. If the final task includes creating something tangible, a rough draft or first pass at the final product is a good target deliverable for the check-in. This keeps the check-in date from becoming merely an agreed-to reminder date. And you often discover a lot in reviewing a first draft. Often, the vision for the end product is not accurately shared, so requiring an early rough draft allows you to discover issues early enough to allow time to adjust plans. For this to be effective you need to convince your staff that you will be very lenient in judgment of that rough draft. Otherwise, they will spend too much time polishing something that may be a false start.

A Delegation and Follow-Up Task System That Really Works

This delegation and follow-up task system really does work. I find it is amazingly effective at clearing my subconscious of loose-end concerns about assignments and guiding me in appropriate follow-up activities. At any given time I can have 20 or more open assigned tasks that are neatly scheduled for follow-ups. They remain out of sight until exactly the right scheduled check-in point, freeing my attention for more important activities. Without a system like this I might forget to check in, and then the task becomes an emergency. I might even check in too often, which is unnecessary and irritating to staff. The system brings order and calm to an otherwise chaotic mess.

How to Follow Up on Delegated Tasks: More Details

I want to discuss in a bit more detail how to follow up with your staff on assigned tasks. So many managers get this wrong and that leads to missed deadlines and poor morale in your workgroup.

When the start date of the follow-up task arrives (in reality, my informal reminder date) and the follow-up task appears at the top of my Now Tasks list, I then have a choice in how I follow up.

I may schedule that date to coincide with the next regular one-on-one meeting. For that meeting, using the MYN All Now Tasks view, I sort on the task name and scroll to the task list for the individual

Avoid Following Up in a Group

You may be tempted to make follow-ups part of a regularly scheduled departmental or team meeting. This is probably the most commonly used technique in the business world today. I recommend you avoid this unless team activity depends on that knowledge. In most cases not everybody needs to hear everyone's tasks and where they are on them. Such sessions lack positive energy and often lead to useless posturing. They usually do not optimize the time spent. Use your one-on-ones instead.

Many tasks, however, move too fast to wait for scheduled one-on-one meetings. Or you may need to cancel a scheduled meeting. You may not have regular one-on-one meetings with your staff. And you may make many assignments to staff who aren't your subordinates; you may not meet regularly with them. This is the beauty of having the scheduled follow-ups as individual tasks on your task list. They trigger and appear at the top of your Now Tasks list at just the right time, whether you look for them or not, and whether meetings are scheduled or not.

Following Up Outside of a Meeting

How to handle follow-ups outside of meetings can vary. If I'm really busy and the actual deadline date is not for a number of days more, I may just shoot off an e-mail to Jon asking, "How are things going on the network performance issue? Let me know as soon as you can, the senior staff meeting is coming up in five days." If this is to a colleague, I would be much more politic: "Hi Karen, just checking in to see if all is okay on getting the product overview presentation together by Friday. Let me know if I can get you any additional information or help in any other way. Really appreciate you working on this. That report is going to make the BigCo sale a success."

If Jon is a member of my staff, though, better yet is to call or walk over to Jon's desk. The personal touch and one-task-at-a-time nature of this check-in is usually effective at getting the task moving. And I am raising the reminder while Jon is at his desk, at his tools, where he can actually act when he gets the reminder and thinks, "Oh man, I forgot about this, I better move on it."

Setting the Next Follow-Up

Whether you follow up in meetings or between them, there is one more critical step that you must do. In case you don't or can't get an immediate answer to your follow-up, or the answer indicates that the task is not yet complete, you should decide and record immediately what day would be the appropriate next day to check in again. Immediately reset the start date on the follow-up task to that new date. This will cause the task to reappear on the task list on that day. If you send an e-mail or voice message as your follow-up action, then set the new date in the task at the moment you send the message (don't wait for a reply; otherwise you will forget). If your check-in takes place in person, enter the new negotiated date into your system as soon as you finalize it at your staff member or colleague's desk.

This is the key utility of using a system to boost your ability to get control of delegated tasks. Such tasks are too numerous and too fast moving to keep their status in your head. You need to keep the status of tasks up to date and in a system, and you need to make those updates immediately. Loose notes or memorized actions will not suffice. Otherwise those tasks will fall through cracks. If you have a mobile device, you can do a status reset right in your meeting with your staff. Whether that meeting is in the hall, in a conference room, or at your staff's desk, make sure you update the status immediately. Keeping tasks updated ensures a steady follow-up approach. It minimizes forgotten agreements and sends a consistent management message to your staff. If your staff learn from experience that you always follow up, they are less likely to relax on deadlines or take chances that you might not notice slipped deliverables.

Escalation

If the reminder scenario repeats itself a number of times on the same task, however, you need to escalate management of this task beyond a simple reminder system. The weekly one-on-one meeting with your staff can be a good forum for this escalation because it allows time to brainstorm solutions to whatever is holding up completion of the task. Or if the deadline is too close, call an urgent ad hoc meeting to review the impact of the problem and together plan out a course of action. The latter only happens after a few check-in points, so all involved will feel the escalation is fair. The beauty of this approach is that you can stay ahead of assigned tasks and manage them in a timely and fair fashion.

Summary

The positive effects of a good delegation system are remarkable. Staff who previously seemed forgetful or even irresponsible suddenly start responding positively to your assignments. People are human and can forget promises they make. This is particularly true if they do not have a good task management system in place themselves. As the sponsor of a delegated task it is up to you to usher the task ahead and ensure its completion. A good delegation system together with your good task management system is a winning combination for helping you succeed in delegating tasks.

You can succeed with delegation if you keep the following in mind:

▶ Effective delegation requires three important components: identifying tasks, establishing buy-in, and using effective follow-ups.

▶ You can implement an effective Outlook task nomenclature to accomplish successful delegation.

▶ Create follow-up tasks to ensure that you check in with delegated staff on a regular basis.

Next Steps

The next lesson explores a number of topics on time management and an array of time-saving suggestions. You may wish to work with the system for a few weeks before digging into that lesson. Or skim through it now and see if there are any techniques that you wish to start using immediately. You will find a wealth of time-saving ideas and insights there.

Lesson 11: Time Management and Other Time-Savers

Introduction

Many people say they need to learn time management. However, what I think most people need to learn when they say that is *task* management. By following the task management principles in the MYN system, you will in fact meet most of your time management needs. You will find you use your time much more efficiently and effectively. You will find you sail through e-mail quickly. You will probably find that you are able to leave work without any nagging doubts about what has been left undone.

Beyond the task management principles taught in this book, however, a few simple time management techniques can be extremely useful.

Note: *This lesson is summarized in portions of videos 19, 20, and 23 of the MYN-Outlook Complete Video Training (see beginning of the Quick Start chapter for more information).*

What's in This Lesson

Some Key Time-Management Techniques

First, if your day is mostly full of appointments, you'll need to set some time aside to work your tasks. I encourage you to schedule general task time right on your calendar. That is discussed next.

Second, you may need to make sure that time spent working your task list is kept well focused. In the sections ahead I provide a number of techniques to ensure that. For example, I provide a simple process for identifying clearly whether you really are overloaded with high-importance tasks or just working inefficiently. Identifying this helps lead to a solution (see section ahead titled "Doing the Math on Your Workweek"). And in the section titled "Cleaning Up Your Task Time" you'll find tips to make sure you use your task time most effectively.

Time-Saving Tips

Finally, the second half of the lesson presents a number of time-saving tips for using Outlook with the MYN system, particularly for e-mail. These include the following:

▶ How to auto-categorize incoming mail.

▶ Quicker ways to maintain the list of Outlook Categories that you apply to e-mail.

▶ Creating an All Mail Search Folder or Smart Folder to find mail more quickly.

▶ How to make the e-mails you write more effective.

Because most of these techniques can stand alone, you may want to scan through this chapter and read only those that currently seem to offer you value. Then plan to return to this lesson after using the system for a while. You will find some sections will become more relevant to you over time.

Time Management: Finding Time to Work on Tasks

Just as important as deciding what tasks to do is ensuring that you have time to do them. Your task list is useless if you have no time to work the list.

Everyone's work patterns are different. Some of you have endless meetings all day long. Others of you may sit at your desk working assignments most of the day. Or you may have operational responsibilities scheduled throughout the day. Some of you may travel extensively. And I'm sure there is everything in between. So you will need to design an approach to making time for working tasks that is appropriate for your workday.

If you are at your desk all day and are not devoted exclusively to operational activities, you may not need to set aside dedicated task working time. Your workday is your task day. If you are in meetings most of the day, the opposite is true. You are going to need to identify periods of time when you will accomplish your task list, and schedule those periods on your calendar to block out that time.

Setting General "Tasks" Appointments

My typical day falls somewhere between the scenarios I just described. I am often 50 to 60 percent booked with meetings, so I usually have time between those meetings for working tasks.

During busy weeks when meetings are more prevalent, I need to schedule specific time for working tasks, and I have no problem doing so if I do it ahead of time. When needed, I place one- to two-hour appointments on my calendar labeled simply "Tasks." During those appointments, I work down my Now Tasks list, trying to complete as many tasks on my list as possible.

There are other weeks when my meeting schedule is so intense that I find it takes some effort to schedule task time.

And farther down that scale, it is not unusual to meet executives whose every workday every week consists of endless meetings. After I teach them these task techniques, they conclude that they need to specifically schedule task time every day of the week, well ahead of time, to prevent the open slots from being claimed by appointment seekers. You may find this works for you too. It is something you should strongly consider because it prevents your only available task time from being after-hours time. Many of the meetings that subsequently cannot be scheduled probably were not critical anyway.

Scheduled Tasks Compared to General Task Time

Given the previous discussion, you may wonder when it is appropriate to schedule tasks individually on your appointment calendar in advance, as opposed to just listing them in your MYN task list and working them during general task time. My rule of thumb is to leave them on the MYN task list as much as possible.

Why not schedule most tasks right on your calendar? You might think this will prevent the accidental overbooking I just described. You might think it will ensure task completion. "What gets scheduled gets done," right?

There are three reasons not to do this. First, because these are self-appointments usually based on nearly random decisions of when to work a given task, you are almost certain to ignore or change the task in that slot due to other priorities, time needs, and inspirations arising at that time. There will always be some other fire drill at the moment, and your lower-priority scheduled tasks will be left by the wayside. When that happens you'll need to reschedule it, and such constant rescheduling is cumbersome. There is too much overhead associated with making and moving calendar entries to make these constant changes worthwhile, so you will quickly start to ignore the appointed tasks, and possibly drop them.

Second, following Lesson 6 instructions, you are mostly listing next actions on your MYN task list, and they tend to be small tasks. Small tasks are more efficiently worked off a list than off individual appointments. Trying to make tiny time slots for each task is tedious. And because our duration estimates for small tasks are usually off, this leads to inefficient completion. You will fill the allotted time even if less time is really needed. It is much more efficient to march down a list of small tasks and attempt to get as many done as possible within a large segment of general task time.

Third, the best time to attack a given task may vary and present itself naturally to you when you least expect it. You will find opportunities to work tasks synergistically with other tasks. You will find that throughout the day priorities change and that you postpone tasks you thought you were going to do today and reprioritize other tasks first. And you'll find that inspiration to work a certain task will hit you at unusual times—you should take advantage of those times and not wait until the scheduled times. Trying to keep track of all these changes with individual appointments on your calendar will be nearly impossible.

For Large or Tough Tasks

All that said, occasionally you will come across a task that is accurately recorded in your Now Tasks list as a next action and yet it is clear that it will take several hours or more to accomplish. So if a long-duration task (two hours or more) needs to get done I may schedule it on the calendar, particularly if I feel I may have trouble clearing other time to do it. Or perhaps you have a task that has a hard deadline that you need to ensure gets completed. In cases such as these, rather than using general "task time" on your schedule, it is better to schedule the specific task by name on your calendar, as I discussed in the "Managing Deadlines" section at the end of Lesson 4. Doing so is a good way to make sure specific tasks have adequate time set aside for them. It also highlights the importance of a task. And it allows you to set an appointment reminder.

Converting Tasks to Appointments in Outlook (Windows)

When you do decide to move an existing task to your calendar to schedule it, notice you can convert the task to an appointment (in Windows) by simply dragging the task from the task list to the appointment calendar. The new appointment window pops up ready for editing. Also notice that if you right-click before you drag you can choose to move the task rather than copy it. I do not recommend doing that. If you delete the task from the task list and the scheduled work time gets away from you due to distractions, the task is no longer on your list day after day reminding you to try again later.

■ ■ ■

Doing the Math on Your Workweek

The Problem

If after following the approaches in the book so far you still find that you're not getting your tasks done, you may need to focus on time management. The top recommendations from the best books on time management are these: avoid interruptions, manage the number of meetings you have, and schedule enough time to work on tasks. Generally, these are commonsense recommendations.

Notice that at the base of the third recommendation is an implicit assumption that you also do a fourth thing: figure out the amount of work time really needed to get all your tasks done. Most of us rarely do this, and from time to time we need to. If week after week you are consistently falling short on accomplishing important tasks, you probably need to do a simple five-minute exercise that I call "Doing the Math on Your Workweek."

Discovery

Here is how I came across this technique. After changing jobs and digging into a busy set of new activities, one month I found myself well behind on my important tasks. I was confused because I had all the tasks prioritized correctly, I had deferred unimportant ones to review in the future, and I had scheduled ahead those that had specific best days to work. And I had set aside and consistently used what seemed like a considerable amount of task time. Yet a number of my most important tasks were not getting done.

I finally decided to do something I generally didn't do, which is to apply some of my routine project management techniques to the collection of tasks I had on hand. Project management techniques are usually not applicable to this system of ad hoc task management, but in this case they were. Let me explain.

In the project management world, when making a formal project plan, one of the first things to do after listing all the steps in a project is to estimate how long each of those steps will take. The project manager uses that information to estimate the total duration and effort of the project, schedule the tasks, and assign people to the tasks. And while estimates are usually just that—estimates—the inaccuracies are usually offsetting and so the result of doing the exercise will usually get the manager to a fairly accurate plan.

So I applied the same technique to my list of tasks. I simply stepped through all the tasks on my list and estimated the duration of each, then summed them up. The results were surprising. Even though I thought I had a good picture of the amount of work on my plate, I found myself amazed at how much time the tasks I had signed up for actually added up to. My previous rough guess was low by a factor of three! Until I did the math, I had no idea how much work I had committed to.

Underestimating Time: a Common Problem

As I work with more and more people on task management, I find that this is a common problem. People consistently underestimate the total amount of time it takes to accomplish the sum of the tasks they sign up for. Individually, the estimates for each of their tasks are usually not that bad. It is just that they never stop to do the math and add up how much *all* their tasks really require in a given week. There seems to be a psychological block we all have toward doing this math accurately. Maybe the cause of this peculiarity lies in how the human brain functions, or, more likely, maybe it is just the result of our habit of optimism. I see this phenomenon again and again.

Part of the problem is the "heat of the workday." As the research cited in the Introduction points out, our brains function differently when under stress or during intense activity. As work stress increases, we lose accurate perspective on the various dimensions of our work, such as good prioritization and, apparently, accurate assessment of the time needed to accomplish work.

Easily Seen in Others

How often have you seen examples of this mistake occur with colleagues or your supervisor? For instance, your boss gets out of a stressful meeting with his or her boss, and in reaction to an urgent situation brought up in that meeting, assigns you a task to fix something. In your detached and calm perspective you estimate three days of work for this task. From your boss's emotional perspective he is amazed that it cannot be done in under a day. You both are experts in your field but you have amazingly different estimates of the effort required. The next thing your stressed boss usually does is accuse you of overengineering the solution. In the end, the estimate done by calm analysis is the accurate one.

You often do the same thing to yourself. Imagine yourself in a stressful work-week where day after day you are collecting tasks on your Now Tasks list and not getting as much done as you had hoped. As the week progresses and you see the list of uncompleted tasks getting larger, what happens? You become more stressed and do an even poorer job of estimating the time that you need to get your work done. You are most likely consistently underestimating the time needed.

The way we usually make up for these errors is to work late into the evening. If you do this only occasionally in reaction to unusual peaks in activity, this works. But if your high workload is consistent and you are pulling one late night after another, the cumulative stress and fatigue only exacerbate the situation. You do not regain your clear perspective but rather, like Don Quixote, you keep chasing your impossible dream, in this case, of *doing it all*. You are getting more and more detached from reality in the process.

The Solution

The solution to this is remarkably simple. You just need to sober up for a moment, take five minutes, and do the math on your workweek. You need to figure out how many hours of tasks you have on your task list in the week ahead and how that compares to committed time. And if in this objective analysis you find yourself overbooked, you need to take some measured and rational steps to account for that now, rather than hoping for a miracle to bail you out as the week progresses. Use this tool to identify that need, and consider using the results to show to your supervisor if you feel your pleas for relief are not being taken seriously.

How far out should you do this math? For ad hoc tasks such as those studied in this book, a week's planning horizon is a good balance between near-term commitments and unknown future changes in priority and available time.

You can make this exercise as simple or as complex as you wish. I prefer to make it simple by doing the following.

Step by Step

1. Windows users can optionally create and use a new Tasks folder view that displays tasks due in the next week. The details for this are in Lesson 12, in the section titled "The MYN This Week's Tasks View." If you don't want to bother with that (or if you are a Mac user), you can also use your Tasks folder sorted on start date, it's just not as easy as the custom view. Don't try to use the To-Do Bar for this, as it filters out future tasks.

2. Next, reconcile the tasks in your task list as follows: Reset all High and Normal priority tasks that don't *really* need to get done in the next week as follows. Either schedule their start dates into a future week or set them to a Low priority (preferably using the Defer-to-Review process in Lesson 9). This removes lower-urgency tasks and leaves you with what *really* needs to get done this week. This is a reasonable activity if you are falling behind on important tasks.

3. Then simply go through all High priority and Normal priority tasks, studying each task with a start date before or inside this week for a moment (those are the only ones listed in the custom view). Do a rough estimate of the number of hours needed to complete each task. Don't worry about being terribly precise. I usually estimate in whole hours. Small tasks I usually list as .25 or .5 hour each.

4. For each task, write the estimate for that task at the end of the subject line. For example: "Summarize staff meeting notes and distribute, 1 hr."

5. Then add the total hours of these tasks (you can do that in your head) and write it down.

6. Compare that sum to the number of hours you have scheduled for task time in the week ahead. I suspect, if you are finding your week has slipped out of control, you will discover that the total hours needed for committed tasks is two to three times greater than your scheduled task time. If so, read the next section titled "Resolution."

7. If not, if the two are roughly equal, you are probably in good shape. But if you find repeatedly that you are estimating correctly and yet you are still not getting your tasks done, see the section ahead titled "Cleaning Up Your Task Time."

You may at first balk at this exercise and think, "Estimating like this is very inaccurate; how can this really help?" My response: Sure, individual task estimates may be off a bit. In truth, however, inaccurate estimates for individual tasks are usually offsetting and the total is often not far from reality.

Another objection is this: "I always schedule more than I can accomplish, so this is not surprising. I'll just do what I can get done." If you really feel that way, go back to step 2 in the previous section "Step by Step," do it right, and repeat the process. Recall that only tasks that really *must* be done in the next week should be on your list for the purposes of this exercise.

Note: *If you know Windows Outlook well, you probably know there are hidden fields in tasks for entering and tracking work hours. You could use those fields instead of entering the hours as text on the subject line. But I am purposely not getting fancy here. The point is to do a very quick estimate of what work is on your plate. Jotting hours onto the subject line and doing a quick summation by eye is fine for our purposes and ensures that you may actually do this check now and then.*

Resolution

So now what? Assuming you have discovered that you are well overbooked, you now know you have a problem, and why. Like many problems in life, this is an important first step toward a solution. At least you now have a clear picture of the problem and can start doing something about it. And you can take some relief in the knowledge that no, you are not a bad or horribly inefficient worker who needs to work harder. Rather, you just really do have too much on your plate and you now need to fix that.

Clearly you have some corrections to make. Either you have to add a lot more task time, find others to delegate tasks to, or start renegotiating some of your commitments. Those next steps I leave to you. The beauty of this is, if you do this at the beginning of the week, well before tasks become due, you have time to start negotiating alternatives. You have time to seek permission rather than forgiveness.

The only thing more amazing than how simple this activity really is, is how rarely it is done. This seems so obvious and yet so few of us ever do it. We fail to recognize that we usually estimate low when mentally adding up the work we have committed to. It is a part of our human nature that we need to work around, consciously, by periodically stepping back and doing this math exercise.

■ ■ ■

Cleaning Up Your Task Time

Inefficient Task Time

Under the topic of time management I recommend one other thing: clean up your task time. Let me elaborate.

First, as mentioned in this lesson in the section "Setting General 'Tasks' Appointments," I recommend for most of you setting aside dedicated time for doing your tasks. You should schedule this time on your calendar. Otherwise, if you only try to "work them in" you will be utterly disappointed; things are just not going to get done. Get this time assigned on your calendar early before others start placing appointments throughout your day. Honor those task-time appointments and do not set other appointments on top of them.

Second, if the analysis described in "Doing the Math on Your Workweek" shows that you have enough task time yet are still not getting your tasks done, you have one more analysis step to do. You need to make sure you are keeping your task time "clean." What I mean by that is you need to ensure that you really work your tasks during your dedicated task period.

Honoring Your Task Time

Here is a common problem. Unfortunately, what people often do when the scheduled task time arrives is to relax into that time. If it is during the afternoon, it is often the first time of the day away from intense meetings or a constant stream of visitors. It may be the first time people can sit at their desk in a while. As a result, as they enter the general task period people tend to shift gears. They unconsciously start to unwind and often look for distractions to help them do so. They might visit cube mates. They might take a "quick glance" at the web, make a few personal phone calls, or go get a snack. Or they may go into information collection mode: reading e-mail, listening to voice messages, reconciling loose papers on the desk, and so on. Before they know it, the task time is gone and they have accomplished very little on their list.

So you need to consciously account for this need for taking breaks, socializing, reading e-mail, and other cleaning-up activities during periods separate from your scheduled task time. One approach is to build separate break and e-mail reading time into your schedule. For instance, I add about an hour or two a day to my task time to account for e-mail reading, paper shuffling, and ad hoc breaks. If your task time is in the afternoon, add the delineated break time just before the start of your task time, with a hard deadline for when you actually start on tasks. That way you are caught up as you enter your focused task period.

Another remedy is to schedule these task times for periods when you are fresh and not in need of unwinding, as discussed ahead in the section "Time Mapping."

Avoiding Interruptions

During the time you set aside to focus on tasks, you need to avoid outside interruptions. Commit to yourself that this is the purpose of this time and that you will discourage visiting, unneeded calls, and other distractions. You may even need to decide that you will not answer the phone, not take incoming e-mails when Outlook beeps at you, and most important, that you will turn away visitors. This can be difficult. The social aspect of work is one reason people don't work alone. They enjoy interacting with coworkers. It feels good to help people who stop by for assistance. It feels good to get up from your desk and chat with others. But you need to solve this problem of interruptions to make your task time effective.

You might try some sort of physical change in your environment to delineate pure task time. This could be closing the door to your office if you have an office. Or if you work in a cubicle, either finding some other physical space you can escape to or putting a Do Not Disturb sign on the edge of your cube. Somehow you need to signal to others and yourself that this is a special time with a distinct purpose.

This is a very challenging problem and you may need to experiment to solve it. It is difficult to turn away visitors, difficult not to take phone calls. In the end, however, you need to find a way to isolate a period of pure task time in your day. You may want to brainstorm with your colleagues on agreed methods to accomplish this, so that you respect one another's private time.

Time Mapping

One technique to improve time usage, highlighted by Julie Morgenstern in her book on time management, *Time Management from the Inside Out*, is something called time mapping. Others call this time zoning. This expands upon a best practice recommended by nearly all the time and task management experts: Identify the times of day that you are best at doing certain activities, and schedule those times throughout the week for their optimum usage (see Figure 11.1).

So, for example, if you like to do tasks in the morning when your mind is clear, make sure that your standing meeting for task processing is at the same time every morning of every day. If you like to keep open office hours after lunch when you enjoy conversations with colleagues and subordinates, schedule a block of open time in your calendar every day at that time. In other words, map each day the same throughout the week. This is often difficult to pull off completely due to previously set standing meetings (Figure 11.1 is an idealized example), but to whatever degree you can, you will optimize your natural cycle and create a habit of doing the activity.

Figure 11.1
Time Mapping, idealized example.

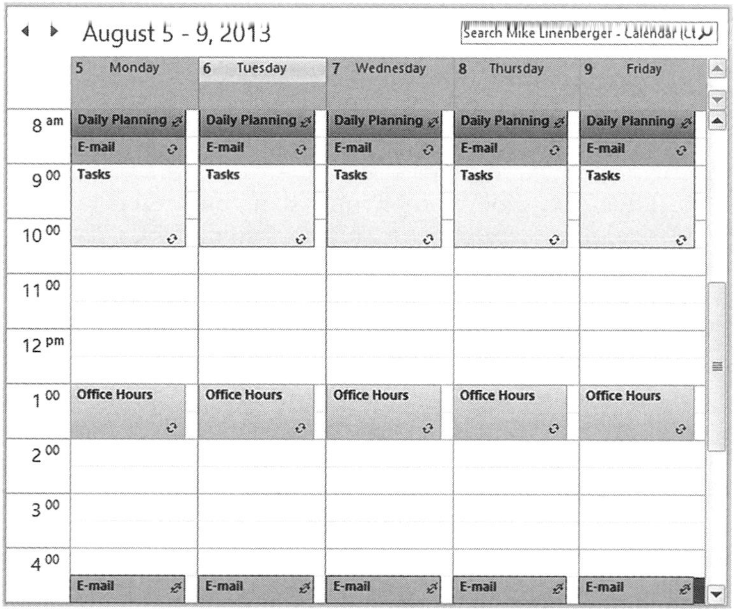

Write Your Long Replies at the End of the Day

Another way to clean up task time and make use of the time mapping approach is to save writing your long e-mail replies for the end of the day. Sure, if you can reply in less than a minute, go ahead and write a quick reply at any time. But if 30 minutes later you are still crafting and recrafting a carefully worded, politically correct message, you have just lost control of your time.

Better is to make longer replies your last action of the day. Why? You are less likely to get carried away. Your excess energy from your morning caffeine is spent by the late afternoon. Your initial emotional response has dissipated. And because your major intent at the end of the day is to wrap up and go home, you will more likely limit your reply to the minimum business words needed before you bolt out the door. So you will spend much less time on what for many is a major time sink. This also potentially minimizes the time spent on all-day e-mail threads. Instead, catch up at the end of the day and have the final word!

Of course, if part of your job role is to monitor and reply quickly to e-mail support requests, then reply as fast as is fitting for your role. But most of us are not in such support roles, so delaying long replies to the end of the day can make sense.

It is also a shame to use the morning, which is often your most creative and productive time, on writing long low-priority e-mail replies. Try waiting to the end of the day for these replies for the reasons I just listed and see if it works for you. As mentioned in Lesson 7, I recommend using the Outlook Follow Up flag tool exclusively for the purpose of marking these deferred replies (which works especially well because that also puts an entry in your MYN task list). I discuss the pros and cons of using that flag thoroughly in Lesson 7.

But note this: If the reason for not replying is that you need to take some action first, instead of deferring the reply with the Follow Up flag, convert the e-mail to a *full* task, following the instructions in Lesson 7.

Turn Off E-mail Notification

Another way to avoid interruptions during task time is to avoid reading incoming e-mails the instant they arrive in your Inbox. To help with this, turn off e-mail notification in Outlook—you know, that little message box that pops up briefly every time you get an e-mail (see next figure for an example of the Windows version, called a Desktop Alert). In fact, I think notifications should always be turned off at work. Instead, I feel that you should choose or schedule a time to read your e-mail all at once, between blocks of work.

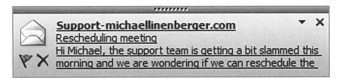

Why? Unless you work in a customer support role where e-mail is your main connection to customers, I strongly feel e-mail should *not* be an instant-response medium. The beauty of e-mail when used correctly is that you can batch up your communications into distinct time blocks and then keep your attention on uninterrupted work much of the rest of the day. Many studies have shown that it can take three to five minutes to reorient yourself to a work task after being interrupted. And the default settings for the desktop alert box in Outlook lead to an especially deep interruption. That's because they show just enough information about the e-mail (including the first sentence) to totally draw you in to wanting to know more. They lead you to think about whether you want to consider the e-mail and to possibly open it, and that often completely drags your focus out of whatever task you are working on, even if you do not end up reading the mail. With hundreds of e-mails coming in each day, the lost time and productivity adds up.

So I highly recommend you turn off the desktop alert notification and instead check e-mail only between blocks of work or at scheduled times. Don't worry, you will survive being out of e-mail touch a few hours at a time—and you will enjoy the focus and time you regain. And you can turn it on only for specific people.

How to Turn Off E-Mail Notification

The controls to turn off e-mail notification are buried surprisingly deep in the 2007 menus. It's a bit easier in later versions.

Outlook 2010 and 2013 users should go to the File tab, choose Options, and then choose Mail on the left, and then scroll down to the Message section as shown in Figure 11.2. At a minimum, clear the bottom check box so the popup alert box is suppressed. The other indicators are less invasive.

Figure 11.2
Turning off e-mail notifications (Outlook 2010 and 2013).

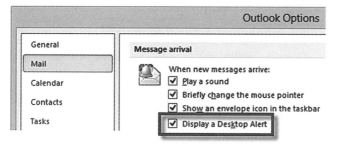

For Outlook 2007, from the Tools menu, choose Options, and click the E-mail Options button and then the Advanced E-mail Options button. In the dialog box that opens, find the segment titled "When New Items Arrive In My Inbox" and, at a minimum, clear the bottom check box so the popup Desktop Alert box is suppressed. The other indicators are less invasive.

Outlook for Mac 2011 users should go to the Outlook menu on the top menu bar, choose Preferences, then in the Personal Settings section choose Notifications & Sounds. Clear the check box labeled Display an Alert on my Desktop, and then perhaps select the check box Bounce Outlook Icon in Dock, if you want some minimal notification.

After general e-mail notification is turned off, you might want to be notified of the arrival of e-mail from specific people (say your boss). You can create an Outlook rule that will pop up the same Desktop Alert you just turned off, but only upon arrival of mail from those select people. Or create a similar rule to alert you upon arrival of mail with High importance. I discuss using Outlook rules a few pages ahead. See the "Other Rules" section after that for a link showing how to get alerts only for certain people.

Identifying Deliverables

One more technique you may want to use to clean up your task time is to clearly identify deliverables you expect to accomplish in a given task time. Here is how this works. At the beginning of a scheduled task period, decide what tasks you intend to accomplish. If you have recently done the "Do the Math on Your Workweek" exercise described at the start of this lesson, the tasks in your daily list each have durations written next to them. Use those durations to determine which tasks you can get done now. Then identify a deliverable, or end product, that must be created to signal the completion of each task. This might be an Excel document, a written report, or a memorandum. Copy that deliverables list right into the subject line of your task appointment in your Outlook calendar.

This is very effective. While working at your desk during the task time, each time you glance at your calendar to see what is up next you'll see those deliverable commitments staring at you. You will know they are due during the next hours, and you will refocus on the task at hand. It's a good way to get serious if you find yourself slipping off track. It's also a good way to manage interruptions. If someone stops by your desk with a request during your task time, you have the focus you need to be able to say something like "I'd like to help you, but I really need to get this memo done in the next half hour; let me talk to you later."

This deliverables focus is a common technique used in large-project-oriented consulting companies to drive project tasks to completion. The association of a distinct deliverable with a task is an effective way of adding structure and ensuring a task's completion.

Declining Low-Priority Meetings

I am still amazed that many people feel they must accept every meeting they are invited to. That's not true! If you're doing that, no wonder you have no time for tasks. Just because someone thinks of a meeting topic does not mean it's *your* priority. Try to decline more meetings and devote that time to working on your own tasks. If appropriate, request that the organizer send a summary of the meeting outcomes to you after the meeting.

The War Room

Here is something to consider if important tasks or projects are not getting completed. The way many large project consulting companies accomplish task efficiency with their junior and midlevel staff working on projects is just the opposite of finding privacy for everyone; rather, they seek out team group work settings and use the peer pressure of the team to keep one another on track. This is commonly done in a *war room* approach: Give a team of colleagues a common goal to reach with a challenging deadline, place them all in a single large conference room working on laptops, and have them work together to complete the tasks. Often the team members decide among themselves which tasks each team member is assigned. Through a combination of urgency, peer pressure, and teamwork, the tasks get done rapidly. In such a setting, because the team's success is measured as a whole, individual interruptions are not tolerated by peers, and staff who wander off on personal errands are met with glares upon their return. Weekly internal team assessments weed offending staff off teams, like "getting voted off the island."

At the consulting company Accenture, where I once worked, entry-level training consisted of several weeks of boot camp where newly hired staff were thrown into team settings solving hypothetical problems under urgent deadlines. The consultants who came out of such training were remarkably adept at knocking off tasks quickly on the real projects they were assigned to later.

If you and your colleagues are having trouble getting project tasks done individually, and you can pull away from meetings for a while, you might consider a war room approach. This works especially well if you are all working on parts of a larger project with clear deadlines. It can be remarkably effective.

■   ■   ■

Save Time by Auto-Categorizing Incoming E-mail (All Versions)

If you are filing e-mail using Outlook Categories, as described in Lesson 8, consider this. Probably the least enjoyable part of any e-mail organization system is filing. It takes time to decide how to file e-mail and assign categories or drag to folders. Wouldn't it be great if your e-mail were categorized automatically? Think how much time you would save. If e-mail arrived precategorized, all you would need to do after you read it is drag mail in bulk to the Processed Mail folder, which is what you do anyway.

While automatic categorization of *all* of your mail is not possible, you can do it with much if not most of your mail. The two primary ways to auto-categorize is to do it based on sender name or based on a keyword in the mail.

Easy on The Mac

On the Mac, if your intention is to categorize incoming mail based on sender, a built-in feature makes this very easy. You merely assign the category to the sender's entry in your Outlook Contacts list, and then check a box at the bottom of the Edit Categories dialog box (see Figure 8.5 in Lesson 8), and it is all automatic. Again, you get to the Categories dialog box by CTRL-clicking any e-mail in its Categories column, and then choosing Edit Categories from the shortcut menu.

Using Outlook Rules (Windows and Mac)

In Windows, you do not have the handy Mac feature I just described. Rather, you enable automatic assignments based on sender by creating Outlook rules.

And on both the Mac and Windows, if you want to automatically assign a category based on other criteria—like a keyword in the subject line—rules are the only way to go.

Rules are a bit complicated to create, but they do not take that long. The small amount of time it takes to create these rules pays off greatly in time saved during e-mail processing.

What do I mean by Outlook rules? Outlook rules are small logical statements that you create and apply against incoming (or outgoing) mail to cause the mail to be processed in a variety of ways. For instance, a common use of rules is to cause mail, based on its contents, sender, or subject line, to be filed automatically in certain folders. Or you can use similar criteria to cause certain incoming mail to be forwarded automatically, display an alert, and so on.

For Folder Filing

As I stated, the most common use of rules is to cause mail, based on its contents, sender, or subject line, to be filed automatically in certain folders. However there are two problems with this. First, in MYN we are only filing into one folder, the Processed Mail folder, and it makes no sense to auto-file into only one folder.

More importantly, even if you do use multiple topic-named folders, the rule moves the mail directly into that folder without dropping it into your Inbox first. So, unless you check all your folders often, you are likely to miss some business-critical messages. For that reason most people use folder rules only for newsletters and similar low-priority e-mail.

For Auto-Categorizing

For the system in this book, the most valuable action is to assign a category automatically to incoming mail based on its contents or sender. The beauty of doing this is that, when assigning categories via rules, Outlook leaves the incoming mail in your Inbox so you can read it.

For example, as mentioned earlier, I have an Outlook rule that assigns the category Personal to e-mail that comes from any of my family members. I have another rule that sets an e-mail's category to a specific project name whenever I receive mail from the project manager for that project. And mail associated with a number of other projects at my work are categorized using rules that search the e-mail subject line for certain keywords that are uniquely associated with those projects. Due to these and other rules, back when I used categories extensively, I enabled nearly 70 percent of my mail to arrive precategorized.

These rules are never foolproof; you should expect the logic of any rule that you write to misfire periodically, skipping or assigning the wrong category. But that doesn't matter. They *usually* work. And even if these rules work only 80 percent of the time, they will still save you great effort setting categories.

Without these rules you would need to classify *all* of your mail, so even if you need to change a misclassified mail every so often, you come out way ahead.

Note: *There is a limit to the number of rules you can create in Outlook if you are running on Exchange Server. It is not count based but storage-based, and that limit is easy to reach. Newer Exchange Server limits can be set by administrators to be much larger than older limits, but the default is low and usually left that way. If you start getting error messages when you create a large number of rules, it is probably due to that limit. If so, contact your administrator and ask them to raise it. If that is not possible or if it does not help, consider switching to ClearContext add-in software. It has a similar rules engine but with no limit on its rule count.*

So how do you create Outlook rules? Outlook provides a simple wizard to create these rules quite easily. The wizard in Mac Outlook is pretty simple, and I show how to use that just ahead. The wizard for Windows Outlook is more complex (because it offers more choices), and is best shown in a video.

Creating a Windows Outlook Rule to Categorize E-mail

Windows Outlook has a flexible wizard you can use to create your rules. It's complicated, so here are a few complimentary online videos I've created to help you: www.myn.bz/mvc.htm. Select video 23a for Outlook 2007, or 23b for Outlook 2010 and 2013, which are near the bottom of that page.

Note: *Outlook 2007 users might see a preset rule in their rule list called Clear Categories on Mail. This strips categories from incoming mail to keep other people's categories from clogging your e-mail (see the section "Dealing with Categories in Mail Sent to You," that follows for more details). If you decide to keep the rule active, you should ensure that any category-assignment rules you make appear below that rule in the list of rules. The reason is rules are triggered in the order they appear in the list, from top to bottom. It would be counterproductive to add a category to an e-mail and then strip it out again. Use the Move Up and Move Down buttons to arrange the rules in the correct order to prevent that.*

Creating a Mac Outlook Rule to Categorize E-mail

On the Mac there is no need to create a rule if your intention is to auto-categorize based on sender name, as mentioned at the very start of this section. However, for any other type of auto-categorization (most likely categorizing based on a keyword in the subject line) you will need to create a rule.

Creating rules on the Mac is much easier than in Windows. But, as with many things on the Mac compared to Windows, you exchange ease of use for power and flexibility. That said, all that we need to create a category rule is present in the Mac controls, and it's easy to do. Because it's so simple, no video is needed; just use the steps I show next.

For this example, let's say you want to create a rule that sets a category based on a keyword in the Subject field.

Note: Exchange users need to be online with your mail server to create these rules.

1. Because you are interested in e-mail that is entering your primary Inbox, you must first select that folder. Select an e-mail that you want to apply the category to. (That's optional, but it makes the next steps simpler.)

2. From the Home tab click the Rules button and click Create Rule. If you did not select an e-mail in step 1, select Edit Rule, select a mail source on the left, and click the plus sign (+) at the bottom of the window.

3. In the Edit Rule dialog box that pops up (Figure 11.3), type a rule name at the very top. Then edit the rule elements as indicated next.

Figure 11.3
Sample Mac Edit Rule dialog box.

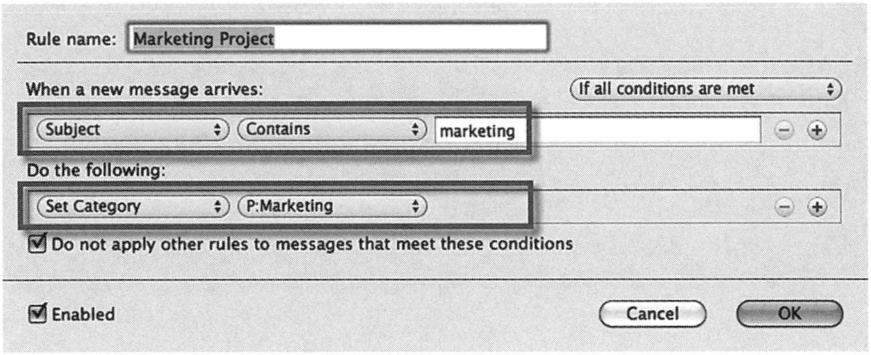

4. In the first drop-down menu in the When a New Message Arrives section, select Subject. In the next block to the right, select Contains. And in the text box to its right, type a keyword or phrase as appropriate. In Figure 11.3, I typed the keyword "marketing."

5. In the Do the Following section, two actions may appear by default and you need only one. If two are there, delete the first action by clicking the minus sign (–) to its right.

6. Then edit the remaining action. In the first block ensure that Set Category is selected, and then select the category name in the next block at right.

7. Consider whether you want to clear the check box that says Do Not Apply Other Rules to Messages that Meet These Conditions (examine your other rules, if any, that may affect these messages). And leave the Enabled check box selected. The complete example is shown in Figure 11.3.

8. Click OK.

You are now done creating the rule. From now on, Outlook will automatically categorize incoming mail that meets the criteria of these new rules. This will occur as you see the mail appear in your Inbox.

Other Rules (All Versions)

Use these principles to create other rules to improve your efficiency in Outlook. The other rule I typically make is to show a Desktop Alert when mail from certain senders comes in (after turning off e-mail notifications, following my earlier instructions on that). See this link: www.myn.bz/Alerts.htm. (Link is case-sensitive)

■ ■ ■

Maintaining Category Names Quickly and Efficiently (All Versions)

In Lesson 8, I showed how to use Outlook Categories to tag and file mail. And in this lesson I've shown how to auto-assign categories. In Lesson 12, I will also show how to use categories to create a projects view of tasks and a goals view of tasks. By now you can see that Outlook Categories are very useful in the MYN system. Getting the category list right, and maintaining it, will become important.

Categories Assigned to Mail May Not Be in the Category List

The first lesson to learn about category maintenance is that the list from which you assign categories in all Outlook versions is really just a pick list from which to make category assignments. If you delete a category name in those lists, doing so may have little influence on categories already assigned to mail—the old assignments will be retained there.

This acceptance of categories not on the master list also occurs in mail sent by other users, if the category name gets through your Exchange filters. In older Outlook and Exchange installations, as you receive e-mail from colleagues who may also be categorizing e-mail, the mail, after it is in your copy of Outlook, can retain the category names from your colleagues (see the section ahead titled "Dealing with Categories in Mail Sent to You"). If so, Outlook will treat these categories almost as though they are your own. As a result, your category-grouped mail will include even those imported ones (sometimes tagged with a note saying *Not in Master Category List*).

This set of behaviors is good and bad. It is good because, for deleted categories, it retains an historical trail of your previous assignments. As for accepting categories on incoming mail, that could save you the effort of assigning it yourself (if you agree with the assignment). It is bad because it seemingly leaves Outlook cursed to accept and retain categories from other senders.

If you find a category name assigned to mail that does not match what's in your list, you may want to rename it or delete it.

How to Rename a Category Name (All Versions)

Renaming a category in Outlook is simple. In the Windows Outlook Color Categories dialog box select the category, click Rename, and then type over the name. On the Mac's Edit Categories dialog box you simply click the category name a few times and by the second or third click it becomes editable. Then type over the name. Changing the name like this causes Outlook to find all the places the old category exists and change it to the new name, *even in other data files in your folder tree* (which is pretty amazing). And the old name now no longer exists in the category list.

Deleting a Category Name (Windows and Mac)

In all Outlook versions, if you delete a category name, then the name is removed or altered in the category pick list, but the assignments remain unchanged in the old mail it is assigned to.

So first consider carefully why you want to delete a category. Do you want to remove a category — but not its old assignments? Or is your intention to also clear the assignment from all old mail messages? Or is it really to reassign them to a new category name? If the latter, just follow the previous steps on renaming categories.

However, if you really do intend to delete a category and remove it from all old mail, you will want to do this correctly. Follow these steps:

1. Go to your Processed Mail folder and group by Categories by clicking the Categories heading.

2. Scroll to the group corresponding to the category you want to remove and select all the mail in that group.

3. With that mail selected, remove that category assignment from all the mail: Open the category assignment mechanism appropriate to your version of Outlook and clear the selection next to the category you want to delete.

4. Delete the category. In Windows Outlook open the Color Categories dialog box (see Figure 8.5, top, in Lesson 8), and click the Delete button at its right. In Mac Outlook, open the Edit Categories dialog box (see Figure 8.5, bottom, in Lesson 8) and click the minus sign at the bottom of the dialog box.

Dealing with Categories in Mail Sent to You (Windows Outlook)

If your colleagues are using categories too, you may start to receive mail that has categories already assigned before it arrives in your mailbox. Newer Exchange Servers are designed to prevent this, but some category assignments may slip through in older installations. This will cause Outlook to group your mail in your category-grouped mail list under categories that are not of your invention.

How should you deal with this? If this is happening consistently, you may want to agree with your colleagues on a standard naming convention for categorizing mail. That way, as e-mail arrives, it will be precategorized in a category that is already in your list.

If you cannot get colleagues to align their category names with yours, all is not lost. You merely need to recategorize the e-mail when you set your categories in your Inbox. The Category or Color Categories dialog box allows you to clear the check box next to those unwanted categories. Then just continue by selecting the categories you want. It is a bit annoying; you need to consciously clear the check box on the old or wrong category before assigning the new category, but it really only takes a second of extra work. The imported category disappears after all references to it are removed. If this happens consistently you can also create an Outlook rule that swaps categories (old and new) automatically.

Microsoft realized importing others' unwanted categories was an issue, so, as a result of changes they made starting in the 2007 suite, this problem no longer exists in organizations that have standardized on Outlook 2007 and Exchange Server 2007 or later. These versions now strip out categories on incoming mail. How? First, the newer Exchange Server is set by default to strip these out at the server level. Second, in case a newer Exchange Server is not in the sending path, an Outlook rule is created when you install Outlook 2007 to do the same on incoming mail at your computer. It is called Clear Categories on Mail and is turned on by default.

Unless you know you are working with Exchange Server 2007 or later, take care with the wording you use when creating Outlook Categories. Someone may see yours in the mail they get from you. The version of Exchange Server is separate from your Outlook version. So even though you may be using Outlook 2010 or later in your office, it is possible that your IT department is still using Exchange Server 2003. Check with someone in your IT department to confirm your Exchange Server version number.

■   ■   ■

Finding Mail Quickly: Creating an All Mail Search Folder (Windows Outlook) or All Mail Smart Folder (Mac Outlook)

In Lesson 8, I showed you how to create Search Folders to display categorized mail in Windows Outlook. And in Lesson 3, I showed you how to use Smart Folders for Mac Outlook. You can also use Search Folders and Smart Folders for other purposes. Here is one perfect example—a way to display all your mail from various folders in one long list.

Why might you want this? Well, have you ever looked for a recent e-mail by visually scanning your Inbox or Processed Mail folder, but not been able to find it on the first pass? If so, you ended up having to look through your

Sent Items folder next, and then maybe in several other folders, opening and scrolling through each one at a time. Sometimes the mail you want is part of a send-reply conversation and you are not sure if the mail you seek is something that you sent (so it's in Sent Items), or something they sent to you (so it's in your Inbox or Processed Mail folder). You could of course use the Outlook search engine. But for recent mail, scanning a folder visually is sometimes the best way to find something.

The Search Folder and Smart Folder I show you next creates a virtual folder that allows you to easily view one long scrolling list of all your "recent" mail—even up to years' worth—no matter where the mail is actually stored in Outlook (with one caveat discussed next). It will make it much easier to find your mail when you are not sure where to look. It's virtual, so it does not duplicate any mail. It just gives you a very convenient single-folder view of all your mail, collecting it from all the folders it may be distributed in. I call it the All Mail Search Folder and using it is a fantastic way to find mail.

Why the All Mail Search Folder and Smart Folder is Useful:

▶ You can easily do a visual search of all your recent mail in one list, even after it has been filed. You can view and scan messages chronologically if you wish, just like in your Inbox. Or you can click on the From heading and easily see all your mail from a single sender. Again, no matter where it is actually stored.

▶ If you are still filing mail into multiple topic-named folders, this custom approach allows you to see all that mail in one long list too—no matter how you split your filed mail across your actual folders.

▶ If you have not filed out of your Inbox for a while, and so are not sure whether to search there or in your files, using this approach allows you to visually search for it all in one place.

▶ Using Instant Search in Windows Outlook in this folder automatically searches all mail on your mail store. You don't have to do two passes and click Try searching all mail items on the second pass to add other folders.

▶ You can see full conversations, including mail in your Sent Items folder. That makes finding mail in long send-reply conversations easier.

One Caveat. Search Folders in Windows Outlook only consolidate mail from one mail store, and that's an important limitation for a few of you. A mail store either means a mail server (Exchange) or a local mail file (a .pst file). That's not an issue if you are using my recommended folder configurations where all recent saved mail is in your main mail store (for example, in the Processed Mail folder in Exchange or in your primary local file for non-Exchange installations; see Lesson 5 or Appendix A). However, if you split your recent mail across mail stores (for example, you place your Inbox on

Exchange Server but you place your recent saved mail in a personal folders file—a .pst file), then this search folder won't include mail in that local file. Nor will it include archived mail. But for most of us, that's not an issue when looking for recent mail.

On the Mac, Smart Folders present none of these problems because they search over all mail stores.

Note: *Using this custom Search Folder somewhat changes my Lesson 8 objection to using multiple topic-named folders. Recall that in Lesson 8, I asserted strongly that using many topic-named Outlook folders to file mail can be a major waste of time. I still regard filing into many multiple topic-named folders to be limiting due to having to choose only one topic. I also think it's too slow to be practical for most people (unless you use add-in software like ClearContext). However, finding mail in those folders can be greatly improved with this Search Folder.*

How to Create the All Mail Search Folder (Windows Outlook)

1. In the Navigation Pane folder list, right-click the Search Folders heading, and select New Search Folder.

2. In the New Search Folder window, scroll to the very bottom and double-click Create a Custom Search Folder the bottom of the list.

3. In the Custom Search Folder window that opens, click the Browse button.

4. Clear the check box in the very top-level item, and then add check marks to all the next-level folders where you purposely store your mail—that's most likely your Inbox, your Sent Items folders, the Processed Mail folder, and maybe more folders if you use several. You will want to leave a lot of folders unchecked like Junk E-mail and Deleted Items. Make sure Search Subfolders is selected at the bottom—that way you do not need to open each checked folder and select all its subfolders—they'll be included. Click OK.

5. Back at the Custom Search Folder window, in the Name field type "All Mail".

6. Click OK, and then click Yes in the error dialog box saying that you have not specified any criteria (we don't want to). Then click OK in the New Search Folder window, and you are done! You can now see the All Mail Search Folder in the Search Folder list.

How to Create the All Mail Smart Folder (Outlook for Mac 2011)

Smart Folders are created by doing a search first, and then saving the search criteria as a new Smart Folder. Here's how to do that for all mail such that you see all folders (except the ones you would want to exclude like Junk E-mail).

1. Click in the Search This Folder box at the top right of your Outlook window.

2. Click the All Mail button at the left end of the Search tab in the Ribbon.

3. Click the Advanced button at the right end of the Search tab in the Ribbon.

4. When you do step 3, an Item Contains button and field appears below the Ribbon. Click the Item Contains button and choose Folder at the bottom of the shortcut menu.

5. An Is button appears to its right; change that to Is Not.

6. Click the None button to its right and select Choose Folder at the bottom. At the top of the next dialog box that opens type "Junk." Select the Junk E-mail folder in the list that appears below, and click Choose.

7. Click the plus sign (+) at the right end of that line and repeat step 6 as many times as needed to include all other folders that you would like to exclude as well—that's most likely your Deleted Items folder, and any other Deleted Items and Junk E-mail folders you may have for other accounts or local mail.

8. Click the Save button near the right end of the Search tab in the Ribbon. A new Smart Folder appears with Untitled selected as its title. Type over that so it reads "All Mail".

Next Steps (Windows and Mac)

Because the All Mail Search folder or Smart Folder is selected by default after you first create it, you'll now see its contents in the main mail list window at the right of the folder list. Note that Windows Outlook may churn awhile as it builds this folder's contents from your various folders, but that only happens the first time you create it. You will not need to wait like this again in the future—it is updated automatically from now on.

Also, in Windows, the folder initially may open with mail grouped by source mail folder, which is not very useful. So click on the Received column to see an Inbox-like date-based sorting.

From now on, if you are looking for an old mail item and you are not quite sure where it is, click on the new All Mail Search or Smart Folder in your folder list, and do your search there. You are much more likely to find what you are looking for—and much more quickly.

Place the All Mail Search Folder
in the Favorite Folders Pane (Windows)

Because the Search Folders group is located a bit low in your folder list, and because your folder list may be large, the new All Mail Search Folder might be hard to locate quickly. So I recommend you drag a link to this new Search

Folder to your Favorite Folders pane; that way it's easy to get at quickly. The Favorite Folders pane (called Favorites in 2010 an 2013) is the little subpane at the top of the Navigation Pane. If you do not yet use it, then you should try it—it makes finding key folders in your folder list much easier. I drag a link to all my main folders there, including my Inbox, Sent Items, Processed Mail, and even Deleted Items; you may want to do that too.

If that subpane is not visible at the top of the Navigation Pane, go to the View menu or tab, then to the Navigation Pane submenu (called Folders Pane in 2013), and select Favorite Folders near the bottom of that menu (called Favorites in 2010 and 2013).

That's it! Start using this new All Mail Search Folder today.

∎ ∎ ∎

More Outlook Time-Saving Tips

Speeding Task Creation (Windows)

Here are some tips related to out-of-the-box Outlook functionality that will save you some time when you create tasks or appointments.

Typing "Today" or "Yesterday" in a Date Field

When entering dates in any date field, you can use the following shortcut: After clicking in an empty date field (or selecting its contents), you can type "today" (see next figure) and press ENTER. Outlook converts this to a real date.

☐	!	Task Subject	Start Date	⟡
		Write Status Report	today ▾	

This saves a little time and can prevent you from selecting the wrong date. You can also type "yesterday" in a date field.

Note: *You might want to type "yesterday" fairly often in the start date of new tasks as part of the Target Now process (Lesson 9). In that process you designate all Normal priority tasks with today's start date as Target Now tasks. These are tasks you really want to do today (but they are not critical). Because many new tasks you create you do <u>not</u> intend to do today, you can avoid clogging the Target Now list by typing the word "yesterday" in the Start Date field of most new tasks. For more details, see the section "Target Now: the Fourth Urgency Zone" in Lesson 9.*

Typing Other Words in a Date Field

You can also type "now" and reach the same results as *today*. You can also type the day of the week if you want to set a date a few days ahead. You can use abbreviations such as mon, tue, wed, thu, and fri. You can type intervals such as "2 weeks" to set the date to two weeks from today. You can do the same with months and years. If you type only a number in the field, Outlook interprets it as the day of the month, and Outlook completes the rest of the date for you when you press TAB or ENTER. You can even type holiday names in the field, but only if they are in the future in the *current calendar year.*

Save Time by Using Recurring Tasks (Windows and Mac)

Recurring tasks are a type of task in Outlook that allows you to create a task once, and then have it recreated automatically after a designated time interval. You can make any task into a recurring task by simply using the Recurrence button at the top of the task window.

An example of why you would create them might be a Monday status report that is due each week. You can cause that task to recreate itself automatically every Monday morning in your Outlook task list. Unlike repeating appointments, however, future instances of recurring tasks are not placed in your task list immediately. Rather, the next one shows up only after the previous one is marked complete or deleted. So they are a convenient way to keep a repeating task on track without burdening your task list with a long list of future tasks.

The Outlook implementation of recurring tasks is quite well done. It provides a lot of flexibility and power. However, there are some subtleties to using recurring tasks with MYN. I have a complete write-up about this online. I encourage you to study that article by going to this link: www.myn.bz/Recur.htm (link is case sensitive).

Save Time by Converting Tasks Back to E-mails (Windows)

In Lesson 7, you learned how to convert e-mails to tasks. But what if you want to convert tasks to e-mails? When might this happen? One example is this: You complete a task and you want to respond to the original sender, including the original e-mail as a reference. But if you did not convert it with Copy Here as Task with Attachment, you have no replyable e-mail attached to the task. Only the text of that e-mail is in the task.

When you want to reply to those tasks, you can look for the old e-mail in your Processed Mail folder, but that takes time. Instead, save time by converting the task back to an e-mail as follows.

Close the task and select it in a list view, and then drag the task to the Mail banner button or to the Inbox icon. That opens an e-mail window with the text of the task inside it. Remove the task header information at the top of this text, and then add any message you want above the remaining original e-mail text. You will need to complete the To field and perhaps adjust the Subject field. Then click Send.

Save Time by Writing Clearer E-mails (All Versions)

Using Clearer Subject Lines

A pet peeve of mine is getting an e-mail whose title makes it seem merely informational, but then inside the e-mail I find an important request. Indicating that request in the subject line would help my business life immeasurably as I try to identify action mail to do or convert to tasks.

With that in mind, I figure the least I can do is set an example for my colleagues and indicate action requests in the subject lines of e-mail I write. Doing so also helps me; it helps ensure that my request will get done. If I am requesting that my staff or colleague take some action, I put it right in the subject line. For example, if the action is *required*:

▶ Action Required: Update Sales Report

If it is an *optional* action, or I want to soften the message, I use the word Requested or something even more innocuous:

▶ Action Requested: Feedback on Conference

▶ Your Response Appreciated: Survey Enclosed

And if there is a deadline, I put it right in the title:

▶ Action Required by Fri 2nd: Update Sales Report

Writing Clearer E-mail Text

A related problem is this: not getting to the point quickly in an e-mail. Sometimes a request for action is buried at the bottom of a long problem statement in the e-mail. This causes the reader to have to dig through the mail to find out whether an action is requested and what it is. Instead, summarize the request right at the top of the e-mail by creating these headings and statements in the beginning of the e-mail text:

Who: All members of the Go-To-Market Sales Team *(write this in case the distribution list is large and readers may think they were wrongly sent the mail; this clarifies exactly who the mail is intended for).*

What: Budget Justification Write-up.

Action Needed: Create draft report and send to me *(describe clearly the next action you are requesting. You might be able to combine this and the What statement into one Action Needed statement).*

When: By Friday February 2nd.

Details: *(if needed include your discussion of why this is required or details of what the result should look like, and so on).*

Repeat this information even if some of it is in the subject line, as sometimes people skip over or quickly forget the subject line.

I find I sometimes create the Who, What, When summary *after* I write a long e-mail and realize it's too long and I need to summarize it. I then leave the original e-mail text in the Details section.

■   ■   ■

Summary

This lesson discussed a large number of optional time management and time-saving tips, including the following:

▶ Making time to work on tasks and, if needed, setting aside dedicated task time, including an exercise to determine if you really are overloaded at work.

▶ How to clean up your task time if it tends to be ineffective.

▶ Several ways to improve your use of Outlook Categories when filing e-mail.

▶ A number of Outlook time-saving tips.

▶ How to write clearer e-mails.

Next Steps

I suspect you skipped over many of the items in this lesson, and that's fine. Consider reviewing it again after using the system for a while to see if any sections become more important or relevant to you.

The next lesson is a similar collection of optional system components that Windows users may find valuable (sorry, they are not applicable to Mac users). I suggest you scan the section headings to see if any resonate with needs you are experiencing in your current workday. In particular I suggest you look at the section "Intrinsic Importance," as it shows a way to focus on not just the urgent but also the important.

Lesson 12: Advanced Topics for Windows Outlook

Introduction

I promised at the beginning of this book that I would focus first on getting your workday, e-mail, and tasks under control and then later advance a level and teach you more ways to improve your work life. By now I hope you *do* have your workday under control using what you have learned so far. So let's take a little of your extra time to look at some advanced perspectives that you can apply.

Unfortunately, these ideas can only by applied in Windows Outlook, not in the Macintosh version of Outlook. That's because they all rely on added task view features available only in Windows Outlook.

Note: *There is no video summary of this lesson. (For more information about MYN videos, see the note at the beginning of the Quick Start chapter.)*

What's in This Lesson

In this lesson I am going to discuss extensions of the MYN system you may want to add to your daily ritual. Here are some of the specific items covered.

▶   Tasks that link strongly to your goals and values are said to have high *intrinsic importance*. I describe the concept and offer a column you can add to your To-Do Bar to track such tasks.

▶   I show a number of ways to track goals and projects and several methods that link them to tasks.

▶   I show you how to add a column to your To-Do Bar that displays task deadlines.

▶ If you work with a narrow monitor, I demonstrate how to add back the compact layout to the To-Do Bar, thus saving space on your screen.

▶ I show how to configure a large number of Outlook task views and view changes to round out your suite of MYN tools.

Consider this entire lesson as graduate level work in the MYN system. It is not a set of prescriptions that you must do. Rather, it is a list of independent suggestions to *consider* doing. So feel free to scan through and pick and choose among the tools and views, finding items that you feel meet your needs.

As an introduction to these advanced concepts, let's start with intrinsic importance, which can be a very important optional add-on to your MYN system.

Intrinsic Importance

Beyond Urgency Management

In today's over-clocked business world, we are more often driven by urgency and recentness of attention than by the core importance of tasks. I call the core importance of tasks their *intrinsic* importance, and it is easy to overlook. When you have way too much to do, you tend to wait till something is urgent to do it. You then get in the habit of only doing the critical things, which means important but not urgent things are often passed by. We say to ourselves, "Hey this can wait, it's not about to boil over," and then we get almost addicted to focusing only on the urgent. An entire book has been written on this topic, *First Things First*, by Stephen R. Covey. There are ways to move beyond this limited focus in a manner consistent with MYN principles.

This sounds pretty important, so why did I wait to the last lesson to introduce it? My contention is that while urgency focus is unfortunate, managing urgent items is necessary. Urgency often comes from sources out of your control, so you can't just make a decision that you are no longer going to pay attention to it and focus only on core importance instead. You really do need to be good at managing urgency and the high volume of work that often leads to it. That's where most of us fail, and that's why the MYN system is focused on identifying various levels of urgency of tasks on your list, and managing them appropriately. MYN says you must put a system in place that manages urgency first.

By this point in the book you have done that. You have brought order to chaos using urgency management, and your workday is generally under control. You know how to manage high volumes of tasks and e-mail, and you can now afford to step back and take a higher perspective. I now want to introduce you to a way to manage and promote *intrinsically important* tasks within your Now Tasks list.

Intrinsic Importance Defined

What do I mean by intrinsically important tasks? These are tasks that link strongly to your values or goals. So, for example, if you had a high-value goal such as "I will have great health and vitality," then tasks such as *go to gym* or *schedule annual physical* should have a high intrinsic importance. But in an urgency-based world you might easily skip over tasks like these.

No system can make you do these tasks. All you can hope for is a way to call them out so you at least acknowledge their importance. I am going to show you a small To-Do Bar change you can make that gives you a way to acknowledge tasks with high intrinsic importance. With this in place, you are more likely to notice these tasks and less likely to defer them without thinking. You are more likely to make them a priority.

Adding Intrinsic Importance to the To-Do Bar

Here's how to implement the MYN intrinsic importance feature. You are going to add a new column to the To-Do Bar and call it "II" (for intrinsic importance). After you add it, you will examine the tasks on your To-Do Bar and either leave that column blank, or put a 1, 2, or 3 score in that column for how high you think their intrinsic importance is. The question is this: Do these tasks link strongly with important goals or values you have? Enter a "3" if they link extremely strongly and leave the column blank or at zero if there is no link.

Then you'll add a custom formatting rule that causes the entire task to be boldfaced *if it has a nonblank or greater-than-zero value* in the II field.

Figure 12.1 shows how the task list looks after the II column is added. Notice the values chosen on the right and the three boldfaced tasks in the list. Clearly these tasks now stand out.

Figure 12.1
Intrinsic Importance (II) column in To-Do Bar.

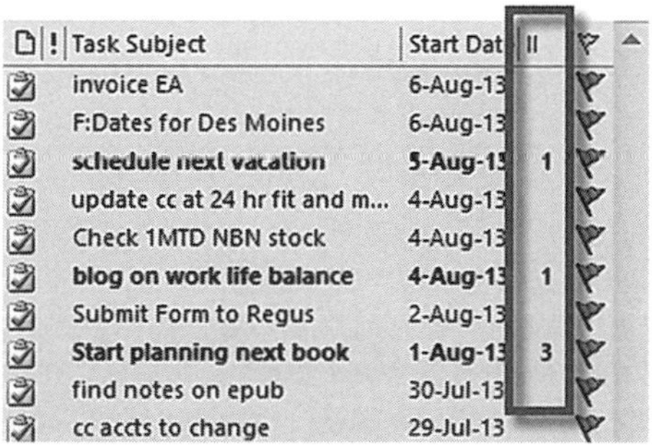

When this feature is in place and tasks are scored, you can use this column in several ways. As you consider which tasks to do on a given day, you might favor any tasks that are boldfaced. As you periodically clean your list you can avoid deferring tasks that are boldfaced. You can also occasionally sort on the II column to temporarily view all high-importance tasks at the top (but be sure to set it back to start-date sorting when finished). You might promote some of those intrinsically important tasks to your Target Now tasks list by setting their start date to today.

Using intrinsic importance won't necessarily cause you to finish those tasks first, but it provides you additional data as you make intuitive decisions on which tasks you will do when. As you glance at your list, it's good to be reminded which tasks have high core value to you.

How to Add the Intrinsic Importance Column

Here's how to add the Intrinsic Importance column and formatting.

Note: *The view change shown next is* not *prebuilt in the MYN-enabled version of the Outlook add-in software ClearContext. You'll need to add it yourself.*

1. Right-click anywhere in the To-Do Bar task list header bar (with the heading Task Subject), and select View Settings. (In Outlook 2007, select Customize Current View or Custom.) The following dialog box with the large stack of buttons opens.

2. Click the Columns button (called Fields in Outlook 2007), which opens the following dialog box.

Show Columns

Maximum number of lines in compact mode: 1 ▾

Select available columns from:

Frequently-used fields ▾

Available columns:		Show these columns in this order:
% Complete	Add ->	Icon
Actual Work		Priority
Assigned To	<- Remove	Task Subject
Attachment		Start Date
Categories		Flag Status
Company	New Column...	
Complete		
Contacts		
Custom Priority		
Custom Status		
Date Completed		
Due Date		
Modified		
Notes		

Properties   Delete   Move Up   Move Down

OK   Cancel

3. Click the New Column button (called New Field in 2007), in the middle of that dialog box. The New Field/New Column dialog box opens, as shown here. Type "II" in the Name field. Set the Type field equal to Number and the Format field equal to All Digits.

New Column

Name: II

Type: Number ▾

Format: All digits: 1,234.567 -1,234.567 ▾

OK   Cancel

To add the field to the field list in the right side of the Show Fields/Columns dialog box, Click OK.

4. Drag the field so it's below the Start Date field, second from the bottom, as shown here. Click OK.

Show these columns in this order:

Icon
Priority
Task Subject
Start Date
II
Flag Status

5. At the large stack of buttons, click the Conditional Formatting button (called Automatic Formatting in Outlook 2007). In the dialog box, click the Add button, and in the Name field type the title "MYN II".

6. With the new MYN II item selected, click the Font button. In the Font window that opens, choose Bold from the Font Style list. Click OK.

7. In the formatting dialog box again, with the new MYN II item selected, click the Condition button. The Filter dialog box opens. Click the Advanced tab.

8. Click the Field button in the middle left of this dialog box.

9. From the Field list, choose User Defined Fields in Folder, and from its submenu, choose II.

10. From the Condition list choose Is More Than, and in the Value box enter "0", as shown here. Click Add to List.

```
Filter                                                    [×]

 Tasks | More Choices | Advanced
  Find items that match these criteria:
  ┌──────────────────────────────────────────────────┐
  │ <Add criteria from below to this list>            │
  │                                                    │
  │                                                    │
  │                                                    │
  │                                          [ Remove ]│
  └──────────────────────────────────────────────────┘
  Define more criteria:
    ┌─ Field   ▼ ┐      Condition:          Value:
    │ II         │      │ is more than │▼│  │ 0       │
                                              [ Add to List ]

                        [  OK  ]  [ Cancel ]  [ Clear All ]
```

11. Click OK. Then click OK in the formatting dialog box, and click OK in the large stack of buttons window. This brings you back to the To-Do Bar.

The II field should appear on your To-Do Bar. Resize the field width so it is just wide enough to show one-digit numbers.

Using the Intrinsic Importance Column

Because this is a user-defined field, the only way you can enter the II value is in the To-Do Bar column. You won't be able to add that field to the Task dialog box. But that's okay, it still works.

Scan through your current list of tasks and enter scores for any tasks that meet your criteria for being intrinsically important. Now, and in the days ahead, consider this score as you pick which tasks to target for the day.

You might wonder: Shouldn't we just leave the Now Tasks list sorted on the II field, placing the high scoring ones always at the top of the list? *Definitely not.* I have concluded that sorting tasks on only intrinsic importance does not work. Our lives do not function that way. For example, which should be sorted higher in your list, a task called *Go to gym* or a task called *Attend office after-work party*? The gym might meet a goal and have a high II score, but the party might be just what you need that day, so it should remain at the top. Intrinsic importance should be only one factor in determining what tasks you will put at the top of your list. Often it's not the highest factor. That's not a bad thing, it's just reality. So instead, keep the list *date* sorted and use the FRESH Prioritization approach (Lesson 4), and reset start dates to force items to the top. Use the intrinsic-importance value among other considerations when deciding which tasks to sort to the top by date.

Note: *If a task with high intrinsic importance is really time critical as well, consider placing it on the calendar instead of just putting it on the task list. Then set aside enough time to make sure it gets done. This is discussed in Lesson 11.*

■   ■   ■

Understanding Outlook Task Views

In the rest of this chapter, I'm going to show you ten custom task views or view changes that will help you manage your MYN tasks. Nearly all are mentioned elsewhere in this book as being optional but perhaps useful. I've collected them all together here because you might want to create them all in one sitting. They use similar skills to create, and because they all are optional, it makes sense to list them together.

I want to start by explaining what custom views are. In Lesson 3, you customized the To-Do Bar to match MYN system principles. This is one form of creating a custom view by modifying an existing view in place and saving the changes.

More often, however, custom views are new views that you create from scratch to view your tasks in different ways. You will give them a new and unique name, and you will save them in your copy of Outlook. That way you can activate them as needed, later, with the change view commands. I'll show you that in the section "Choosing Between Optional Task Views" that follows.

The custom view capability of Windows Outlook separates Outlook from many of its competitors. It separates it from the Mac version of Outlook, too. It gives Windows Outlook great power for creating custom solutions.

Before showing you how to build new custom views, I want to discuss the preinstalled task views that come with Outlook. I also want to discuss the Tasks folder itself and Outlook folders in general. This discussion will help you understand what you're doing when you create and use the new custom views.

Tasks Folder and Preinstalled Tasks Folder Views

You access the Tasks folders by first putting Outlook in the Tasks mode (see Lesson 2). You do that by clicking the Tasks icon or banner button in the lower-left corner of your Outlook window. After that you can change which tasks folder you are viewing by picking it from the My Tasks list at the top of the Navigation or Folders Pane. Typically, you will pick either the To-Do List folder or a Tasks folder.

What's not covered much in Lesson 2 is that the To-Do List folder and the Tasks folder (and all other major folders in Windows Outlook) come with *preinstalled views* that enable you to vary the way you see your data in each folder. The default view for the To-Do List folder is also called To-Do List. It's optimized for a mixed view of flagged-mail tasks and true tasks. But you can choose a different view, as I'll show you.

The default view for the Tasks folder view is called Simple List. It's basically a list of all tasks in the system with only the task subject name and the due date displayed. It is this view that opens when you open the Tasks folder the first time (see Figure 12.2).

Figure 12.2
Simple List view in Tasks folder.

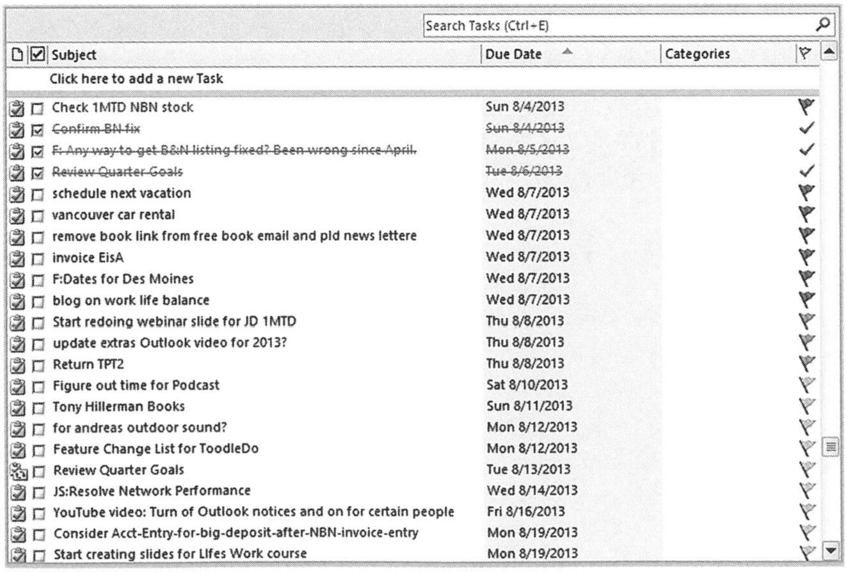

Even though it's not configured for MYN, the Simple List view is very useful. For example, it displays completed tasks (designated with strikethrough lines and a dimmed font). I use this view if I accidentally mark a task complete in the To-Do Bar and want to find it and make it active again. This view shows the Due Date column and not the Start Date column, but because due dates are set equal to start dates automatically, the columns are usually interchangeable when viewing tasks. So you can use this view to scan your future-dated tasks by sorting on the Due Date column. That said, a custom view that follows is better for that (called MYN All Now Tasks).

You can display a number of optional Tasks folder views. For example, Outlook 2010 ships with 11 Tasks folder views you might want to use. Think of these views as filtered or selected subsets of your entire task list that also vary by showing different columns.

There are good reasons to use these other preinstalled views. For example, let's say you want to see a list of your tasks without viewing the completed tasks. To do that you choose the view labeled Active Tasks. Or, you can choose a view labeled Completed Tasks to see only those, which is useful for selectively deleting old completed tasks. Many more views exist. Next, let's see how to activate those views.

Choosing Between Optional Task Views

There are a number of ways to choose between the various Outlook views, and they vary by Outlook version.

Using the View Menu or Tab (All Versions)

In all Outlook versions, you can select views from the View menu or tab. In Outlook 2007, open the View menu and choose Current View. In Outlook 2010 and 2013, on the View tab, click Change View (at the very left end of that tab). All versions: After you do that, all available views for the currently selected folder are displayed, ready for you to choose from. For instance, from within a tasks folder, select Detailed List. Notice that the task view now changes to a new view (one very similar to Simple List but containing a few more columns). Select Simple List again from that box to return to the default view.

In Outlook 2010 and 2013, because this control displays view *icons* rather than a scrolling list of view names, it can be hard to find custom views that have long names—the icon labels don't show enough text to distinguish them. To make finding them easier, click Manage Views at the bottom of that control, and select your views from the scrolling list of view names displayed there. Once you find the view, click Apply View to activate it.

When switching views, you may want to turn off the Reading Pane that is often displayed the first time you use a new view. Go to the View menu or tab, click Reading Pane, and select Off.

Advanced Toolbar (Outlook 2007)

Outlook 2007 gives you a another way to see at a glance which view is open and to select others. It requires that you add another toolbar called the Advanced Toolbar. Here's how you do that. Go to the View menu and click Toolbars. Then choose Advanced on the submenu. You'll see a new toolbar added to the top of your Outlook window, as shown here.

In this toolbar you will see a box that lists names of task views, with (most likely) the view named Simple List shown by default. This is the Current View Selector.

Select Data Type and Folder First

One important lesson to learn about choosing views with menus or the Advanced Toolbar is this: You should choose the data type and folder your view applies to first before trying to choose the view from the view list. So if you are trying to open a specific Tasks folder view, make sure you activate the Tasks data type, and then click either the To-Do List or the Tasks folder. Only then should you select the view name in the menus or Advanced Toolbar.

Current View Section in Outlook 2007 Navigation Pane

In the Navigation Pane of Outlook 2007, when in the Tasks mode, there is an additional way to select views and it's probably the easiest method of all. Unfortunately, this method is not available in 2010 or 2013. In the 2007 Navigation Pane, look for the Current View section partway down the pane (see Figure 12.3).

That section should appear after you click the Tasks banner button. However, if you have lots of tasks folders, you might need to scroll down to the middle portion of the Navigation Pane to see it. After you find the Current View section, you might need to toggle it open by clicking the arrow next to it. After it's open, notice that you can select various task views like Simple List and Detailed List.

Note: *If this 2007 Current View section is not visible at all, activate it as follows: From the View menu, choose Navigation Pane, and select Current View Pane from the submenu.*

To-Do List Tasks Folder

Before you start creating custom views, notice that when creating views it is important to understand the To-Do List folder. You learned something about this folder in Lesson 2, but I also encourage you to read the Appendix A section "Windows Outlook: The Mysterious To-Do List Folder," for an even more complete discussion.

Figure 12.3
The Current View selector in the 2007 Navigation Pane.

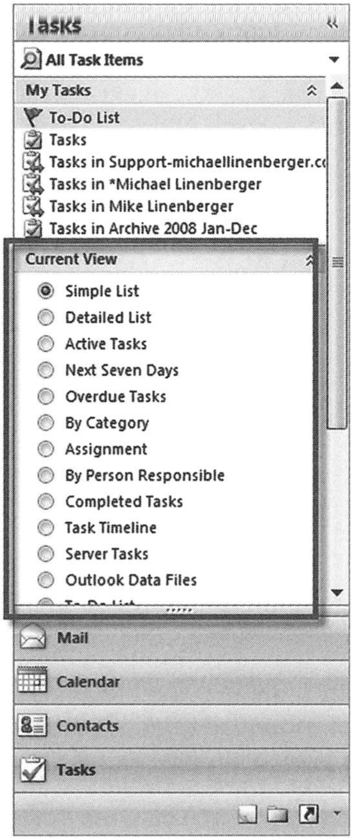

In the meantime, know this: Many of the Task view creation instructions you will follow in this lesson ask you to select the To-Do List Tasks folder when creating the view. Be sure you do this, and then be sure to select the To-Do List Tasks folder when you *use* the view. Why? Because it is the only way to see flagged-mail tasks.

You will also see one other thing that is related to this when using the instructions that follow. Views you create in the To-Do List folder that hide completed tasks should usually have two filter conditions in the Advanced tab of the Filter dialog box, as shown in the next figure.

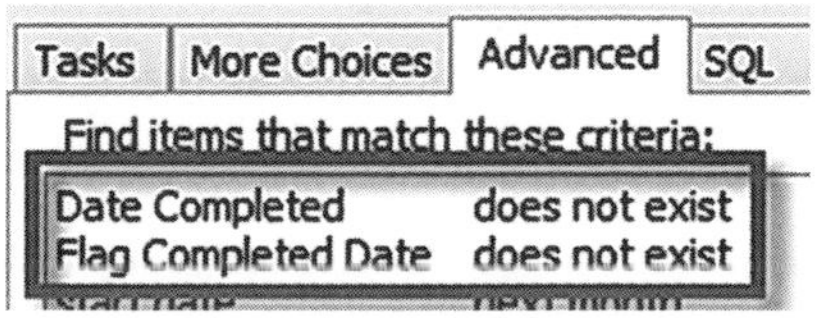

I call these *Outlook transition filter conditions,* because they handle a problem that can occur if you transition your Outlook data from older versions of Outlook to Outlook 2007, or later. They fix an odd behavior in how some Outlook views display completed flagged-mail tasks created from pre-2007 mail. You'll notice that these two conditions always appear by default in any new view you create in the To-Do List folder, so be sure to leave them there for all views that *filter out completed tasks.* Remove them for any view in which you want to *see* completed tasks.

Tasks Subject Field Compared to Subject Field

As you build the views in this lesson, you might notice the use of the Tasks Subject field. In earlier Outlook versions, a similar field called Subject was always used in the tasks folder views. With the introduction of flagged-mail tasks, Microsoft added the Task Subject field to all tasks and uses that field in any view that shows flagged-mail tasks (such as the To-Do Bar task list). Make sure to use the Task Subject field in any views where it is called out.

Why the different field? Explaining this is a little tricky, but here goes. It's to enable users to change the title of a flagged-mail task without changing the Subject of the original e-mail. Recall that a flagged-mail task in the To-Do Bar is just a virtual copy of the e-mail. The two items really are the same entity. An unfortunate outcome of that is if you change the title of a flagged-mail task (to better indicate the action), you also change the Subject of the corresponding e-mail. That can get confusing for various reasons. For example, say you were to later reply to that e-mail — the recipients could be confused by the new name. So to prevent that problem, Outlook copies the e-mail Subject contents to the new Task Subject field, which becomes the displayed title of the task. That way, if you change that displayed task title, the Subject of the corresponding e-mail in your Inbox does not change. This Task Subject field enables that, so you should use it in most custom views.

One downside to using Task Subject is you cannot sort on it. So if you're creating a view in which you might need to do that, feel free to use the Subject field instead of the Task Subject field. For example, in Lesson 10 on delegation, I give instructions on how to sort alphabetically on the Subject field with the MYN All Now Tasks view. That's why that view is constructed with *Subject* instead of Task Subject. (I show how to make that view later in this lesson.)

Close the Reading Pane

As you create the new views in the sections ahead, you might notice that Outlook has a bad habit of opening the Reading Pane on new views. You will probably want to close it. Use the View tab or menu, click Reading Pane, and choose Off.

Using Multiple Windows, or Side by Side

After you start using different Outlook folder views, you might find you want to open several different task views simultaneously, so you can plan your work. Something many users of Outlook do not realize is that you can open multiple windows in Outlook, showing different views in each one. This makes it possible, for example, to keep your Calendar folder open in one window and your goals and projects view open in another. To do this, right-click the icon or banner button for the data type that you want to open in the second window, and select Open in New Window from the shortcut menu. If you have a very large monitor, you can display both windows in different parts of your screen. If you have a smaller monitor and the windows overlap, you might want to use the keyboard shortcut ALT + TAB to move between the windows.

If you use multiple Outlook windows like this and you want to have the same windows reopen automatically the next time you start Outlook, be sure to use the File menu's Exit command to exit rather than the Close button on the windows. When you use the Exit command, all the multiple windows will reopen automatically the next time you launch Outlook.

In Outlook, you can, of course, open the To-Do Bar next to any data-type view. So when you create a goal or project list (described in the next section), you can open the To-Do Bar next to it and view your Now Tasks at the same time. This is very useful as you plan how to complete goals and projects.

That concludes the introduction to custom views in Outlook. Next, I'll show you a number of business scenarios where you can create specific views.

■   ■   ■

Tracking Goals and Projects in Outlook

If you manage several goals or projects, this next topic will be very important to you. It shows you a few different ways to track goals and projects on your task list in Microsoft Outlook, and it highlights one technique in particular that requires you to create a custom task view.

First of all, starting with goals, you may have noticed that I deliberately do not say much about creating or tracking goals in this book. Not because they are not important, but because most people's problems with tasks and e-mail are not related to a shortage of goals or inattention to the ones they have. Instead, most people's problems are in dealing with the barrage of incoming e-mail and action requests at volumes that seem to defy an eight-hour work-day. This dilemma is not solved by merely having and working goals.

The same is true of projects. Unless you are managing relatively large projects, I don't see lack of project management skills as being the main cause of an out-of-control workday. Again, mastering management of the daily deluge of e-mail and tasks should come first.

That said, after successfully using MYN to conquer the disarray of your e-mail and tasks, it is fitting to take the next rung of the achievement ladder and yes, *do* start focusing on your goals and projects. Again, this is graduate-level MYN.

In my book *Master Your Workday Now!* I write extensively about goals—how to create them and how to achieve them, whether you use Outlook or not. That books takes a higher-level view of goals that will help you create the right ones and relate them to your life. So check out that book. In the following pages I take a more operational look at goals: how to track them in Outlook.

Tracking Goals

By now the distinction between goals and tasks should be clear, but if not let's just use this distinction: a task is *actionable*, and a goal is *plan-able*. Specifically, tasks, when you glance at them in the middle of your workday, should be something you can *do*, that you can *act* on. Goals should be something you can plan tasks against to achieve the goal.

This means you should not place goals on your Now Tasks list. For example, if you have a goal to lose weight, don't write "Lose weight" on your Now Tasks list. Why? Because in the heat of a busy workday if you see that item pop up on your list you won't know what to do with it. What you *should* write on your Now Tasks list is an action (task) toward that goal: "Call Sam the personal trainer." Or "Go to gym today." This is essentially the next-action concept that I discussed in Lesson 6, and it is an important element of getting your tasks done.

So if not on the Now Tasks list, where *do* you place your goals in order to plan against them? Notice that you should record them *someplace*, because you want to continue to refer to them often and create actions against them. I suggest you create a goals list, and Outlook is one good place to put it. I show you some options for that in a moment, options that work well also with projects.

Tracking Projects

There are two ways this system can help you with projects. First, as with goals, you might want to list your projects somewhere in Outlook so that you can periodically identify next-action tasks and place them on your Now Tasks list. And, as with goals, you should not list them in your Now Tasks list itself because they are too big to place there. Second, projects tend to have a sequence of dependent tasks. I'll show you a few ways to track these tasks together in Outlook.

But not all projects are usefully tracked in Outlook the same way. That really depends on how complex the project you're talking about is. Let me list the two extremes of project types and then show how the MYN system can help.

Types of Projects

Large Formal Projects are multiweek, multimonth, or multiyear activities, usually worked independently of your operational duties. They often include some fully dedicated staff. Such projects are large enough to warrant their own set of planning and follow-up meetings and should be managed using formal project management techniques, not the Outlook Task system. The discussion here does not really apply to these. That's because you need to separate project planning and management steps from the execution of individual tasks, and Outlook is not a large-project planning and management tool. Instead use a tool like MindManager and Microsoft Project to identify and schedule the long string of dependent tasks that result.

That said, if you are assigned a number of individual tasks from a large formal project, you could put those on your Outlook task list and use the MYN system to help you execute them.

Background Projects or Miniprojects fall well below the large size and intense focus of a formal project. I define these as work units that require multiple associated or linked tasks but that overall are not large enough to be managed as a formal project. These may be spin-offs from a larger project, or they may stand alone as simple multitask activities. Your attention on these projects is usually part-time. It starts and stops throughout the week as you try to fit these into your other operational duties. A lot of what you do at work probably falls in this category. The MYN system can be useful for executing and even managing these small projects, if the task list for the project is small and not complicated. Outlook can help in two ways. First, as a place to create a list of these projects, as you do with goals. And second, as a place to list next-action tasks (in your Now Tasks list) that apply to those projects. Ways to do that are listed next.

Outlook MYN Solutions for Projects and Goals

Now that you know the various types of goals and projects, let's look at how to list and track them.

Ways to List and Manage Goals and Projects in Outlook

There is a large range of possible approaches on where to record goals and list projects, and I don't feel any one of them is the best. I think this varies by individual and the number and size of goals or projects. Let me throw out a few approaches that you can pick from, most of which use Microsoft Outlook. For the following six Outlook-based methods, I'll provide implementation details later in this lesson. Pick one of the following that works best for you.

1. Create Outlook Categories with your goal or project name, and then assign those categories to tasks that help achieve those goals or projects. Put a *G:* or *P:* designator in front of the category name (G:LoseWeight; P:LandscapeFrontYard). That way all project or goal items clump together in the Outlook Categories list and you can scan them there. Then you can configure an Outlook view in your Tasks folder that groups tasks by each goal or project, to help plan your steps to achievement. I'll cover that ahead. Use this approach only for a small number of projects and goals; otherwise the category list can get quite cluttered. So you might want to reserve them for the largest and most important.

2. Enter each goal or project as an individual task in your master tasks list (covered ahead). You can then periodically glance at that list and, if appropriate, create new Now Tasks against some of those goals and projects. You can brainstorm and record future actions in the Notes text field of each master task for later reference. Again, put a *G:* or *P:* designator in front of the master task name (G:Lose weight; P:Landscape front yard) and sort alphabetically on that view. I'll show how to create that ahead. This is suitable even for very numerous projects and goals.

3. Recognizing a natural Goal→Project→Next Action hierarchy, some people create nested Outlook tasks folders using the goal and project names and then store next actions as Outlook tasks in the lowest-level folder. The advantage is that it lets you create hierarchical relationships if you need that. More on this ahead.

4. Or just list your goals or projects in an Outlook Note data type, and don't make any attempt to link them to tasks. Ultimately, having a place where you can record and review your goals and project names is often enough.

5. Use some application other than Outlook. I really like the software Mind-Manager. I use it for brainstorming many things, including my goals and projects. And there are many other software titles available that can help. Just do an Internet search on goal setting software and project management software.

6. Use paper. Tape a printed goal list or project list (or graphic representation of it) to your wall next to your computer monitor. If you have one main project, paste the printed project plan in clear sight. Paper is actually an excellent approach. Sometimes we try to be too clever with technology and lose sight of good old-fashioned paper. The advantage to this is that your goals and projects are always in sight, and you can format the list in any way that helps you to understand and focus on them, say using hierarchies, pictures, maps, and so on. And you will see them daily, which many experts say is essential if you hope to realize your goals and move your projects forward.

What to Do with a Goals or Projects List

The key to all these approaches is to refer to the goal or project list *often*, and then periodically toss next-action tasks that support them on your To-Do Bar task list. I feel strongly that after you get e-mail and tasks under control with MYN, you should do the following: As you finally relax enough to consider your higher work objectives, commit to completing—every day—at least a few tasks related to your key goals or projects. Otherwise you can get so accustomed to just knocking tasks off your list that you forget to specifically target important ones.

Series Tasks

One reason to consider a project tasks perspective in Outlook is due to something I call series tasks. With these tasks, after you complete one, the next one is eligible for doing and then the next one and the next. These are also called linked tasks, or dependent tasks, and they are typical in project environments where a complex stream of activity is required to meet the end goal. They are also common when you start using next actions (Lesson 6), because, after you break down a task to identify its very next action, you are likely to end up with other steps to reach the final desired outcome.

How do you designate these in Outlook? Should you attempt to show those linkages in Outlook?

Large Projects

If you have a large, complex project with many tasks displaying complicated dependencies, use a good project management tool like Microsoft Project. That software has the tools you need to link tasks and auto-update start dates of all tasks if parts of the project are delayed. I have found no good way to do that in Outlook. Every time I have tried to find logical ways to link across a large number of tasks in Outlook, too many exceptions arise that make it too complicated. Instead use a tool built just for that. Although Microsoft Project is a good one, the application MindManager is simpler and also has ways to display linked tasks.

Small Projects

If your project is a simple background project or miniproject, and it has a relatively small number of tasks, it *can* be useful to make some links in Outlook. Why? Because when you complete one task, it's good to know which ones need your attention.

So how do you show those linkages? One thing you should *not* do is copy all the dependent tasks to your Now Tasks list. The visible Now Tasks list is only for tasks that you can consider working on *now*—dependent tasks don't pass that test. You should write only next actions on the Now Tasks list; otherwise it becomes cluttered with nonactionable items and slowly becomes unusable (Lesson 6).

Also avoid entering a series of future-dated project tasks with estimated future start dates. For example, don't export all the tasks for a project from Microsoft Project and import them into Outlook. Even though hidden from view (due to their future start dates), these estimated future dates will come back to haunt you as soon as the project timing changes. The tasks will show up either too late or too early. Instead, there are two better ways to handle linked tasks.

Use any of the options that are listed in the earlier section "Ways to List and Manage Goals and Projects in Outlook," where multiple actions are associated with a project and are reviewable. Then, when you complete one project task, remember to come back and review the project list to decide which next action to activate in your Now Tasks list. In that list both the project-categories approach and the master-tasks-list approach (options one and two) work. Implementation details for these are covered later in this lesson.

While this list-review process can work well, the weakness is that, as you complete a given project task, you might forget to look again at the associated project list to find the next. Then the sequence stalls.

The MORE and PigPog Methods

Another two solutions that help solve these problems are the MORE method and the PigPog method. They work especially well with the multiple steps arising from next-action decomposition. There are a number of variants of this solution written up in other sources. The common elements of each solution variant are as follows: List the multiple steps to complete a miniproject in the Notes field of a single Outlook task item. Then, place the next action of that series in the Subject field of that task. Finally, also indicate in the Subject field somehow that multiple steps are associated with this next action. I like this method and encourage you to try it. Here are the most common ways to do this:

▶ Use the MORE method (see Lesson 6) where you place the first task of a sequence as a task item in your Now Tasks list. At the end of the Subject field enter the word MORE with an ellipsis before it. For example: "E-mail Ted about proposal …MORE." Then in the task Notes field, list the subsequent tasks. When you complete the first task, don't mark the task complete; rather, open the task and look for subsequent actions. The …*MORE* in the task name reminds you to do that. Change the Subject field of the task to the next action in the list. Keep doing that until the sequence is complete. This idea was contributed by Don Morgan.

▶ The PigPog method is similar to the MORE method, but instead of …*MORE*, put a project or outcome name after the task subject, in brackets. For example, "E-mail Ted about proposal {Newco Sale}." Seeing brackets around the project name will remind you to look inside. It also reminds you why you are doing this task. The PigPog method was created by a number of people in the GTD Palm Yahoo! Group and documented by Michael Randall. For more information, go to www.pigpog.com/node/1031.

▶ Mark Ashton contributed the following idea. Do the same as I just described but put a → at the *beginning* of the subject line. This is to ensure that you do not accidentally delete a series task after partial completion, when long task names cause the word MORE (or the project name in brackets) to scroll out of sight at the right. You might try other codes at the front, a *P:* for example.

▶ Feel free to include other information about the project in the notes section. For example, date information if it is pertinent, say deadlines or start dates. Or you may want to write up a vision statement for the project in that space.

This technique is best suited for either large tasks or very small projects that have relatively few steps to complete. I would not use it as your only way to track a large project with many steps.

Some small projects may have parallel work streams, each with its own series of dependent tasks. In those cases create a MORE task or PigPog task for each work stream.

Using ClearContext for Tracking Project Tasks

The Outlook add-in software ClearContext that I highlight throughout this book has a nice set of features for tracking project tasks. Its Dashboard view can be used instead of the project views I show ahead, and offers much stronger integration with the other elements of Outlook that may be related to your projects (e-mail, contacts, appointments, and more). Take a look at it.

■   ■   ■

Category-Based MYN Goal and Project Views

Now that you understand ways to manage goals and projects, and now that you understand Outlook views, let's create some custom views that help you manage your goals and projects.

These first two parallel views are currently my favorite approaches to tracking goals and projects. They assume you will create your goals and projects as entries in the Outlook Categories list and that you will link tasks to these Categories. These Tasks folder views enable you to view a list of all tasks for a given goal or project grouped with the goal or project name, so that you can plan ahead, pick next actions, defer longer-term associated tasks, and so on.

Some Background

To make this work, you should only use this approach for less numerous (probably larger) goals or projects. For those who use David Allen's Getting Things Done system, or who used my system in the first edition of this book, a little discussion is needed to describe why that's important and how this differs from the first edition of this book.

In the past I did not use categories to list projects, because my project lists tended to be long. I tended to create a lot of project names. Why? Because one premise of the first edition of this book was that any time you have a multistep activity you should identify it as a miniproject and put it on a project list (in the Master Tasks view). That's also a teaching of David Allen's Getting Things Done approach. The idea is, after you complete the current next action you can review the project list and determine if additional next actions are needed for these miniprojects.

But I found I gradually stopped reviewing that long project list. Many of those miniprojects were for next actions I had deferred out a ways, so I did not need to review the corresponding miniproject weekly. And that approach does not make sense now that I am using the Defer-to-Review method (Lesson 9). So I skipped reviews a lot, and the whole project list approach for all multistep activities no longer worked for me.

So I now no longer recommend converting all multistep activities into projects. Instead I now recommend using the MORE approach for linking tasks (described earlier in the section "Series Tasks"). Using that, you don't need to create a miniproject for every multistep activity.

One outcome of this is that the project list gets much smaller and only lists "real" projects—those that might have long time frames and substantial collections of related tasks. With a much shorter project list, using the Outlook Categories capability to list projects is much more practical now. The advantage of using Outlook Categories for listing projects is that you can link individual tasks to project names with category assignments. Then you can create views that show all the tasks associated with a given project. Those views are useful for planning projects and identifying next actions. They also help during execution, as you may find that related components of the project are done more easily together. The project tasks list helps you plan that out.

Using P: and G:

As you will see, both the projects view and the goals view use the same logic with category names. For these views to work, you need to put a *P:* in front of project names and a *G:* in front of goal names in the category list. The view filters look for these character strings. I find using this nomenclature works well when picking projects or goals out of the Outlook Categories list because they group together in the list.

Figure 12.4 shows how the projects version of this view will look when it is completed. The steps to build that follow.

Figure 12.4
Category-based MYN Projects view.

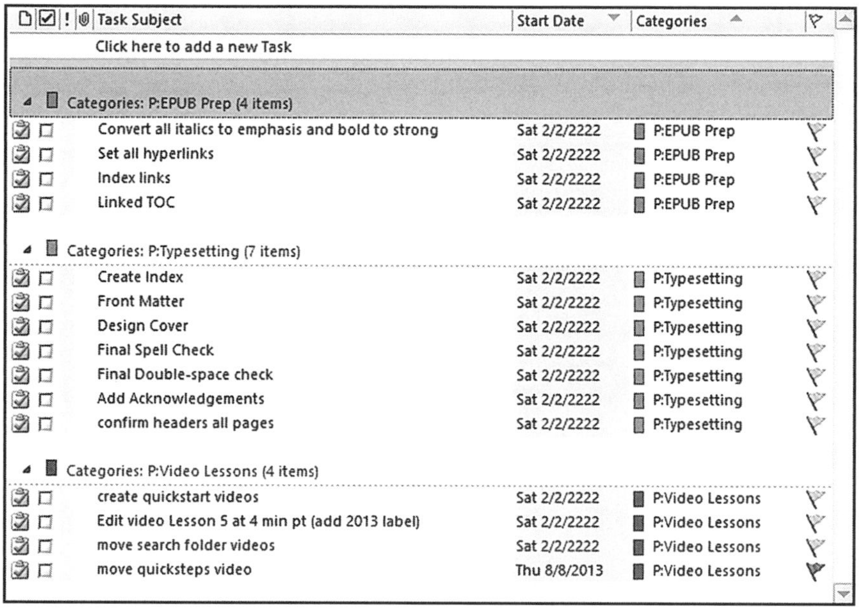

☐	☑	!	⚲	Task Subject	Start Date ▽	Categories ▲	⚑
				Click here to add a new Task			
▲ ⬛ Categories: P:EPUB Prep (4 items)							
				Convert all italics to emphasis and bold to strong	Sat 2/2/2222	⬛ P:EPUB Prep	⚑
				Set all hyperlinks	Sat 2/2/2222	⬛ P:EPUB Prep	⚑
				Index links	Sat 2/2/2222	⬛ P:EPUB Prep	⚑
				Linked TOC	Sat 2/2/2222	⬛ P:EPUB Prep	⚑
▲ ⬛ Categories: P:Typesetting (7 items)							
				Create Index	Sat 2/2/2222	⬛ P:Typesetting	⚑
				Front Matter	Sat 2/2/2222	⬛ P:Typesetting	⚑
				Design Cover	Sat 2/2/2222	⬛ P:Typesetting	⚑
				Final Spell Check	Sat 2/2/2222	⬛ P:Typesetting	⚑
				Final Double-space check	Sat 2/2/2222	⬛ P:Typesetting	⚑
				Add Acknowledgements	Sat 2/2/2222	⬛ P:Typesetting	⚑
				confirm headers all pages	Sat 2/2/2222	⬛ P:Typesetting	⚑
▲ ⬛ Categories: P:Video Lessons (4 items)							
				create quickstart videos	Sat 2/2/2222	⬛ P:Video Lessons	⚑
				Edit video Lesson 5 at 4 min pt (add 2013 label)	Sat 2/2/2222	⬛ P:Video Lessons	⚑
				move search folder videos	Sat 2/2/2222	⬛ P:Video Lessons	⚑
				move quicksteps video	Thu 8/8/2013	⬛ P:Video Lessons	⚑

How to Build the Category-Based Projects View

Note: The views shown here are included with the MYN-enabled version of the Outlook add-in software ClearContext, which is available on my website (www.myn.bz/clearcontext.htm).

1. In the lower-left corner of the Outlook window, click the Tasks button. Select the To-Do List folder near the top of the Navigation or Folders Pane.

2. **Outlook 2007**: In the View menu click Current View, then click Define Views (it's at the bottom of the submenu).
    Outlook 2010, 2013: From the View tab, click Change View, and then click Manage Views.
    All Versions: The following dialog box will open. Click the New button in the upper-right corner.

3. In the Create a New View dialog box that opens, name the view "MYN Projects" as shown here. Make sure Table is selected in the middle. Select the All Task Folders button at the bottom. Click OK.

4. The dialog box which I call *the large stack of buttons* opens. Click the Columns button (Fields in 2007). Build a field list with the items in the order as shown:

> Icon
> Complete (optional)
> Priority
> Attachment
> Task Subject
> Start Date
> Categories
> Flag Status

Note: If you have trouble finding any of the field names, try selecting All Task Fields in the Select Available Fields/Columns From list box. Task Subject and Flag Status are displayed by selecting All Mail Fields.

5. Click OK.

6. In the large stack of buttons, click the Group By button.

7. If it is selected, clear the Automatically Group According to Arrangement check box in the upper-left corner.

8. From the Group Items By list, select Categories. Select Ascending to the right of that list box. Click OK.

9. In the large stack of buttons, click the Sort button. Sort items by Priority, Descending, and then by Start Date, Descending (as shown here). Click OK.

10. Back at the large stack of buttons, click the Filter button, and in the dialog box that opens, click the Advanced tab. Using the skills you learned in Lesson 3, add the following conditions:

   ► Make sure the two transition filter conditions are set as follows:

Date Completed	does not exist
Flag Completed Date	does not exist

   ► Add the following conditions as shown in the next figure:

Categories	contains	P:
Status	not equal to	Completed

11. Click OK.

12. Click the Conditional Formatting button (Automatic Formatting in 2007). In the scrolling list of rules, clear the Overdue Tasks check box. Click OK, and then OK again. Click Apply View.

13. You may want to remove the Reading Pane if active. From View menu or tab, click Reading Pane, and select Off.

If you ever want to return to this view, you can activate it with the methods in the earlier section "Choosing Between Optional Task Views."

Using the Category-Based Projects View

Start creating Outlook Categories that match your project names (see Lesson 8 for more information on how to create and assign Outlook Categories). Insert a *P:* in front of each category name. Make sure there is no space between *P* and the colon. Then start assigning those categories to tasks that are associated with that project. Here are some tips:

▶ **Share categories with e-mail**. Recall that these category names are shared with e-mail, appointments, contacts, and all other Outlook data types. So if you are categorizing e-mail, plan to label project e-mail and project tasks with the same project's category name.

▶ **Renaming categories**. If you are already using Outlook Categories as project names and you want to use this new view, you'll need to rename that category everywhere it is assigned so that it now contains *P:* in front of the name. Use the Rename button on the Color Categories dialog box.

▶ **Dating dependent tasks**. This view will encourage you to start brainstorming what future tasks are needed to complete a project. You can drop those into that Projects view anytime. That's good. However, stick to the rules. Do *not* try to create a list of project tasks with start dates of dependent (linked) tasks estimated in the future. This gets complicated quickly, especially when dates of early tasks change. Instead, label all future dependent tasks with the date 2/2/2222. Why? This future date prevents these tasks from dropping into your To-Do Bar (your Now Tasks list) randomly. You want them to appear there *only after* they graduate to next-action status. The date 2/2/2222 is easy to type, and it's a very long time in the future, so a good way to keep tasks out of your Now Tasks list. One day, when you're reviewing the project list for this project, you'll decide one of these tasks is now ready to activate as a next action for the project. Then you change the date to the date you want to start it. That said, if a project task is truly *independent* (not linked to other tasks in that project), feel free to enter an actual future start date on it. That's the same as entering a Defer-to-Do task (Lesson 9).

▶ **Project work streams**. Many projects have parallel and independent work streams, each with its own string of dependent tasks. For example, a house-painting project might have separate crews painting the main house and the detached garage, and their paths never cross. They work separate schedules and their tasks are not dependent on each other. You want to identify the next action for *each* work stream, and place it on the Now Tasks list.

▶ **No hierarchy**. There is no provision in this process for hierarchical projects or for displaying relationships with goals. For one approach to handle this, see the section "Hierarchical Goal, Project, and Tasks Folders" later in this lesson.

Periodically, open this view and do some project planning. The most important planning action is to identify any tasks that are now eligible for action. When you do, move them out to your Now Tasks list as a next action by giving them a near-term date. Remember to write these tasks in next-action language (Lesson 6).

Project tasks tend to be large, so chances are when you start to activate a project task, you will turn it into a MORE or series task. You will likely do this after you identify the true next action of each. (For more information, see the earlier section "Series Tasks" in this lesson).

How to Build the Category-Based Goals View

The category-based goals view is nearly identical to the category-based *project* view. Rather than repeat all those steps at this point, let me show you how to modify the earlier steps. Do this: follow all the earlier steps except for two changes:

▶ In step 3 name the view "MYN Goals."

▶ In step 10 replace *Categories contains P*: with "Categories contains G:"

All the other steps are identical. This view is available in MYN ClearContext.

Using the Category-Based Goals View

After you create the view, you now need to start creating Goal categories with a *G:* in front of their names (see Lesson 8 if you need to review how to create and assign Outlook Categories), and then start assigning those categories to tasks that are associated with that goal. Some thoughts on this, similar to those just described for the Projects view, are repeated here in case you skipped that section:

▶ **Share categories with e-mail**. Recall that these category names are shared with e-mail, appointments, contacts, and all other Outlook data types. Take advantage of that if possible.

▶ **Renaming categories**. If you're already using Outlook Categories as goal names and you want to use this new view, you need to rename that category everywhere it is assigned so it now contains *G:*. Use the Rename button on the Color Categories dialog box.

▶ **No hierarchy**. There is no provision in this process for hierarchical goals or displaying relationships with projects. For one approach to handle this, see the section later in this lesson, "Hierarchical Goal, Project, and Tasks Folders."

As with projects, study this view periodically and adjust dates on tasks to best help you achieve that goal. Add new tasks that you think might advance each goal. If new goal-based tasks are already next-action tasks (that is, they can be done now if time and priorities allow), give them a near-term date now. Dependent tasks are less likely with goals, but if you encounter any, use the 2/2/2222 date approach described earlier for projects, to keep them out of sight on most Now Tasks types of views.

Adding a Categories Column to the To-Do Bar—Use Caution

When using these Category methods on goals and projects as just described, you might want to be able to see what categories are assigned to tasks right in the To-Do Bar.

One way to do that is to add a Categories column to your To-Do Bar. Be very careful, however, if you do add this column, because you must *never group or sort on that column* (such as clicking the label at the top of the column). If you do, it is very difficult to get back to the MYN grouping and sorting. Clicking the other header labels will not restore it. Rather, you will need to redo the grouping and sorting steps shown in Lesson 3—clearly too much work to do routinely. Even if you never intend to purposely re-sort the To-Do Bar on Categories, adding the Categories column makes the To-Do Bar much more sensitive to stray clicks on the header bar. *Be Careful.* Do not click the Categories column heading. For these reasons, I advise against adding the Categories column to the To-Do Bar. Instead, use a configuration trick I've recently developed that displays Categories there, but prevents accidentally sorting on them. Go to: www.myn.bz/cat-column.htm.

Assigning Other Categories to Tasks

To use the category-based goals and projects views, you assign goal and project categories to tasks. There are other types of categories you might want to use with tasks. One nonproject or goal category I commonly assign to tasks is the category "Errands." I assign that to shopping items or other out-and-about type activities. That way, when I'm out doing errands, I can filter my tasks by *Errands* on my mobile device, and see my shopping list or errands list. For more about using mobile software that syncs with Outlook tasks, see Lesson 6. That lesson also describes using MYN with Getting Things Done, or GTD. It includes how categories can be used on tasks to assign GTD Contexts.

■　■　■

The MYN Master Tasks View

In the first edition of this book the Master Tasks view was a very important part of the system. If you read that edition you may recall that tasks were divided into two types: daily tasks and master tasks. Master tasks represented long-term tasks you were not yet ready to work on (as well as the place to list project and goals). The master tasks concept is common to many task systems and books, including FranklinCovey and the long-famous book *The Time Trap*, by Alec Mackenzie.

Starting in the second edition of my Outlook book I stopped using master tasks as a storage place for long-term tasks. It's not that there is no need for long-term tasks; there still is. It's just that I decided the master tasks list does not work well as a way to manage individual long-term tasks. I discuss why in Lesson 9, and discuss there as well why the new Defer-to-Review process solves this problem so well.

But there could still be a place for a master tasks list, and that's to use it solely to list projects, goals, roles, agendas, and so on. This view enables that. However, this view has a number of disadvantages as well, which I'll list shortly.

Note:　*If you followed the first edition but have recently reconfigured your To-Do Bar following Lesson 3 of this book, you should delete your old Master Tasks view, as it will no longer work with the new To-Do Bar settings. Reason: These new settings no longer filter out tasks with no dates. If you still want to use the master tasks approach, create the new folder and view described next.*

Master Tasks View Compared to Category View

You can use this new Master Tasks view as an alternative to the category-based project and goals views described earlier. Why might you want to do that? If you like to identify all multistep tasks as projects and so have a long list of projects, this Master Tasks view will work better for you because it will prevent clogging your Outlook Categories list with too many project names. And if you have no need to link individual next-action tasks to higher-level goals or projects, the new Master Tasks folder and view is simpler to use. Or you can use it along with the category-based views.

How This Folder and View Works

Very simply, the way this new master tasks list and view works is this: You list a project as a task entry by placing a task with a *P:* in front of the name there. Add as many as you like. List goals by placing a *G:* in front of the task (see Figure 12.5).

Figure 12.5
Master Tasks folder and view.

			Subject	Start Date	Due Date	Status	Catego...
			Click here to add a new Task				
	☐		P:Update Videos for 2013	Sat 8/31/2013	Mon 9/16/20...	Not Started	
	☐		G:Perfect Home Life	None	None	In Progress	
	☐		G:Create Life Changing Teaching Material	None	None	In Progress	
	☐		G:Expand Business	None	None	In Progress	
	☐		G:Health and Vitality	None	None	In Progress	
	☐		P:Website Redesign	Tue 4/30/2013	Mon 9/9/2013	Waiting on s...	
	☐		P:Marketing Campaign	Fri 2/1/2013	Fri 12/27/2013	In Progress	
	☐		P: Lesson Changes	Sun 6/2/2013	Wed 8/28/20...	In Progress	
	☑		~~P:Free Intro Lesson~~	~~Mon 3/4/2013~~	~~Tue 7/2/2013~~	~~Completed~~	
	☐		P:Outlook Book Edition 4	Mon 4/1/2013	Sat 8/31/2013	In Progress	
	☐		R:Industry Leader	None	None	In Progress	
	☐		R:Husband	None	None	In Progress	
	☐		R:Compay Leader	None	None	In Progress	
	☐		R:Brother	None	None	In Progress	

And one other very important point: This view is applied in a brand-new Tasks folder. In the old system you shared your current primary Tasks folder for this use, indicating master tasks as tasks with no dates. But no longer; you are now going to create a whole new Tasks folder and call it Master Tasks.

Disadvantages of Using this Folder and View

There are several disadvantages of adopting this master tasks approach. One is you need to modify your To-Do-Bar and To-Do List views so they filter out these entries (as shown in steps ahead). That's because those lists should only show next actions (Lesson 9). Making the filter change is especially a hassle in the To-Do List because you need to do it for all views you are likely to use there. And if you ever find you must reenter the Lesson 3 settings for the To-Do Bar (sometimes needed due to server changes), you'll have to remember to put the filter in there. And finally, those filter modifications cannot be combined with the optional In Folder filter shown in Lesson 3 to remove flagged mail items from the To-Do Bar; you have to choose one or the other.

Because of these many issues, you may *not* want to use Outlook for your master tasks list, but instead use alternate software (such as Excel). That makes sense because you are using very few features of Outlook here — it's just a simple list. If you *do* want to do it in Outlook, here's how:

Create the Master Tasks Folder and View

Note: *The view and folder shown here are* not *included with the MYN-enabled version of the Outlook add-in software ClearContext. You'll need to create it with the following steps.*

There are three distinct steps to creating the master tasks list. First is to create the folder; next is to create the view; and last is to create filters in other views.

Create the Master Tasks Folder

1. Activate the Folder List mode in the Navigation or Folders Pane. To do that: In 2007/10, click the Folder List button at the bottom of the Navigation Pane (Lesson 2). In Outlook 2013, the Folder List button is called Folders, and is probably hidden under the ellipsis at the right end of the data type buttons in the lower-left corner of the Outlook window. Click that ellipsis to find it (Lesson 2).

2. Right-click the primary folder group name in your Outlook Folder list (top of the folder group your Inbox currently resides in) and select New Folder. The Create New folder dialog box is displayed.

3. In the Name field, type "Master Tasks Folder".

4. From the Folder Contains drop-down list, select Task Items.

5. In the Select Where to Place the Folder box, select the name of your main folder group again (as in step 2). Click OK.

   You should now see that new folder appear in your Folder List, as shown here. Again, make sure you activate the complete Folder List view (as described in step 1), or it will not be listed. The new folder should have an Outlook tasks icon (a clipboard with a check mark) next to it. Next you will create the view in that folder.

Create the Master Tasks View

1. Click the new folder in the folder list so it opens in your main Outlook window. It will of course be empty.
   Outlook 2007: In the View menu select Current View, then select Define Views (it's at the bottom of the submenu).
   Outlook 2010, 2013: From the View tab, click Change View, and then click Manage Views.

2. In the upper-right corner, click the New button. Name the view "MYN Master Tasks View". Choose This Folder, Visible Only to Me. Or if you know you will be sharing it, choose This Folder, Visible to Everyone. Click OK.

   Note: I did not select All Task Folders in step 2. This is because I only want this view applied to this specific tasks folder. It might be confusing if I saw this view in other tasks folders, as it is not applicable.

3. In the large stack of buttons click the Columns button (Fields in 2007). Build a field list with the items in the order as shown:

   Icon
   Complete

> Attachment
> Subject
> Start Date
> Due Date
> Status
> Categories

4. Click OK. Click the Sort button and set sorting to (none).

5. Click OK. Then click Apply View.

Filter Master Tasks Out of the To-Do Bar and To-Do List

The To-Do Bar task list and the To-Do List folder views show tasks from all Outlook folders that hold tasks, so these master tasks will show up there. But you don't want that. To keep master task entries from appearing there, you will need to add one more filter to the To-Do Bar and to any views you use in the To-Do List folder. Starting with the To-Do Bar:

1. Right-click anywhere in the To-Do Bar task list header bar (with the heading Task Subject), and select View Settings. (In Outlook 2007 select Custom or Customize Current View.) The dialog box with the large stack of buttons opens.

2. Click the Filter button. Click the Advanced tab.

3. Click the Field button on the left. Select All Task Fields. From the (very long) submenu, select In Folder.

4. Select the condition Doesn't Contain.

5. Type the phrase "Master Tasks" (with the quotation marks) in the Value box. Make sure this wording matches exactly the first two words of your new Master Tasks folder name.

6. Click Add to List.

7. Click OK. Click OK again to return to the To-Do Bar.

8. Repeat these steps for any views you use in the To-Do List folder such as the To-Do List view.

Using the Master Tasks Folder and View

In the future, after selecting the Master Tasks folder, you might need to activate this new view. If so, use the methods in the earlier section "Choosing Between Optional Task Views."

This is a very simple view. Use it this way: Place an entry for each project by creating a task for each one and naming the task <*P:Project name*>; for example, *P:Landscape Front Yard*. Do that now for all your projects. Use a similar *G:* notation to list your goals. Open each project and goal and, in the Notes field for each item, list future tasks that someday might become next-action tasks. You might also want to write in the text field a short narrative of the expected outcome of this project and even a short vision statement.

After all your projects and goals are listed, review the complete project list periodically. During that review, be sure to move to your Now Tasks list any next actions that advance each project or goal. I suggest doing that review in your Monday morning Defer-to-Review session (Lesson 9).

Note: *Readers of the first edition of this book, if you have created this view because you want to continue your previous practice of storing most lower-priority tasks here, you now have a new process for doing that. In the first edition, you set the date fields of a daily task to None to move it to the Master Tasks view. With this new approach, to convert a Now Task to a master task, you drag the task from your Now Tasks list to this new Master Tasks folder. Drag the other direction to promote a master task to a Now Task. Again, however, I highly recommend using Strategic Deferrals instead.*

Other Points

Notice that the start date, due date, and status fields are optional but useful. They are especially useful for projects. Unlike next actions, all projects *could* have distinct due dates; and projects might exist at various levels of status. So use these fields in their traditional ways.

I also left off the Priority field because it is less useful in this view, but feel free to add it if you feel you need it. And I do not filter out completed projects or goals. Those I feel you want to admire for a while. You can delete them later. The Categories column is optional. I use it in case I want to show which project category maps to which project in this list. Usually it's a one-to-one match.

Notice that the sorting was set to None in the configuration steps. This allows you to drag entries into any order you wish, which is useful. Later, you might be tempted to sort by other columns like Due Date or Subject, by clicking at the top of those columns. But after you do that you will lose your ability to drag entries. To get the drag capability back, from the View menu or tab select View Settings (in 2007, Custom or Customize Current View), click the Sort button, and reset the sorting to (none).

Also note that in the first edition of this book, I placed very low-priority tasks, tasks that you may or may not ever get to, ideas, whimsies, low-priority interests, all in the Low priority section of the Master Tasks view. I reviewed that section on a very long cycle and often skipped that review. However, after rethinking this, I've realized that *no matter how low priority a task may seem, you ought to glance at it periodically to see if your interest in it has increased.* Each such item can have a different appropriate schedule to review. So these types of tasks are now made part of the Defer-to-Review process, with generally long review periods assigned (at least six months or more), which are determined individually for each item. For more information, see section "Defer-to-Review Tasks" in Lesson 9.

∎ ∎ ∎

Adding the Concept of Roles to Views

All the views I've shown you so far, whether category based or master-task based, can be expanded to include the concept of *roles*. Stephen Covey in the book *First Things First* talks about periodically reviewing the list of roles and responsibilities you have in your life. He suggests making sure tasks related to those are routinely added to your daily activities. Roles, such as spouse, parent, committee chair, and so on, require more than reactive actions. They require proactive and thoughtful consideration of new activities you might take in the weeks ahead. Around each of these roles it helps, for a brief moment, to consider creative ideas, leadership needs, stakeholder expectations, and even, if the relationships are personal, random acts of kindness—all in support of that role.

Proactive planning like this separates a leader from just a doer. Without proactively placing specific activities on your Now Tasks list or appointment calendar to support these important, but nonurgent, roles, leadership activities toward these roles and responsibilities likely get no attention in the heat of a busy week. When making these entries in your master list, consider using the code *R:* for roles and responsibilities: *R:Team Lead* or *R:Husband.* For examples of how this approach was applied in the Master Tasks view, see the bottom of Figure 12.5.

∎ ∎ ∎

Hierarchical Goal, Project, and Tasks Folders

When you start planning your goals, projects, and tasks, it won't take you long to realize that there is a natural hierarchy that goes something like this: From our goals we create projects and from our projects we create tasks. So we should be able to trace many tasks back to a project and then to a goal. In fact, some people say that *every* task we list we should be able to trace back to a goal, and tasks that are not related to our goals should not even be in our task list.

The logic in this is undeniable. However, the utility of doing much work on it is debatable. Every time I spend much time creating goal→project→task hierarchies I don't get much value out of it compared to the time it takes to create the hierarchies and maintain them. But that's just me, and a large and vocal group of task system users feel very strongly about using such hierarchies in task systems. So to that end, at this link I show you one way to do this in Outlook that works relatively well: www.myn.bz/hierarchy-tasks.htm.

The To-Do Bar Deadline Column

Let's move away from projects and goals and again focus on general tasks. This next view change fulfills a promise I made in Lesson 4 to show you how to add a Deadline column to the To-Do Bar—to replace Outlook's unusable Due Date column.

A Review of Using Task Deadlines

As discussed in Lessons 4 and 6, hard deadlines are not common in next-action tasks. You don't want to create fake deadlines because that will lead to disrespect for any deadline date. Instead, you should use the Target-Now or Defer-to-Do approach (Lesson 9) for tasks that you have strong feelings about completing but that don't have true deadlines.

If you truly have a hard deadline, you can use the DUE [date] designation in the subject line, as described in the Lesson 4 section "Managing Deadlines." I also mention there the option of creating a second task with the start date set to the deadline date and set to a High priority. That's for a bit of insurance.

I mentioned that you cannot use the task Due Date field that already exists in Outlook as a deadline field. That's because it is self-populating; whenever you enter a start date on a task a due date is automatically entered. This defeats the purpose of highlighting only those tasks with true deadlines.

This DUE [date] in the subject line technique works if you have an occasional deadline task. If you tend to have a lot of true deadline tasks, that approach can get tedious, especially if you decide to make duplicate tasks as I just described. So if you have a lot of true deadline tasks, using the new Deadline column is a better way to do this, as I show next.

Create a New Deadline Column

As with the Intrinsic Importance field and column described at the beginning of this lesson, you can create a new user-defined Outlook field and place a corresponding column on the To-Do Bar. In other words, you will have a dedicated column just for deadlines. That way deadlines stand out and you can view them easily. You can sort on the Deadline column to see all upcoming deadline tasks together. Just click on the Deadline column title in the header. You can even create a rule that will highlight a task in red when the deadline is due (that rule is included in these configurations).

However, only add this column if you really need this—only if you really have a lot of true deadlines. I state that caution because this field will occupy a considerable width of scarce screen real estate in the To-Do Bar. I advise users to avoid adding extra columns to the To-Do Bar unless they really need them.

One more point. Like the Intrinsic Importance (II) column defined earlier in this chapter, because this is a user-defined field, the only place you can enter the deadline value for a given task is directly in the To-Do Bar column. You will not be able to show or enter that field within the Task dialog box. You can of course add it to other Tasks folder custom views if you so choose. Here is how your To-Do Bar will look with the Deadline column added:

Adding the Deadline Column to the To-Do Bar

To add the Deadline column and formatting:

Note: *The view change shown here is not included with the MYN-enabled version of the Outlook add-in software ClearContext. You'll need to create it yourself.*

1.   Right-click anywhere in the To-Do Bar task list header bar (with the heading *Task Subject*), and select View Settings. (In Outlook 2007, select Customize Current View or Custom.) The dialog box with the large stack of buttons opens.

2.   Click the Columns button (Fields in 2007). The following dialog box opens.

3. Click the New Column button (New Field in Outlook 2007) in the middle of the dialog box. The following dialog box opens.

4. Matching that dialog box, in the Name field, type "Deadline". Set Type to Date/Time and set Format accordingly.

5. To add the field to the right-hand field list in the Show Fields/Columns dialog box, click OK. If this doesn't work, from the list box in the upper left (Select Available Fields From), select User-Defined Fields in Folder. Then find the Deadline item in the new list that appears on the left. To add it to the list on the right, click the Add button.

6. Move the Deadline field up or down so it is the second from the bottom, as shown in the following figure. Click OK.

7. In the large stack of buttons, click the Conditional Formatting button (Automatic Formatting in Outlook 2007).

8. In the formatting dialog box, click the Add button, and type the title "MYN Deadline Due".

9. Click the Font button. The Font window opens. From the Font Style list in the upper middle section choose Bold. Set the color (lower-left corner) to Red. Click OK.

10. In the formatting dialog box, click the Condition button. In the Filter dialog box that opens, click the Advanced tab. Build the following filter:

   Deadline   on or before   Today

Note: To find the Deadline field, click the Field button and then click User Defined Fields in Folder.

11. Click OK. In the formatting dialog box click OK. In the large stack of buttons click OK. The To-Do Bar is displayed.

You should see the Deadline field in your To-Do Bar. Resize the field width so it's just wide enough to show any dates you enter.

Using the Deadline Column

The only place you can enter the deadline value is in the To-Do Bar column. You cannot add that field to the Task dialog box. In some versions of Outlook, you need to tab over and *type* the date in the field. The date drop-down list does *not* work. I am not sure why.

Use this field only for true deadlines. When the deadline arrives, the task name will be displayed red and bolded. At that point you should immediately move it up to your Critical Now section (by dragging or by resetting the priority to High), because it now meets that definition.

It only makes sense to use this field if the deadline is in the future. If the deadline of a new task is today, placing the task in the Critical Now section accomplishes the same goal: showing the task is due today.

■ ■ ■

Adding the Compact Layout

If you have added the two optional fields described earlier (II and Deadline), the To-Do Bar is probably starting to get too wide. Unless you have a wide-screen monitor, this might encroach on other Outlook columns. If this happens, you can add back in a modified version of the compact task layout (we removed the compact task layout in Lesson 3). That way, you can see more of the other columns and resize your To-Do Bar to be narrower. Figure 12.8 shows the To-Do Bar in compact layout with all other MYN settings.

Figure 12.8
Compact layout in To-Do Bar task list with MYN settings.

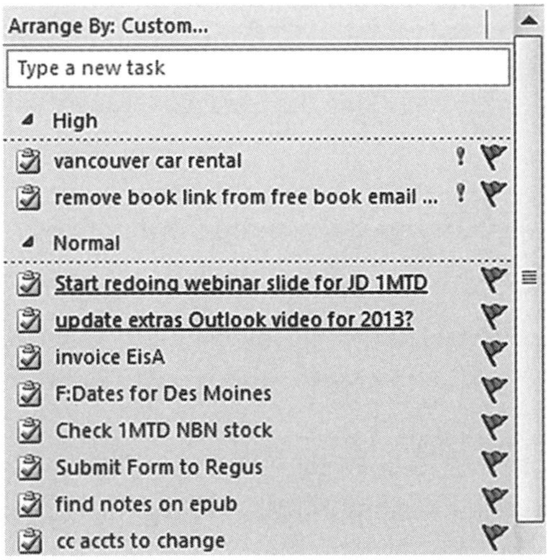

Recall that the compact layout hides fields and combines others (Lesson 2). It also removes the field names from the header bar. In Figure 12.8, the compact layout hides three MYN fields: Start Date, II (Intrinsic Importance), and Deadline. It also merges the Priority field with the end of the Task Subject field.

Notice that while three fields are now missing, most of the MYN information you need is displayed. You don't really need to see the start date, because the sorting gives you the information you need on that. And if you need to change the start date, you can right-click the flag and use some presets, or double-click the task and edit the start date in the Task dialog box. Most of you are probably not using the optional II and Deadline fields, so not seeing them is probably not an issue either. But even if you are, there is still little impact to hiding them. That's because if the II value is above 0 the task will be bolded. And if a Deadline field is set today the task will be bold and red. So really, all your most important information is still visible in the compact layout.

Some key information you cannot see in compact mode is deadlines in the future if you marked them only in the deadline column—not until you drag the To-Do Bar wider than 40 characters. But this is not a showstopper if you use this layout only occasionally, such as when you work on your laptop or Windows 8 tablet while on the road.

To enable the compact layout, follow these steps:

Note: Changing the view as shown here is not included with the MYN-enabled version of the Outlook add-in software ClearContext. You need to create it; however, the changes are minor.

1. Right-click anywhere in the To-Do Bar task list header bar (with the heading Task Subject), and select View Settings. (In Outlook 2007, select Customize Current View or Custom.) The dialog box with the large stack of buttons opens.

2. Click the Other Settings button.

3. At the bottom of that window, in the Other Options section, select Use Compact Layout in Widths Smaller Than. Type "40" in the box. Forty characters is an appropriate threshold given our field count, but feel free to experiment with other values.

4. Click OK, and then OK again.

Now try dragging the left edge of your To-Do Bar wider and narrower, and notice how at some point it switches over to the compact layout. If you want to change the width at which that switch occurs, repeat the steps just shown and change the number 40 to some other value.

After this compact layout is displayed, be mindful of using the controls at the top of the task list. If you click the header and change the Arranged By setting, you will lose the MYN grouping and sort settings and you cannot get them back by clicking something else. You will need to go back into the large stack of buttons dialog box and reset the Priority field grouping and the start date sorting by hand (Lesson 3).

■   ■   ■

Modify the Simple List View

Normally, I don't recommend changing existing Tasks folder views that ship with Outlook. Instead, I have you create new ones with new names. But here is one case where I do recommend changing a default view: the Simple List view.

You should make two small modifications to the Simple List view in all Tasks folders. That's to add the Start Date column and to add the Modified Date column.

As discussed in Lesson 4, the start date is now your main task management date. That's why you are adding the Start Date column. The reason for adding the Modified Date column is less obvious. Here's why to add it: The primary use of the Simple List view, at least for me, is to find misplaced tasks—tasks I accidently marked completed, or tasks I marked to a future date and want to confirm, and so on. Usually I do such a search right after I take the (possibly wrong) action on the task. So by having the Modified Date column and sorting on it, I can see the last task I modified right at the top of the list.

You also may want to add columns commonly used in the To-Do Bar such as Priority and, if you use them, Categories, II, and Deadline, so you can edit them in-line. The last two may be especially important because you cannot edit them when you double-click the task.

Use skills from Lesson 3 to add all these columns.

■ ■ ■

MYN Defer-to-Review View

In Lesson 9 you learned how to use Defer-to-Do and Defer-to-Review MYN processes to defer tasks and keep your Now Tasks list short. You were shown how every Monday a group of Defer-to-Review tasks might pop into your Low priority section, and how you should process those tasks out of there as soon as possible.

You can do all your management of these Defer-to-Review tasks right in the To-Do Bar. But there is a new Tasks Folder view discussed in Lesson 9 you might want to build that gives you a way to do some proactive management. It shows all future Defer-to-Review tasks in a nicely divided collection grouped by week and then by month into the future (see Figure 12.9).

With this view, as you scan each group and see any tasks that you need to reassess sooner, or later, you can simply drag the tasks from one group to the next and the start dates are automatically reset. One benefit of this view is to see what week or month tasks are piling up in, to avoid putting too many tasks into the same review period.

Figure 12.9
MYN Defer-to-Review Tasks custom view.

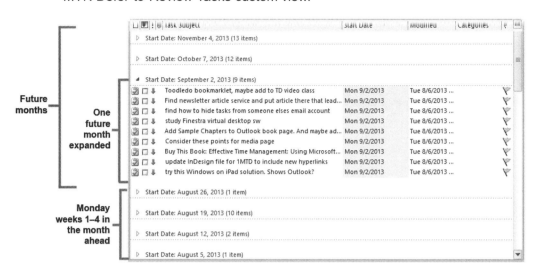

The view is pretty easy to create. You are going to group by Start Date and set the filter to show only Low priority uncompleted tasks. Also turn off the overdue tasks rule in that view—the one that marks old tasks red. I also like to show the Modified Date column—that's so I can see when I last reassessed a particular item. To implement these features, follow these steps.

Note: The MYN Defer-to-Review view shown next (without the optional II column) is included with the MYN-enabled version of the Outlook add-in software ClearContext, which is available from my website (www.myn.bz/clearcontext.htm).

Building the Defer-to-Review View

1. In the lower-left corner of the Outlook window, click the Tasks button. Select the To-Do List folder near the top of the Navigation or Folders Pane.

2. **Outlook 2007**: In the View menu select Current View, then select Define Views (it's at the bottom of the submenu).
   Outlook 2010, 2013: From the View tab, click Change View, and then click Manage Views.

3. In the upper-right corner, click the New button. Name the view "MYN Defer-To-Review Tasks". Select the All Task folders option at the bottom. Click OK.

4. In the large stack of buttons click the Columns button (Fields in 2007). Build a field list with the items in the order as shown:

Icon
Complete (optional)
Priority
Attachment
Task Subject
Start Date
Modified
(optional: add the II user-defined field from earlier)
Categories
Flag Status

Note: If you have trouble finding any of the field names, try selecting All Task Fields in the Select Available Fields/Columns From list box. Task Subject and Flag Status are displayed by selecting All Mail Fields.

5. Click OK.

6. Click the Group By button. Group by Start Date, Descending. To activate the Group By drop-down menu, you might need to clear the check box in the upper-left corner. Click OK.

7. Click the Sort button. Sort on Start Date, Descending. Click OK.

8. Click the Filter button. The Filter dialog box opens. Click the Advanced tab. With the dialog box that is displayed, build the following filter conditions:

   ▶ Make sure the two transition filter conditions are set as follows:

Date Competed	does not exist
Flag Completed Date	does not exist

   ▶ Then add the following:

Priority	equals	Low
Status	not equal to	Completed

9. Click OK.

10. Click the Conditional Formatting button (Automatic Formatting in 2007). Clear the Overdue Tasks rule check box. Click OK, and then OK again. Click Apply View.

Now you can activate this view with the methods in the earlier section "Choosing Between Optional Task Views."

Warning: When using this view, be careful not to click the Categories column heading. The custom grouping will be deleted, and you will need to reconfigure the view to add it again.

Use this view to plan out future task reviews.

.   .   .

MYN All Now Tasks View

The MYN All Now Tasks view is formatted the same as the task list in the To-Do Bar list except it displays all *future* Now Tasks, as well. This view is useful for studying future commitments, or for confirming or editing any future dated tasks you may have just entered.

Use this view primarily for studying future High and Normal priority tasks. For studying future Low priority tasks, I recommend you use the MYN Defer-to-Review view described in the previous section.

Note: *This view replaces the All Daily Tasks view in the first edition of this book.*

Just like in the MYN To-Do Bar settings, this view groups on Priority and sorts on Start Date. It also filters out completed tasks. The II and Deadline fields, described in previous sections of this lesson, can be added as an option, as well.

To add the MYN All Now Tasks view, follow these steps:

Note: *The MYN All Now Tasks view (without the optional columns) is included with the MYN-enabled version of the Outlook add-in software ClearContext, which is available from my website (www.myn.bz/clearcontext.htm).*

1.   In the lower-left corner of the Outlook window, click the Tasks button. Select the To-Do List folder near the top of the Navigation or Folders Pane.

2.   **Outlook 2007**: In the View menu select Current View, then select Define Views (it's at the bottom of the submenu).
Outlook 2010, 2013: From the View tab, click Change View, and then click Manage Views.

3.   In the upper-right corner, click the New button. Name the view "MYN All Now Tasks". Select the All Task folders option at the bottom. Click OK.

4.   In the large stack of buttons click the Columns button (Fields in 2007). Build a field list with the items in the order as shown:

    Icon
    Complete (optional)
    Priority
    Attachment

Task Subject (optional: use Subject so you can sort on it)
Start Date
(optional: add here the II and Deadline fields described earlier in this
lesson)
Categories
Flag Status

Note: *If you have trouble finding any of the field names, try selecting All Task Fields*
in the Select Available Fields/Columns From list box. Task Subject *and* Flag
Status *are displayed by selecting All Mail Fields.*

5. Click OK.

6. Click the Group By button. Group by Priority, Descending. To activate
   the Group By drop-down menu, you might need to clear the check box
   in the upper-left corner. Click OK.

7. Click the Sort button. Sort on Start Date, Descending. Click OK.

8. Click the Filter button. The Filter dialog box opens. Click the Advanced
   tab. In the dialog box that is displayed, build the following filter
   conditions:

   ▶ Make sure the two transition filter conditions are set as follows:

Date Competed	does not exist
Flag Completed Date	does not exist

   ▶ Then add the following:

Status	not equal to	Completed

   Click OK.

9. Click the Conditional Formatting button (Automatic Formatting in 2007).
   In the scrolling list of rules, clear the Overdue Tasks check box. Click OK,
   and then OK again. Click Apply View.

Now you can activate this view with the methods in the earlier section
"Choosing Between Optional Task Views."

Use this view for studying future commitments or for confirming or editing
future dated tasks you just entered. This is the view you use most with delegation (see Lesson 10). Make sure you use the optional Subject field in step 4
for that purpose.

■   ■   ■

The MYN This Week's Tasks View

I described in Lesson 11, in the section "Doing the Math on Your Workweek," a method to figure out how much work you have on your plate by totaling the hours of tasks due this week. I said you could create a special Tasks folder view to help you with this exercise. Well, here are the instructions for creating that view.

There are really two approaches to creating the view needed for the "Doing the Math" activity. You can use one or the other, or both, according to your needs. The first approach identifies all tasks due in the next seven days. If you are doing this exercise on a Wednesday, it will list all tasks scheduled through Tuesday of the following week.

Note: *You might already have a Tasks folder view delivered by default with Outlook called Next Seven Days. This view is* not *configured correctly for our needs. Do* not *use it.*

This seven-day view may (or may not) be what you want. That's because many people use Friday as a natural deadline for a week's worth of tasks. In this case, if you are doing the exercise on a Wednesday morning, you want to see only tasks for the next three days. For this, instead, you need to create a view that displays all tasks in a given calendar week. To create either or both versions of the This Weeks's Tasks view, follow these steps:

Note: *Both views shown next are included with the MYN-enabled version of Outlook add-in software, ClearContext, which is available from my website (www.myn.bz/clearcontext.htm).*

Creating the Views

1. In the lower-left corner of the Outlook window, click the Tasks button. Select the To-Do List folder near the top of the Navigation or Folders Pane.

2. **Outlook 2007**: In the View menu select Current View, then select Define Views (it's at the bottom of the submenu).
    Outlook 2010, 2013: From the View tab, click Change View, and then click Manage Views.

3. In the upper-right corner, click the New button. Name the view "MYN This Week's Tasks". Select the All Task Folders option at the bottom. Click OK.

4. The dialog box with the large stack of buttons opens.

5. In the large stack of buttons click the Columns button (Fields in 2007). Build a field list with the items in the order as shown:

    > Icon
    > Complete (optional)
    > Priority

Attachment
Task Subject
Start Date
Categories
Flag Status

Note: *If you have trouble finding any of the field names, try selecting All Task Fields in the Select Available Fields/Columns From list box.* Task Subject *and* Flag Status *are displayed by selecting All Mail Fields.*

6. Click OK.

7. Click the Group By button. Group by Priority, Descending. To activate the Group By drop-down menu, you might need to clear the check box in the upper-left corner. Click OK.

8. Click the Sort button. Sort on Start Date, Descending. Click OK.

9. Click the Filter button. The Filter dialog box opens. Click the Advanced tab. In the dialog box that is displayed, build the following filter conditions:

▶ Make sure the two transition filter conditions are set as follows:

Date Competed	does not exist
Flag Completed Date	does not exist

▶ If you want to view the Friday week, add the following:

Status	not equal to	Completed
Start Date	this week	
Start Date	on or before	today

Note: The *This Week* filter includes Saturday as well.

▶ If you want to view the seven-day week, instead add:

Status	not equal to	Completed
Start Date	in the next 7 days	
Start Date	on or before	today

If you did these steps correctly, you will end up with five conditions.

10. Click OK.

11. Click the Conditional Formatting button (called Automatic Formatting in 2007). Clear the check box Overdue Tasks.

12. Click OK, then OK again. Click Apply View.

Now you can activate these views with the methods in the earlier section "Choosing Between Optional Task Views."

To use this view, see the section "Doing the Math on Your Workweek" in Lesson 11.

. . .

Summary

We covered many things in this lesson:

▶ To track tasks that relate strongly to your goals and values, consider adding the Intrinsic Importance (II) column to your To-Do Bar.

▶ More about the various task views that come with Outlook, and how to select them.

▶ To ensure that a series of small dependent tasks are tracked together, use series tasks (MORE and PigPog method).

▶ If you plan to track goals and projects, many optional methods are available, including creating some new project and goal views, and a new version of the Master Tasks view.

▶ To create tasks that support your various roles, you can list your primary roles—such as team lead, spouse, parent—on the Master Tasks view and use that list.

▶ It's recommended if many of your tasks have hard deadlines to add the Deadline column to your To-Do Bar. Do this if you have a relatively wide monitor, because it takes up significant screen real estate.

▶ I described adding the compact layout, which is one solution to narrow screens.

▶ To round out your suite of MYN tools, consider adding or making a number of optional Outlook views and view changes.

. . .

Next Steps

It is likely that you selected a small subset of the items in this lesson to actually implement right now, and that makes sense. Over time, however, other tools described in this lesson may become important to you. So do this: Put a task on your task list timed for one month from now to reread this lesson, to see if anything you previously skipped looks useful to you.

. . .

Wrapping Up Total Workday Control

This is the last lesson in the book. Your journey is now complete. You have learned the best task management system available—one based on the most effective practices in the industry. You have learned how to move tasks out of your e-mail and into your task system, thus removing the most common source of out-of-control e-mail. You know how to empty your Inbox and file your mail, helping to keep your workday clear and focused. You have worked through all the principles and applied them in Outlook. Congratulations!

Next is only practice. Plan, a few months from now, to skim through the book again, rereading selected lessons. The book is packed with suggestions, many of which may not sink in until you have used the system awhile. Your use of the system will evolve over time. Rereading will suggest ways of using this information that become apparent to you as you use the system. In particular, Lessons 1, 4, 6, 9, and 12 contain much rich information that subsequent reads can bring to your notice.

But most of all, use the extra time you achieve from this system wisely. You have now mastered something few are able to do: getting everything important done, keeping easy pace with your e-mail, being in control of your workday. These are important skills that will make you more efficient, so use that extra time to leave work at a reasonable hour for a change and spend time with your family. Use that time to do some strategic thinking and planning. And when you do, think big. You are ready for the next level, so start planning to be there.

One last thing. If you find this system is as powerful as I expect at getting your workday under control, consider introducing these concepts to your colleagues. Raising the efficiency of your whole organization is a worthy goal. Notice this, however: While you may be proficient at learning from a book, many people are not. So consider the webinar and in-person training options you can find at my website: www.myn.bz. While there, sign up for the free monthly e-mail newsletter so you are notified of system updates and enhancements.

Appendixes

Appendix A:
Understanding Outlook Folders
in the MYN System

Introduction

Most Outlook users work for years in Outlook without ever really understanding its built-in folder system. For example, few Outlook users realize that an expanded Folder List pane is available. Most do not really understand the file setup behind the mail folders. And a majority of users do not know the difference between an Exchange-based Outlook configuration and a local file–based one. For simple Outlook usage, not understanding those topics is fine. But a whole expanded set of capabilities is available to those who are willing to dig a little deeper.

A deeper understanding of folders will particularly help you get the most from this book. For example, it is worth figuring out whether you are using Exchange Server or not (I discuss that here), because having Exchange gives you access to mobile solutions not possible otherwise. If you are using a Processed Mail folder as in Lesson 5, you may benefit from creating a more intelligent Processed Mail folder placement—I discuss that here as well. The Navigation or Folders Pane in Outlook can be a mystery to use. That mystery is unlocked at the end of this appendix. If you save a lot of e-mail, you need to understand folders to set up an effective archive system. You can learn those folder details here—and you should—before moving on to Appendix B, "Archiving Your Mail in the MYN System."

Let's explore the topic of Outlook folders and their underlying data sources to create the groundwork for a deeper understanding of using the MYN system with Outlook.

Outlook Folders Explained (Windows and Mac)

By Outlook folders I am referring to the hierarchical structure of Outlook data optionally displayed in the Navigation or Folders Pane on the left side of the Outlook window.

Note: Lesson 2 provides an introductory discussion of the Outlook window layout including the Navigation or Folders Pane, along with details on how to manipulate the folder views. If you have not read that yet, I recommend doing so now.

Viewing Folders

The Navigation or Folders Pane on the left side of the Outlook window nearly always displays folders. Figure A.1 shows examples of this pane, across all Outlook versions covered in this book, with the mail folders open.

Figure A.1
Navigation or Folders Panes for Windows Outlook 2007, 2010, 2013, and Outlook for Mac 2011.

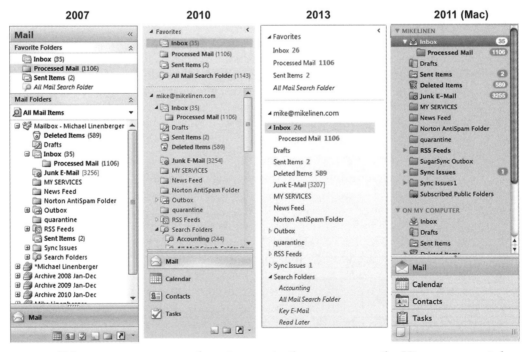

If for some reason you do not see a similar pane, open the View menu or tab and click Navigation Pane or Folders Pane (2013) to activate it (2007/10 users also choose Normal from the submenu). To see the list of mail folders, click the Mail button near the bottom of the left side of the Outlook window.

The Navigation or Folders Pane often shows only a partial list of folders. To see a *full* list of Windows Outlook folders, in Outlook 2007/10, click the Folder List icon at the very bottom of the Navigation Pane (it looks like a folder). Or on the Go menu (2007), choose Folder List. In 2013, click the ellipsis (the three dots) at the right end of the major folder labels in the lower-left corner of the Outlook windows and find the Folders command. The Mac does not have an equivalent capability.

All these actions display the full folder structure across all data types in Windows Outlook. Try that now. When you do, your complete list of all Outlook folders should be displayed on the left side of your screen.

Note: *Later in this appendix you can find a full description of the Outlook Navigation or Folders Pane and the many ways to use it to manipulate folder views.*

Similar to Operating System Folders, But Not the Same

The complete Outlook folder collection I just described may remind you somewhat of your computer's operating system folder and file list as displayed in Windows Explorer (Windows 7 and earlier), or in File Explorer (Windows 8), or in the Mac Finder. The reason they are called folders in Outlook is because if you open any one of them you are likely to see a collection of items contained within, just like physical file folders. But in this case, only a certain type of item exists in each folder. For example, the Inbox folder contains only e-mail items and the Contacts folder contains only contacts items—you can't mix the two types in the same folder. As with operating system folders, you can drag items from one folder to another of the same data types to organize them better. The actual graphics for these folder icons do not look like traditional operating system folder graphics, however. Rather, the artwork represents some reference to the type of data contained within. Nonetheless, they act like the hierarchical folders you have become accustomed to in the Windows Explorer (File Explorer) or Mac Finder file interface.

These Outlook folders are not really operating system folders. They do not correspond one-to-one to actual folders in your computer's file system. Rather, they are *virtual* folder structures visible only from within Outlook. In Windows Outlook, other than the folders in your Exchange mailbox (if you use Exchange Server), a given group of Outlook folders is usually stored together, invisibly, within a single Microsoft Windows file. Knowing about this file and its name will be helpful to you later in this discussion when I show how to create additional folders. It will also be useful when you think more carefully about where to put your Processed Mail folder in Windows. It is similarly helpful when you learn how to archive your mail.

In contrast, Outlook for Mac 2011 uses one file for each e-mail message and Outlook folders there are completely virtual.

Because all Outlook folders are solely owned by Outlook, all your folder creation and manipulation activities must take place from within the Outlook menu system.

Four Major "Buckets" in Outlook

The folder list within your copy of Outlook may have just one high-level group of folders (see the 2010 section of Figure A.1), or it may have multiple high-level groups of folders (as in the 2007 section of Figure A.1). Each group represents a different "bucket" of information and each group corresponds to different Outlook data files. Each group might have similar-looking items in it (there may be an Inbox within each group, for instance), but each default group or bucket of information has a distinct and different functional purpose within your usage of Outlook. Furthermore, the files corresponding to these buckets may be stored in different locations: some on a server, some on your local hard drive.

Outlook can typically have up to four different buckets or types of information that correspond to these groups of folders (three on the Mac):

► Exchange Server Mailbox (usually one, but there may be several if you have multiple accounts)

► Local Folders (usually called Personal Folders or My Outlook Data File in Windows, and called On My Computer on the Mac)

► Archive Folders (not present on the Mac)

► Public Folders (optionally present if you use Exchange)

Note: If you use Outlook add-in software, such as Business Contact Manager, you may see additional types of folder groups. And you may see RSS feeds and other informational "folders."

Exchange Server Mailbox

The first group type, the Exchange Server Mailbox, is the most common data type in large companies. If you have more than one e-mail account, you may have multiple groups. The folders displayed in this group represent data stored on a central Microsoft Exchange Server. Server-based data like this enables several advantages. I provide more information on this ahead.

Local Folders

A local folders group represents mail stored on your computer or on a locally networked file system that acts similarly to data stored on Exchange Server, but it is somewhat limited in its capabilities. If you are using Outlook at home, or in a small business without Exchange Server, this will be your only choice for displaying recent Outlook data. Even if you are working in a company with Exchange Server, adding local folders is a good way to store local copies of your Exchange Server–based data. You might have several local folder groups. You may have additional e-mail accounts here.

In Windows Outlook 2007 or older, local folders are called Personal Folders, but they may be labeled differently. In 2010 and 2013, new local folders are initially labeled My Outlook Data File, but they may be labeled differently on your computer. On the Mac local folders are called and labeled as On My Computer folders. I describe all of these ahead in the section "Local Folders."

Note: In addition to Exchange and local folders/Internet mail, there is IMAP server–based mail that acts similar to Exchange but has fewer features. I do not cover IMAP in this appendix.

Archive Folders (Windows)

The third type of data folder you may have if you use Windows is the Archive Folders group. The Archive Folders group is really just another local folder group, with the added feature of automatic copying of data into it. In Outlook 2010 and 2013 this group may be labeled Archives. You can optionally use Archive Folders in the MYN system. See Appendix B for a full discussion of archiving, the Archive Folders group, and how to archive in the MYN system.

Public Folders (Windows and Mac)

The last of the major data buckets in Outlook that you are likely to see in your folder list is Public Folders. You will see these folders only if you are working within an Exchange Server environment. They are usually configured by your Exchange administrators and show up automatically in your folder list. These are shared Outlook accounts that multiple users can read and in some cases contribute to. The most common use of public folders in the companies where I have consulted is to display public calendars containing the schedules of shared resources in the company (conference rooms, equipment, and so on). These do not play a role in the MYN system.

Folder Group Contents

Each of these four types or buckets of folder groups can, within them, hold one or more Mail folders, Calendar folders, Contacts folders, Tasks, Notes, and so on. While a single bucket is really all you need, you may want to use more than one bucket to help organize your information. The additional groups of folders allow you to create alternative structures to separate your information logically. They also provide optional data archiving structures. And depending on your work environment, you could actually be required to use certain types of these folder sets — you may have no choice. Let's explore these concepts.

■   ■   ■

Exchange Server Mailbox

The most important thing to know about these groups of folders is whether your copy of Outlook is set up as part of Microsoft Exchange Server. Many large corporations (and even many medium-size and small businesses) use Exchange Server as part of their Outlook deployment. In contrast, if you work with Outlook from a home business, you most likely do not use Exchange Server (but you can—see the "Hosted Exchange Accounts" section ahead for more information).

Determining If Your Copy of Outlook Uses Exchange Server

There are a number of ways to determine whether you are using Exchange Server. Ask your technical staff; they should know. But, if you want to check for yourself, do this:

▶   In Outlook 2007, go to File menu>Data File Management>E-mail tab, and look for the word *Exchange* under the Type column.

▶   In Outlook 2010 and 2013, go to the File tab>Info>Account Settings>Account Settings>E-mail tab, and look for the phrase *Microsoft Exchange* under the Type column.

▶   On the Mac go to the Outlook menu>Preferences>Accounts (under Personal Settings) and select your default account. Look for the word *Exchange* on the right, at the top.

If you are in an Exchange environment, the key distinction is that your primary e-mail, appointments, contacts, and tasks folders are stored on a central mail server shared by others in your company. If you are not in an Exchange environment but are solely using local folders (Windows) or On My Computer folders (Mac), your primary folders are instead stored within a simple file structure on your computer. Their content is periodically updated, most likely by accessing an Internet mail service.

Why Use an Exchange Server?

You may wonder: Why do companies often use Exchange? What does an Outlook user gain by using Exchange Server over just local folders with an Internet mail server, or over other types of servers? The advantages include extra features such as mobile access, potentially lower costs, and security.

Exchange Server Feature Advantages

The primary advantage of using Exchange is the wide set of features that Exchange offers to Outlook users—like seamless integration with other Microsoft Office applications. Exchange has extra intelligent features such as scheduling tools, shared e-mail distribution lists, ability to recall messages, Out of Office Assistant, public folders, integration with SharePoint, and voting capabilities, to name a few. For MYN users, one useful advantage of working with Exchange Server is the ability to add wireless synchronization of your tasks with multiple mobile devices. Because of these extra capabilities, many companies opt for Exchange Server.

Note: *Other than mobile connectivity, most of these features are not pertinent to this book. Knowing whether you are on Exchange Server, however, is necessary for making some decisions later in this appendix regarding Processed Mail folder placement options.*

Exchange Server Cost and Security Advantages

The other advantage can also be a lower cost to the business. The usual alternative to Exchange Server, when using Outlook as a client, is Internet-based e-mail. This is usually cheaper if you have few users, but at high user counts, Exchange may be cheaper. Why? With Exchange Server, your company hosts the e-mail accounts "internally." Costs for all users can be spread across your internal Exchange Server investment, so it can be cheaper (but not always). Also, many companies like the idea of having their e-mail on their own internal servers—for security reasons.

Other Exchange Server Advantages

Another advantage when using Exchange is that, like browser-based e-mail, you are essentially looking at the live contents of a server, not a local copy of your latest mail download (although Outlook does cache server mail so you can work offline). Because it is server based, compared to using local folders only as described below, you can usually move from computer to computer within your organization and, with a few setup steps, access all your mail.

Hosted Exchange Accounts

Even if you work from a home office or for a small business that has not installed Exchange Server, you can gain the extra benefits of Exchange by signing up with a hosted Exchange service you can reach over the Internet. It provides an experience nearly identical to having Exchange in your organization without any of the server maintenance headaches. With most hosted service providers you can purchase either an individual account (for example, you work alone at home) or a set of accounts (you own a small business with multiple employees). Accounts go for as little as $3 for each user per month. Although you reach these servers over the Internet, this is not your typical Internet e-mail account, but a full Exchange account with all of its benefits. Search the Internet on the term *Exchange Hosting* to find such a provider. Microsoft offers them in a service called Exchange Online. GoDaddy.com also offers Exchange Server hosting. My company uses an Exchange Server hosting service called Intermedia.

■ ■ ■

Local Folders

Local folders are Outlook data files stored on your local hard drive (and possibly on a corporate file server). They are used as your primary data storage if you are using an Internet-based mail account. And they can be used for secondary "offline" storage; more on that ahead. In Windows they are often labeled Personal Folders or My Outlook Data File. On the Mac they are labeled On My Computer.

Local Folders in Windows Outlook

Windows Outlook users, if you know that you are *not* working in an Exchange Server environment, then you are likely storing your primary e-mail, appointment, contacts, and tasks folders in an Outlook personal folders file. What does this mean? It means that your primary Outlook data is probably stored on your local computer. When you open your Inbox, for example, you are looking at a list of mail stored within a file on your computer. You must periodically synchronize that Inbox with your Internet e-mail provider to keep it up to date (this is probably set to happen automatically). Many Exchange users also add local folders to Outlook so they can move mail to it from their Exchange mailbox, if that starts to get full.

On My Computer (Mac)

Outlook for Mac 2011 shows its local files in its On My Computer folders, and you may see that term in various places on the Navigation Pane (see Mac section of Figure A.1). On My Computer folders are usually there because you are using an Internet mail account. But even with Exchange they may appear in the Navigation Pane depending on settings in your Outlook Preferences. They'll appear either as an additional Inbox, or as an entire ON MY COMPUTER section lower in the Navigation Pane, as it is in the Mac section of Figure A.1. I discuss how to make those settings in the section ahead "Viewing and Creating Local Folders on Outlook for Mac 2011."

Outlook Calendar, Contacts, Tasks Are Usually Not Known to Internet Mail

Looking beyond your Inbox, the other folders visible in Outlook—Calendar, Contacts, Tasks, and so on—are also only on your local folders file if you do not have Exchange. These other folders usually have nothing to do with your Internet mail provider. They are concepts known only to Outlook and only stored locally when using local folders as your main mailbox. That greatly limits your mobility and is why, especially if you use Outlook tasks, I recommend you get an Exchange account. That said, there are several services which can be utilized to keep those local files synced with online calendar and contacts lists. Microsoft, Apple, Google, and others offer cloud services for this (beyond the scope of this book).

Mixing Local Folders with Exchange Folders

While local folders are *required* if all you have is an Internet e-mail account, local folders can be *optionally* used or added if you have an Exchange account. If used, they exist in addition to the Exchange mailbox set of folders. The 2007 section of Figure A.1 shows such a situation in Windows. The top group of folders represents the Exchange folders, and the bottom group represents a set of local folders. Same with the Mac portion of Figure A.1. In some MYN e-mail storage scenarios (described ahead), if you are an Exchange user you will want to also use local folders in your mail filing strategy.

Local Folders as Locally Saved Mail or Archives

A more significant reason for using a set of local folders along with an Exchange Outlook configuration is this: The mailbox on Exchange Server tends to fill up quickly and, in companies with hundreds or thousands of users, these mailboxes consume considerable central server storage. Excess Exchange Server storage can slow mail performance. Your IT staff does not like this, so they put size limits on the amount of mail you are allowed to store on Exchange Server. It is likely that you will reach those limits well before your interest in the old mail stored there has passed.

So you need to find a place to store your old mail, either as a place where you can get at it quickly, or for long-term archiving. Local folders created on your local computer (or elsewhere) are perfect for this. They look just like folders on Exchange Server but are accessible separately from Exchange. Therefore, as your mail ages, you can manually drag it from your Exchange mailbox to your local folders, thus freeing up the Exchange space and providing long-term storage of your older mail.

Note: *This is one advantage of having an Internet account over a typical space-restricted Exchange account. With an Internet account and a local folders–based Inbox, you have complete control over your primary Inbox and can let it fill up with much more mail before needing to invoke space management techniques (but don't forget to add a backup capability).*

Local Folders as a Filing System

Another reason for using local folders is this: Within a local folders group you can create multiple folders and nested folders with names that match filing classifications or for mail archiving. For example, as you finish reading mail in your primary Inbox you can move that mail to a variety of intelligently named folders and folder groups where it will be easier to find later if needed. This is a very common technique used by many Outlook users to help organize their massive amounts of mail, and to save space on their servers. Creating multiple personal folders for filing works whether you use Exchange or an Internet mail server.

Notice that you do not have to create these custom folders within local folder groups. You can create your own named folders right within your Exchange

344 Total Workday Control Using Microsoft Outlook

Server folder group if you want, and still file out of your Inbox. That is what you did in Lesson 5. If you store those new folders on Exchange you may be limited by server storage, so keep that in mind. I address that issue below.

In all cases, you can add as many additional folders as you like. You can nest folders within other folders to create as deep a folder hierarchy as you like.

Local Folders as a Possible Place to Put the MYN Processed Mail Folder

In the MYN system, as we saw in Lesson 5, you file throughout the day by dragging all mail from your Inbox to a *single* folder called the Processed Mail folder. From there you can use various filing strategies (described in Lesson 8). In Lesson 5, you learned one way to set up that Processed Mail folder, but you can actually use a few different scenarios for setting that up. Internet mail users will of course store that folder in a local folder group—you have no choice. If you use Exchange, and if you have storage limits on your Exchange mailbox (most Exchange users do), two optional setup scenarios allow you to store that Processed Mail folder in a local folders group, which you might like. I will cover that below.

Local Folders and Outlook Web Access/App or Mobile Devices

While local folders are a great way to get mail off Exchange Server, there is one aspect of their use along with Exchange you need to consider. Local folders you create outside of Exchange are not visible to Outlook Web Access/App or to your mobile devices that synchronize wirelessly to Exchange Server. The synchronization process does not see them.

Note: *Outlook Web Access (Called Outlook Web App in newer versions of Exchange Server) is also referred to as OWA. It is the Internet web browser version of Microsoft's Outlook e-mail. If when away from the office you access your company's Outlook e-mail through Internet Explorer or some other browser, you are probably using Outlook Web Access/App.*

Normally, using OWA or a mobile handheld device with Exchange is not a problem because most people do not empty their Inbox for weeks or months at a time and so can easily see older mail; it is all still on Exchange. In the MYN system, however, I encourage you to empty your Inbox daily. In Lesson 5, I instruct you to place the Processed Mail folder in a place that is still on Exchange; if you do that, all still works. But ahead I suggest you consider alternative scenarios that place the Processed Mail folder in a local folders group. So if you want to use OWA or a synchronized mobile device to read older mail (mail moved out of your Inbox), that will be a factor when deciding if those alternatives will work for you. You'll see all that when you get to the next section. But notice this for now: If all you do with OWA or a mobile device is check *brand-new mail*, you are fine with Lesson 5 configurations. The new configurations described ahead are only important if you use these devices to work with mail older than a day or so. Again, that's because, in the MYN system, you will move that mail out of your Inbox.

Considerations When Creating Local Folders in Windows

Local folders in Windows Outlook will usually be organized in groups and each group usually represents a separate file. Let me explain what that means and why that may be important.

The .pst (PST) File

If you decide to change your Processed Mail folder setup as described in the sections below, or if you choose to set up an archive plan in Appendix B, then you may be creating a local folder group and file. In case you have never created a local group before, notice that adding a local group is a two-step process. First, you create a special Outlook data file (which is stored within the Windows operating system). That adds the new group to the folder list in Outlook. You will see the new group appear on the left side of your Outlook window. Second, you add logical Outlook folders to that group.

It should be clear now that each group of local folders in your folder list corresponds to one Windows operating system data file that you (or your IT staff) added. If you were to look at that file in Windows, you would see that it is named by default either Outlook.pst or PersonalFolders(n).pst, or, in Outlook 2010 and 2013, My Outlook Data File(n).pst (where n is an incremented number that starts at 1 and gets larger as you add additional personal folders files). Notice the file extension ".pst" — that is unique to the Outlook local folders data file. You will see references to .pst files (often called PST files) elsewhere in this book and in other Outlook books. Knowledge of this data file becomes important for several reasons. The first is for deciding what file format to use when creating new local folders groups.

The .pst File Format Starting in Outlook 2003 and Beyond

In the steps below, when creating a new local folders file, you may be asked to select which .pst file format you want to use. Let me explain the background behind that because the choice is very important.

Starting with Outlook 2003 (and continuing with Outlook 2007/10/13) Microsoft introduced an optional new local folders file format that has a much larger personal folders file size limit. Where the technical limit of the older format is 2 GB, the technical limit of the new format is 20 GB.

If you use the newer format when you create your Processed Mail local folders group, it provides a number of advantages when planning your folder strategy. The primary advantage is that, because its capacity is so large, in many folder scenarios archiving old mail out of that folder group is needed much less often (perhaps years between each archiving).

The only slight disadvantage is that this new file format may not be backward compatible with Outlook 2002 or older mail you may have stored prior to upgrading. You may need to keep these two data types separate. If you have just upgraded from 2002 or older (to 2003 or 2007/10/13) and are trying to mix your older mail into a new local folders group, you may see Outlook errors. Rather, to be safe, stay completely with the old format, or use the new file format only for new mail.

The steps below specify clearly how to choose the new format. You just need to decide if you are happy with segregating old Outlook 2002 (or older) mail storage. My recommendation is to do that segregation. Leave the old mail in its own old file and always go with the new file format when creating new personal folders files.

Why is this so important? As I said earlier, the older format is officially limited to 2 GB of storage, which may seem like a lot. However, in my experience, and the experience of others, when the file gets larger than 500 MB it can become unstable and unusable without warning. I know many users who have lost entire mail collections as a result. And with high mail volumes or large attachments, many users can reach 500 MB in well under six months.

That said, many IT departments using Outlook 2003 or 2007 still choose the older format by default when they help their staff create personal folders, either out of ignorance or because they are concerned about compatibility with older mail. That's why in the steps below to create the Processed Mail folder, even if you already have an old local files group in place in your folder list, I want you to create a new group. That way you can ensure that you use the new larger file format.

Note: *You may be wondering how you can determine whether a .pst file currently in use in your copy of Outlook has the new or old format. Here is how. From Outlook's File menu, Outlook 2007 users choose Date File Management. Outlook 2010/13 users from the File tab select Account Settings, and Account Settings again. Then, click the Data Files tab. Select the file of interest in the list of data files, click the Settings button, and in the window that opens, examine the Format field. If you see Personal Folders File (97-2002) in that field, that .pst file is in the old format.*

Note: *The .pst file approach is gradually being replaced in newer versions of Exchange. In Exchange 2010, a new server-based Personal Archives option was introduced. In Exchange 2013 it's now called In-Place Archiving. Both give the option of placing archived mail in a central server location. Check with your IT department to determine if this is available in your organization. For more information, see: www.myn.bz/PersonalArchives.htm. Because this new option is not yet in widespread use, all instructions in this lesson assume you are still using a .pst file approach.*

Deciding Where to Store the Local Folders File

The first step when adding a new local folders group is to consider *where* to store the data file. If this is a home or very small business computer, the default location proposed by Outlook as you start to create the file is probably the correct location; it is usually on your local hard drive. Just make sure you are backing these files up.

If you work in a larger organization, the choice might be more complicated. Ask your IT department. If your IT department has no policy on where to store Outlook personal folders files, read below to help decide where to put these new files.

If Your Company Uses File Servers for Local Files

Some companies require or recommend the use of central file servers for all "local" files. This is to enable easier automatic backups and easier movement of employees between multiple computers. In this case you will probably want to store the .pst file on that central file server instead of on your hard drive. For instance, a company I consulted with had a central file server available and encouraged its staff to store their local files there. It issued file server space to all of its employees and mapped that space on all corporate computers to a logical drive called the "P: drive" ("P" stood for "Personal"). Other organizations may use a different letter like *H:* or *S:* and so on. At this company, in their standard configuration, the Windows My Documents folder was also mapped to this server space. So, all "locally" saved files were actually saved to this file server, which was backed up nightly. If you work in a company with a similar arrangement, this automatic backup service is quite valuable and something you will probably want to take advantage of when deciding where to store your Outlook .pst file. Storing your .pst files on the server also enables you to get at your stored mail if you are logging on from another computer on the corporate network, or if you are working remotely over a wide area network connection or VPN. So if your company uses file servers for local files I recommend you store the personal folders file there.

If Your Company Does Not Use File Servers for Local Files

If your company does not use file servers for local files, determine if your company provides over-the-network backup services for your desktop computer, and which drive on your desktop computer is normally backed up. That's where you want to put your .pst file. This is not a common IT service, however, so it is unlikely that you have this.

If no over-the-network backup is available, determine if you have multiple hard drives or partitions in your desktop computer and see if one is dedicated to data storage: plan to use that one. You may need to ask your IT department about that. It is probably called the *D:* drive, but it might be something else. If you only have one drive or partition, probably the *C:* drive, use that; most likely Outlook will default to it.

If you do use your computer's hard drive, I would also ask your IT department if they can arrange a backup solution for it. I consider saved mail important data and would insist on some sort of backup plan.

Viewing and Creating Local Folders on Outlook for Mac 2011

As stated earlier, local folders on Outlook for Mac 2011 are called On My Computer folders. To ensure that you can see your On My Computer folders in the Navigation Pane, go to Outlook>Preferences>General and clear the check box next to Hide On My Computer Folders. Also, to make the list of local folders more clear, in that same general settings dialog box, clear the check box next to the setting Group Similar Folders, Such as Inboxes, from Different Accounts. I discuss this control more later in this appendix, but leave the check box cleared for now.

Next, look in the Navigation Pane. If you have an Exchange account, you will see the folders associated with Exchange at the top. Below that you will see a section called ON MY COMPUTER with (if Mail is selected) a set of five folders below it by default.

These default folders in this lower section start out empty. They are local storage areas that you can use to offload data from Exchange Server.

Note: Unlike Windows Outlook, local folders in one group on the Mac are not stored in one Mac OS file. Rather, they are a collection of Mac OS files (one for each e-mail message).

You can use the predelivered mail folders under ON MY COMPUTER to store mail moved from your Exchange account. Or you can add more folders there by selecting the ON MY COMPUTER label and CTRL-clicking it, and then choosing New Folder—perhaps adding a Processed Mail folder. Or you can add subfolders to the existing five folders. Notice that you cannot delete or rename the original five folders; they are part of the system.

Of course, if you have no Exchange account, the ON MY COMPUTER section will be your only section.

■   ■   ■

Strategies for Setting Up Your Processed Mail Folder

The previous section can help you in defining a strategy for setting up your Processed Mail folder. If you were directed here from Lessons 5 or 8 to enhance your Processed Mail folder configuration, now you are ready. Let's start with some review of how the Processed Mail folder is used in the MYN system.

In Lesson 5, I described a simple filing system of dragging mail from your Inbox to a single Outlook folder called the Processed Mail folder. The main goal was to empty your Inbox daily, after you extracted tasks. After mail was in the Processed Mail folder, you were invited to leave it there and search it in bulk when needed, preferably using one of the new fast search engines available in Outlook. In Lesson 8, I took filing to the next step. If you wanted topic-based filing, you applied Outlook Categories to mail in the Processed Mail folder, and grouped on Categories when searching for mail.

So, central to the MYN system filing approach is the Processed Mail folder. It is what makes daily emptying of your Inbox possible. It is what makes Outlook Category–based filing so useful.

Refining the Processed Mail Folder Configuration

In Lesson 5 you created the Processed Mail folder as a subfolder of your Inbox. That placement is the most flexible and it is a quick solution for the early stages of using the MYN system. However, you now might want to refine that setting. First, I want you to answer a few questions. After the answers are explained, you can decide to keep your original Processed Mail folder configuration, or extend it, or replace it.

▶ Which do you use: Exchange-based mail or Internet-based mail?

▶ Is there a highly-restrictive size limit on your Exchange mailbox?

▶ Are you using Outlook Web Access/App (OWA) or a mobile device synchronized with Outlook to view mail older than a day or so?

Your answers to these questions will lead to one of three Processed Mail folder configurations (A, B, and C). The bullets below help you decide which configuration to choose, and the table that follows summarizes the same information. After that, full descriptions of each configuration and how to implement them follow. Here is how to determine which of the configurations is for you:

▶ If you are using an Internet-based mail service in Outlook, use configuration A, which is simply to leave the settings as they were in Lesson 5, with the Processed Mail folder as a subfolder of your Inbox.

▶ With Exchange, if there is no size limit (or it is very large, say six months' worth of mail or more), do the same as the previous bullet: use configuration A. That is, leave the settings as they were in Lesson 5, with the Processed Mail folder as a subfolder of your Inbox.

▶ If your Exchange implementation *does* impose a highly-restrictive size limit but you are *not* using OWA or a mobile device synchronized with Outlook to view older mail, use configuration B, which is to create a local folder group and to place the Processed Mail folder in there. This prevents "Your Mailbox Is Full" messages and possible inability to use mail. I'll describe how to set that up in a moment.

▶ If your Exchange implementation does have a highly-restrictive size limit and you *are* using OWA or a mobile smartphone or tablet device synchronized with Outlook, use configuration C, which is a combination of configuration A and B. That is, leave the Processed Mail folder as a subfolder of your Inbox and *add* the configuration B local folders group as a place to move your oldest Processed Mail folder mail, every few days. This allows you to see your old mail on your OWA or mobile device and it gives you a place to put the oldest mail when you get the "Your Mailbox Is Full" message.

All this is summarized as a table in Figure A.2.

Figure A.2
Processed Mail folder configuration options.

MYN Processed Mail Folder Configurations	Restricted size limit on Exchange Inbox	No limit or generous size limit on Exchange Inbox (or using Internet mail)
Using OWA or mobile device to view older mail	Processed Mail Configuration C	Processed Mail Configuration A
NOT using OWA or mobile device to view older mail	Processed Mail Configuration B	

Processed Mail Folder, Configuration A (Windows and Mac)

This configuration is for those without restrictive size limits on their Inbox. You might be an Exchange user lucky enough to be in an organization that does not impose limits, or you might be an Internet mail user. The action in this configuration is simply to just leave the settings as they were at the end of Lesson 5, where the Processed Mail folder is made a subfolder of your Inbox. In case you did not do that yet, go to the Lesson 5 section "Emptying Your Inbox—Step 1: Creating the Processed Mail Folder," and follow the instructions there.

After that is done, your folder should be indented as shown here.

Processed Mail Folder, Configuration B (Windows and Mac)

If your Exchange implementation *does* impose a restrictive size limit but you are *not* using OWA or a mobile device synchronized with Outlook to view older mail, use configuration B, which is to place the Processed Mail folder in a local folders group. This prevents you from exceeding your Exchange limit because, using MYN processes, you are constantly dragging mail out of your Exchange Inbox into your local folders. So you will probably never again get the "Your Mailbox Is Full" message.

The steps below show how to create this setup. But Windows users, before proceeding, be sure to read all the prior sections of this appendix so you fully understand how local .pst folder files work and how to create them. You will need this understanding for the next steps, and you should decide before you start where you are going to store the new personal folders file.

Mac users have it easier; you simply create a folder in the ON MY COM-PUTER section.

The steps for Windows are covered first, followed by instructions for the Mac.

Configuration B in Windows Outlook

1. Open the File menu and choose Data File Management (2010/13 users open the File Tab, choose Account Settings, and Account Settings again). The following dialog box will open. Activate the Data Files tab as shown here.

2. Click Add. Outlook 2010 and 2013 users, go to next step. In 2007 a dialog box opens showing two types of storage. The file type you want is labeled Office Outlook Personal Folders File (.pst). Click OK.

3. A Create or Open dialog box appears, where you can name the file and indicate where in the file system to store it. In 2010 and 2013, at the

bottom of that dialog box is a drop-down menu labeled Save As Type. Choose Outlook Data File (.pst). All versions, in the Name field type "Filed E-mail" or something similar. Name it in a way that distinguishes it from your other folder groups. In 2010 and 2013, this will become the name of the new local folders group in your folder list (for 2007 you set that name in step 4).

All versions, in most cases you simply click OK on this dialog box to accept the default file location. Home or small office users will probably do that.

You may have decided, though, when reading the section "Deciding Where to Store the Local Folders File," to use a different location. Your IT department may require a specific location. You change locations by using the standard file system controls in that dialog box to navigate through your folder and file system. If you have no idea how to do that, ask a knowledgeable colleague or your IT department for advice (there are so many possible locations, being more specific is beyond the scope of this book). After you have navigated to the correct location, click OK in the dialog box.

4. 2010 and 2013 users, skip to step 5. For 2007, whether you use a local location or a network location in step 3, the following dialog box opens:

In the Name field type "Filed E-mail" or something similar to match the name you gave in step 3. This will be the name of the new local folders group in your folder list, so name it in a way that distinguishes it from your other folder groups. You are able to assign a password to the file if you like. I recommend the default choice—no password. In other words, after typing the name, simply click OK. (You might consider using a password if this file is stored in a location accessible to others.)

5. For all versions, you'll be returned to the Outlook Data Files dialog box shown in step 1. There you will see that your new data file has been

added. Click OK to close that. More important, if you look in the Navigation or Folders Pane on your main Outlook window, you will see that a corresponding new folders group has been added (in 2007 it will have the same name you entered in step 1).

6. Next, you will create the new folder within that new folder group. Do this by right-clicking the folder group in the Outlook folder list (in the Navigation or Folders Pane), then choosing New Folder from the shortcut menu, which opens a dialog box. In the Name box type "Processed Mail" and leave all the other settings alone. Click OK, and you should see the new folder appear in your Navigation Pane, within that group, ready for immediate use.

7. If you are collecting all your sent mail in the Sent Items folder, then I also recommend you create another folder, called Saved Sent Mail, within the same folder group. Use this to periodically drag mail from the Sent Items folder; doing that also helps you avoid exceeding your Exchange limits. Repeat step 6 to do that, just changing the folder name to Saved Sent Mail.

Configuration B in Outlook for Mac 2011

If you are using Exchange with Outlook for Mac 2011, you can use the On My Computer Inbox as a place to create your Processed Mail file. You can either create it at the same level as the other existing five folders there (my recommendation), or perhaps make it a subfolder of your Inbox; but I see no advantage to the latter. To do the first, select the ON MY COMPUTER group, CTRL-click it, and choose New Folder. Then rename the new folder Processed Mail.

This Processed Mail folder is where you will place mail dragged from your Inbox every day. Similarly, use the existing Sent Items folder there to store older sent mail. Or create a new folder and call it Saved Sent Items, to prevent confusion.

Processed Mail Folder, Configuration C (Windows and Mac)

If your Exchange implementation *does* have a size limit and you *are* using OWA or a mobile device to view older mail, use this Processed Mail folder configuration. This is simply a combination of configurations A and B. This allows you to see your new and moderately old mail on OWA or a mobile device, and it gives you a place to move your much older mail when your Exchange mailbox fills up.

Note: *Windows users, this scenario, of the three, will benefit most from using Windows Outlook AutoArchive recommendations in Appendix B. If you decide to do those, only do step 1 below (which you may have already done), and then skip to Appendix B and use AutoArchive scenario 2 there. However, only consider doing that if you have a half day to read and follow those instructions; they are complicated. If you do not have that time, continue with step 2 below for now, in which case you are building a form of manual archiving into the configuration. You can always come back to Appendix B AutoArchive steps later.*

Here are the steps for Windows and Mac:

1. Per configuration A, leave the Processed Mail folder as a subfolder of your Inbox (as in Lesson 5) or follow the configuration A steps to create it now.

2. Next, follow the configuration B steps (Windows or Mac as appropriate). There is one small and optional modification to the steps I just showed. Name the folder Older Processed Mail, or something similar. That way you do not get it confused with the Processed Mail folder in the upper part of the Navigation Pane.

Here's how to use the folder created in step 2. The next time you get a "Your Mailbox Is Full" message from Exchange, drag the oldest mail from the Processed Mail folder under your Inbox to the folder created in step 2. Or do that every few days just to stay ahead of those messages. One way to stay ahead is to check the folder group size of your Exchange mailbox and compare it to known limits. I show how to do that next. And when you do move mail, do not forget to drag mail from the Sent Items folder periodically to the folder you have decided to place saved sent mail in.

Note: These instructions correspond to the scenario 2 manual-archiving setup in Appendix B.

∎   ∎   ∎

Checking Outlook Folder Sizes (Windows and Mac)

Configuration C has you move mail from your Exchange mailbox into local folders, after your Exchange mailbox gets close to its limits. So it is good to know what your mailbox limits on Exchange are (ask your IT staff; they know). That way you can monitor the size of the Exchange mailbox and start moving mail after it gets close to the limit. You can of course wait until you get a message saying it is full, but that usually happens at the worst possible time and often shuts down your ability to send or receive mail.

Here is how to check your folder size. In Windows you can use this both on Exchange Server folders and on local folders. You may want to check local folders as well because, at least in Windows, they have limits too, as discussed near the beginning of this appendix. On the Mac you can only check the size of Exchange-based folders using the method I show next. On the Mac, *local* folder limits are based on your hard drive size; just monitor free space on that to see if you are running out of local folder room.

No matter whether you are checking an Exchange folder or a local folder (the latter in Windows), you will always check the size of the highest-level folder or group as a whole.

Steps to Check Folder Size

1. Right-click (CTRL-click on Mac) the Exchange mailbox group in the Navigation Pane (or the local folders group if checking local folder sizes in Windows). Always select the highest level of the folder group hierarchy.

2. Choose Properties (Folder Properties on the Mac) on the shortcut menu (it might say "Properties for" or "Data File Properties" and then, if given a choice, the group name).

3. In Windows, in the dialog box that opens, click the button in the lower left titled Folder Size, and then either click the Server Data tab or the Local Data tab (depending on which you are checking). On the Mac, select Storage. The following dialog box opens (or something similar).

	Folder Size	✕

Local Data	Server Data

Folder Name:		mike@mikelinen.com
Size (without subfolders):		0 KB
Total size (including subfolders):		1598541 KB

Subfolder	Size	Total Size
BCM Contacts Server Copy	243 KB	243 KB
Calendar	21671 KB	21695 KB
Calendar\ms8013329-60059...	25 KB	25 KB
Contacts	1407 KB	3807 KB
Contacts\ClearContext Cont...	209 KB	209 KB
Contacts\Saved Contacts	2184 KB	2184 KB
Deleted Items	34175 KB	34175 KB
Drafts	0 KB	0 KB

Close

Notice the third line down is titled Total Size, and to the far right of that label is a number in KB. This is the number you are looking for. Of course, you should divide by a thousand to get MB; divide by a million to get GB. If you see that it is getting close to your known mailbox limit, it is time to move mail out of this folder group.

In the example I just showed, this file contains approximately 1.6 GB. If the folder group you chose were from a Windows .pst folders file in the old pre-2003 format, I would say it is well past time to freeze this file and start a new one, or time to move mail out of the folder group. If it were larger than 15 GB and you were using the newer .pst format file, I'd say it was time to replace it.

If this is an Exchange account, 1.6 GB is also way over the Exchange storage limits of most corporate systems and you would have had messages by now telling you that. My Exchange account in this example has a much larger limit than that in most corporations, so I am fine.

You can also examine the sizes of individual folders within the folder group by studying the scrolling list at the bottom of this window. This is useful if you are at or close to your limit and you want to identify which folders you need to drag items from. Depending on the MYN configuration, it is usually on or more of the following folders that get too big: Inbox, Processed Mail folder, or Sent Items folder.

Note: *In Outlook with Exchange Server 2007, 2010, or 2013 you can also access the Folder Size dialog box from within the "Your Mailbox Is Full" alert window (called Mailbox Cleanup). Just click the View Mailbox Size button at the top of that alert window. With Exchange Server 2010 and newer, you can also see your folder sizes in Outlook 2007 and 2010 by clicking the File tab, choosing Info on the left, and clicking the Cleanup Tools button.*

Again, on the Mac, this technique only works on Exchange Server folders. You cannot use it to check the size of local folders because an Outlook for Mac 2011 folder group does not correspond to a file as it does in Windows. Rather, it maps to a database entry that points to individual files on your Mac (one for each mail message). So your real limits on the Mac are your hard drive limits, and you can check space remaining for local files by referring to your Mac Finder.

·   ·   ·

The Outlook Navigation or Folders Pane (Windows and Mac)

I am going to switch direction here and present a large section discussing how to understand the folder access that the Outlook Navigation or Folders Pane provides. The Navigation or Folders Pane has some subtle designs to it. I know many users who have used the Navigation Pane for years but still do not really "get" how it works. I am going to spend some time on this because knowing these details will help you understand why it is a great design, but with a few shortcomings. If you think you fully understand it, feel free to skip the rest of this section and move on to the section "Windows Outlook: The Mysterious To-Do List Folder."

Understanding the Navigation or Folders Pane

The Three Functions of the Navigation or Folders Pane

The Navigation Pane in Windows has three main functions in both the Windows and Mac versions, and they may seem fairly obvious. First, the Navigation or Folders Pane is used to select or locate Outlook folders so you can see what's inside. After you select a folder, its contents are displayed in the main window to the right of the Navigation Pane. Second, you can drag Outlook items directly to folders displayed in the Navigation Pane, to file intelligently Third, you can rearrange folders and change properties of folders in this pane.

And depending on your Outlook version, there are three other features that may be there that are less obvious. In Windows you can drag items within the Navigation or Folders Pane to convert them into other data types. In Outlook 2007 the Navigation Pane provides controls to change the folder data *views* you see on the right side of the screen. And in Outlook 2007 the Navigation Pane sometimes presents commands to change the structure of the pane itself, or to control Outlook Instant Search.

The Three Modes of the Navigation or Folders Pane

Locating and manipulating Outlook folders is the Navigation or Folders Pane's primary function. To fully understand how to use it to locate folders, and this is the part most users do not get, you need to know that the Navigation Pane can exist in one of *three modes*. You activate each by clicking buttons at the *bottom* of the Navigation Pane. Outlook Windows offers all three. Outlook for Mac 2011 offers only the first, but it does have two variants (see next section).

▶ **Data-type mode (Windows and Mac).** When in this mode, one and only one of the six Outlook data types (Mail, Calendar, Contacts, Tasks, Notes, and in Windows, Journal) is highlighted, and all folders of that data type are displayed no matter where they are stored. This was discussed near the start of Lesson 2. You just click one of the data-type buttons near the bottom of the Navigation or Folders Pane to activate the data-type mode for that type. The Mail data type shows a folder list tree. All others display a mostly one-dimensional list of folders of their type. Notice that Journal is not displayed by default in this list, but you can add it in Windows 2007 and 2010.

▶ **Folder List mode (Windows Only).** The Folder List mode emphasizes data location and displays together all data types in a each location. By location I mean which server or local folder group. When in this mode, a folder tree is displayed that highlights data storage locations at the highest level, and then the multiple data types within each location. For example, mail, calendar, tasks, and contacts folders on Exchange Server are shown first, then below that mail, calendar, tasks, and contacts folders on your first .pst, and then the same on the next .pst, and so on. This can be a powerful indicator of an item's context and importance. Folder List mode was also discussed in Lesson 2. To reach this view in 2007 and 2010, use the Folder List icon (looks like an like an image of a folder, as shown at the bottom of Figure A.3). In Outlook 2013 you find that by clicking on the ellipsis (…) at the right end of the major folder labels in the lower-left corner of the Outlook window and choosing Folders.

Figure A.3

Folder List and Shortcuts icons at bottom of Outlook 2007/10 Navigation Pane.

▶ **Shortcuts mode (Windows Only).** Only folders you have specifically created shortcuts for are displayed when this mode is active. To select this mode, click the Shortcuts icon (looks like an upper-right-pointing arrow in a box as at the bottom of Figure A.3) or click the icon or banner button labeled Shortcuts. In Outlook 2013 you find that by clicking on the ellipsis (…) at the right end of the major folder labels in the lower-left corner of the Outlook window. This mode allows you to create and view shortcut icons to your favorite folders across all Outlook data types. However, I never use the Shortcuts mode. That's because the Favorites pane at the top of the Navigation Pane is an equivalent for mail, which is all I set shortcuts for.

Selecting one of these three modes from the bottom of the pane (and switching among the six different data types within the first mode) dramatically changes the appearance of the upper part of the Navigation or Folders Pane. The pane reconfigures itself to manage the selected mode only.

After you understand the functions of these three modes, a lot of the mystery of the Navigation or Folders Pane goes away. Most of the complaints I hear from people who do not like the Navigation or Folders Pane stem from lack of knowledge of these three modes. After a brief discussion of the variants in the Mac's Navigation Pane, I cover two of these modes and the six data types in more detail.

The Mac's Two Navigation Pane Variants

Outlook for Mac 2011 offers an innovative two-way variant within its data-type mode. It allows you to group folders within each data-type mode either by folder type or by account. For example, in the Mail data type, you can group all the Inboxes from various accounts together at the top of the Navigation Pane, then all the Sent Items, then all the Drafts folders, and so on. Or instead you can choose the other perspective, where you group all folders from a given account together in its own account group. We saw earlier how to toggle between these two modes. You go to the Outlook menu>Preferences>General, and select or clear the check box next to the setting Group Similar Folders, Such as Inboxes, from Different Accounts. I recommend leaving that check box cleared. I think it gets too messy otherwise.

Data-Type Buttons (Windows and Mac)

The banner buttons and icons that correspond to the six Outlook data types (Mail, Calendar, Contacts, Tasks, Notes, and Journal in Windows) I call collectively *data-type buttons,* as they determine which one data type the Navigation Pane is displaying when in the data-type mode.

The first time you click a data-type banner button or icon near the bottom of the Navigation Pane (or a data-type label in 2013), you open the *default* folder for that data type in the main Outlook window to the right. So for Mail, you open the Inbox. You also expose panes in the upper two-thirds of the Navigation or Folders Pane. These allow you to open other folders of the Mail data type, such as the Sent Items folder, or any local folders of the Mail data type you might have created.

If you are new to Outlook and have not created many other folders, then not many other folders will be exposed in that pane at the top of the Navigation or Folders Pane. The Mail data type is likely to be the only data type that exposes multiple folders in that upper pane. Contacts and Calendar initially only show one folder each, for example (the Mac is slightly more complex). However, if you have been using Outlook for years and have collected many years' worth of folders and data stores, or if you are in an organization that has many servers with different Outlook data, you may see many folders in the upper part of the pane for all data types. In those scenarios, the pane becomes a convenient way to find similar data types across multiple data stores. So, in summary, clicking a data-type button essentially shows you all folders associated with that data type and *only* folders associated with that data type.

Note: *There is one exception to this segregation of data. The Deleted Items folder only shows up when you select either the Mail data-type button or Folder List, yet it is the collection point for all items that you delete from any of the data types.*

Also note, for data types other than Mail, the upper pane is more *list-based* rather than *folder–based.* For example, click Contacts. You will probably see one or two contacts folders displayed at the top, in a list (on the Mac they will have check boxes next to them). But whether it displays a list or folder tree, that upper pane still accomplishes the same thing: It shows other folders of that same Outlook data type you have currently selected, and you can display the contents of those folders, one at a time, by clicking them. If check boxes are present, clicking more than one of them lets you merge data from the various folders on the left into the display on the right. This is especially useful for combining various calendars into one view.

In Outlook 2007, clicking a data-type button can also expose the Current View Selector in the middle of the upper pane (depending on whether it has been activated for that data type). I discuss the Current View Selector in Lesson 12 in the section "Current View Section in Outlook 2007 Navigation Pane." I especially like this feature in the Tasks folder, and I'm unhappy it was removed in Outlook 2010, 2011, and 2013. In Windows the upper pane can also show a variety of type-specific tools like mini-calendars, shortcut groups, and even menu commands; I won't cover those here. Outlook 2007 Instant Search also uses a small portion of this upper pane, as described at the end of Lesson 5.

The Default Folder Can Change

After you use the upper portion of the Navigation or Folders Pane to open another folder for a given data type, it "sticks" and becomes the default folder when you return to this data type. So, for example, after entering the Mail data-type mode, if you select the Sent Items folder in the pane I just described, it becomes the default. If you navigate away from the Mail type, say by clicking the Calendar data-type button near the bottom of the Navigation Folders Pane, when you click the Mail data-type button again later, the Sent Items folder is what will open first. This often confuses new users, so you might try that sequence of steps now to get used to how it works.

One more point. You can also use the Go menu on the main menu bar of Outlook 2007, and in the View menu of 2011, to switch between the data types and modes just as you do using the buttons or icons near the bottom of the Navigation or Folders Pane. Outlook 2010 and 2013 do not have this menu.

Summary of Using the Data Type Buttons

Let's summarize what we've just covered. There are three modes to the Navigation or Folders Pane (one on the Mac) and the main one is the data-type mode. Clicking one of the six data-type buttons near the bottom of the Navigation or Folders Pane causes the pane to enter that mode, and opens the current default folder for that data type in the main Outlook window to the right. And it also opens detailed controls for that data type in the upper portions of the Navigation or Folders Pane. After those controls are open, you can pick from various other folders that may exist for that data type, opening their contents in the Outlook window as you click them. Whichever folder is last opened for a given data type will reopen when you return to that data type.

So as you can see, the first step when navigating among folders is to always start with data type buttons at the bottom of the Navigation (Folders) Pane to pick your data type mode. Then use the upper portions of the Navigation (Folders) Pane to accomplish your Outlook navigation. This two-step requirement is important, and many people lose track of where they are if they do not understand this.

Folder List Mode Advantages (Windows Only)

As mentioned, the Folder List mode, the second of three modes in Windows Outlook, is very useful. Back in Outlook 2002, the Folder List was the primary way to navigate among Outlook folders. After opened it never went away, which I liked. But, unfortunately, in these later versions, the Folder List mode is hard to keep active. It disappears as soon as you click one of the other data-type buttons. In a way, that is unfortunate. The more segmented, one-data-type-at-a-time focus of later versions can feel restrictive and confusing. Many of us prefer to use this more complete and simpler Folder List approach so we can consistently view how folders relate by data store. Why? First, because seeing the data location adds context in how the various data-type folders relate to one another. But mainly, because with the complete Folder List *all* folders are in view at once, so opening one is a one-step process. With the segmented data-type modes it is a two-step process: You need to click the data-type button at the bottom to activate that data type, and then you need to find the folder and click it. That can be slightly slower and confusing. And with the Folder List view, the folder-tree data-store location information is intuitive for many of us. After you are used to it, you feel like you are missing information when you see just a list of folders of a single data type.

One solution that helps to keep the Folder List mode in view is this: If, after you open the Folder List, you make a point of not clicking any of the data-type banner buttons or icons at the bottom, you'll be able to keep that Folder List tool open and use it exclusively. But I usually forget that and end up losing it by clicking one of the other banner buttons.

Data Type mode Advantages

All that said, there are times when the Folder List is not the best navigation approach, and the data-type mode is better. First, if you have many storage locations, it can become tedious to scroll through a long folder tree looking for a particular folder. It is often nice to see only single data-type folders together in one list. Second, there are some folders you cannot see in the Folder List mode. For example, when navigating Tasks folders in Outlook 2007 you need to enter the Tasks data-type mode to see the To-Do List folder. It is not visible in Folder List mode. Third, there are some special new Outlook capabilities that become active only in the data-type mode. For example, using the Calendar data-type mode allows you to overlap appointments from multiple Calendar folders on one calendar display (by selecting multiple check boxes in the Navigation Pane). So there are many advantages to using the Navigation Pane data-type modes, and you should learn them well.

Configuring Buttons and Icons at Bottom of Navigation Pane

I mentioned earlier that you can configure whether to expose a data-type button (or other mode button) near the bottom of the Navigation Pane, and whether it appears as a banner button or as an icon.

Five Ways to Configure

Here are five ways to configure whether you see a particular data type and how you see it. Only the first of these ways works on the Mac, and only the last one works in Outlook 2013.

▶ First, in Outlook 2007, 2010, and 2011 you can enlarge the banner button area by clicking and dragging the boundary at the top of that area. As you drag up, Outlook will convert the small icons at the bottom of the banner button area into full-sized banner buttons, one at a time.

▶ Alternatively, in Outlook 2007 and 2010 you can click the small Configure Buttons drop-down arrow in the very bottom right corner of the Navigation Pane (it's a small, faint triangle, located to the right of the icons). This will open a shortcut menu that allows you to show more or fewer banner buttons in the Navigation Pane. After that shortcut menu opens, click the Show More Buttons command as shown in Figure A.4.

Figure A.4
Menu at bottom of Navigation Pane, Outlook 2007/10.

As you repeatedly click this menu item, you will sequentially convert the small icons from the very bottom row to banner buttons. Click the Show More Buttons command as many times as needed. The Show Fewer Buttons command reverses this.

▶ The third way to modify these buttons, Outlook 2007 and 2010 only, is to use a control to choose which data types and modes to show as buttons or icons in the Navigation Pane. For example, by default, the Journal is not included in the list of buttons or icons, but you can use the control to add it here. To select these, click the Add or Remove Buttons command on the Configure Buttons shortcut menu shown in Figure A.4.

▶ A fourth way to modify the button configuration, again Outlook 2007 and 2010 only, is to click the Navigation Pane Options command (using the same Configure Buttons shortcut menu shown in Figure A.4) to change that list. Unique to this method, you can change the *order* of the list as well. So if you want the Tasks banner button just below Mail, or even at the top, use this method.

▶ To do the equivalent in Outlook 2013, because the major data-type labels are shown horizontally across the bottom, your adjustment adds or subtracts labels in this list. Do that by clicking the ellipsis at its right end, choosing Navigation Options, and adjusting the count and order there.

Minimizing the Navigation or Folders Pane (Windows Outlook)

One last thing to say about the Navigation or Folders Pane. If you lack screen space or just do not like seeing the Navigation Pane, in Windows Outlook you can minimize it but still show the major data-type buttons. To do that just click the left-pointing chevron (2007) or left-pointing arrow (2010 and 2013) in the header of the Navigation or Folders Pane, or use the Minimize function reached from the View menu or tab, and then the Navigation or Folders Pane submenu.

■ ■ ■

Windows Outlook: The Mysterious To-Do List Folder

This next lesson is primarily for Windows users because the To-Do List folder only exists in Windows Outlook. However, Mac users might want to read this as well, because it helps clarify how your Tasks folder works.

If you start using flagged-mail tasks (Lesson 2 and Lesson 7) and you want to see them while in Tasks mode, Windows users need to start using the mysterious To-Do List folder. Why do I call it mysterious? Because its presence in the My Tasks portion of the Navigation or Folders Pane seems out of place. That subpane is suppose to list tasks folders. But where is this tasks folder? And why is it there in addition to the Tasks folder? They seem to show essentially the same information. But do they?

As described in Lesson 2, it's all about flagged-mail tasks—the To-Do List folder shows them, and the normal Tasks folder does not.

In Outlook for Mac 2011, there is no To-Do List folder. That's because the Tasks folder on the Mac acts just like the To-Do List folder in Windows: It always shows both tasks and flagged-mail tasks (the latter if you click the Flagged Items box on the Home tab of the Ribbon).

There are, of course, more details to this. Before we look at them, let me say something to Windows users. If you follow my recommendation to use flagged-mail tasks only for delayed replies (Lesson 7), you can ignore the distinction between tasks and flagged-mail tasks. You should be able to handle your small number of flagged-mail tasks completely on your To-Do Bar. Consequently, visibility of flagged-mail tasks in the Tasks folder views will be mostly irrelevant in those circumstances. However, if you don't plan to use that recommendation and plan to use flagged-mail tasks more extensively—or you just are curious—then you'll want to learn more about this To-Do List folder and how it works.

In case it's not clear, let's look at how the To-Do List folder displays flagged-mail tasks and how the Tasks folder does not.

1. To activate the Tasks data type, click the Tasks button, icon, or label near the bottom of the Navigation or Folders Pane.

2. Click the To-Do List folder choice at the top of the Navigation or Folders Pane in the My Tasks section.

Any e-mails you might have flagged (flagged-mail tasks) appear within the task list at the right, along with all your ordinary tasks. They are mixed together. This is similar to the To-Do Bar task list, just filtered and sorted differently. If you haven't already, create a few flagged-mail tasks from the Mail folder so you can see them in there. Then return to the Tasks view and the To-Do List folder.

To confirm the difference, just below the To-Do List folder in the My Tasks pane is the standard Tasks folder. Try clicking back and forth between the Tasks folder and the To-Do List folder in the My Tasks subpane to see how flagged-mail tasks are shown and not shown. (You might need to sort on a date field to see your new flagged-mail tasks.)

The main reason to use the Windows To-Do List folder is so you can see flagged-mail tasks mixed in your task list. On the Mac, flagged-mail tasks are mixed with normal tasks in *any* tasks folder.

Note: *The additional functionality of the To-Do List folder and the To-Do Bar task list goes well beyond just showing flagged-mail tasks. For example, the single To-Do List folder also displays tasks from other tasks folders elsewhere in your folder list (if you have them); every task in any tasks folder is displayed. They also display flagged Contacts. With proper links, you can also see tasks from SharePoint, OneNote, and Project Server. So be aware that this list can get very busy. If you find these features useful, these are other reasons to become proficient with the To-Do List folder. They're also reasons to be cautious with the To-Do List folder. It can get confusing.*

Okay, so now you know *how* to show your flagged-mail tasks when viewing the Tasks data-type folders. But do you understand *why* this special To-Do List folder is needed? I sure didn't at first. I was confused by this because the To-Do List folder is not really a separate data folder. To confirm that, click the Folder List icon at the very bottom of the Navigation Pane (Folders icon in Outlook 2013). The entire Outlook data folder hierarchy is displayed. You can see true Tasks folders there, but not the To-Do List folder—it's missing.

The Story behind the To-Do List Folder

What's going on here with this very unusual folder behavior? The underlying story is a little complicated. It starts with the introduction of the To-Do Bar (first added in Outlook 2007). To show flagged e-mail (flagged-mail tasks) on the To-Do Bar along with true tasks, the tasks list there is implemented with modified Search Folder technology. (For more information on Search Folders, see Lesson 8.) This means that it is a virtual folder view of items resulting from defined search criteria. In this case, the search criteria is hard-coded in the To-Do Bar to search both e-mail and task data.

But what if a user wants to view a similar collection of true tasks and flagged-mail tasks in a *folder* view where they can see more columns and create custom views? That's what the To-Do List folder is for. Like the To-Do Bar task list, the To-Do List is a Search Folder. In other words, the To-Do List folder *is not a real Outlook folder*. It is a virtual view.

So why didn't Microsoft just *replace* the Tasks folder icon with this To-Do List Search Folder? After all, it shows all the ordinary tasks, too. The answer is that Search Folders are very limited tools. They do not have all the features of a true folder. You can't share them, you can't drag items to them, and you can't create subfolders in them. So if you want these functionalities in your Tasks folder, you need to use the original Tasks folder (and forgo access to flagged-mail tasks). That's why Microsoft is showing *both* folders in the My Tasks pane of the Navigation Pane—to give you the option.

Another reason is that flagged-mail tasks that you have removed the flag from look just like completed tasks in the To-Do List. So if you are looking just for completed *tasks*, you'll want to open a tasks-only folder, such as the Tasks folder.

Note: *In Outlook for Mac 2011, Microsoft did replace the normal Tasks folder with the equivalent of the Windows To-Do List, but it's still called just Tasks. The Mac default Tasks folder can show flagged-mail tasks along with normal tasks. As a Search Folder, it also has some of the same disadvantages as Windows. For example, unlike all other folder types on the Mac, you cannot create a subfolder in it. (If you try to create a subfolder, it gives you another tasks folder at the same level, but it doesn't show flagged mail.) But it is sharable and you can drag items to it. So, the Mac design team did this correctly by removing the confusion of two types of folders and merging them into one simple folder. That said, creating additional tasks folders reintroduces the distinction and the confusion.*

A few more points on this To-Do List folder in the Navigation Pane:

▶ Just like the To-Do Bar task list, this To-Do List folder collects tasks from *all* data sources: Exchange, local folders, and so on. That's another reason it isn't displayed when the Navigation Pane is in Folder List mode, because that tree of folders is organized at its highest level by data-store-location. Because the To-Do List shows tasks across *all* data stores, there is no place to logically put it in that folder tree.

▶ What if you enter a new task in this To-Do List folder. Where is it actually stored? It's stored in your primary Tasks folder, the one that is in the same folder group as your primary Inbox.

▶ While the To-Do List folder is a Search Folder, it is not an ordinary Search Folder because it does not show in the Search Folders folder in the folder list, and it displays multiple data types. So it's a *special* Search Folder created by Microsoft just to help us with viewing flagged-mail tasks (and other special items). It *does* act like a real folder in many ways, though. For example, you can define custom views for it (Lesson 12).

That's the new To-Do List folder, why it exists, and how to use it. In nearly all cases, I advise you to use it whenever you visit the Tasks data type to view your tasks in specialized views. In Lesson 12, I guide you to select this To-Do List folder option as you create all custom Tasks folder views (except one, which is avoided on purpose). Switch to the Tasks folder primarily when using views that include completed tasks.

■   ■   ■

More on Flagged-Mail Tasks

In Lessons 2 and 7, flagged-mail tasks are described in detail. But there are additional features to flagged-mail tasks that might help you in your daily task management efforts, as follows.

Date Fields on Flagged-Mail Tasks

When you create a flagged-mail task by setting a flag on an e-mail, Outlook sets a hidden pair of start and due date fields—fields that parallel the functionality of the Start and Due Date fields of *true* tasks.

Note: If you'd like to examine or change those flagged-mail task date fields, open a flagged e-mail. On the Ribbon's Message tab at the top of the e-mail message, find the Tags section. Click the Follow Up button, and then click Custom on the submenu to display those dates.

What do I mean when I say they parallel the functionality of true tasks? Let's look at an example: If you look in the To-Do List folder and see a flagged-mail task there, the flagged-mail dates are displayed in the Start Date and Due Date columns—the same columns that display the date values for true tasks.

By default, both flagged-mail task date fields are set to today when you first flag the e-mail. Then, if you do not clear the flag by tomorrow, the entire e-mail turns red, indicating the action is overdue. That's a useful feature because in MYN you use flags only to indicate deferred replies. And because I recommend you reply within a day, the red color reminds you the next day to write those replies.

In Windows you can also right-click the flag on an e-mail, which displays a shortcut menu with a choice of dates other than today (as well as a few other operations). However, with the MYN system, there's rarely a reason to choose those other dates, so I recommend you ignore that right-click menu from now on.

Why not choose other dates? In MYN flags are set only to mark e-mails that you intend to reply to within about 24 hours. Because of that, there is rarely a good reason to set its date fields to anything other than today. You won't be doing long-range management of flagged-mail tasks. If you find it necessary to delay such a reply, then convert the item to a true task, and manage it with all your other tasks, setting the date as needed.

Understanding the Flags at the Right Edge of All Tasks in the Windows Outlook To-Do Bar

The To-Do Bar displays a flag at the right edge of every task in the task list. That flag looks just like the flag you see at the right edge of flagged mail items in your Inbox, which might make you think these are indicators of the flagged-mail tasks. Not so. Rather, *all* items in the To-Do Bar task list have flags, whether they are flagged e-mails or true tasks. No, these flags are here for one main reason—to provide a shortcut to set a task's completed status—just left-click the flag.

But in Windows Outlook you can also use the flag to change the date on tasks—to do that use a right-click. Normally I don't recommend using the right-click commands on task flags when you're using the MYN system; however, there are some valid uses.

For example, let's say you want to delay, for exactly one day, the start date of several tasks. Select them all. Then right-click one of them and select Tomorrow. They are all redated to tomorrow. However, while the Tomorrow choice works well, there are subtleties to many other choices in the right-click menu. For example, if you select Next Week from that menu, the Start Date field is set to next Monday and the Due Date field is set to next Friday. That can lead to some issues in MYN, so avoid the Next Week selection.

If you want to set a date different from the preset list, use the Custom choice and you can set any dates you want. Unfortunately the Custom choice is not available when selecting a group of items.

One caution when using this flag in the To-Do Bar is this: When you *left*-click an item in the To-Do Bar and it marks the item complete, in most cases it also *removes* the item from the To-Do Bar. For new users of the To-Do Bar, this can be a bit disturbing; most users are accustomed to left-clicking flags on mail items *without* having the item disappear. But don't worry, you will get accustomed to this after a while.

If you mark a task complete accidentally and it disappears, how can you get it back? You can easily restore tasks in Outlook 2007 by selecting Undo Flag from the Edit menu (not present in 2010 or 2013), or use the keyboard shortcut, CTRL+Z (CMD+Z on the Mac). Or, you can go to the Tasks folder and clear the check mark from the Completed check box for that task. For more information on these operations, see the section "Changing Task Views to See Completed Tasks" in Lesson 2.

▪   ▪   ▪

The Daily Task List under the Windows Outlook Calendar View

I am going to diverge from the topic of folders for the last section in this appendix. Instead I am going to talk about a whole new tasks structure available in Windows Outlook. Starting in Outlook 2007, and continuing with Outlook 2010 and 2013, Microsoft has created a new place to view tasks: underneath the Calendar folder view (Day and Week views only). It is called the Daily Task List. See the bottom of Figure A.5.

Figure A.5
The Daily Task List in Outlook 2013, Calendar folder (Day and Week views only).

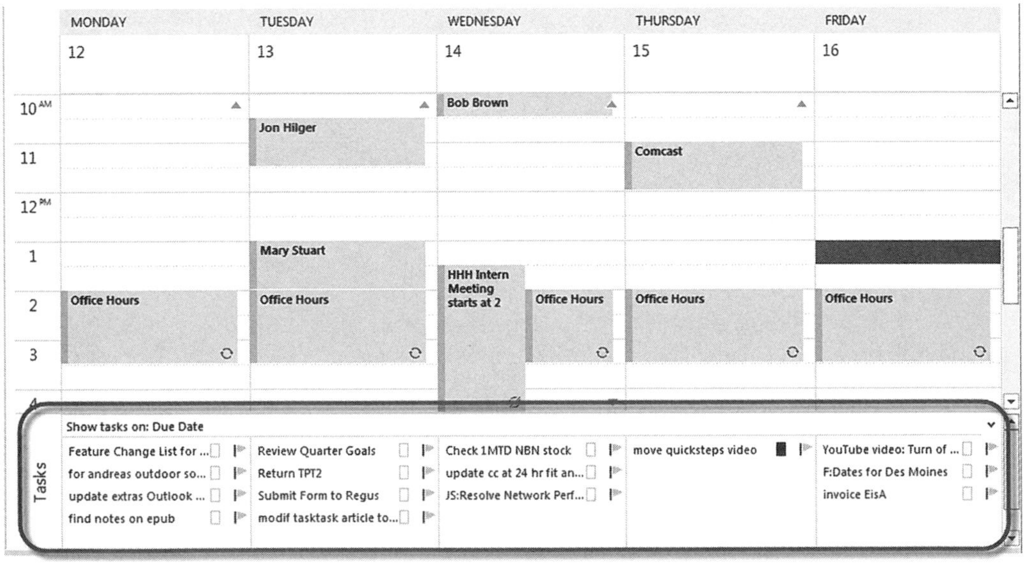

Note: *If you cannot see that section, make sure you are in the Week view, and then from the View tab or menu, choose Daily Tasks, and choose Normal.*

This new structure is useful to MYN users for looking at future tasks. Unfortunately, though, this list is not designed very well to support the MYN system's use of tasks on *today's* list. Let me explain it a bit more.

If you look at the days *after* today on the week calendar, you can see tasks that you have deferred to those days. I have always wanted a way to view upcoming deferred tasks directly in the main Outlook views. The Daily Task List makes that possible. You can also drag tasks to various days as a way to set the defer date. This display also has a nice feature that shows which tasks you completed on what days in the past.

If, however, you look at *today's* date, the list below the calendar for that date shows all tasks with a date of today *and earlier*. This is much like our To-Do Bar filter, which does the same. So you might think this is another way to view your MYN Now Tasks. Unfortunately, though, this view always sorts the *older* tasks to the top of the list (the opposite of the MYN system), and that sort order is not configurable, including no way to sort on priority. So assuming you are allowing 15 or 20 near-term tasks to move forward from day to day, as I teach in the MYN system, the *least* important of those tasks may be at the top of today's list in this display and the most important scrolled off the bottom. So the configuration of this new task display makes the today's list portion of the Daily Task List not useful for MYN users. Instead, open the To-Do Bar to view today's tasks.

One other thing. While Due Date is the initial filter in this display for deciding which tasks to show on which days, you can also set the filter to use Start Date. You select this by right-clicking the header of the list. A menu opens as shown here, where you can set it to By Start Date.

You will want to do that for the MYN system. The same action can be used to turn off the completed tasks display. Unfortunately, these are the *only* configurations you can make on tasks in this display.

You can hide the Daily Tasks List section if you want and make more room on your Calendar view by doing this: From the View menu or tab, choose Daily Task List, and click Off in the submenu. You can hide it temporarily by clicking the small arrow at the right end of its top edge. Or you can adjust the height of the view by dragging its top edge.

∎   ∎   ∎

Next Steps

Now that you understand the details behind using folders in Outlook, you're ready for Appendix B. Let's look at how to use those folders to archive old mail.

Appendix B:
Archiving Your Mail
in the MYN System

Introduction (Windows and Mac)

If you use a Windows version of Outlook, you may periodically get messages from Outlook offering to archive your old mail. New installations of Windows Outlook are configured to display these messages automatically. This feature is called AutoArchive. If you were like me, you quickly canceled out of those messages and perhaps scratched your head wondering what they really meant. You probably wondered where the mail went after you archived and if you would be able to see old mail again easily. Or perhaps you actively accepted those messages and are using the AutoArchive features of Outlook, but you don't really understand the process. Few people take the time to figure out what is really going on.

And you might have come to this appendix solely to learn how to turn Auto-Archive off so you no longer get those nagging archive invitations. That is one of the first things I cover in the AutoArchive section ahead.

And whether you use Windows or the Mac, you are probably wondering what options there are for archiving old mail in Outlook.

Many people archive their mail manually, by dragging it to other storage folders, but have wondered if there are better ways to archive mail, either manually or automatically. Due to Exchange Server limits you may be forced to archive mail often and feel there ought to be better ways to automatically keep folders below those limits.

All of these things, and more, are covered in this appendix. I pay particular attention to the Processed Mail folder and how to archive mail from it. Where you put the Processed Mail folder strongly guides whether you need to archive and how to do it. For that reason, this appendix works hand in hand with Appendix A, where distinct Processed Mail configuration scenarios are identified. I match those scenarios with corresponding archive strategies here.

Understanding Archiving (Windows and Mac)

From here on, when you see the word *archiving* in this appendix I am referring to archiving in general, whether done with Outlook AutoArchive (in Windows) or by manually dragging mail (in all versions).

Archiving is a difficult topic, especially when learning to use the Windows Outlook AutoArchive feature. Most users trying to use it end up with a jumble of folders and difficult-to-find mail. Corporate support departments have a tough time teaching a uniformly applicable approach, so users are often left on their own to figure this out.

One of the first steps to solving this confusion is to get the terminology straight, so let's do that.

Archiving Compared to Filing

In Lessons 5 and 8 you learned ways to file e-mail. Many users get the terms *filing* and *archiving* confused, and for good reason; the distinction is subtle. How is filing mail different from archiving mail? Filing is usually done with the intention of fast retrieval. Archiving, in contrast, usually implies a deeper storage, storage that may be harder or slower to search through or retrieve from. These days, though, with lots of local storage available, that distinction is less important.

Filing also usually involves identifying distinct folders or topics to store messages in so you can find them quickly later. Archiving usually refers to moving older mail to another location, regardless of topics or search strategy. This definition is the one I will use.

Archiving Compared to Backing Up

Let's put another terminology confusion to bed. Because archiving is sometimes done onto external drives, some people confuse *archiving* mail with *backing up* mail. These are very different activities. Archiving mail *moves* mail from one location to another, thereby removing mail from the first location. Backing up mail, in contrast, makes a *copy* in the second location, but does not remove it from the first. Archiving solves a storage problem, whereas backing up is preparation for disaster recovery. So just to be clear, in this discussion we are not talking about backing up mail.

Archiving Due to Age or Storage Limits

There are two schools on why you should archive. One says you should archive when your documents become less important, usually due to aging. In some cases this is true. For instance, staff on a project or a legal case that comes to an end may collect all the related mail and archive it in separate storage, out of the way, but still reachable in case old issues arise. And others package up *all* mail older than, say, one year and archive it into a date-named storage space.

For most people, though, it is not an aging or project-end trigger but rather a storage-limit trigger that drives them to archiving. Archiving is what they do when their most convenient file cabinet (for example, the Outlook Inbox) fills up and they want to get the oldest stuff out of the way to make room for more of the new.

The filled-up Outlook Inbox might be an Outlook Exchange mailbox reaching its limit. Or it could be a local file filling up, which is possible if you are working with an Internet mail server in Windows Outlook—in this case the .pst file described in Appendix A can get too large. But a filled-up Inbox is most likely an issue in an Exchange-based mail setting because the policy trend among corporate IT departments has been to keep individuals' Exchange Inboxes very small. Because that policy leads to constant messages saying "Your Mailbox Is Full," archiving is more important than ever for corporate Exchange users.

Does the MYN System Avoid Storage Limits?

You might think that because, in the MYN system, you are dragging mail from the Exchange Inbox every day, and with ample local hard disk space available as a place to store that mail, archiving could be avoided. But if you study Lesson 5 and Appendix A you will see that in one scenario this is not true. That's making the Processed Mail folder a subfolder of your Inbox. If you do that on Exchange, the server mailbox will continue to fill. So you will need to move mail again—to keep the Processed Mail folder from driving through your Exchange limits—and archiving is the best way to do that. You will see that solution among others described ahead.

If You Have Mail Retention Policies

Many companies these days have mail retention policies where mail older than a certain number of days is automatically deleted from the Exchange Inbox. In some cases you are allowed to store that mail in local Outlook folders before it is deleted. In other cases, no local storage is allowed. If you are in the first case—if you are allowed to save old mail locally—this appendix is for you, so read on. If you are in the latter case, well, there is really nothing to be done—you can't store old mail, and archiving is a moot point. In this case you may want to export very important e-mails as text files on your computer, but I offer little advice on how best to do that.

Manual Archive Compared to AutoArchive (Windows)

Let's get back to AutoArchive, which is the Windows Outlook feature at play when you get those messages asking if you would like to archive your mail.

You may ask yourself, Is this form of archiving different from manually moving mail into another folder or hard drive? Where does this mail go? How do I retrieve it? Is this the only way to do archiving in Outlook?

Archiving can be done either way, manually or automatically, and the outcome is the same. The mail is moved from one folder to another folder. This is confusing to new users, so I'll say it a different way. After mail is moved automatically by Windows Outlook AutoArchive, it is no different than if you had dragged it there manually. You can open and read and use that mail just like any other mail. The source of this confusion is that with default settings, AutoArchive seems to hide your archived mail in an arbitrary location (and sometimes it does). But it doesn't have to. And the naming of the Archive Folders group may make you think it is special, but it's not. Actually, you can set AutoArchive to place the mail in practically any local folders group you want, and after it is there, you can continue to use that mail as you would regular saved mail. So mail stored by AutoArchive is no different from mail you archive manually.

The power of AutoArchive is that it is a highly configurable way to move mail *automatically*. There are user-controllable settings that control *which* mail goes, *where* it goes, and *when* it goes. You can change those settings folder by folder. These settings can make AutoArchive a very useful tool for you.

Out of the box, however, Outlook comes with default AutoArchive settings that are one-dimensional, a bit confusing, and not suited for the MYN system. But with a little instruction you can learn how to improve on those settings and make them do what you want. We'll get to those instructions later in this appendix.

Outlook for Mac 2011: No AutoArchive Per Se, Other Solutions

Outlook for Mac 2011 does not have AutoArchive built in as Windows does, so you'll probably be using the instructions below for *manually* archiving mail. That said, there are ways to create AppleScripts and to use Apple's Mac OSX scheduling tools to accomplish virtually the same thing as Windows Outlook AutoArchive—but programming those is beyond the scope of this book.

You may want to look at third-party tools as well. Keep your eye on Mac online sources to see if an automated archive solution is released. One product I saw, but that I have not tested, is Outlook Exchange Accounts Optimizer. It is designed to do essentially the same thing on the Mac that AutoArchive does on Windows Exchange e-mail (but it appears to lack the folder-by-folder control offered in Windows AutoArchive). It does look like it could work for MYN. See www.softhing.com/oeao.html.

Should You Use Windows AutoArchive or Manual Archive?

I just mentioned that Windows Outlook AutoArchive can be very useful, so you might be itching to try it. Before I show you how to use AutoArchive, I want you to think long and hard about whether you really should set it up and use it.

Setting up and using AutoArchive is not for the faint of heart, particularly the way I recommend you do it in MYN. AutoArchive, if you choose to apply it just right, can get complicated. The steps ahead are a bit extensive. You probably should set aside about two hours to work through the configuration steps. If you feel overly challenged by these steps and yet feel strongly about saving old mail, stick with the alternative *manual* methods described below. In the long run the manual methods take more work and are inherently more risky, but they require less up-front configuration and understanding. You can always *start* with manual archiving, then move to using AutoArchive after you get the hang of archiving and feel the need for some automation.

That said, there is one case where I do recommend using AutoArchive immediately if you are using the MYN system, and that is the case I described earlier: You are in an Exchange Server environment and are consistently using OWA or a mobile device to view *older* mail and have strict storage limits on your Exchange account. If this describes you, I recommend configuring and using AutoArchive right away when using MYN. More on that ahead.

■   ■   ■

Archive Solution Scenarios (Windows and Mac)

I'll cover how to do both manual and automatic archiving. First I want to show you the typical Outlook and MYN configuration scenarios where you will *need* archiving (and point out scenarios where you clearly do not need it). Then for each of those scenarios, I'll show you how to archive manually (Windows and Mac) and then by using AutoArchive (Windows only).

Note: *This appendix assumes you are using my recommended MYN filing method of storing all mail in the Processed Mail folder. I do not specifically include archive scenarios for mail moved into multiple topic-named folders. There are just too many possible combinations of setup to cover that option here. Users in that situation may still want to read this appendix to learn more about archiving and how you might design a solution to fit your needs, because the same principles apply.*

Now let's get started.

In Appendix A, I went over local folders in Windows and the Mac. I also covered the difference between the old Windows .pst file format and the new one. I went over Exchange-based mail versus Internet-based mail and how to tell the difference. And I covered the impact of using OWA or a mobile device on how you set up your Processed Mail folder. The combination of these variables makes a big difference in what kind of archiving I recommend you do and whether to do it at all, so be sure you have read those sections and understand them.

Figure B.1 ahead condenses these variables into three scenarios, each with recommended archive approaches. These are not the same configuration scenarios described in Appendix A (though they do overlap a bit), so be sure to study the ones below as well. Then I'll explain how to do those four archive scenarios both manually and, for Windows, with AutoArchive.

Using the Archive Scenario Table

Using Figure B.1, identify where your Outlook usage fits on the chart. The column headings show where you store your Inbox and whether you use OWA or a mobile device (MD) to read old mail.

Figure B.1
MYN archive scenarios.

1) Limited Exchange *without* OWA/MD 2) Using Internet Mail	Limited Exchange *with* OWA/MD	Exchange with essentially no limit
Solution Scenario 1	Solution Scenario 2	Solution Scenario 3

Make sure you have identified your scenario before proceeding. If needed, restudy this material and relevant portions of Appendix A to identify where your Outlook usage fits.

Some notes on Figure B.1:

▶ "OWA/MD" stands for using Outlook Web Access (also called Outlook Web App) or a mobile device (MD) for reading older mail (mail older than today).

▶ "Limited Exchange" means you are in an Exchange environment and have typically small storage size limits on your Inbox, and/or a fairly restrictive age-based mail retention policy that allows off-server storage.

Note: As mentioned in Appendix A, the Windows .pst archiving approach is being replaced in Exchange environments. In Exchange 2010 a new server-based Personal Archives option was introduced. In Exchange 2013 it's now called In-Place Archiving. Both give the option of placing archived mail in a central server location. Check with your IT department to determine if this is available in your organization. For more information, see: www.myn.bz/PersonalArchives.htm. Because this new option is not yet in widespread use, all instructions in this lesson assume you are still using a .pst file approach.

The What and Why of the Three Archive Solution Scenarios

First I will discuss *what* these three solution scenarios are and *why* you will use them. In the subsequent section I will tell you *how* to use them.

Solution Scenario 1

You got to this scenario because you are using Exchange for your Inbox (with restrictive size limits, or with retention policies that allow off-server storage). And using MYN you have probably created one Processed Mail folder within a local folder system that has generous space. By local folder system, I mean you are using a newer .pst file in Windows Outlook or using an On My Computer folder on the Mac. And you are not using OWA or a mobile device to read old mail. This describes configuration B in Appendix A. Alternatively, you are using Internet mail with a local folder system to store the Inbox, which is configuration A in Appendix A.

Archiving is rarely needed in this case, because the Processed Mail folder is stored in a very large data store and you are keeping your Inbox relatively empty as taught in Lesson 5. However, you may want to limit the number of years' worth of mail you see in a given Processed Mail folder to reduce clutter. And some people report slower Windows Outlook performance with a very large local .pst file. You may eventually reach the 20 GB limit of the .pst file in Windows. If you think you are reaching that limit, feel free to do manual archiving as described in the scenario 1 steps ahead, perhaps once a year. And be sure to back up your mail files often.

For the Mac, because there is no single file that may get too large, you are limited only by the size of your hard drive, or perhaps sluggish performance. With today's large hard drives, it is unlikely you will reach that limit very soon. And if it does get overloaded, you really do not have another Outlook-based storage option. Because of all this, Outlook archiving is not needed and not an option for you. You may want to move mail into different date-named local folders just to keep clutter down. If you eventually do start to reach Outlook limits on your local files, your only option would be to drag the files to a Mac OS folder located on another hard drive.

Solution Scenario 2

You got to scenario 2 because you are using configuration C in Appendix A. That means you are using Exchange for your Inbox, with typical restrictions on its size, and you are using OWA or a mobile device to read older mail. Because you want to see older mail while mobile, you have a Processed Mail folder on Exchange Server that you copy into every day. But because of the Exchange size limits, you have placed another Processed Mail folder on a local folder system to archive mail into periodically. Because this scenario corresponds to configuration C in Appendix A, due to instructions there you may already be doing the manual archiving steps described below.

This is the one scenario most in need of archiving, which is why manual archiving was built in to the configuration C setup instructions in Appendix A. It is probably the most likely scenario that readers who need archiving will fall into, because Exchange limits and mobile mail are common. It is also the scenario most ripe for AutoArchive.

The reason it is ripe for AutoArchive is that, in this scenario, it is to your benefit to keep the Exchange-based Processed Mail folder as full as possible. Why? Because, when you visually search for mail there by scanning your folder contents, you want to see as much recent mail as possible. That way, your mail searches in that folder are most productive and you can avoid looking in older archive files. Therefore you do not want to archive too much at a time.

For example, you would not want to empty the entire Exchange-based Processed Mail folder during archiving because the next time you used OWA or a mobile device to search for mail you would not see any mail older than a day or so. Ideally you will only archive a little of the oldest mail at a time and keep that Processed Mail folder just below the Exchange storage limit.

AutoArchive is perfect for this. You can set it to run every day, taking just a little mail out each time. Your Exchange-based Processed Mail folder stays nearly full, and you don't reach your Exchange limit.

So I commonly recommend AutoArchive for this scenario. That said, you still can use manual archive if you want to avoid the AutoArchive setup steps. Both options are described ahead.

Solution Scenario 3

This scenario is for Exchange users with nearly unlimited mailbox sizes. This corresponds to configuration A in Appendix A.

In some organizations, the Exchange administrators never get around to setting a limit on user mailboxes. This is especially true for new installations, where the server hard drives have not started to fill yet, or in small companies with few employees. With nearly unlimited storage, you can get by (for now) with no archiving. Just make sure your Exchange administrators are backing up Exchange Server data (nearly all do).

However, for these cases, even though your Inbox is currently practically unlimited, it is likely that eventually your Exchange administrator will chase you down and complain about your storage. So you might want to get ahead of this by following the manual archive steps below for scenario 2 and save your oldest mail to another storage area. Just use a larger threshold or an age-based approach. For instance, you might decide in step 3 below (in the scenario 2 manual archive instructions) to drag all mail older than, say, two years to your archive storage, or older than three years — you be the judge of where to draw the line. Again, you might as well start doing this now before you are asked on short notice to "clean your mailbox." You may not be as prepared as you are now to think this through. And your IT staff will appreciate it.

.   .   .

How to Do Archiving: Manual Archiving, All Scenarios

Okay, now let's talk about *how* to do archiving, and let's start with manual archiving. It is what most people do, it requires the least study, and it certainly requires the least *up-front* investment in time. Manual archiving means dragging mail manually from one overflowing data store to a less full one. Let's cover manual archiving for each of the scenarios.

Scenario 1 and Manual Archiving (Windows Only)

Recall that this scenario is for Windows only, and it assumes you are using a local .pst file for your Processed Mail folder. You have a limited-size Exchange Server without OWA or mobile access. This is essentially configuration B of Appendix A. Or you are using Internet mail with the a local file (in which case OWA is not an option), which corresponds to configuration A in Appendix A. Manual archiving works fine for this scenario. You will need to do it very rarely, and it is fairly straightforward. You are simply going to drag a large chunk of old mail from the bottom of the date-sorted Processed Mail folder to another Processed Mail folder in a local folder group. See Figure B.2 for the Exchange view of this, and Figure B.3 for the Internet mail view.

Figure B.2
Manual archive scenario 1 (Exchange-based Inbox).

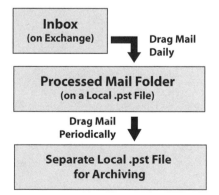

Figure B.3
Manual archive scenario 1 (Internet-mail variant).

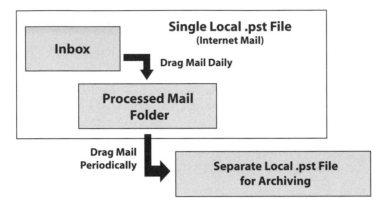

Scenario 1: Timing of Manual Archive (Windows Only)

In Windows Outlook, if you recently created your Processed Mail folder in a brand-new .pst file when you first set it up, this folder will not fill up for some time, say several years. I would set a task, now, to appear in perhaps 12 months, to check the file size of the folder group containing your Processed Mail folder. After it starts reaching 15 GB, I would start doing the manual archiving described next. Internet mail users, start checking size now because you may already have lots of mail in your local file.

Note: *Why 15 GB? Well, if you recently added a new .pst file, I assume you used the newer file format as instructed in Appendix A. That format has a size limit of 20 GB, but I recommend you never allow it to reach the absolute limit. Files in the older file format performed poorly and were often corrupted if they got near their absolute limit, and I have to assume files in the newer one could be too. So I have arbitrarily picked 15 GB. Feel free to try more, but back up often.*

Scenario 1: Manual Archive Steps (Windows Only)

1. You are going to periodically check the size of your main Processed Mail folder group (say once a year), and if it gets close to or over 15 GB, go to step 2. Instructions on how to check a folder group size are in Appendix A.

2. Create a new .pst file using the instructions in Appendix A, section titled "Processed Mail Folder, Configuration B." Set it up with a Processed Mail folder as described there. However, use the name *Older Processed Mail.*

3. Open the original Processed Mail folder, sort by date with newest on top, select the bottom (oldest) third of mail, and drag it to the new folder called Older Processed Mail that you created in the last step.

4. In three months or so repeat steps 1 through 3. You may want to set a task to remind you.

5. After three or four of these copy routines in step 4, check the file size of the file containing the Older Processed Mail folder. If it is at or over 15 GB, you'll want to replace it. At that point rename the folder group with a descriptive date-range name (like *Archive-Jan12-Jul13*). Use steps 1 to 3 of the instructions later in this appendix in the section "Renaming a Folder Group" to do so.

6. I also recommend you rename the .pst file underlying this folder group using the same naming convention. This is a little cumbersome, but doing so will help avoid confusion later. Follow instructions in the section later in this appendix titled "Renaming Your Active Archive."

7. Now repeat step 2 to create another Older Processed Mail folder as a place to periodically drag mail.

Be sure to make the archive files just created a part of whatever backup routine you have for your computer.

Scenario 2 and Manual Archiving, Overview (Windows and Mac)

Recall that in this scenario you have a constrained Exchange Inbox and are using OWA or a mobile device to view older mail while out of the office. This corresponds to configuration C in Appendix A. If you recall from Appendix A, to set up this archive you create an Older Processed Mail folder on local storage to store your oldest mail moved frequently from the Exchange-based Processed Mail folder. Figure B.4 is how that process would look.

Figure B.4
Manual archive scenario 2.

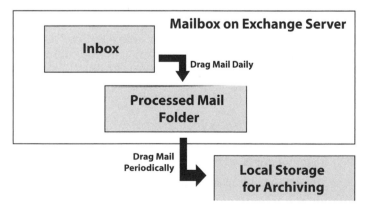

Scenario 2 Manual Archive Steps (Windows and Mac)

1. Continue to drag mail from your Inbox to your Processed Mail folder as you process mail and empty your Inbox daily. When you are starting to get size limit errors from your Exchange system, go to step 2.

2. You probably already did this step in Appendix A. But if not, you now need to create a new local folder using the instructions in Appendix A, section titled "Processed Mail Folder, Configuration B." That means creating a new .pst file in Windows, or creating an On My Computer folder on the Mac. Set it up as described in Appendix A. However, use the name *Older Processed Mail.*

3. Open the original Processed Mail folder, sort by date with newest on top, select the bottom (oldest) third of mail, and drag it to the folder called Older Processed Mail folder.

4. Repeat step 3 the next time you start to get size limit error messages. This may be in as little as a few weeks.

5. Keep doing this for a long while. On the Mac, you probably will have no maintenance to do unless your hard drive fills up. In Windows Outlook, because newer .pst files have such a large size limit, you may not need to do the file replacement in step 6 for several years.

6. Windows only from here on. After a year or so (set a task to remind yourself), check the file size of the file containing the Older Processed Mail folder. If it is near full (say at or running over 15 GB; see note in previous section) you'll need to replace it. At that point rename the folder group with a descriptive date-range name (like *Archive-Jan012-Jul13*). Use steps 1 to 3 of the instructions later in this appendix in the section "Renaming a Folder Group" to do so.

7. I also recommend you rename the .pst file underlying this folder group using the same naming convention. This is a little cumbersome but doing so will help avoid confusion later. Follow instructions in the section later in this appendix titled "Renaming Your Active Archive."

8. Now repeat step 2 to create another Older Processed Mail folder as a place to periodically drag mail.

Be sure to make the archive files just created a part of whatever backup routine you have for your computer.

Scenario 3 and Manual Archiving

Scenario 3 archiving is optional. In this scenario the Processed Mail folder is stored on Exchange Server, probably as a subfolder of your Inbox. With no

Exchange limits (or very large limits), the Processed Mail folder will essentially never fill up.

If you do decide you want to archive (say to reduce clutter), you can do it rarely, say every six to 12 months. Just select a large subset of your oldest mail at the bottom of your Processed Mail folder and drag it to a locally stored folder. The process and diagram in scenario 2 should be used here.

Wrapping Up Manual Archive

That's it for manual archiving. As you can see, it is relatively simple but just a bit time-consuming. And in scenario 2 it can become tedious, so next, I will cover AutoArchive and how to apply it to scenario 2.

■   ■   ■

Using AutoArchive Intelligently (Windows)

Again, the sole value of AutoArchive is to automate the movement of older e-mail between folders (or deletion of old e-mail, which I describe ahead). Assuming you are emptying your Inbox almost every day as instructed in Lesson 5, scenario 2 is the only candidate for using AutoArchive. Using manual archiving in this scenario, you may find you will get size limit errors every week or so, so you will need to drag mail that often. This can get tedious. Even worse, if the folder size jumps fast due to arrival of a big attachment one day, you can actually get locked out of sending e-mail (assuming your Exchange Server administrator has implemented that policy). What if you are on the road using only your mobile device when that happens? Auto-Archive can be a real life saver for scenario 2, not just a convenience.

If AutoArchive is so desirable, why didn't I just skip the manual archive lesson in scenario 2 and take you right here? Because using AutoArchive is complicated. And unless you use the default settings (not recommended for MYN users), it takes a while and a lot of steps to set it up. Some people just would rather not deal with it. So read ahead and see if this is for you.

The AutoArchive controls have not changed over the full range of Windows Outlook versions covered in this book, so everything in the following section will apply to all Windows Outlook versions.

Turning Off Outlook AutoArchive Completely (Windows)

If your sole reason for coming to this appendix is to learn how to turn off Outlook AutoArchive completely, to eliminate those pesky "would you like to archive your mail" requests every couple of weeks, here is how to do that.

Out of the box, Outlook ships with some folders configured for AutoArchive and some not. You could go to each folder and turn AutoArchive off if it is on. An easier method is one that turns it off for all folders simultaneously. Here is how:

1. Right-click your Inbox folder, choose Properties, and click the AutoArchive tab. You will see a dialog box similar to the one below:

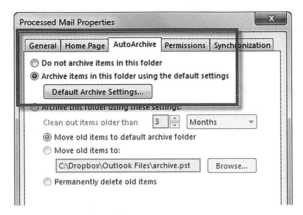

2. Click the second option button, Archive Items in This Folder Using the Default Settings.

3. Click Default Archive Settings.

4. In the dialog box that opens, *clear* the first check box at the very top labeled Run Archive Every. Click OK and OK again to close all dialog boxes.

That's it; that will turn off AutoArchive for all folders, and prevent the periodic messages asking for permission to archive.

Preparing to Use AutoArchive

If you are using scenario 2 and you decide that Outlook AutoArchive is for you, you will need to dig into the configuration screens and set AutoArchive up intelligently. Rather than just turning it on, it is worth taking the time to set it up right so that you can work with it for months and years ahead.

And again, you would not normally use AutoArchive with scenario 1 or 3.

Realize that you can set up AutoArchive in a number of different ways, depending on your goals. The goals of the steps ahead are to keep both your Processed Mail folder and your Saved Sent Mail folder at a safe but reasonably large size, without the need to periodically empty them manually. And the steps assume that, given the system in this book, you will be manually dragging mail from your Inbox (and in some cases the Sent Items folder), so you will not set AutoArchive on those.

For this system, three main operations need to be set up to use Outlook Archive:

▶ Determine the Older Than setting.

▶ Set up and configure AutoArchive.

▶ Run your first archive manually and fine-tune your settings.

What follows are detailed steps for these operations

Note: I recommend you read Appendix A before embarking on using Outlook AutoArchive. It will give you the understanding of Outlook folders that you need to be successful.

Determine the "Older Than" Setting

AutoArchive works like this: When it runs, all mail older than a certain number of weeks or months from today (the Older Than setting) is removed from any folder that has AutoArchive activated for it and placed in a folder of the same name, stored in an Archive folders group (a local folders group on a .pst file). That Archive folders group, along with the matching file folders within, is created automatically the first time AutoArchive runs.

Note: If desired, items can instead be deleted during AutoArchive. I'll show cases of doing that at the end of this appendix.

All mail younger than the Older Than setting is retained in the original folder. So the Older Than setting is the maximum age of mail you would like to keep together in the folder you are archiving from. The Older Than setting is a value that you enter in the AutoArchive configuration screens (described ahead) before you allow AutoArchive to run the first time. Getting it right is essential to preventing those pesky "Your Mailbox Is Full" messages. How do you choose the correct value?

For scenario 2, your limiting factor is your Exchange mailbox storage limit. Calculating the Older Than setting is fairly simple. Just wait until the next time you get a mailbox-over-limit message. At that point stop and check how old the oldest message in your Inbox/Processed Mail folder is, and use approximately that age period, minus four or five weeks (for a safety buffer), as your Older Than setting. This is not an exact determination, but it should be close enough. If in the steps ahead you still get a "Your Mailbox Is Full" message shortly after running archive with that value, shorten the age period some more and rerun archive. Repeat until you stop getting the messages.

Set Up and Configure AutoArchive

There are many different ways to configure AutoArchive. The easiest way is to set the default settings (while configuring the first folder) and subsequently apply those to multiple folders.

Here is how you configure your first folder and create the default AutoArchive settings.

1. Right-click your Processed Mail folder, choose Properties, and click the AutoArchive tab. You will see a dialog box similar to the one below:

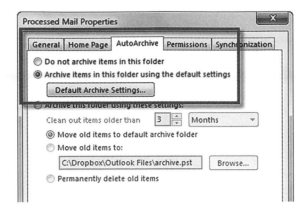

2. Click the second option button, Archive Items in This Folder Using the Default Settings.

3. Click Default Archive Settings. A dialog box similar to the one below opens:

Configuring Default Archive Settings

To configure this dialog box:

1. Select all the options as shown in the previous figure, except as noted below.

2. Enter 1 in the box at the top labeled Run AutoArchive Every. With the small sizes of most Exchange mailbox limits, you will want to clean the oldest mail from your Processed Mail folder every day.

3. Set the Clean Out Items Older Than setting to the Older Than value you determined earlier. Make sure you studied that section carefully and have the correct value.

4. Next, click the option button labeled Move Old Items To. This tells Outlook where to place the archive.pst file, which is the file that holds all your archived items. Use the same considerations you used when deciding where to create your other .pst files. See Appendix A for a full discussion of that. Use the Browse button to locate it.

5. Click OK, and then OK again.

You have completed settings for your first folder, and the AutoArchive default settings have been created. Notice that the Archive folders group will not show up in your folder list until after the first AutoArchive session is run (as described below).

Configuring Sent Mail and Saved Sent Mail AutoArchive Settings

Next, configure your Sent Items folder to be archived as well:

1. Right-click your Sent Items folder and choose Properties, then click the AutoArchive tab.

2. Click the second option button, Archive Items in This Folder Using the Default Settings. Because you have already set the default AutoArchive settings, there is no need to define them again for this folder; no other configuration is needed.

3. Click OK, and OK again.

Clear AutoArchive Settings for the Inbox

After you turn on AutoArchive in Outlook, it runs the default settings against all folders, all folder groups, and potentially all data sources in your folder list. Most folders other than those just listed you do *not* want to archive in the MYN system. So you need to explicitly remove archive settings from each of those excluded folders, one at a time. If you have a lot of old folders, this can be tedious but it must be done. And it must be done at all levels of a hierarchical folders list.

You will first turn off archiving for your Inbox folder and the Tasks folder. Why? Because you manually drag your Inbox mail to your Processed Mail folder daily as you empty it, so archiving the Inbox is not needed or desired.

And in general I do not recommend archiving Tasks. Instead of archiving tasks, I recommend you clean out your completed tasks periodically. See the very last section of this appendix, in the subsection titled "Purging Old Completed Tasks," for a discussion.

So to turn off AutoArchive, do this.

1. Right-click the Inbox, and choose Properties, then click the AutoArchive tab.

2. Click the first option button, Do Not Archive Items in This Folder.

3. Repeat steps 1 and 2 for the Tasks folder, so it is not archived either.

4. Follow the same steps on Drafts, Junk, Deleted Items, and any other system folders that do not make sense to archive.

Clear AutoArchive Settings for Any Other Local Folders You May Have

Repeat those steps for any other local folders that may have been left over from your previous mail-saving systems. You want to clear the settings so as to not disturb these folders during archiving. Otherwise these folders may lose much of their mail, and you will unnecessarily move it to the Archive Folders group. Recall that after you turn on archiving in the default settings, it runs again *all* folders, *all* folder groups, and potentially *all* data sources in your folder list, unless you make settings at each folder to prevent that. So be thorough in clearing existing archive settings from all old folders. Of course, if you are using a hybrid approach and filing out of the Processed Mail folder into multiple other folders, you may want to leave these folders with archiving turned on, so you can control their size as well.

Note: *If you have multiple hierarchical folders, here is an important point: Settings made to a parent folder are <u>not</u> inherited by child folders. You need to apply or remove Auto-Archive settings to all the folders individually, at every level of the hierarchy. Yes, this can take time.*

Do the First Archive and Fine-Tune Your Settings

You next need to run a first AutoArchive manually to create the new Archive folders group in your Navigation or Folders Pane, and to fine-tune and confirm the settings of your AutoArchive configuration.

Normally AutoArchive is an automatic process and you would not run it manually. While configuring your settings for the first time, however, run it manually once so that you can see the effects of your settings and confirm that they are correct. Here's how:

1. Check to see if you already have an archive file in use. Have you been accepting the Outlook periodic archive requests in the past? If so, or if you accidentally did once, you already have an archive file created. Look for a folder group with the name Archive Folders (Archives in 2010 and

2013). You'll need to rename the file behind that group so that you can start fresh. Follow steps 1 through 4 in the section titled "How to Swap Your Archive Files" later in this appendix to rename the underlying archive file.

Note: This file might not be visible as a folder group in your folder list pane, so to accurately determine if an archive file exists, do this: In Outlook 2007, from the File menu, choose Data File Management. In Outlook 2010 and 2013, from the File tab choose Account Settings and then Account Settings and then click the Data File tab. In all versions, in the dialog box that is now open, if you see archive.pst in the file name list at the right, you currently have an archive file in use. If so, you will need to rename it following the instructions referenced in step 1.

2. Before running Archive for the first time, open your Processed Mail folder, sort by date, and write down the date of the oldest mail in that folder. You will need that date in a moment.

Note: To be most accurate, you should add the Modified field to the Processed Mail folder view and write that down, because AutoArchive actually uses the modified date rather than the received date when deciding whether to archive an individual piece of mail.

3. You are now ready to start the first archive. In Outlook 2007, from the File menu, choose Archive. In Outlook 2010 and 2013, choose the File tab, then Cleanup Tools, then Archive. The following dialog box will open:

4. Select the first option button at the top.

5. Click OK. This starts AutoArchive, using all the settings in all the folders you have just configured.

6. You will see a message in the lower margin of your main Outlook window (the Status Bar) stating that Archive is in progress.

7. Archiving runs in the background while you do other work. If you have a lot of aged mail, it may take five to ten minutes or even more.

8. When it is complete, you will see a folder group appear in your Folder List named Archive Folders. In 2010 and 2013 it will be named Archives.

Note: *If you do not see the Archive Folders or Archives group appear in your folder list, go back to the section "Configuring Default Archive Settings" earlier in this appendix and confirm that you selected the Show Archive Folder in Folder List check box in the AutoArchive dialog box.*

Examine Archive Folders to Confirm Success

A number of things can go wrong with your archive settings, so now is the time to check results.

Confirming That Mail Was Moved

The first thing you should confirm is that a Processed Mail folder now exists in the new Archive Folders group (called Archives in 2010 and 2013). When Archive runs the first time and creates the Archive Folders (Archives) group, inside that group it creates copies of the folders it is copying from. So you should find a Processed Mail folder inside this new folder group.

Open the new Archive Folders (Archives) group and find the Processed Mail folder and open it. Is there mail in there now? If yes, skip to the subsection below titled "Mail in Archive Folders Group."

If No Mail in Archive Folders Group

If there is no mail in the Processed Mail folder that's inside the Archive Folders (Archive) group, the first thing to check is the age of the oldest mail in your Processed Mail folder, the date that you wrote down a moment ago before you ran Archive. Was your oldest mail younger than the Older Than setting you used when you set up AutoArchive?

Note: *You may need to add the Modified field to the Processed Mail folder view to confirm this and the next test, because AutoArchive actually uses the modified date rather than the received date when deciding whether to archive an individual piece of mail.*

If yes, then no mail *should* have moved and everything is fine. In fact, you probably didn't need to set up AutoArchive yet. In this case, there is not much to confirm yet, so figure out how many days before your oldest mail will reach that Older Than setting and then come back to this section at or beyond that time to do the rest of the confirmation steps.

If on the other hand your oldest mail *was* older than the Older Than setting, mail should have been moved to the Archive Folders group and something is wrong. Don't forget to examine the modified date, not the received date, as described in the previous note. If it looks like it should have run, but didn't, you may need to go through the configuration steps again.

Mail in Archive Folders Group

If there *is* mail in the Processed Mail folder in the Archive Folders group, check the date of the youngest mail there. Compare that to the Older Than setting. It should roughly correspond. Don't forget to examine the modified date, not the received date, as described in the previous note. If the dates look right, so far, so good.

Too Many Folders with Mail in Archive Folders Group

If you see folders other than the Processed Mail folder inside the Archive Folders group, and they have mail in them, and you did not expect this, it is probably because you failed to remove archive settings from some of your source folders. Find those folders now and turn off Archive for them. Copy the archived mail back to the original folders.

Assuming you got this far, all is working so far. Now for a few more steps.

Setting the Order in Your Folder List

Over time, if you collect multiple Archive folder groups with named date ranges, you may want to order the groups within the Navigation Pane in date order. In Outlook 2010 and 2013 you can simply drag them to where you want them. In earlier versions that does not work—they sort alphabetically. So you will want to rename them to distinguish the order of various date ranges. Follow the steps below.

Renaming a Folder Group

Here is how to rename a local folders group:

1. Right-click the top level (the group level) of the new Archive folder.

2. Choose Properties (it may be named Data File Properties). The name looks editable in the dialog box that opens, but it isn't.

3. Click Advanced.

4. In the Name box, type "Z - " in front of "Archive Folder" (or another letter or word that will place it in the order you want, alphabetically).

5. After you click OK and OK again, you should see the new name in your list, and the modified order.

Periodic Archive File Swap

The archive.pst file will fill up eventually, perhaps over a year or two, and you want to catch it before it does and swap it out for a new one. As it fills up you probably won't get an error message; rather, you may experience data corruption, which is not a good thing. So you will want to monitor its size using the instructions in Appendix A on how to check a folder size. I recommend you examine your Archive folders group size about a year after you create it, and then, if not yet full, perhaps every two to three months after that so you can catch it when it is full. You may want to set a recurring task to do this. If it is larger than 15 GB, do the file swap as instructed below.

How to Swap Your Archive Files

Swapping archive files is a two-step process.

First, you need to rename the current active archive file and corresponding folder group to something else, which removes it from the current archive process. Doing this also makes the archive.pst file name available for use in a new archive file, which will be created next.

Then run AutoArchive manually. Because no archive.pst file now exists, when AutoArchive runs, it will create a new blank archive.pst file and corresponding Archive folders group. This becomes your new target archive store. You now are left with your retired and renamed archive file and group (which you can view your old mail in) and a new near-empty archive file ready for your continuing batch of archived mail.

Here is how to do each of those two operations.

Renaming Your Active Archive

The AutoArchive process we have defined always writes to a data file named archive.pst. This file is linked to the current Archive Folders group (called Archives in 2010/13) displayed in your Navigation or Folders Pane. The file and group start with the same name (Archive or Archives), but you can name them differently. To swap archive files you must find that data file and rename it. Then, Outlook 2007 users should rename the corresponding Archive folders group in the Navigation or Folders Pane as well. Preferably you rename both with names representing the date range of the retired archive group. And finally, because renaming a data file breaks the link to the folder group, you need to relink the two. Here are those steps:

1. Find the archive.pst file wherever you stored it during the initial configuration. To do this, in Outlook 2007, open the File menu and choose Data File Management. In Outlook 2010 and 2013, open the File tab, then choose Account Settings, and then Account Settings again. Click the Data Files tab. Select the archive.pst entry in the file name list that opens, and click the Open Folder or Open File Location button. This opens the Windows folder that contains that file, with the file selected.

2. With that Windows folder open, but without yet renaming anything, exit Outlook (you cannot rename an Outlook data file while Outlook is running).

3. In the open Windows folder, which will still be present after you exit Outlook, rename the archive.pst file to something like *Archive-Jan12-Jun13.pst* (using dates as appropriate for the month and year range it represents). Keep that window open because you may need to refer to the file path in step 5 below.

Note: *In some instances, even if you exit Outlook, the file system does not let you rename this file, stating that it is still in use. In such cases you will (unfortunately) need to restart the computer to fully release the control Outlook has over that file. After restarting your computer, rename the file before you start Outlook again. To make this easier, before you restart your computer, write down or save the file path of the open folder so you can find the folder again after you restart.*

4. After the file is renamed it will break the link to the original folder group in your Navigation or Folders Pane, so you must recreate that link. Here is how:

5. When you restart Outlook you will get a File Not Found error message due to the broken link. Click OK to accept it (you may need to click the old folder group to generate that error). A file dialog box opens showing the contents of the folder where the archive files are stored. In that dialog box select the newly named file and click Open. This will relink the folder group in your Navigation or Folders Pane to the correct .pst file.

6. Exit and restart Outlook one more time to test that you did all this right and clear out any remaining old links. Then, in your Navigation or Folders pane, click and open the folder group corresponding to the file that you just renamed to confirm that you have relinked it correctly (it should open without error; restart Outlook again if you do get an error).

7. If needed, now rename that Archive folders group using steps 1 to 3 of the renaming technique in the section titled "Renaming a Folder Group," earlier in this appendix. (Outlook 2010/13 users do not need to do this—Outlook renames it to match automatically.) Rename this to something similar to the file name you just used, like *Archive-Jan12-Jun13*. It does not have to match the file name, but it makes sense to make it match because if you ever need to reinstall Outlook, you'll need to add these files manually and you'll be happy you gave them logical names.

Creating the New Archive Store

You next need to run AutoArchive manually to create the new Archive Folders group and corresponding archive.pst file. The steps below accomplish this.

1. Run AutoArchive manually using instructions in the earlier section "Do the First Archive and Fine-Tune Your Settings." This recreates a new archive.pst file. You'll see a new Archive folders group appear in your folder list.

2. Set a task to check your folder size again in 12 months or so.

This is all you need to do when swapping files. Your previous archive settings for all folders are retained, and your previously scheduled AutoArchive sessions will continue, but will now move old e-mail to the new empty archive.pst file.

Now you have old saved mail stored in frozen and renamed archive files. I call them frozen because you have no reason to ever modify these again; they are for search and view only. You can view mail in those old files and search them with Outlook Instant Search (running in the background, it may take a day or so for indexing to finish on the new files).

Backing Up Your Archive Files

These frozen archive files are valuable files, so you should add those files to your backup strategy. Take this requirement seriously. If you work in a big company, your best backup strategy is that described earlier, where your archive files are originally saved and updated to a networked file server that is part of a regular corporate backup plan. Many corporate IT departments have this available.

Note: *If you are not in a corporate environment, but rather work in a small office or from home, purchase a high-quality external hard drive and backup software, or use an online backup service, and ensure that these files are included.*

As these frozen archive files build up, the space these files require may exceed your available space. In that case, or if you have no backup scheme at all, do this: Store these files on your hard drive and then burn a copy to a CD or DVD for backup. This is a reasonable backup approach because these files are now frozen (no longer modified). Label and store the CD or DVD in a safe place.

But even better is to have an overarching backup strategy that you simply add these files to. You need one anyway. Ask your IT department to advise you on how to set one up. If you have no network backup available, the software I use for local backup is called ShadowProtect Desktop. It creates a full-disk image and makes incremental backups. However, adding this is an option only if you are allowed to install software on your computer in your organization. Many online backup services also exist.

Wrapping Up AutoArchive

That completes the instructions for configuring your AutoArchive settings to best serve the system described in this book. As you can see, it is a bit complex to set up and maintain. Everything AutoArchive does you can do manually, so use manual archiving if you wish to avoid the complex setup scenarios. However, even if you can successfully archive your Outlook mail manually, you will find that the AutoArchive approach, because it is automatically done more often, will allow you to keep the maximum amount of mail in your Processed Mail folder.

Notice that AutoArchive can assist with a variety of other special requirements for saving and purging old mail and other Outlook data. The section below describes a number of these features.

. . .

Other Uses of Windows AutoArchive to Prevent Exchange Mailbox Size Limit Messages

Even in this system, where the Exchange Inbox is kept well maintained through our filing and archive steps, you will still find your Exchange mailbox group periodically overrunning your corporate limits. Remember, no matter what Outlook version or Inbox archive scenario you are using, if your organization has imposed a limit on your Exchange mailbox size you will get "Your mailbox is over its size limit" messages when the sum of all Outlook data in the folders within the Exchange mailbox gets too large. With your Inbox emptied daily, and Processed Mail folder now under AutoArchive control, error messages will be due to four other folders filling over time: Deleted Items, Sent Mail (scenario 1), Tasks, and Calendar. Let's go over these one at a time and discuss maintenance strategies and how AutoArchive might help.

Emptying the Deleted Items Folder

Your Deleted Items folder, as it fills, may help drive your Exchange mailbox over its size limit. Rarely do you want to save deleted items more than a day or two. Yet I often forget to empty it. You can use AutoArchive to do that for you. To configure this, right-click the Deleted Items folder, choose Properties, click the AutoArchive tab, and configure the settings to look like those shown in Figure B.5.

Cleaning Out Old Sent Mail

In scenario 2 the Sent Items folder is well controlled using the AutoArchive scheme just shown.

For scenario 1 users, however, your Sent Items folder, as it fills, can drive your Exchange mailbox over its size limit. What I do when I see the size limit warning message is this: Open the Sent Items folder, sort descending by date, select approximately the bottom half of the messages, and drag them to the Saved Sent Mail folder (created in Appendix A). This works for me.

Figure B.5
Settings for AutoArchive of Deleted Items folder.

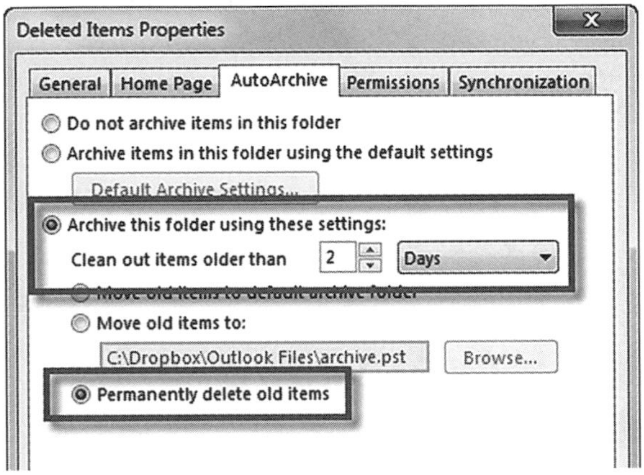

There is unfortunately no easy AutoArchive configuration that works well in the MYN system. Rather, I stick with the manual approach of periodically dragging my sent mail to the Saved Sent Items folder.

Purging Old Completed Tasks

Completed tasks can start to build up and impact your Exchange Server storage space. You can manually purge those old completed tasks by going to the Tasks folder and opening the Completed view (I show you how to find and open Tasks folder views in Lesson 12 in the section:"Understanding Outlook Task Views"). Then scroll to the bottom and delete your oldest completed tasks using the DELETE key (you may want to save some recent ones to review for status reports, and so on). Make sure you are using the Tasks folder and not the To-Do List folder; otherwise you will also delete old mail that was previously flagged. Instead, you can clear completed flagged mail from the To-Do List folder without deleting the e-mail by right-clicking the flag and choosing Clear Flag.

You can also use AutoArchive to automatically purge old tasks. Luckily, AutoArchive archives tasks based on the Completion Date, which is exactly the behavior we expect. As with Deleted Items, there is no reason to save the archived tasks; you just wish to delete them.

To configure this, right-click the Tasks folder, choose Properties, click the AutoArchive tab, and configure the settings so they look like those shown in Figure B.6. Notice I used an Older Than value of 2 months; adjust that according to your preferences.

Figure B.6
Settings for AutoArchive of Tasks folder

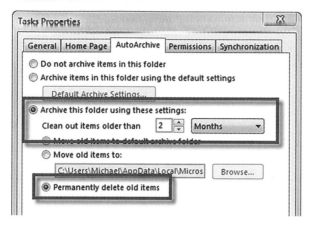

Calendar

Your Calendar is probably the least likely source of an overloaded Exchange mailbox, but it can contribute, particularly if you create appointments with file attachments. To use AutoArchive for the Calendar, follow the instructions I just showed you for Deleted Items, using a much larger Older Than setting. Many people like to be able to look back in their calendar over the past year to see when certain meetings were held, so 12 to 18 months may be a reasonable setting for the Older Than setting.

Appendix C: Resources and Quick Guides

Websites for This Book and Michael Linenberger

www.michaellinenberger.com—Sign up for my monthly newsletter there to get book updates and useful tips.

www.michaellinenberger.com/blog—Follow my blog for weekly updates on my system and relevant Outlook news.

www.facebook.com/masteryourworkdaynow—Follow me on my Facebook page for tips related to the MYN system.

www.twitter.com/mikelinenberger—Follow me on my twitter page.

Note: *Although my main website is www.michaellinenberger.com, you can also use a shorter link to get there: www.myn.bz. However, some web servers block redirected links. If you receive an error using www.myn.bz, then substitute the longer link. Also, all links are case sensitive, so match capitalization exactly.*

Some Useful Books

▶ *The One Minute To-Do List,* by Michael Linenberger. In this 2011 book, I demonstrate the quick-start method for learning MYN. It includes a more complete discussion of the contents of the Quick Start chapter of this book. It also teaches non-Outlook methods for using the MYN system.

▶ *Master Your Workday Now!,* by Michael Linenberger. Released in 2010, this book describes my approach to setting goals and matching your career to your highest purpose in life.

▶ *Total Workday Control Using Microsoft Outlook, 3rd. Ed.*, by Michael Linenberger. Use this older third edition if you need support for Outlook 2003.

▶ *Total Workday Control Using Microsoft Outlook, 2nd. Ed.*, by Michael Linenberger. Use this older second edition if you need support for Outlook 2002 (and 2000).

▶ *Seize the Work Day: Using the Tablet PC to Take Total Control of Your Work and Meeting Day*, by Michael Linenberger. This older book is largely out of date (and it is out of print); however, many concepts in it can still be applied to today's Windows 8 tablets. You can find copies from resellers on Amazon.

▶ *Getting Things Done*, by David Allen.

▶ *First Things First*, by Stephen R. Covey, A. Roger Merrill, Rebecca R. Merrill.

▶ *The 7 Habits of Highly Effective People*, by Stephen R. Covey.

▶ *To Do... Doing... Done!*, by G. Lynne Snead and Joyce Wycoff.

▶ *The Time Trap*, by Alec Mackenzie.

▶ *Time Management from the Inside Out*, by Julie Morgenstern.

Software and Product Links

ClearContext

▶ ClearContext Windows Outlook add-in software, special MYN version: www.myn.bz/clearcontext.html

Non-Outlook Task Solution: Toodledo

▶ Toodledo, all about: www.myn.bz/ToodleDo.html

▶ Toodledo MYN special edition: www.myn.bz/TD.htm

▶ Toodledo iPhone & iPad app: www.toodledo.com/info/iphone.php

▶ Toodledo Android app called PocketInformant: www.myn.bz/PocketInformant.html

▶ Toodledo Android app called Ultimate To-Do List: www.myn.bz/blog/ultimate-to-do-list-configuration-instructions/

Apps for Accessing Outlook Exchange Tasks on Mobile Devices

▶ iPhone and iPad TaskTask: www.myn.bz/TaskTask.htm

▶ Android TouchDown: www.myn.bz/TouchDown.htm

▶ BlackBerry To-Do Matrix: www.myn.bz/TDM.htm

Exchange Hosting

▶ Intermedia: (three mailbox minimum)
www.intermedia.net/exchange-hosting/exchange-hosting.asp

▶ Microsoft: (one mailbox okay)
www.microsoft.com/online/exchange-online.aspx#

▶ GoDaddy: (one mailbox okay)
www.godaddy.com/email/hosted-exchange.aspx

Microsoft Outlook Links

▶ Microsoft Office Outlook, main product page:
office.microsoft.com/en-us/

▶ Outlook 2007/10 add-in software, Calendar Printing Assistant for Microsoft Office Outlook:
www.microsoft.com/downloads/en/details.aspx?FamilyID=e7bab4eb-d032-46cd-908e-a7a6af2ef404&displaylang=en

▶ Microsoft Office Web Apps (part of Office 365):
office.microsoft.com/en-us/web-apps/

Search Engine Software

▶ X1 full product list: www.x1.com

▶ Google Desktop: desktop.google.com

▶ Xobni: www.xobni.com

Voice Mail to E-mail Services

▶ Google Voice (also includes single-number routing of calls):
www.google.com/voice

Data Backup and Archiving Products

▶ ShadowProtect backup software (my current favorite):
www.storagecraft.com/shadow_protect_desktop.php

▶ Acronis True Image backup software: www.acronis.com/

▶ Retrospect backup software for small to medium-size businesses:
www.retrospect.com/products/software/retroforwin/

▶ Outlook Exchange Accounts Optimizer, software for archiving mail in Outlook for Mac 2011: www.softhing.com/oeao.html

Master Your Now! System Tear-Out Quick Guide:
Outlook Task Management Principles

(See Lesson 4 for a complete discussion of these principles.)

1. Assign a High and Normal priority only to tasks you must do or would consider doing now. (These are your Now Tasks.) Give must-do-today tasks a High priority (your Critical Now tasks), and all other tasks a Normal (medium) priority (your Opportunity Now tasks).

2. Set the Start Date field of all new tasks to today or to a future day you would like to start seeing the task on your MYN task list. If the date is in the future, the task will not appear on your list till that day. Do not leave any tasks with a start date of None.

3. Do *not* set Outlook reminders on *tasks* (*do* set them on *appointments* if the task is time-of-day sensitive).

4. Keep the High priority (Critical Now) list to five or fewer items. Work those tasks early, and complete all your High priority (Critical Now) tasks by end of day.

5. If a task has a future deadline, but you'd like to start work on it before that deadline, set the start date earlier. Use Normal priority, and enter "DUE" and the deadline date in front of the task title. Alternative: Use the Deadline field as described in Lesson 12 instead.

6. Review your Critical Now tasks about once an hour, and review your Opportunity Now tasks once a day (morning is best).

7. When reviewing your Normal priority (Opportunity Now tasks) section, if you find tasks near the bottom of the list that are important, and so need to be promoted in the list, set their start dates to a date near today. This moves them to near the top of the list. This is part of the FRESH Prioritization approach.

8. Limit the Opportunity Now section of your MYN task list to no more than about 20 items. If it gets much larger than 20, first try deleting or delegating. If that is not possible, set some tasks to a future date that you really intend to do them, or better, move tasks to the Low priority section by setting their Outlook priority to Low. (This is the same as tossing them over the Now Horizon as described in Lesson 1.) Review your Low priority section once a week in case any tasks there become more important over time.

MYN-Outlook E-Mail/Task Processing Workflow

Ver. 1.7

- Do or Capture All Actions as Outlook Tasks
- Empty Your Outlook Inbox

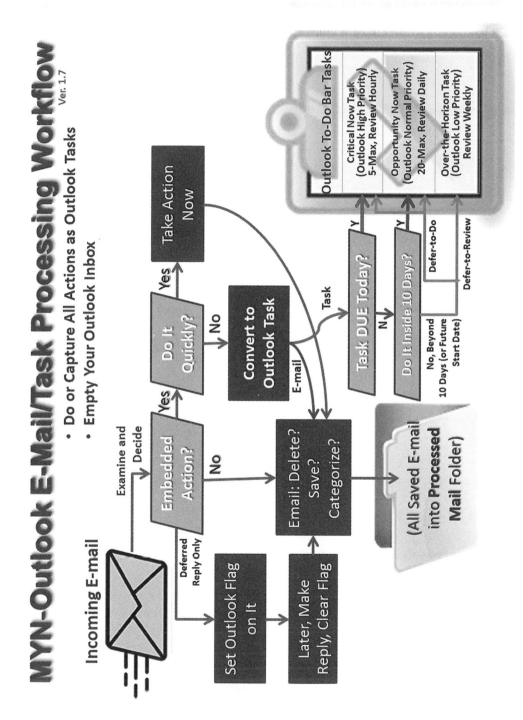

Incoming E-mail

Examine and Decide

Embedded Action?

Deferred Reply Only → Set Outlook Flag on It → Later, Make Reply, Clear Flag

Yes → Do It Quickly?

Yes → Take Action Now

No → Convert to Outlook Task

E-mail → Email: Delete? Save? Categorize?

No → Email: Delete? Save? Categorize?

(All Saved E-mail into Processed Mail Folder)

Task → Task DUE Today?

Y → (To-Do Bar)

N → Do It Inside 10 Days?

Y → (To-Do Bar) — Defer-to-Do

No, Beyond 10 Days (or Future Start Date) — Defer-to-Review

Outlook To-Do Bar Tasks

- Critical Now Task (Outlook High Priority) 5-Max, Review Hourly
- Opportunity Now Task (Outlook Normal Priority) 20-Max, Review Daily
- Over-the-Horizon Task (Outlook Low Priority) Review Weekly

Index